ON PAINTING

ALSO BY GILLES DELEUZE

PUBLISHED BY THE UNIVERSITY OF MINNESOTA PRESS

Cinema 1: The Movement-Image
Cinema 2: The Time-Image
Essays Critical and Clinical
The Fold: Leibniz and the Baroque
Foucault
Francis Bacon: The Logic of Sensation
Kant's Critical Philosophy: The Doctrine of the Faculties
Proust and Signs: The Complete Text

BY GILLES DELEUZE AND FÉLIX GUATTARI

Kafka: Toward a Minor Literature
A Thousand Plateaus: Capitalism and Schizophrenia

ON PAINTING

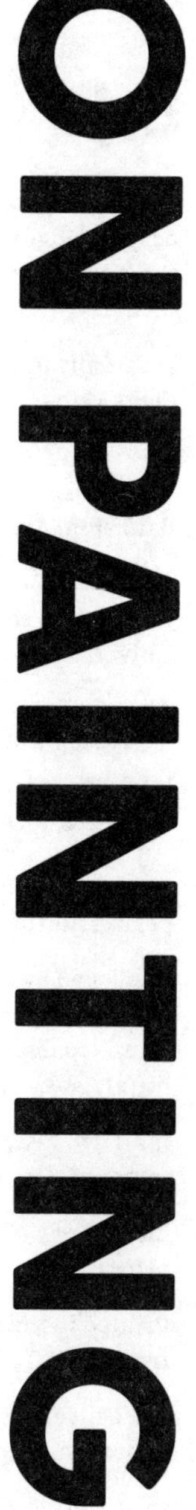

COURSES, MARCH–JUNE 1981

Gilles Deleuze

Edited by David Lapoujade
Translated by Charles J. Stivale
with the Deleuze Seminars
Translation Collective

A UNIVOCAL BOOK

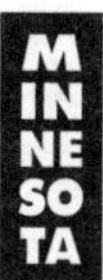

University of Minnesota Press
Minneapolis
London

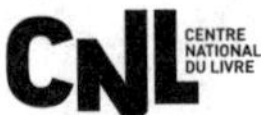

The University of Minnesota Press gratefully acknowledges the generous assistance provided for the translation of this book by the Centre national du livre.

Originally published in French as *Sur la peinture: Cours Mars–Juin 1981* copyright 2023 by Les Éditions de Minuit.

The publisher acknowledges the work of Samantha Bankston, Alina Cherry, and Billy Dean Goehring on a prior translation of portions of this work.

Published by the University of Minnesota Press
111 Third Avenue South, Suite 290
Minneapolis, MN 55401-2520
http://www.upress.umn.edu

ISBN 978-1-5179-1839-2 (hc)
ISBN 978-1-5179-1840-8 (pb)

Library of Congress record available at
https://lccn.loc.gov/2025001947

Printed in the United States of America on acid-free paper

33 32 31 30 29 28 27 26 10 9 8 7 6 5 4 3 2

CONTENTS

PREFACE

Charles J. Stivale

The translation of a text such as these sessions on painting by Gilles Deleuze is rendered doubly complex due to the necessity of accurately transcribing the text from the original recording, undertaken admirably by David Lapoujade, who discusses the circumstances of this seminar and conditions for preparing the edited transcript for *Sur la peinture* in the introduction that follows.[1] My remarks here offer certain guideposts for reading these sessions as well as some conventions that I followed in preparing the translation.

Deleuze's seminar on painting unfolded during the springtime of his first year (1980–81) on the new campus of Vincennes–St. Denis, following a long seminar on Spinoza that began the preceding fall and ended as the first segment (omitted in *Sur la peinture*) in the same session with which the painting seminar begins. Readers of Deleuze will no doubt be aware that this seminar coincided with Deleuze's publication of *Francis Bacon: Logique de la sensation* in the same year, and between this concise work and aspects of the seminar there are evident overlaps to which I briefly refer in these notes.[2] In giving the simple title *Sur la peinture* to this first print transcription of a Deleuze seminar, Lapoujade follows the lead of Richard Pinhas for the seminar's initial transcription on the WebDeleuze site. On the other hand, on the Paris-8 transcript site, La Voix de Gilles Deleuze en ligne (Gilles Deleuze's Voice Online), the title is "Painting and the Question of Concepts," the title we also adopted for the transcripts and translations on the Purdue University Deleuze Seminars site.[3]

This revised title suggests succinctly a concern to which Deleuze returned frequently during the 1980s as he slowly developed the elements contributing to his final collaboration with Félix Guattari, *What Is Philosophy?*—namely, the importance of developing concepts based on specific problems as the basis of doing philosophy.[4]

Just as Daniel W. Smith suggests that *Francis Bacon: The Logic of Sensation* is best approached "as a book of philosophical concepts" (FBLS, xi UM),[5] the reader will note that in session 1 Deleuze immediately asks if one of the concerns of painting might be concepts, suggesting that if he takes up such a broad topic as painting, it's so that painting might delight him with new insights, that is, with glimmers of philosophical concepts. In this light, I propose to consider three concepts among many developed by Deleuze in this seminar that help to conceptualize a broad organization of the eight sessions: diagram, modulation, and color.[6]

As Deleuze opens the seminar on painting, he immediately raises the importance of the catastrophe in painting and how it affects the act of painting, notably, the relation of catastrophe and the birth of color. From these early remarks, one can understand the entire seminar as developing, over eight sessions, as the movement from a fundamental imbalance at the heart of painting to the triumph of color and, indeed, ultimately to answer the question "what is a color concept?" Deleuze employs the first four sessions to examine the process through which color might emerge, a process that falls under the broad heading of the "diagram." Whereas Deleuze seems to devote only one chapter in *Francis Bacon* to this term (chap. 12), he introduces it in the seminar at the end of session 1 and then develops and enriches it during the next three sessions. Specifically, Deleuze describes the pre-pictorial condition of a painting, to wit: catastrophe as a germinal chaos from which a "diagram" might emerge and then lead to the pictorial "fact" as the advent of painting.

Hence, in these early sessions, Deleuze situates the diagram both as a specific step in the creative process—from chaos, through the diagram, to the pictorial fact—and as a notion taking on greater import. For, having introduced the broad conception of the diagram in session 1, Deleuze opens session 3 by insisting that a goal of this continuing discussion of painting is to constitute the diagram as a properly philosophical concept. Let us note that Deleuze indicates that he derived this term from Francis Bacon,[7] and that Deleuze's shift in usage corresponds to this broad understanding of the term. In fact, Deleuze signals this broad understanding by initially writing the term with a capital D, *Diagramme,* in the original edition, accurately presented as *Diagram* in the translation.[8]

As derived from Bacon, this broad conception of diagram is directly juxtaposed to the more specific conception of the diagram as an "act" leading to "pictorial fact," hence what Deleuze calls "the turning point of the painting" (*FBLS*, 82 UM; 101 C), part of a specific tripartite process. Deleuze also insists that the diagram—as "the operative set of traits and color-patches, of lines and zones"—has a more sweeping breadth, corresponding to works of specific painters, hence a painter's diagram writ large, and suggesting that "we can also date the diagram of a painter," that is, "the moment when the painter confronts it most directly" (*FBLS*, 83 UM; 102 C). Whereas Deleuze moves quickly past these distinctions in *Francis Bacon,* he develops the importance of the diagram at great length in the seminar, devoting much of session 3 to its pictorial characteristics and to the dangers that confront the diagram.

Then, to render this analysis more concrete, Deleuze turns to three "categories" or manners of painting, that is, "diagrammatic positions" (session 4), through which characteristics and dangers emerge: the "abstract," the "Expressionist," and the "figurative." He particularly emphasizes their respective hand-eye dynamics, that is, asserting the manual aspect of diagrams and distinguishing these from "codes" as modes of articulation. Session 4 constitutes a crucial turning point in the seminar because, through a detailed discussion of the distinction between the diagram (as analogical) and code (as digital), Deleuze turns to the importance of painting as a medium that is modulated based on a signal, that is, the motif or model, modulating light and/or color, resulting in the figure on a canvas. Deleuze thereby makes the specific link between focal concepts, for the diagram is the matrix of modulation, the modulator, moving the discussion into a second conceptual phase (sessions 5 and 6). On the one hand, Deleuze examines three lines of analogy or similitude, the physical analogy of "mold"; the organic analogy of the "module," or internal molding; and the aesthetic analogy of "modulation," taken in a strict sense. On the other hand, much as he did with the diagram, Deleuze develops modulation toward a broader conceptual understanding, grouping the three instances of analogy under the conceptual heading of modulation while maintaining the "strict sense" of modulation along the analogical sequence. Moreover, Deleuze defines painting as "modulating" light and color, transmitting a signal onto the space of canvas, and this assertion (in session 5) leads (in sessions 5 and 6) to Deleuze's reflection on two problems that support the conceptual understanding of modulation: the existence of major signal-spaces in painting, and how modulation worked in each of these spaces.

In pursuit of these signal-spaces as they relate to modulation, Deleuze outlines their successive reversals, contrasting Egyptian and Greek spaces, and then Egyptian and Byzantine spaces. Drawing from work by Aloïs Riegl on the optical and tactile (or "haptic") eye of Egyptian space, corresponding to the mold-modulation defined as geometric crystalline contour,[9] Deleuze shifts to the disjunction of planes in Greek art, a tactile–optical art (following Riegl) with a corresponding space and linked to modulation via an internal mold, and then to Byzantine space, followed by Renaissance space with a double tactile referent and also a collective line with strong multiplicity. With the seventeenth century, Deleuze observes the shift toward a purely optical space, the line corresponding to a collectivity (as in Da Vinci and Raphael), but also to the background having primacy, unleashing light and even color (with Vermeer).

Then, Deleuze turns to the conceptual shift that he anticipated from the start of the seminar, even seeded in session 6 through the somewhat parenthetical study of Goethe's theory of color, color triangle, and chromatic circle. In the two final sessions, he addresses the shift toward an in-between, neither foreground nor background, but a third plane, an accident or fall between planes through an imbalance or organization in the process of coming undone. This is the seminar's final overlapping conceptual focus, on color, with color signal-space having a modulation all its own, what Deleuze calls (with Cézanne) "modulating color." Deleuze justifies this first hypothesis through the evidence of colorism generally and Impressionism specifically, referencing Van Gogh's and Cézanne's writings and painting, inspired by the work of Delacroix. Calling also on Paul Signac's writings about the Impressionists' palette restrictions, Deleuze asserts that Seurat's pointillism took this much further.

These bases allow Deleuze to address two problems in the final sessions: first, the definition of regimes of color with their specific characteristics through which one can envisage these regimes as sometimes referring to previously defined spaces and to previously defined modulations, and sometimes to a space peculiar to color and to a chromatic modulation not yet defined. Through critical perspectives offered by Xavier de Langlais (characterized by Deleuze as both reactionary and instructive), Deleuze reviews technical aspects toward the development of a space through color and of color, united by accent, which he explores in stages: Impressionism's painting of accents, a punctual constitution of space, referring to the laws of contrast and of analogs; then in painters for whom everything is organized around diametric oppositions to the Impressionists, first, in Neo-Impressionism (e.g., Seurat), then, Cézanne's relief-effects with color, finally the break with Impressionism occurring with Van Gogh and Gauguin. Deleuze distinguishes the Gauguin formula and the Van Gogh formula, flesh and figures done in broken color, conquering a new space of color as spatializing energy and as weighable energy, thereby producing two elements of modern color, "color-structure" and color-weight, that is, "color-force." The interplay of these two elements at once defines this colorist space and creates a new form of modulation, with Deleuze concluding the final session simply by saying that these color modulations are numerous. Thus, while the work of Bacon indeed provides an occasional reference point within this seminar, my overview of these three key concepts shows the extent to which Deleuze addresses an extremely broad range of artistic works, styles, and techniques.

I should add a note on Deleuze's approach to teaching that is quite evident in these sessions. Besides preparing carefully organized lessons in which he systematically lays out the unfolding reasoning to support successive hypotheses, Deleuze based his teaching on a principle that he elucidated on different occasions, but most succinctly in session 4 of the Leibniz and the Baroque seminar:

> Reading philosophy means doing two things at once: it means being very attentive to the linkage of concepts, that's what philosophical reading is; but there is no philosophical reading without there being a nonphilosophical reading. And the nonphilosophical reading, without which the philosophical reading remains dead, provides all kinds of sensible intuitions that must emerge within you, but extremely rudimentary sensible intuitions, and because of this, are extremely lively. (*TDS* Leibniz and Baroque 4–161286)

Deleuze insistently encouraged students to *sentir,* to feel the flow of linked concepts and how these intersect not just in terms of the importance of emotion in the learning process but, in these sessions, also as a way to understand how the aesthetic, painterly, and pictorial elements provide another layer for understanding these linked philosophical concepts. I mention this aspect of Deleuze's teaching so that the reader might be attentive to this deliberate yet otherwise subtle current within each session that we have tried to render clearly in each translation.[10]

Whereas Lapoujade explains in the Introduction the challenges he faced given the basic principle of readability that informs his approach to editing *Sur la peinture,* the team of translators that undertook the translation of these sessions for the Purdue Deleuze Seminars site (Samantha Bankston, Alina Cherry, Billy Dean Goehring, and myself) followed a different principle, that of faithfulness to Deleuze's spoken word, however hesitant, repetitive, or even prone to misprisions the formulations might have been. For the translation of this new edition, the principles guiding my work have been:

1. To remain entirely faithful to the edited transcription in *Sur la peinture,* not just in the basic text, but also in the decisions made by Lapoujade on paragraph breaks and textual revisions, as well as in the scholarly apparatus added to the French edition, with any variations signaled and justified.
2. While adhering fully to principle 1, to undertake a necessary reconciliation of the transcription in *Sur la peinture* with the oral version of the transcripts on which The Deleuze Seminars translations are based and which forms the basic groundwork for this translated edition, with particular attention given to regularizing terminological choices.
3. To employ as key reference the textual support provided in Daniel W. Smith's translation of Deleuze's *Francis Bacon: The Logic of Sensation,* especially since Lapoujade frequently refers to the French edition of this work.

I updated the original translations on The Deleuze Seminars site so that these correspond to Lapoujade's extensive and commendable revisions and have also translated the scholarly apparatus created for *Sur la peinture.* Where necessary and as little as possible, I translate citations from Deleuze's or Lapoujade's original sources, but I otherwise adopt these from extant translations of the various works cited. Nonetheless, the edition rendered here is based on the work of the aforementioned translators whose work I wish to acknowledge fully.

Among the conventions employed in this edition, the complete reference to each text cited is presented in the initial note where the reference appears. Notes in *Sur la peinture* may be supplemented (indicated with *Trans.*) with occasional necessary details added to the original notes; occasional notes containing editorial additions, corrections, and clarifications; and notes originating from the individual translators. While adhering to the transcript editing and deletions in *Sur la peinture,* I indicate certain classroom events (e.g., laughter, significant omitted interventions) either in brackets or in notes.

Also, given that time markers appear throughout *Sur la peinture* corresponding to breaks in the recording, readers who might wish to access the recordings based on these markers should be aware of a significant anomaly: two separate sets of the same recordings are available on YouTube, one attributed to WebDeleuze (notable for the picture of Deleuze in a fedora), the other attributed to SocioPhilosophy (notable for the photograph of a younger Deleuze *sans chapeau*). Lapoujade's time markers correspond to the former recording set and differ from the latter set by about eight seconds. While admittedly a minor difference, this distinction may be disconcerting for anyone attempting to locate a segment within the recording flow.

ACKNOWLEDGMENTS

The French edition of this seminar would not have been possible without the support, encouragement, and confidence of the copyright holders for Gilles Deleuze, who receive our deepest thanks. Also to be thanked for this edition are Pierre Butic for his inestimable assistance, Richard Pinhas for his extensive work, and Anne Querrien, Pascale Criton, and Odette Lazrak.

—*David Lapoujade*

This translation owes its existence to the perseverance of Daniel W. Smith in seeking the funding necessary to develop The Deleuze Seminars site, to recruit transcribers and translators, and to guide the project toward its conclusion. Special gratitude is owed to the translators whose initial work in The Deleuze Seminars forms the basis of the translations developed here: Samantha Bankston, Alina Cherry, and Billy Dean Goehring. No endeavor of this scope is possible without a strong editorial team, and the careful attention from the University of Minnesota Press has been exemplary: warm thanks to Doug Armato, Drew Burk, Zenyse Miller, Jeff Moen, Paula Dragosh, and Rachel Moeller. Special thanks to support from Taylor Adkins and Cooper Cherry in their work on the Machinic Unconscious Happy Hour, and immense love and respect for the unflagging help from the family "unit," both the four-legged clowder and the wonderful support and patience of Nancy Ciupek Kozak.

—*Charles J. Stivale*

INTRODUCTION

David Lapoujade

The seminars that Gilles Deleuze (1925–1995) taught from the 1970s through the mid-1980s are inseparable from the creation of the Experimental University Center at Vincennes (EUCV) in the autumn of 1968. "Vincennes" was created by a decision of the minister of national education, Edgar Faure, in response to the student movement of May 1968. In the minister's words, this was an attempt at a "pilot experiment" of offering to students and employees without "baccalauréat" [the French terminal high school diploma] an interdisciplinary training corresponding to new degrees and an unprecedented pedagogical organization. This new location was immediately perceived as the result and continuation of the May 1968 movements. The individuals enrolled in courses there were students, workers, unemployed persons, activists, foreign visitors, artists, the curious public, and so on. The turbulent history of Vincennes continued until August 1980, when the campus buildings were razed in three days, on the orders of Alice Saunier-Seïté, the minister of universities who was fiercely opposed to the existence of the center, and with the support of Jacques Chirac, mayor of Paris.[1] This was the beginning of what Félix Guattari would call the "Winter Years."[2] The university was transferred to Saint-Denis, and teaching resumed on these new premises, on the grounds of a modest IUT.[3]

Deleuze was originally contacted to teach at Vincennes by Michel Foucault, who was entrusted with the responsibility of the chair of the philosophy department at the time of its creation. Due to serious health problems, Deleuze would eventually join the faculty at Vincennes beginning in academic year 1970–71. In the interval, Foucault was elected to the Collège de France, and François Châtelet, a lifelong friend, then became chair of the department. To protect Deleuze's very fragile health, Châtelet allowed him to teach only one session per week, on Tuesday mornings. His seminars during the first year,

"Spinoza's Logic" and "Logic and Desire," were the result of his initial collaborations with Guattari, whom he met during the summer of 1969, and would result in the publication of *Anti-Oedipus* in 1972. Each session lasted around three hours, including a break.[4] Having always refused to teach in a large lecture hall, Deleuze held his classes in a prefabricated building until his final seminar in June 1987.[5]

In a 1979 collective work in defense of the increasingly threatened Vincennes campus and programs, Deleuze explained how he conceived his courses while arguing for the innovative teaching practices at Vincennes:

> In the traditional arrangement, a professor lectures to students who are acquiring or already possess a certain competence in some discipline. These students are working in other disciplines as well; and let's not forget interdisciplinary studies, even if they are secondary. Generally speaking, then, students are "judged" by their degree in some discipline abstractly defined.
>
> At Vincennes, the situation is different. A professor, for example, one who works in philosophy, presents lectures to an audience that includes to varying degrees mathematicians, musicians (trained in classical or pop music), psychologists, historians, and so on. However, instead of putting these other disciplines aside to facilitate access to the discipline they are supposedly being taught, the students instead expect philosophy, for example, to be useful to them in some way, to intersect with their other activities. Philosophy will matter to them, not in terms of the degree to which they possess this kind of knowledge, even the zero degree of initiation, but in terms of their immediate concerns, in other words, the other subjects or material that they already possess to whatever degree. Students attend a lecture looking for something they can use for themselves. In this way, what directly orients the teaching of philosophy is the question of how useful it is to mathematicians, or to musicians, and so forth, even and especially if this philosophy does not discuss mathematics or music. This kind of teaching has nothing to do with general culture; it is practical and experimental, always outside of itself, precisely because the students are led to participate in terms of their own needs and competences.
>
> [. . .] The presence of numerous workers, as well as numerous foreigners, confirms and reinforces this situation. [. . .] Every student

> shows up with his or her own domain already in place, and rather than tossing such domains aside, the discipline being taught must "grow" from that domain. This resonance is the only way to grasp a subject in itself and from within it. Far from being opposed to the norms which the minister demands, the teaching at Vincennes should be an integral part of these norms. [. . .] This method is in fact connected to Vincennes's specific situation, to its particular history, and no one can dismantle Vincennes without at the same time undermining one of the most important attempts at pedagogical renewal in France. The real problem facing us today is a kind of intellectual lobotomy of teachers and students, against which Vincennes offers its own particular capacities of resistance.[6]

When Deleuze came to teach each session, he brought with him only some brief notes and a few books from which he cited excerpts (or even pages torn from books when the reference texts were too big). He never composed any courses. His written efforts were exclusively destined to published works, articles, and interviews. But, in the well-known interview with Claire Parnet, the *Abécédaire,* Deleuze explains that he prepared greatly for his courses and would rehearse "in his head":

> It's like in theater, in popular songs (*chansonnettes*), there are rehearsals, and if one hasn't rehearsed enough, there's no inspiration. In a course, it means having moments of inspiration, without which the course means nothing. [. . .] Reworking mentally and managing to find that what one is saying is interesting. And that doesn't go without saying, finding that what one is saying is interesting, impassioned. And this isn't a form of vanity, it's not finding oneself passionate and interesting; it's the subject matter that one is treating and handling that one has to find passionate. And to do so, one sometimes has to drive oneself, truly whip oneself hard. [. . .] One has to get oneself stimulated to the point that one is able to speak about something with enthusiasm: that's what rehearsing is.[7]

The sessions were very often the laboratory for books to come, but with the material presented in another form, following another rhythm, with another kind of clarity than in the books. This approach is a completely different way of exposing philosophical concepts, as he said regarding Leibniz for whom the density of his presentations varied with different readers. In this sense, the seminars do not repeat the books but present them differently, in another light, illuminating certain complex passages through their exceptional pedagogy, also thanks to their digressions, to the pathways ultimately abandoned or modified, with moments of varying inspiration. Certain developments in the books that are condensed into a few lines, or a few pages, are patiently developed at length in the seminars. Deleuze's readers very often encounter explanations in them that, through their great clarity, help provide a renewed understanding of the published works.

Of all the seminars taught by Deleuze during that time, many of which were recorded, we currently possess only a few of them in their entirety, despite the vast amount of audio material. Of the seminars from 1970 to 1979, the only available recordings and transcriptions are those carefully produced by Richard Pinhas, a regular seminar participant and close friend of Deleuze.[8] But as Pinhas did not attend all the seminar sessions, significant gaps exist. Only starting in 1980 do we begin to have the quasi-totality of the recordings available, when the university was brutally transplanted to Saint-Denis.[9]

The sound quality of the recordings is relatively good, with a few exceptions.[10] With tape recorders placed on Deleuze's desk, certain public interventions, too far from the microphones, were inaudible. The sessions' recordings were often regularly halted because of interruptions and the time required for a cassette change.

Our edition offers the most faithful transcription possible of these recordings with the aim of avoiding two pitfalls. We have not wanted to preserve the entire oral dimension of the courses by reproducing interjections, hesitations, repetitions, and errors in spoken language. There are several reasons for this: first because this speech exists, available online, and also because strict respect for the oral aspect would have detracted from the text's readability. The same concern for readability has led us sometimes to modify certain deliberately awkward formulations that Deleuze liked to use (e.g., "what is it he says, Kant, and how does this work for us?"), sometimes to preserve them in order not to break the rhythm of the presentation. The other pitfall would have been the reverse, to suppress the entire oral dimension. We have therefore decided to preserve the oral aspect of Deleuze's thought during his lectures whenever it does not hinder reading, thus, to propose a written form that retains the inflections of the spoken word, as Deleuze did when he composed the interviews that he granted. Finally, in relation to the existing transcriptions that are sometimes deficient or filled with gaps, this current publication of his seminar on painting offers a complete and corrected version.

Regarding the interventions by participants, we integrated them into the body of the text each time that Deleuze pursued them extensively. In the opposite case, they are either reproduced in notes or briefly summarized in brackets. We mentioned the names of the speakers with their agreement when they are identifiable.

Furthermore, we pointed out, also in brackets, inaudible passages and interruptions due to cassette changes by indicating the time marker to which the recording corresponds, as well as the duration of the longest interruptions. Also presented in brackets are words, groups of words, or phrases added by the editor for purposes of readability (missing words, modified grammatical construction, etc.).

The notes have a strictly informational purpose. Sometimes they indicate Deleuze's usage of a term, a concept, or an author by referring to the works in which he mentions them significantly; sometimes they indicate the explicit or implicit references used in the session. In this case, we occasionally cite at length the texts mentioned so that the reader can see the usage that Deleuze introduced during the seminars. Finally, certain notes cite excerpts from other sessions closely related to what Deleuze is discussing.

Finally, when a session's progression closely follows a published work's development, we indicate in the body of the text the work's abbreviated title and the relevant pages, for example, for *Francis Bacon*, FBLS, 39–40.

CATASTROPHE AND DIAGRAM

SESSION 1

31 March 1981

The subject of this seminar will be painting.[1] I am not yet convinced whether or not philosophy has anything meaningful to say or offer painting. I don't know. Perhaps this isn't the way to pose questions. But I'd rather ask the question in reverse, namely: the possibility that painting has something to offer philosophy and that the answer would not be unambiguous, an answer that may not be applicable for the other arts such as music in the way it applies to painting . . . What can philosophy expect from art forms like painting or music? I would suggest that what philosophy can expect from painting is unique to that art form alone.

So, what can philosophy offer painting? Perhaps philosophy can provide it with some concepts, but doesn't painting already concern itself with concepts? I believe we have already found our question: Is color a concept? I don't know. What is a color concept? What is color as a concept? If painting offers such a concept to philosophy, where does this take philosophy? I mean, how would we then proceed? There's obviously a problem: speaking about painting. What does "speaking about painting" mean? I believe that it means precisely: forming concepts that are in direct relation with painting and with painting alone.

In fact, at this point, the reference to painting has become essential. If you understand what I'm getting at, even in a vague way, I've already resolved a question. I assume that those of you who participate in this discussion will know as much as me about painting, and sometimes much more. What I don't want to do is to display any reproductions of artworks because we'd no longer have any desire to talk. We'd say: "Well, yes, what's there left to say?" So, I will call upon your memory. Only in some very rare cases will I show a small image, when it's absolutely necessary for us to do so. But what we do will take care of itself, with no real need to make use of any reproductions.

Nor am I claiming to attempt a response to the question: What is the essence of painting? For those attending the sessions on this research topic, I will try to provide you with specific themes that I'll pursue each time as well as the specific painters I'll be referring to because attempting to discuss the unity of painting poses a problem. There is no reason to establish some kind of unity. For example, regarding a painter's specific materials, we'll eventually have to consider if there is a common genre of painting today for watercolors, for oil, for acrylics.[2] I don't know. We have no reason to take this as a given. I've chosen themes that are of interest to me, and sometimes they will flow into philosophy. These will be the moments I'll relish: the moments when painting inspires some kind of spark within me, something new for me, which I can then apply to philosophical concepts. Fine, so let's give it a try.

Today I want to focus my discussion on the topic of catastrophe in relation to painting, which I briefly mentioned before.[3] This obviously presupposes that painting has a very special relation to catastrophe, and initially, I won't try to establish [the relation] theoretically. I'm basing this initial insight on an impression. This would suggest that writing and music wouldn't have the same relation with catastrophe as painting, or not the same kind, or not as direct.[4] The painters I've chosen to think with all reside within a relatively recent period in the history of painting. I point this out because I'd like to have you sense the extent to which the painters we will be discussing are limited examples. This will then allow us to consider whether or not these painters indicate something more general about painting or if this connection to catastrophe is valid only for certain painters. I'm starting off with no preconceived notions here. For this segment on catastrophe and painting, I am choosing Turner as an example, one of the great English painters from the nineteenth century—I'm choosing only the greats, of course!—Cézanne, Van Gogh, Paul Klee, and another more modern English painter, Bacon.

That's what I want to say, and I am being prudent: when we visit a museum, we are all struck by a certain number of paintings that depict a catastrophe. What kind of catastrophe? For example, when painting discovers mountains: we begin to see the creation of paintings of avalanches and storms, and so on. For me, I'm intrigued by how these paintings of catastrophes tend to extend and envelop the entire painting with something often already present in painting. These sorts of paintings tend to generalize a kind of imbalance, of things falling and collapsing. And in a certain way, painting has always meant painting local imbalances. Why is this theme of the thing in disequilibrium so important? Paul Claudel is one of the writers who wrote the most profoundly about painting, notably in a splendid book called *The Eye Listens,* which specifically analyzes the Dutch [painters]. And Claudel gets right to the heart of the question.[5] He says: What is a composition? You see, this is a pictorial term. What is a composition in painting? And Claudel's reply: he states that for the Dutch masters, a composition is always a whole. It's a structure that is always in the process of becoming imbalanced or in the process of coming apart.[6] We will hold on to this only for the moment: the point of collapse, a glass that appears about to tip over, a curtain that appears about to fall back down.[7]

There is no need to refer to Cézanne's pots, the strange imbalance of his pots, as if they were really grasped by Cézanne at the actual golden hour of the morning, at the very birth of an ensuing collapse. There's a contemporary of Cézanne who spoke about "drunken pottery."[8] Paintings of an avalanche can be said to capture a generalized disequilibrium. But in the end, this doesn't get us very far, since, at first glance, we still remain at the level of what the painting represents. And when I wonder about the importance of a category in painting such as catastrophe, I am also going to refer to another catastrophe, specifically a catastrophe that would affect the act of painting itself. You see, in the process of our reflection, we are moving from the catastrophe represented in a painting—whether a local catastrophe or catastrophe as a whole—to a much more secret catastrophe that affects the act of painting itself. My question here becomes the following: Can the act of painting be defined without this reference to a catastrophe that affects it? Doesn't the act of painting, at its most profound level, confront and perhaps even encompass this catastrophe, even when what is represented is not a catastrophe? In fact, Cézanne's pottery isn't a catastrophe; there was no actual earthquake. The same goes for Rembrandt's glasses: there was no real catastrophe involved. So, it's a question of a deeper catastrophe that affects the act of painting within itself to the extent that the act of painting could not be so defined otherwise.

The fundamental example, indeed a typical one, is the artwork of Turner. He had something like two periods. In the first one, he paints a lot of catastrophes. Storms are what interest him in the sea; in the mountains, avalanches are often what interest him. In this early period, he already shows great genius. What happens around 1830? Everything unfolds as if Turner somehow encountered a new element, in fact so deeply that this encounter remains forever tied to his first manner of painting. What is this new element? Catastrophe. Catastrophe is at the heart of the act of painting. As has been said before, forms suddenly vanish. What is painted and the act of painting tend to be identified with each other. But what form do they take on? Ephemeral forms like gusts of steam and balls of fire where none of the forms maintain their integrity, where the brush strokes are merely suggestive. Turner proceeds through such strokes carrying onward into a kind of inferno, as if the entire painting he was creating were itself emerging from an inferno. A ball of fire. Turner's famous dominant trait: golden yellow. A kind of great oven, on which boats are splintered and cracked wide open.[9]

A typical example is a painting with a complicated title: *Light and Color (Goethe's Theory, the Morning after the Deluge)*. We will have to make use of every last detail in this title. So try to go see a reproduction of this work by Turner. The painting is dominated by a gigantic and admirable ball of fire, a golden-hued ball that appears to bestow or ballast the entire painting within a kind of gravitation.[10] Why do I find this title important? Turner left stacks of watercolors in bundles. As has already been mentioned, he was so very far ahead of his time that he didn't even exhibit his paintings; he stored them away. He bequeathed everything to the State, to England, where his paintings remained for years in crates. And then there's the admirable yet infuriating John Ruskin, Turner's passionate admirer, who burned many of the works for reasons of what he considered pornography. In the end, that was catastrophic as well. There's a statement by Ruskin that makes one shiver—well, in the end, no one can condemn anyone—in which Ruskin says: I'm proud, quite proud to have burned all kinds of bundles of Turner's drawing and watercolors.[11] Ruskin's merit remains for having been one of the few to understand Turner in his lifetime. Ruskin baptized all kinds of bundles of watercolors: the birth or the advent of color. For this introduction, I don't want to say any more on the topic.

So, I'm making use of Turner's work to contend the following about painting: here we have the specific example of a painter and his paintings that at first appear to represent what we could call an avalanche or storm type of catastrophe, but which will lead to an infinitely deeper catastrophe that concerns the very activity of painting itself, a catastrophic process that affects the very depths of the act of painting. And what I'd like to suggest here is that this catastrophe inherent in the act of painting is inseparable from a kind of birth. A birth of what? The birth of color. There appears to be a problem here that we may have involuntarily created. Was it necessary for the act of painting to undergo this catastrophe as a means of engendering its main concern, namely, color? Was it necessary to undergo catastrophe in the act of painting for color to be born, color as pictorial creation? We have to accept that whatever this catastrophe affecting the act of painting is, it is also something other than catastrophe. So far, we haven't made much progress. If you look at a work by Turner through the lens of the end of his career, it's much easier to accept the term *catastrophe*. How is it that at that time, we seemingly have a number of painters coming to our rescue who use the word, who say: yes, painting, the act of painting must undergo and journey through chaos or through catastrophe? And they appear to suggest that only in this way does something emerge from this ordeal. Our idea is confirmed: there is some kind of necessity for catastrophe in the act of painting in order that something might emerge.

What emerges from this? Perhaps I'm simply choosing painters of the same tendency; I don't know, but the answer appears to be the same: [what emerges from this is] color. Who are these painters? Catastrophe—this is Cézanne's fine phrase—catastrophe affecting the act of painting in such a way that, according to Cézanne, color arises. And Paul Klee as well: there is a need for chaos so that what he calls the egg or cosmogenesis emerges. And at the same time, panic. My God—or at least the painters' God! Who prevents catastrophe from overwhelming everything? What happens if catastrophe overwhelms everything so that nothing emerges? In this regard, would the act of painting also perhaps pose some kind of danger? If the painter confronts this catastrophe in the act of painting, if he or she cannot paint without a catastrophe affecting his or her act at the most profound level of the work, the catastrophe likewise must be controlled. What happens if nothing emerges from this act, if the catastrophe simply proliferates and makes a total mess? Haven't we all glimpsed the possibility that, in certain cases, a painting is a failure? Painters almost do nothing but fail; they are always throwing out their paintings. It's astonishing. There's a kind of destruction where the painters and the painting become consumed by the chaos in the process. Can one control a catastrophe? With certain paintings by Van Gogh, one says: he is getting close to something. Where does Van Gogh's madness come from? From his relations with his father or from his relations with color? [*Laughter.*] I have no idea. In any case, that it's a result of color is perhaps more interesting.

So, our task now will be to look at two texts. I have yet to refer to any specific writings by painters themselves. The manner in which a painter speaks about his or her painting is not the same thing as the way in which a musician speaks about his or her music. I am not saying one is better than the other. I am simply saying that there is something unique about the way that painters write about their work. I want to refer to some texts presumably by Cézanne and a formal text by Klee, which have in common that they both speak deliberately about catastrophe in its relation to painting.[12]

[*Brief pause in the session,* time stamp: 1:18:08.]

Gasquet created a very important book on Cézanne.[13] In this book, he takes himself as being a bit like Plato for Socrates, that is, he reconstitutes dialogues many years later from conversations with Cézanne. This is not a transcription. What does Gasquet—who wasn't a painter, but a writer—add on his own? Many critics are suspicious of this text. On this point, I tend to agree with Maldiney, who, on the contrary, considers this a text that truly risks being very faithful to Cézanne, since it includes some fairly strange arguments.[14] You know that there is a kind of legend and rumors circulating about painters: painters are always treated a bit as if they were uneducated creatures and not very clever. As soon as we read what painters write, we're reassured; neither of these stereotypes is true. And one of the reasons why the matter of the authenticity of Gasquet's text often gets raised is that, from time to time, Cézanne strangely starts speaking like a post-Kantian.

On the other hand, Cézanne was actually very well educated; he didn't reveal it, or did so rarely. He seemed to enjoy playing the role of a peasant, a yokel, whereas he had considerable knowledge, and read quite a lot. Painters always pretend to have seen nothing, to know nothing. I think that they read a lot at night. [*Laughter.*] One can easily imagine that Gasquet even told Cézanne some things about Kant. What Cézanne understood is quite fine because he understood much more than someone with a university education. At one point, Gasquet has Cézanne say something incredible: "I would like to paint space and time and make them become forms of the sensibility of colors, since I sometimes imagine that colors are like great noumenal entities, living ideas, creatures of pure reason."[15] Commentators have said: Cézanne couldn't have said that; it's Gasquet who attributes it to him. I'm not so sure, myself. It's plausible that, one evening, they were having a conversation about Kant whom Cézanne understood quite well, because, when I say that he has a better understanding than a philosopher, what I mean is that he could see that the noumenon/phenomenon relationship in Kant's work was such that, in a certain way, the phenomenon was the appearance of the noumenon. Hence the theme: colors are noumenal ideas, colors are the noumena, and space and time are the form of the appearance of noumena, that is, of colors. Colors appear in space and in time, but in themselves, they are neither space nor time. This seems to me to be a very, very interesting idea; based on this, I'd gladly make the case that Cézanne said it. So, of course, at the same time, Gasquet's text steals things from letters sent to him by Cézanne, thereby creating some kind of hybrid mixture of their exchanges. Yes, but as for what's essential, everything suits us fine.

In the text that I am going to read from, Cézanne distinguishes between two moments in the act of painting.[16] His reflections will lend themselves precisely to the crux of our problem. In one of these moments, he refers to "chaos" or the "abyss," and in the second moment—if you read the text closely, since it's not clear, in fact, but it's a supposed conversation—he calls the second moment:

"catastrophe." The text is organized very logically and very rigorously. The activity of painting consists of the moment of chaos followed by the subsequent moment of catastrophe, and from this, something emerges: once again, what emerges is color. That is, when color emerges at all . . . since there is still the possibility that nothing emerges. One is never certain; this process and activity of painting guarantee nothing in advance.

So let me read to you from the text itself, starting with what Cézanne has to say about the first aspect. "In order to paint a landscape correctly, first I have to discover the [geological] strata. Imagine that the history of the world dates from the day when two atoms met, when two whirlwinds, two chemicals joined together. [I can see rising] these rainbows, these cosmic prisms, this dawn of ourselves above nothingness."[17] What is significant for us here? In my view, Cézanne's comments provide us with an original viewpoint that gets to the heart of the very practice of painting, namely, the theme of "only one thing ever truly gets painted: the beginning of the world." That's what matters to painters, painting the beginning of the world. What is the beginning of the world? It's the world before the world, that is, something that exists, but that is not yet the world. It's actually the birth of the world itself. How then does such a comment relate to painters who are Christians? Why would the history of creation be of interest to them? Insofar as they are painters, it's obvious. It's obvious that they are involved in something that concerns the creation of the world. I mean, this is an essential concern of painting.

"Imagine that the history of the world dates from the day when two atoms met, when two whirlwinds, two chemicals joined together."—[For] Turner, it's about chemical dances, yes, chemical dances of color—"this dawn of ourselves above nothingness, I can see them rising, I immerse myself in them when I read Lucretius." In fact, Cézanne read lots of Lucretius. And, Lucretius's interest concerns atoms, of course, the dance of atoms, but just as strangely, colors and light. There's no point in trying to understand anything in Lucretius if one doesn't first pay attention to what he says about color and light in relation to the atom. "These great rainbows, these cosmic prisms, this dawn of ourselves above nothingness, I see them rising, I immerse myself in them when I read Lucretius. In this fine rain . . ."—He's standing under a fine rain; it's precisely this fine mist that begs to be painted, this fine rain. Even if Cézanne is painting a portrait, a vase, a pot, even if he is painting his wife, the work always returns to this initial expression of the fine rain or expressing something of this order—"In this fine rain, I breathe the virginity of the world." What is this virginity of the world? It's the world before man and before the world. "A sharp sense of nuances works on me. I feel myself colored by all the nuances of infinity. At that moment, I am as one with my painting." This is strange, "I am as one with my painting" . . . What does that mean? We must comment on this precisely, my painting *yet to be created* . . . Since, as the rest will remind us even more precisely, he hasn't yet begun to paint. Perhaps we even have a basis for better understanding, for anticipating why the catastrophe belongs to the act of painting. It belongs so much to the act of painting, since catastrophe exists *before* the painter begins his or her act. [The catastrophe, it begins before.] Catastrophe will exist during as well, but it begins *before*. The painting is yet to be painted.[18] "In this fine rain, I breathe the virginity of the world. A sharp sense of nuances works on me," this is the pre-pictorial work. The catastrophe is already pre-pictorial. It's like the condition of painting; it comes before the act of painting. "A sharp sense of nuances works on me. I feel myself colored by all the nuances of infinity. At that point, I am as one with my painting."

"We are . . ."—the painting and I, the painting not yet undertaken, and the painter not yet having started to paint—"We are an iridescent chaos. I come before my motif"—you see, he hasn't painted anything yet—". . . I lose myself in it. I dream, I wander."—He loses himself through the very confrontation with his motif, in confronting a kind of chaos.—"Silently the sun penetrates my being, like a faraway friend [who] warms my idleness, [fertilizes it]. We germinate." And this idea of the germ or seed will literally recur when Klee makes use of it as well.[19] "We germinate. When night falls again, it seems to me that I shall never paint, that I have never painted." All this is pre-pictorial; it's the "before painting" for eternity. "I need night to tear my eyes away from the earth, from this corner of the earth into which I have melted. The next day, a beautiful morning . . ."—And here I find myself still within the first moment mentioned by Cézanne, and you see, this pre-pictorial moment of chaos has taken place. He merges with his motif; he no longer sees anything, and night is falling. As he explains in a letter, his wife scolds him because when he returns, his eyes are red.[20] He no longer sees anything. We have to ask: What is the painter's eye? How does an eye function in painting? Well then, it's a reddened eye, already. "The next day, a beautiful morning, slowly, [geological] foundations appear, the layers, the major planes form themselves on my canvas. Mentally I compose the rocky skeleton." If you see the landscapes of Aix by Cézanne, you immediately see what he refers to as the rocky skeleton. "*Mentally* I compose this . . ." You see, he hasn't started yet. "Mentally I compose the rocky skeleton. I can see the outcropping of stones under the water; the sky weighs on me. Everything falls into place. A pale palpitation envelops the linear elements. The red [patches of] earth rise from an abyss." The abyss is the previous evening's chaos. Red patches of earth emerge. What form of red? These must be brownish red patches of earth; these must be darkish purple, tending toward black. "I begin to separate myself from the landscape, to see it."—You see, this is also a genesis of the eye, this tale. At the moment of pure chaos, no eye, it has melted. The eye is completely red, it no longer sees anything. "With this first outline, I detach myself from these geological lines. Geometry measures the earth." In other words, geometry is identical with geology.

To summarize, I'm saying that this first pre-pictorial moment is the moment of chaos. One has to pass through this chaos. And according to Cézanne, what emerges from this chaos? The frame. The frame of the canvas. Here we have the great planes being sketched out. "Everything falls into place": this is already dangerous. There's a letter in which Cézanne says, this isn't going well. He says, "Planes fall one atop the other."[21] From this moment onward, everything could collapse; it's the first coefficient of a possible collapse. The distinction of planes might very well not succeed in occurring. The distinction of planes occurs starting from chaos. If chaos lays siege over everything, if nothing is capable of emerging from out of this chaos, if chaos remains chaos, the planes fall onto each other instead of falling upright. The painting, then, is already ruined before having even begun. This kind of shit happens. Any painter will tell you they have these kinds of experiences where everything is going fine, and then, suddenly, it's a mess. I'm blocked off, then I'm not blocked off.

[*Interruption of recording,* time stamp: 1:33:45.]

ANNE QUERRIEN:[22] This reminds me of what architects experienced during the late eighteenth century regarding the great debate around the sublime and the picturesque. And indeed, within the picturesque, there is passage through three stages, whereas in the sublime, only two stages are retained, with the sublime elevated to a higher level through its opposition to chaos. And what we see here is that chaos comes first . . . From chaos, they construct the sublime, and either they remain within the sublime, that is, geometrical lines, and so forth, or they manage to move into the picturesque, that is, into color and all that. I'm thinking about what my architect friends told me regarding architectural compositions in their debates about the sublime and the picturesque and about what you were telling us about Kant, and the sublime and chaos in Kant . . .[23]

DELEUZE: For those who might find this point of interest, there's a book by Kant that, I believe, is one of the most important books in all of philosophy, the *Critique of Judgment,* which Kant wrote at a very old age, and which includes one of the first great philosophical theories of aesthetics. Kant distinguishes two aspects or two moments of the sublime: one, he names the geometric or mathematical sublime, and the other, the dynamic sublime.[24] If we really wanted to, we probably could sketch out a comparison of Cézanne's two moments with Kant's two moments of the sublime, the first one being a geometrical or "geological" sublime, according to Cézanne's very expression, and the second being something of a dynamic sublime. Kant's text is extraordinary. These are the great founding texts of Romanticism.

We are now going to talk about the second moment. As a reminder, in the first moment, something emerges out of chaos, specifically the frame of the artwork. The second moment: "A feeling of tenderness comes over me. Some roots of this emotion raise the sap, the colors. It's a kind of deliverance. The soul's radiance, the gaze, exteriorized mystery are exchanged between the earth and the sun, [ideal and reality], colors! An airborne logic." Before, we were in a terrestrial, earthly logic, within geological strata. "An airborne, colorful logic quickly replaces the somber, stubborn geometry."[25]

Such a beautiful text. And now the elements are changing. "Everything becomes organized: trees, fields, houses." Wasn't everything already organized? Yet the planes somehow fall into place. "Everything becomes organized" as if he were starting all over again from zero. Cézanne proclaims, "I see." A second genesis of the eye. "I see, by patches, the geological strata." This is what will reveal the secret to us. It's odd, he doesn't specifically say it; but he seems to be starting again from nothing. He already said, "I see," and here, he acts as if he were seeing for the very first time.

What happened? There's only one answer: it's that what emerged during the first moment, the frame, collapsed once again. He says it formally: the entire first moment was a preparatory, pre-pictorial labor: "the geological strata, the preparatory work, the world of drawing all cave in and collapse as if in a catastrophe." That's why this text is very interesting to me since [Cézanne], in his own name, in his own experience, distinguishes two moments in what we can call "the catastrophe" in general: a moment of chaos-abyss from which the "strata" or "the framework" emerge, and then a second moment, the catastrophe that sweeps away the strata and the framework, and from which, what is going to emerge? "The geological strata, the preparatory labor, the world of the drawing cave in, collapse as if in a catastrophe. A cataclysm has carried it all away, [regenerated it]. A new era is born. The true one! The one in which nothing escapes me, where everything is dense and fluid at the same time, natural. All that remains is color, and in color, brightness, clarity, the being who imagines them, this ascent from the earth toward the sun, this exhalation of the depths toward love."[26] This is odd because, as Maldiney points out here, we could make a connection not only with Kant's texts on the sublime, but the same equivalent can also be found, term for term, in texts by Schelling, who is closely associated with painting.[27] "I want to take hold of this idea, this burst of emotion, this smoke of existence"—color that is rising—"above the universal fire." Here as well, it's as if he were describing Turner's paintings. But he's not talking about Turner here; he's referring to how he conceives of his own paintings, about what he wants to create.

Let me take it once more from the beginning. We have an initial moment of decomposition into two aspects: first, there is the chaos-abyss, where I see nothing. Then a second aspect emerges from this initial moment. Something emerges from the chaos-abyss: the great planes, a kind of framework, a sort of geology. Then there is a second moment: catastrophe sweeps away the strata and the great planes. That is, we must start all over again. And yet if the first moment hadn't taken place, none of this painterly practice would function. Once again, there's always an inherent danger that catastrophe might take hold of everything and that the birth of color might not happen. So this procession toward color constitutes a bit of progress: What happens when color does not emerge, when color does not somehow coalesce into a form within the fire? Color has to emerge from this kind of fiery furnace of catastrophe. If color does not forge itself, if it doesn't become properly formed or set . . . Is the painter concerned with ceramics? Yes, of course. He uses other means, but he has his fire. There is no color that doesn't emerge from this kind of fire, which is at the same time on the canvas. Here we can think of a sphere of fire, Turner's sphere of light. What will this furnace of chaos elicit for Cézanne? What shall we call it? We don't know yet. Color is supposed to emerge from this chaos. Color rises . . . Must we simply understand it as a metaphor? No, it's not just a metaphor, clearly not for Cézanne. Color, for Cézanne, becomes a matter of ascension, of an ascending array. It must rise. Is this true for all painters? No, not at all. There are painters for whom color is conceived of as a descending array. It just so happens that, for Cézanne, and we'll see why, color arises as an ascending array. As a result, what appears to be metaphorical is not metaphorical in the slightest.

ANNE QUERRIEN: Color ascends toward white.

DELEUZE: It ascends toward white? No, not really.

ANOTHER STUDENT:[28] [It's] toward blue.

ANNE QUERRIEN: [*Inaudible comments.*] At this moment, there's an ascending array or spectrum of color toward black; it's the intense black body.[29]

DELEUZE: Yes, but for Cézanne, it doesn't ascend toward white. It rises . . .

ANNE QUERRIEN: Ah, toward light . . .

DELEUZE: No, these are ascending arrays. Anyway, we will be discussing how this takes shape.

ANNE QUERRIEN: No, I'm mentioning this because during the exhibition on forms of realism of the interwar years, if I recall correctly, there are painters who began promoting black and darkness as intensity.[30]

DELEUZE: Yes, but here, we're talking about Cézanne, right?

What does it mean when the color does not rise? When it doesn't receive its form or become forged? Earlier, we saw the danger of the first moment. The planes fall on top of each other; they are not upright. There is a kind of geological failure that takes place. What does "upright" mean, since these planes exist only in the painting? It's not the uprightness of resemblance. If the planes fall one atop the other, the painting is already ruined. You see, this is much more important than the problem of depth. The problem of depth is completely subordinate to the problem of planes and the collapsing of planes. Planes must fall but not on top of each other. We always manage to deal with depth. As far as depth is concerned, all creations are permitted. But of course, we always seem to elicit the depth we deserve depending on the way in which we cause the planes to fall. That is the painter's problem. The painter never has any problems dealing with depth. A problem of depth is a joke.

So, in the second moment, what happens if colors don't emerge? What is the danger? Painters express it quite well. The danger is swampy colors; it's a swamp, a marsh. A mess. Everything becomes a heap of grey [*grisaille*]. The planes start falling on each other, and there's total confusion. When colors don't emerge, there's nothing but a dull grey. At worst, this results in soiled paintings. Gauguin once became very annoyed because a great critic of the era claimed that in Gauguin's paintings, all the colors were "muted and scabby" [*sourdes et teigneuses*].[31] [*Laughter.*] In response to such a comment,

[Gauguin] was unforgiving; twenty years later, he still remembered that someone said this about his work. Color is difficult; it's difficult to get away from the muted, the scabby, and dull greys. Why am I introducing this idea? Because there's a famous text by Delacroix to which all painters seem to refer, where Delacroix exclaims: grey is the enemy of color; it's the enemy of painting.[32] And now we can understand what that means. At the most basic level, what is grey? It's where white and black become mixed together, and in the most extreme examples, it's where colors are mixed together and do not rise. It's just dull greyness.

And not long after this text which I just read to you, we find the same Cézanne telling Gasquet: "I was at Talloires. [. . .] You want grays? Well, you've got them! And greens, all the greenish grays in the whole world. The surrounding hills are high enough, it seemed; they appear low, and it rains! [. . .] There's a lake between two gorges, a landscaped English lake. Sketchbook pages fall, already watercolored, from the trees. Surely that's still nature . . . But not as I see it. Do you understand? . . . Gray on gray. You're not a painter if you haven't painted gray. Delacroix said that gray was the enemy of all painting, but he was wrong. You have to know how to paint gray to be a painter."[33] What does he mean? He's wrong to criticize Delacroix. Delacroix's text is as important and fascinating as Cézanne's, and furthermore, they are saying exactly the same thing.

There may well be two greys or else there are a lot of greys, a huge number of greys. There's a grey of colors mixing together, which is the grey of failure. And then there's another grey, which perhaps is like the grey of fiery cinders, an essentially luminous grey from which colors emerge. One must proceed very carefully here when speaking of grey because it's well known that there are two manners of creating grey. Kandinsky also speaks about this. He has a beautiful text about the two greys, a passive grey and an active grey.[34] At the same time, we can't limit ourselves to that. I'm emphasizing this immediately to avoid objections. There's a grey that's a mixture of black and white, and the great grey that is a mixture of green and red—or even, in a more extended manner, that's a mixture of two complementary colors, but above all, a mixture of green and red. And Delacroix spoke about this other grey, that grey of green-red. It's obviously not the same grey.

It would be easy for us to say: yes, there's a grey of colors that are mixed—a white-black grey—and a grey that is like the matrix of colors, the green-red grey. In Kandinsky's color theory, he calls the green-red grey a truly dynamic grey, a grey that rises, that rises to color.[35] Why is it not enough simply to make such a claim? Because if we look at Chinese or Japanese painting, for example, it's well known that they were already capable of obtaining an infinite series of nuances of grey beginning with white and black. So, we cannot say that the mixture of white-black is not also a matrix. I am simply laying the groundwork for a specific question concerning the color grey. Why? No doubt, to move from Cézanne to Klee. Because we're going to see the story of grey return again later on.

So, let me quickly summarize everything we just discussed about Cézanne. Here's what he tells us. He still gave us invaluable information: catastrophe belongs so much to the act of painting that it's already there before the painter can even begin his or her task. He has provided us an important detail that we haven't yet quite worked out completely, you see? What is it that we are in the process of grasping, or beginning to grasp? And this is a question that I personally find very interesting. It's not enough simply to place painting in relation to space because this is obvious. And even then, it seems to me that in order to understand its relation with space, we have to place it [painting] in relation to time, a time that's specific to painting. [We have] to treat a painting as if it already performed or carried out its own synthesis of time. [We have] to say: a painting implies a synthesis of time. [We have] to say: be careful, painting concerns space only because, first, it embodies a synthesis of time. And this concerns a properly pictorial synthesis of time, with the act of painting itself defined by this synthesis of time.

So, this would be a synthesis of time that is specific only to painting. If this hypothesis is correct, how do we discover and manage to define the synthesis of a time that we could call properly pictorial? Let's suppose that the act of painting refers necessarily to a pre-pictorial condition and, on the other hand, that something has to emerge from what this act confronts. The act of painting must confront its pre-pictorial condition in such a way that something emerges from it. And here we indeed have a synthesis of time. But what would this specific form be? In the form of something pre-pictorial—prior to the painter even beginning to paint—in the form of an act of painting and of something emerging from this act. These forms would be within the painting. This would be the time belonging to the painting. To the extent that I would have the right to ask about any painting whatsoever: What is the pre-pictorial condition of this painting? We're not talking about general categories; we're asking rather: Can you show me where the act of painting is in this painting? And: What emerges from this painting? So then, I would have my properly pictorial synthesis of time. If I attempt to summarize Cézanne's theme based on this perspective, I would say: first, the pre-pictorial conditions would be chaos or the abyss, from which the great projected planes emerge. The second moment would be the act of painting as catastrophe. The great planes must be swept away by catastrophe. And what emerges from this? Color.

Above all, stay with me; now's not the time for you to relax or reflect. I am moving on to Paul Klee. Paul Klee's concern was always very strange. There is a recurrent theme in a number of his writings about what he calls the grey point. We sense that he has a relation with the grey point. It's his own personal concern. He somehow makes use of this to explain what painting means to him. For example, in what has been translated under the title *Theory of Modern Art* (in the French edition Médiations), there is a text by Klee titled "Note on the grey point," page 56.[36] Throughout his entire career, never once does he abandon his idea of the grey point and the adventures of the grey point. He discusses it everywhere, or rather, quite often. Here's what he tells us: "Chaos as the antithesis of order is not properly chaos; it's not true chaos. It's a 'localized' notion, relating to the notion of cosmic order [. . .]. True chaos couldn't place itself on the disc of a scale, but forever remains imponderable and incommensurable. It would correspond rather to the *center* of the scale." In fact, it doesn't correspond; he says "rather." You are going to see why it doesn't correspond. What does he tell us here? He is very philosophical; he is saying, if you talk about chaos, it's not something that you can just take on because, if you do, you cannot escape from it. He is saying, I'm ready to take it on because I'm a painter. But from a logical perspective, you cannot take on chaos as if it were the antithesis of something because chaos takes hold of everything and risks consuming everything. You cannot simply call chaos the opposite of order. Chaos is relative to nothing. It is opposed to nothing; it consumes everything. From the start, Klee already calls into question any possible logical thought regarding chaos. Chaos has no opposite. If you take on chaos, how are you going to escape from it?

Klee is going to try to tell us how, for himself, he's able to escape from a chaos with no opposite, a chaos that's not relative. He says, so chaos is a nonconcept. That's interesting for my question: Can painters offer us concepts? He starts by telling us: you know, if you take seriously the idea of chaos, it's a nonconcept. Here we're on the alert. We must allow ourselves to discover Klee's text with pleasure and wonder. We shouldn't seek to argue with him or question him about why he thinks what he does; we have to allow ourselves to enter into the text. "The symbol of this nonconcept is the 'point,' not a real point but a mathematical point." In other words, a point with no dimension. "This being-nothingness or this nothingness-being"—Klee is very philosophical—"is the nonconceptual concept of noncontradiction." This is quite joyful. About chaos, he says: "This being-nothingness or this nothingness-being is the nonconceptual concept of noncontradiction"—of noncontradiction, since it is opposed to nothing, since it's not relative, it's absolute. Chaos is absolute. "To bring it into view"—that is, in order to have a visible approximation of it—"coming to something like a decision on this matter [. . .], one must reach out to the concept of grey, to the *grey point,* the fateful point between what becomes and what dies." You see: it's the grey point that is responsible for being like the pictorial sign of absolute chaos. "This point is grey, because it's neither white, nor black or because it's white as much as it's black . . ." You see, this grey that's in question, it's the grey of black-white. He says it explicitly. "It's grey because it's neither high nor low, or because it's above as much as it's below. [It's] grey because it's neither hot nor cold." In terms of colors, you have hot colors with expansive movement, cold colors with contracting movement. "[It's] grey because it's neither hot nor cold. Grey because [it's a] nondimensional point." Klee's text is very beautiful; we don't know exactly where he's going, but he's going there with a sense of rigor. "Grey because [it's a] nondimensional point, a point between dimensions, between the dimensions and at their intersection, at the crossroads of paths."

And so here we have this idea of Klee's grey-chaos point. I am going to need to include some other writings by Klee; in the text I was citing, he continues to talk about this grey: "To establish a point in chaos is necessarily to recognize it as 'grey' by reason of its principled concentration and to confer on it the character of an original center from which the order of the universe is going to spring forth and emanate in all dimensions. To realize a point with a central virtue is to transform it into the locus of cosmogenesis. To this advent corresponds the idea of every Beginning, [. . .] or better yet, the concept of the *egg*." He has offered us two concepts: the nonconceptual concept of grey and the concept of the egg. That's where we are, on this second level; we are at the genesis of dimensions. The first grey point is nondimensional. The second paragraph is obviously referring to a second grey point. What is this second grey point? It's the first one, but affixed and centered. If you are starting to grasp something in this, you can see here an echo of Cézanne's text. Planes topple down. I have affixed the nondimensional grey point. I've made it the center. In itself, it's not a center at all. But once I've affixed it, I've made it a center in a way that it becomes the matrix of all dimensions. The first point mentioned by Klee was one-dimensional. The second is the very same point, but it has become affixed and centered. In another text, he has an even stranger expression, it's very, very odd: "The established grey point"—that is, once the grey point is affixed, once it's taken as center. It's a cosmogenesis of painting that he is trying to create here, I believe. "The established grey point leaps over itself into the field where it creates order."[37] The first point was the grey-chaos, nondimensional point. The second one is the same, but the same in another form, at an entirely different level, at another moment. This time, it's the grey point [that's] become center, henceforth the matrix of dimensions, to the extent that it is established, that is: between the two, it has leaped over itself. As Klee adored creating little drawings of its cosmogenesis—you see quite well the grey point that leaps over itself [see next page].[38]

I'm going to cite another text by Klee where he speaks of the grey point—the tale of the grey point obsesses him so much—and I think this excerpt will be extremely valuable: "If the grey point expands"—this is the second grey point, taken as center, that's

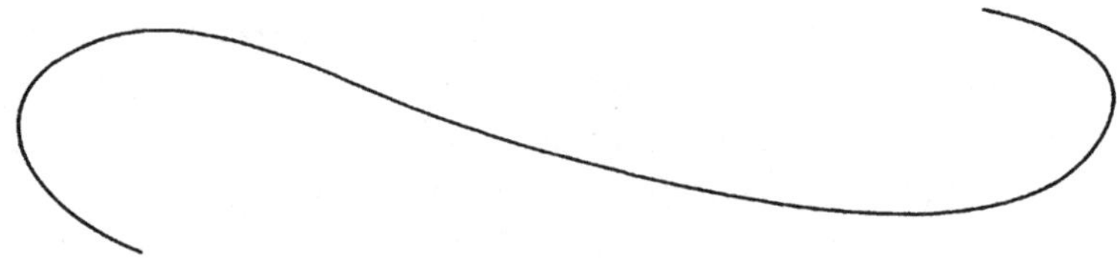

Paul Klee's grey point leaping over itself.

become the matrix of dimensions—"and occupies the totality of the visible, then chaos changes its meaning and the egg creates itself dead."[39] This is the Paul Klee version of the question we were asking earlier: What if chaos consumes everything? We have to pass through chaos, but something has to emerge from it. And if nothing emerges, if chaos seizes everything, if the grey point doesn't leap over itself, then the egg is dead. What is the egg? It's obviously the painting. The painting is an egg.

So what exactly is Klee's grey? As a way to create a parallel with Cézanne's text, I'd say the first moment: it's the grey-chaos point, it's the absolute. Obviously, this is prior to painting. One can't paint this grey-chaos point. When does the act of painting begin? It's on both sides at once [*à cheval*]. The act of painting, if I dare say, has one hand in the pre-pictorial condition and the other hand within itself. The act of painting is the act that seizes the grey point in order to affix it, in order to place it into the center of the dimensions. It is the act that causes the grey point to leap over itself. In leaping over itself, at that very moment, the grey point engenders order or the egg. If it doesn't leap over itself, it's ruined, the egg is dead. So, we have the two moments: the grey-chaos point and the grey-matrix point. Between the two, the grey point has leapt over itself, and that's the act of painting. The passage necessarily occurs through chaos because within chaos, the pre-pictorial condition is located.

Since here Klee does it explicitly, even more directly than Cézanne, can we reconnect with the problem of color in relation to grey? Is this the same grey? It would seem that the answer is: yes, the first grey-chaos point is the grey of black-white. The grey point that leapt over itself, the second one, is not the same. It's the same and not the same. Wouldn't this be the grey of green-red, the grey matrix of dimensions and colors? Is this something we can affirm? Yes, but is this enough? No, because it would be stupid simply to claim that the grey of black-white isn't already the entire egg as well—the entire rhythm of painting. So, all this is just a manner of speaking . . . How can we go about resolving this paradox? We are very slowly making progress, that is, we are beginning to perceive this synthesis of time that is present. It's really more like a question of attribution. This evidently seems to work for Turner. It works for Cézanne. And certainly for Klee as well. You are observing why all these painters can be tied so fully to the idea of a beginning of the world. The beginning of the world is their direct concern. Does music have a relation with the beginning of the world? Yes, yes certainly. But is it in the same way? I really don't know.

We feel stuck. Each time we feel like we've reached a dead end, we must move on to another painter. I'm attempting to find something else to help me advance just a bit. In this case, I'm going to discuss a contemporary painter, Bacon, whose work has really made quite an impression on me. And I will stick to referring to writings by the painter himself. Perhaps next week, I'll make an exception and show you one of Bacon's paintings so that you see what he is trying to say. But perhaps it's not necessary. Bacon did some interviews that were published with Skira Editions.[40] There's one passage that I find completely bizarre because, as I should mention, he is lucky enough to be English, or well, Irish. He uses a term that the English greatly admire—and it's perhaps through this term that we will find some kind of salvation. Why have I chosen to cite this interview at this point in today's session? Because Bacon says that, prior to beginning a painting, there are many things that have occurred, and this is precisely why painting implies a kind of catastrophe weighing on the canvas. Why? In order to jettison everything that has preceded it, everything that weighs on the painting before the painting has begun to emerge. What is the name we give to such things that he has to get rid of? What is this struggle with ghosts that precedes painting?

Painters have often provided an almost technical term in their own vocabulary: clichés.[41] We might say that clichés already reside in the canvas before painters have even begun to paint, that the worst of clichés is already there, that all the abominations of what is bad in painting already reside there within the potential work. Cézanne knew about clichés, about the struggle against the cliché before even starting to paint, as if clichés were there like animals rushing in, already there on the painting before the painter had even picked up his brush. Here we understand why painting is necessarily a flood: one has to drown all that, block all that, kill all that, prevent all these dangers that already weigh down on the canvas by virtue of its pre-pictorial condition. Even if they're not visible, they exist there. Where do such ectoplasms reside? In one's head and in one's heart: they're everywhere, in the room, hovering around. It's amazing how these clichés are like ghosts. If you don't commit your painting to endure a catastrophic dynamic like that found in a furnace or a storm, you will only produce clichés. People will say, oh! what a lovely brush stroke, really, from a decorator. Yes, it's well done, quite lovely! Or else a fashion drawing. Fashion designers know how to sketch quite well, and it's shit at the same time, with no interest, none, zero [*FBLS*, 71–74 UM, 86–90 C].

This is not to suggest that great painters are able to evade this danger any more than others. Rather, the painter is fully conscious of the risks inherent in what matters to him or her the most. They all know how to create a perfect drawing. This may not always appear to be the case, but they have acquired such mastery; sometimes they have even learned to draw like this in the great art academies. For a long period throughout history, this was quite simply how painters were trained. It's hard for us even to imagine a painter who hasn't mastered these sorts of sketches and reproductions. All great painters have spent time acquiring this skill of painting, all of them. But they are also well aware that this acquisition of the art of painting must then engage with a kind of catastrophe. Perhaps I'm not explaining as well as I should; I'm not saying that this is all there is to the act of great painting. I am saying: if the act of painting is essentially concerned with a catastrophe, this is because, on the one hand, it establishes a necessary relation with a pre-pictorial condition, and, on the other hand, within this necessary relation, it must negate the emergence of any potential danger on the canvas, in the room, in onc's head, and in one's heart. The painter must throw himself or herself into the eye of this kind of storm that will thus eliminate all these clichés or cause them to flee.

If someone devotes his or her whole life to painting and struggling against the cliché, this is no mere academic exercise. You must understand how unbearable this process is. Without the necessary passage through catastrophe, one will remain doomed to the cliché. And even if you say, ah, this painter's work is really beautiful, not in the least bit with clichés—while these works may not be clichés for certain people, for the artist himself or herself, they will be. There are some works by Cézanne that we would not consider clichés. But for him, they certainly were. This is why great painters are the most critical about their own works and why they throw out so many things. So, this is the first danger. The artist doesn't dare engage with the catastrophe, but rather avoids it. Are there great painters who avoided catastrophe? Or else they manage to reduce it to such a minimum that catastrophe is no longer visible at all. Perhaps there are great painters who were . . . I don't know, a bit whorish. They appear to endure this passage [through catastrophe] but don't do so at all. And then there's the second danger: one engages with and passes through catastrophe, and the painting remains stuck within it. This occurs all the time. As Klee says, the grey point has expanded instead of leaping beyond itself.

So, now is a good time to look at one of the texts by Bacon, [who says]: I am making marks. It's about the moment when Cézanne reaches the great planes. It's what [Bacon] calls random marks or what he calls cleanup. He takes a brush or a rag and cleans part of the painting. *One part.* Always remember that the catastrophe doesn't dominate everything. The artist himself is establishing his catastrophe. "The [random] marks are made, and you survey the thing"—that is, the painting with one part cleaned—"like you would a sort of [diagram]."[42] This is marvelous! This is going to help us progress in our inquiry. Try to file this word in your memory, a diagram. "And you see within this [diagram] the possibilities of all types of fact being planted. This is a difficult thing; I'm expressing it badly. But you see, for instance, if you think of a portrait, you maybe at one time have put the mouth somewhere, but you suddenly see through this [diagram]"[43]—it's important to understand that, for Bacon, it's bad if the work does not proceed through some kind of diagram. For without doing so, that would yield a caricature, that is, something not very strong—"You [. . .] at one time have put the mouth somewhere, but you suddenly see through this [diagram] that the mouth could go right across the face." An immense mouth. You stretch the line. You will declare in huge letters that this is a diagrammatic line. "And in a way"—this is what matters most to me—"you would love to be able in a portrait to make a Sahara of the appearance." To transform the painting into a Sahara. "To make it so like [a Sahara] yet seeming to have the distances of the Sahara." This means: one must establish in the painting a diagram from which the work will emerge—this is completely the equivalent of the grey point—and this diagram is exactly like a Sahara, from which the portrait will emerge. "To make it so like [a Sahara] yet seeming to have the distances of the Sahara."

What is this, and why does this word *diagram* interest me?[44] Is this random? I don't know, but I assume that, like so many painters, Bacon is well read. Diagram is a notion that has taken on great importance in contemporary English logic. That's good for us. Notably it's a notion with which a great logician named Peirce created an extremely complex theory: the theory of diagrams that has great importance today within logic.[45] Wittgenstein rarely uses the word *diagram*, but on the other hand, he speaks frequently of possibilities of fact.[46] So I don't exclude the possibility that Bacon here is hinting at people about whose concepts he might be vaguely aware and whose books he read, because the word *diagram* is strange. At the very least, he may well have not done any reading and merely chose the word *diagram*, which has a certain contemporary usage, I believe, in English. What is Bacon trying to say to us here? Why do I find this commentary on the diagram so intriguing?

You see, the diagram functions as a kind of cleanup zone that creates catastrophe on the painting, that is, erasing all the previous clichés, even if they were only virtual [*FBLS*, 81 UM; 99–100 C]. It sweeps everything up into a catastrophe, and it's from the diagram, that is, the initiation of this Sahara desert within the painting, that what Bacon calls the Figure will emerge. Can the word *diagram* be useful to us? Yes. Following Bacon, let's conceive of the diagram as this dual notion—around which we've been circling from the start—of germinal catastrophe or germinal chaos. As much for

Cézanne's work as for Klee's, as we discussed, there is this very special instance—the catastrophe—out of which something emerges that is rhythm, color, whatever you'd like. The diagram would be this unit that causes this germinal catastrophe, this germinal chaos, to become comprehensible. Henceforth, the diagram would indeed contain all the preceding aspects, specifically: the tension in catastrophe toward the pre-pictorial condition, on the one hand; on the other hand, the diagram would be at the heart of the very act of painting itself; and finally, it's from within the diagram that something must emerge.[47]

And yet, if the diagram extends across the entire painting, everything is ruined. But if there is no diagram, if there's no cleanup zone, if there isn't this kind of maddening zone unleashed from within the painting so that both the multiple dimensions as well as colors emerge, if there isn't this green-red kind of grey from which all colors will arise and create their ascending arrays, then there is nothing left. We've made some slight progress here: everything that has appeared complex to us within these dual ideas of chaos—catastrophe and germ—we can now tie them all together within the proposition of a notion that would be properly pictorial, specifically, a diagram.[48]

The diagram must become pictorial again. In doing so, it will open lots of new logical horizons for us, creating a kind of logic of the diagram. Perhaps this would be the same thing as a logic of painting if it's oriented in this direction. But on the other hand, would it be possible for a painter to have one or several diagrams? What would a painter's diagram be? A diagram wouldn't be the same for all painters, otherwise it's a notion that wouldn't be pictorial. We would have to uncover each painter's diagram. This might be an interesting undertaking, and it's even possible that they change diagrams. We might even be able perhaps to assign them dates. What would a diagram be that could be revealed in the painting, variable according to each painter, perhaps even variable according to eras, that could be dated? Here's what I am getting at: What would it mean to refer to "a Turner 1830 diagram"? Are these Platonist Ideas? No, since they have dates, they have proper names. And this is what is perhaps most profound about painting. What is Turner's diagram? I'm not going to try to summarize it within a single painting.

How about a Van Gogh diagram? Here perhaps we breathe more easily because he is one of those painters whose diagram is the most readily deciphered and grasped. That doesn't mean he necessarily had a formula. But in Van Gogh's work, everything occurs as if the relation with catastrophe were so greatly exacerbated that the diagram almost appears in a pure state. Everyone knows what a Van Gogh diagram is: it's this infinite world of tiny scratches, tiny commas, tiny threes that sometimes cause the sky to throb, sometimes cause the earth to rock, sometimes completely sweep away a tree—and which has nothing to do with a general idea—that you are also going to find in a tree, in the sky, on the earth, and which will exist as Van Gogh's treatment of color [*FBLS*, 83 UM; 102 C]. I can say: yes, this diagram of tiny commas, of tiny crosses, of tiny threes, and so on, I can show how, from the start, in a rather obtuse and stubborn way, Van Gogh deliberately sought that kind of thing.[49]

As we are coming to the end of today's session, let us ask this: Is it by chance—and perhaps for our own comfort—that Van Gogh discovers color quite late, that such a genius who devoted so much of his time to color spends his whole life in noncolor? Remaining in black and white, as if color filled him with terror, always putting off his apprenticeship in color to the following year, wallowing in greyness [*grisaille*], but really in the grey of black-white, and that he somehow lives from this greyness and sends his drawings to his brother? He is constantly requesting that his brother send him mountain chalk. I don't know what mountain chalk is, but it's the best chalk. He says, send me mountain chalk, I'm not finding any here. So Van Gogh ends up spending his time with charcoal and mountain chalk. And it all goes badly, very badly. How will he enter into color? What will occur when he enters into color, and what entry will he make into color after having held himself back for so long?

Here, Klee's story becomes vital, even dramatic. The grey point leaps over itself. The grey point of black and white becomes the matrix of all colors. It becomes the grey point of green-red or the grey point of complementary colors. It has somehow leapt over itself. Van Gogh entered into color and did so because he confronted his diagram. And what is his diagram? It's the germinal catastrophe, specifically these kinds of tiny commas, tiny colored hooks with which he is going to undertake his entire apprenticeship and mastery of color. And I can even give this moment a precise date [*FBLS*, 83 UM; 102 C]. Just as for the Turner diagram, I can say: 1830, because however strongly Turner may have sensed his own diagram before this, that's when he directly confronts it. And for Van Gogh? The date would be 1888. It's at the start of 1888 that his diagram truly becomes something mastered, and at the same time, something fully varied, since his little commas—you'll notice them in all works by Van Gogh—are sometimes straight, sometimes curved, without ever having the same curve, and so on. That's what the variability of a diagram is. The diagram is, in fact, an infinite opportunity for paintings. It's not at all a general idea. It's dated, it has a proper name: one painter's diagram, then another's, then another's, and in the end, that's what creates a painter's style. So a Bacon diagram certainly exists. There are painters who change diagrams. There are others who don't change, but that doesn't at all mean they repeat themselves. It means that they never finish analyzing their diagram. And so, we finally have a notion adequate for this long history of the catastrophe and the germinal state within the act of painting: it's the notion of the diagram.

SESSION 2

7 April 1981

PAINTING FORCES

At the previous session, I tried to identify something very specific about painting. I'll remind you all again that it goes without saying that what I am suggesting has no universal value. It's up to you to see if something in these reflections suits you or not. To summarize the last session briefly: what struck me in the works of a certain number of painters was the presence on the canvas of a true catastrophe. My question was: What is this relation, not between painting and catastrophe, but a more profound relation between a catastrophe and the very act of painting itself? [It's] as if the painters I mentioned had to traverse or pass through this catastrophe. Then, following this hypothetical claim, I tried to explore the idea of what might be called, using a very vague term, a first concept specific to painting, a kind of pictorial concept. By drawing on some specific texts written by the painters themselves, we then developed a kind of initial concept of a germinal state of this catastrophic process inherent in painting, a germinal catastrophe or a germinal chaos, as if the painting included this germinal catastrophe from which something might eventually emerge. And as I sought to demonstrate, this germinal catastrophe is visible in the works of a certain number of painters.

So, this obviously presents a problem. For painters in whose works this germinal chaos is not visible, can we say that it is there anyway, but remains virtual or invisible? That's something that I don't even dare consider. One must have more solid grounding even to ask this question without it becoming just talk or entirely literary. But in the works of certain painters, we know this to be a process that is clearly present. They speak to us about this catastrophe they're experiencing, once again not personally—although this engagement with chaos might have many personal consequences for their own mental equilibrium. But I'm not talking about how they personally experienced this catastrophe because that's quite secondary. No, what I'm focusing on is how this catastrophe resides specifically in the painting itself: it's painting, *their* painting that experiences this. Perhaps the most striking text regarding this was the one I mentioned by Paul Klee, who spoke of these two moments: the grey point as chaos, and this grey point that leaps over itself to spread forth like a spatial germ. I was trying at least to understand or interpret this as if I were dealing with two states of grey, the black-white grey that leaps over itself and becomes the green-red grey, that is, the matrix of color.

With this in mind, is this germinal chaos what painting must traverse in order for light or color to be born? In this regard, [we have] the admirable titles of bundles of Turner's watercolors, "Birth of Color," "Color Beginning," and this theme runs through all painters for whom ultimately a painting or a painter is situated at a creation or beginning of the world. What else would this mean other than to experience this initial chaos-catastrophe? He or she establishes it on the canvas so that something might emerge that is obviously no longer of the world of objects—there is no way in which this something is of the world of objects—but rather of the world of color-light. And you understand that there is no general formula for chaos-catastrophe, germinal chaos, or germinal catastrophe. It is obvious that Van Gogh's germinal chaos is completely different from Cézanne's, completely different as well from Gauguin's, and quite understandably from Klee's. So these are very singularized kinds of germinal chaos in which something we'll call the painter's style will be in play, and what will emerge from this will also be quite different. I believe that in painters of light who strive for color through light and in painters of color who themselves strive for light through color, it goes without saying that these techniques are entirely different.

So, when I speak of a germinal chaos, what am I getting at? I don't mean something undifferentiated, quite to the contrary. This initial spark of chaos is already present in the work, it exists as if inscribed; the painter's signature is already there. During the last session, you'll recall that I referred to a contemporary painter—Bacon—who proposes a term that I find intriguing and quite useful, which I am therefore going to make use of: Bacon speaks of this germinal chaos as a diagram. He says: in a painting, there is a diagram, even in a portrait. It's the quote that I read to you.[1] What exactly is the diagram he's talking about? He tells us—and we must pay careful attention to the way he explains this—a diagram is a possibility of fact. From this, I almost glean the idea ultimately of what we are doing here as we speak about painting. If we were involved in creating a kind of logic of painting, which would not at all consist of bringing painting into logic, but of considering that painting has its own logic, then this expression *diagram* would be all the more useful for me, since, as I mentioned, it is used so much of late by certain American or English logicians. To connect to some more logical or philosophical considerations, what I would like to do, among other things, is to try to see if painting couldn't provide us with some elements for a theory of the diagram.

I've tried to situate this diagram or this germinal chaos with the very time of the act of painting. It might be possible to say quite simply, understanding we can correct this later, that this is like the second moment in the act of painting's three moments. This is what I meant by saying: you know, in a painting, implicitly there is always a synthesis of time. What are these three moments? I said that the painting is in immediate communication with a before-painting. The painting cannot be conceived prior to an initial before-painting. Fundamentally it possesses a pre-pictorial dimension. On this point, you'll recall that I referred to Cézanne's text in which he discusses all that occurs before he begins to paint.[2] This pre-pictorial dimension indeed appears already in the painting. And, as a function of this initial pre-pictorial dimension, the diagram asserts itself as a second step. Here we are led to a subsequent question: How will the diagram act regarding the initial moment?

If we find in the painting, whether visible or nonvisible, an adherence as well as a pre-pictorial dimension, we still do not know what this dimension encompasses. All I can say is that the necessity for germinal chaos, that is, in the form of the diagram, is located in a certain function that painting performs in relation to this initial pre-pictorial dimension. What is the diagram going to do? It will act as a kind of zone for blurring and erasing, undoubtedly allowing the advent of painting. If the third moment is to emerge, a kind of blurring and vagueness and an initial erasure are needed. So, I have what I call my kind of temporal dimension for the act of painting:

the pre-pictorial dimension, the diagram that will act on this dimension in ways that we still cannot discern, in such a way as to make us wonder, what exactly will emerge from the diagram?

Let's return to Bacon's words. The diagram is not yet the pictorial *fact*. Okay, does this imply that an eventual pictorial fact would exist? Perhaps. Why is it, then, that when painting is discussed, there always seems to be a specific term used by everyone, or by a lot of people, by critics, namely, the theme of *presence*? Presence, presence. It's the simplest word to describe the effect that painting has on us. I'm making no distinctions for the moment; we have no grounds for any. Whether it's a Mondrian square or a figure in a very classical painting, a kind of presence exists. What do critics mean when they use this word? It is clearly used to tell us what we indeed know thanks to the paintings, something we also know for ourselves: it's not representation. The painter causes presence to emerge. A portraitist doesn't represent the king, doesn't represent the queen, doesn't represent the little princess, but rather causes a presence to emerge.[3] This is a convenient word, another way of saying that a pictorial fact exists [*FBLS*, 44 UM; 50–51 C].

After all, every vocabulary suits us. So here we have my three moments: the pre-pictorial moment, which in a way—again, I'm insisting on this—is inherent to the painting; then the diagram; then the pictorial fact that emerges from the diagram. Again, this is a hypothesis because we'll have reasons to revise all this. I'm thinking of a text by Kant, in a completely different field, in which he uses Latin terminology—this is a beautiful passage—to distinguish the *datum* and the *factum*.[4] In French, it's less pretty: the given [*le donné*] and the fact [*le fait*]. He says: you know, the fact is something completely different from the given. So, what I'm referring to as the first moment, the first moment of the painting—the pre-pictorial dimension—is the world of givens. So, what is given? And suddenly, my question becomes more specific, and it will help us: What is given on the canvas prior to the very beginning of the painting?

I'm insisting on this because recently we've seen the emergence of what I would consider to be a kind of disastrous platitude, because it so grossly distorts the real problem, inherent in writing or in painting, that it makes everything childish. I believe that people who adhere to this theme generally claim to be influenced by

Blanchot—which is simply an erroneous interpretation of Blanchot, who never said anything stupid—whereas the theme they derive from him is incredibly stupid. This theme, which is quite ruinous in literature, is that of the writer facing the blank page. This is so stupid that it makes me want to weep. From this perspective, the problem inherent in writing is: My God, how I am going to fill this blank page? [*Laughter.*] There are people who write books about this, about the vertigo caused by the blank page. [*Laughter.*] You understand, why someone would want to fill a blank page is really unclear, since there is nothing missing from a blank page. This has to be one of the stupidest themes I've noticed recently, inspiring all sorts of platitudes: the anguish of the blank page, you can even add a bit of psychoanalysis to this. Some people write novels sometimes of up to eighty, a hundred and twenty, a hundred and forty pages about the writer's relationship with the blank page. This is unfathomably stupid because if someone sits down facing a blank page, it's inevitable that he or she runs no risk of filling it up. Moreover, this is linked to such a stupid conception of writing . . . You understand, it's precisely the opposite: when someone has something to write—I'm making no distinction between true and fake writers; this is more general—it's the third party, the one looking over your shoulder who says: oh, there's nothing written yet . . . Okay, I haven't written anything yet. But what is the difference between my poor head, my excited brain, and the page? None. There are already many things there, and I'll add: there are far too many things on the page; there is no blank page. Objectively, there is a blank page, that is, a false objectivity for the third party who is watching; in contrast, your own page gets cluttered, so utterly cluttered that there is no room to add anything at all, and, as a result, writing will fundamentally become a process of erasing, of deleting.

So, what is on the page before I start writing? An infinite world. An infinite world of bullshit and stupidity [*connerie*], if you'll pardon my expression. So how does this explain the way in which writing is a true ordeal? Well, you just don't write with nothing in your head; you have lots of things in your head. But in your head, in a way, everything is on the same plane, namely, what is good about an idea and what is facile, ready-made, all reside on the same plane. Only when you shift toward acting, through the activity of writing, does this bizarre selection occur in which you become the act. I'd say the same thing for speaking. Before opening your mouth, there are plenty of things running through your mind. Although you may attempt editing in your head, you have to undergo some kind of ordeal of shifting toward action, whether by speaking or by writing, which is a fantastic act of elimination, of purging.

Otherwise, your page is full of ready-made ideas. That doesn't necessarily mean ideas that others also have. You may very well have your own ready-made ideas, entirely your own, although they are ready-made, facile ideas like you have when you are eighteen years old and that are a source of shame when you wake up. Once again, the world of ideas has never been answerable to the true and the false. It is answerable to much finer categories: the important, the essential and the inessential, the remarkable and the ordinary, and so forth. As long as the ideas are in your head, you can consider that something very ordinary is remarkable. And this kind of confusion is not innocent. When you take something ordinary for something remarkable, it affects the content of the idea, not just formal stuff.[5] This is why we've all experienced books where we say—I don't know if you've had this experience—: no, everything the author is saying is wrong, it's childish. We might have a hard time saying in what respect it's all nonsense. No, it's not even nonsense, it's simply nothing. Whereas the guy who has written the work seems to find his ideas to be tremendous. And in this, there are no grounds for discussion. That's why discussions are always kind of bullshit, you know. I can't say to someone: this is why your idea isn't that great, it's impossible to say. Simply put, this is what we have in our heads, the world of ready-made ideas, either collective ideas or even personal ones. Some ready-made ideas that are nothing but my very own are nonetheless facile. At best, I can drop them into a conversation, but were they to pass through the test of writing, I have to ask myself: What on earth is this? What am I even saying? Is this worth writing down? If we are questioning ourselves like this, I don't claim that this leads to success, we can make mistakes like everyone else, but already we can reduce some of our own nonsense. It is so important to pursue such questions.

Anyway, now let me turn back to painting. It is just as idiotic to think that the canvas is a blank surface like a sheet of paper. A canvas is not a blank surface, and I think that painters know that well. Before they begin any painting, the canvas is already full. Here again, for the guy walking around and happens to see a painter, he looks closely and then says: you haven't done much there; there's nothing. But it's just the opposite: if the painter has trouble getting started, it's because the canvas is already full. Full of what? Full of everything that is the most awful. Otherwise painting wouldn't be a form of work. The problem will be to remove these things, however invisible, and *that have already taken hold of the canvas.* Evil is already there. What are the ready-made ideas in painting? Painters have always used a word to designate this initial state—well, not always—but there is a word that's prevailed for designating what fills the canvas before the painter begins. It's cliché. The canvas is already filled with clichés.

Consequently, the act of painting, just like the act of writing, will involve a series of subtractions and deletions, and for painting, the constant necessity to clean the canvas. So, would that be the diagram's negative role? The necessity to clean the canvas to prevent clichés from setting in? What's so awful about clichés? We could simply proclaim that painters today are worse than in prior periods. I have no desire simply to repeat these kinds of analysis. For example, authors like Klossowski have done them entirely too well regarding the existence of a world of simulacra.[6] Although Klossowski understands simulacrum in a very erudite way, it also includes this aspect: the cliché, the ready-made. We are often told that we live in a world of simulacra, in a world of clichés. No doubt, it is necessary to question certain technical developments in the field of images, the photo-image, the cinema-image, the television-image, and so on, this whole world of images. But such simulacra don't exist only on screens; they also exist in our heads and out in the world. It's truly Lucretian, when Lucretius talks about simulacra strolling around the world, crossing through spaces in order to come from some place to crack us in the head, to smack our brains.[7]

We live in a world of clichés. In the end, all of that is *on* the canvas before the painter even begins. What is disastrous is that as soon as a painter has found something, nowadays it becomes a cliché very quickly. There is a production, an infinite reproduction of the cliché, which turns consumption into something quite rapid. And I believe that this struggle leads to the painter's battle cry: War against the cliché! And the painter knows quite well that there are personal clichés as much as collective clichés. The painter can have his or her little cerebral idea, some little idea about something new, but every cerebral idea in painting is a cliché. Even if it's one's own private, personal cliché, it's still a cliché. There's a quote always attributed to Oscar Wilde—one that I don't particularly like personally—: it is Nature that starts to resemble a particular painter.[8] We notice how some people tend to describe a kind of landscape, "oh look, this is a Renoir." To me, this doesn't seem so complimentary for the painter, since such a description only shows the speed with which an act of painting becomes a cliché. Suddenly, while gazing at a woman's figure, I start saying: "Ah, a real Van Dongen," and while gazing at a landscape, "Oh, this is a Renoir." Cliché, cliché, cliché. You'll tell me that these clichés have no objective existence on the canvas. Fine, I'm saying that they have a virtual existence, with a force, with a weight. How will the painter avoid clichés, at once the clichés that intrude from the outside while simultaneously forcing themselves onto the canvas, and the clichés welling up from within the painter? And this war against clichés for the painter will be a struggle with shadows because his or her clichés don't exist objectively. Once again, while belief in the blank surface holds sway, that's precisely where clichés still exist. In any case, for the painter, that's where they still exist. All painters have endured this drama: How to avoid clichés, even a cliché that would merely be their very own? It's a frightening struggle.

Let me bring up a topic that I'd like to discuss later, about the relations between painting and photography, because it seems quite relevant at this point, namely, about these relations and what painters may have learned from photography, or the relevance of photography in relation to painting, things that all seem to me very questionable, but no matter . . . ,[9] some distinctions are necessary. Why is it that today we see certain painters who make use of photos in their work? I'm thinking of a painter—I don't know what you think of him, maybe he suffers only from an excess of talent—Fromanger.[10] In one of his periods, Fromanger used photos in a way that seems very interesting to me. Here, we'll have to see whether or not we stumble across our notion of the diagram. What was he doing by making use of photos in his paintings? During a period when he used photos the most, his way of searching for a motif was to go walking around in the streets. He'd go strolling in the streets with a press photographer. And he would take several shots of street scenes, especially shops. So, in light of how his artistic process began with photography, I ask you to reflect on where in Fromanger's process the act of painting actually begins? To be clear: Fromanger wasn't the one taking the photos, that was the press photographer's role. He firmly insists on this arrangement, which is all the more obvious when we see a photo he makes use of: it's aesthetically worthless, with no aesthetic pretense. Does the photo have the right to seek aesthetic pretenses? That seems to me a very interesting problem. But that wasn't even in question, since the photos were purposely instant press photos. The press photographer would take twelve shots of the same scene or the same shop.

Fromanger would then select from among the twelve photos. With that selection process, the act of painting was already starting, and he had yet to paint anything. There was already a painterly act on Fromanger's part through this process of selection. On what basis was he choosing a photo? He already had an idea in his head. So, what was his idea? He clearly had an intention as an artist. And in Fromanger's case, from the point of view of this technique, what was he seeking to paint? He would choose a photo from among ten or twelve, depending on a color that had already become the dominant color of the painting that he would create. And I forgot to mention: these were all black-and-white photos. He would look at the technical quality of the photos and would pick one, even one of a lower technical quality, because the scene vaguely brought a color to his mind. Let's imagine a scene that would evoke in Fromanger a violet, a very specific violet. He would say: well yes, that scene, I see it in violet. Then, he would choose the photo that seemed to him the most compatible with this violet he already had appearing in his head that the photographed scene had vaguely recalled for him. This was already a painter's choice. And for me, it's clear: the act of painting was already starting with this initial selection of the photo.

And so, after this initial selection, what would he do? He would project the photo on the canvas. I like this technique a lot—a painter can make a series of works using this technique, but he will eventually have to give it up; if he stays bound to that, it obviously becomes a cliché in its turn. So, Fromanger had an idea. In fact, Pop Art made use of similar techniques, but not the exact technique used by Fromanger. This was a little variation, it was a Fromanger-variation. And then, after this projection, what was his process with the canvas? Well, we could say that he certainly wasn't painting at all on a blank canvas, even apparently. There was a kind of truth of painting already emerging from the start of the process. There was the photo's projection on his canvas, a photo with no aesthetic value, deliberately worthless. I get the idea that if there had been a photo with even the slightest artistic pretense, he wouldn't have been able to make a work from it. His canvas was filled with the image of the image, through the projection of the photo.

[*Interruption of the recording,* time stamp: 35:00.]

He would begin making an initial array that I'm going to call, you'll see why, an array of light. You will have to ask me the question I won't answer: Would he replace the initial cliché with a new cliché? That's obvious, and it's why he couldn't carry on with this technique for very long. He created his array of light. He would have the photo projected, and he would paint everything in violet, the chosen violet, but going from light zones to dark zones. For the light zones, he mixed his violet with white (this is an act of painting), and for the dark zones, there was less and less white and, in the end, no white at all, it was the pure violet that gushed straight out of the tube. So he would create this array or spectrum of light obtained through the variable mixture of white with this violet. For those who already are familiar with this color, the violet that Fromanger chose was technically what is called a "warm" color: a Bayeux violet.

Later on, when we discuss color more specifically, even though I know most of you already know this, we will see that the fundamental opposition between colors—from the point of view of tonality—is between warm colors and cool colors, warm defining a color with a movement of expansion, cool with a movement of contraction. Among the elementary colors, yellow is considered warm, blue is considered cool. You can ignore this for now because I don't want to get into it yet. The main thing is that Fromanger's choice of Bayeux violet was a warm violet. He had thus established his spectrum of light, and he was therefore already moving toward a certain color array. He was forging an ascending array toward the pure Bayeux violet. He did this for the background or, for example, for the shop. But the photographer had shot a street scene, that is, people passing in front of the shop or people coming out of the shop. He would then create a spectrum of colors. The dominant violet being warm, he was going to paint a man in green, for example, a cool green, the warm and cool being relative and dependent on hues.

So, from a color standpoint, there was this opposition between the little guy painted using a cool green and the use of a dominant violet. The juxtaposition of the cool green zone in relation to violet was intended, as painters say, to make the violet even warmer. Fine, let's accept that. We'll look at all this from the point of view of a very simple conception of colors. For instance, when you find yourself observing an Impressionist painting, you constantly have these themes: relations of complementaries, relations between warm and cool colors, how a cool color can actually generate more warmth for a warm color, and so on. So, the cool green warmed the violet even more. But in relation to the cool green as a new element, what was Fromanger going to do? At that moment, a whole circuit of colors appears. He was going to paint another guy in warm yellow. This time, the warm yellow wasn't in direct relation with the violet, but was in relation, rather, with the violet through the cool green as intermediary, and so on. And this was how he was going to create his spectrum of colors until the entire painting was filled.

To return to our earlier concept: In what way does a kind of diagram emerge? Where was the diagram located? This is a bad example. We'll have to ask ourselves if that's not always the case with the painters who developed a relationship with photos. Far from using the photo as if it were an element of art, he would completely neutralize the photo and the cliché. He would project the cliché on his canvas (but in doing this, he completely averted using the cliché, since the act of painting started only from the very moment the photo was going to be canceled out in favor of an ascending array of light and a spectrum of colors). And it's here that we rediscover what I referred to as the three moments of painting: the pre-pictorial moment; cliché, cliché, nothing but clichés. The necessity of a diagram that will blur or muddle any concise form, that will clean or erase the cliché so that something else might emerge, the diagram existing only as a possibility of fact. The cliché is the given, that which is given, given in my mind, in the street, in the perception, given everywhere. The diagram intervenes, then, as that which will scramble, erase, or wash away the cliché so that the painting might emerge [*FBLS*, 71–75 UM; 86–92 C]. So, here we rediscover my three moments.

So, here's what I'm getting at: perhaps nobody has waged the war against the cliché as passionately, as—I would say, even if I had to justify this word later—as hysterically as Cézanne.[11] It seems to me that Cézanne possesses an acute awareness of this: my canvas is full of clichés even before I start painting. And this leads Cézanne to be obsessed with overcoming this paradox: How to get rid of all these clichés that are already invading the canvas? Once again, we see how this is a struggle with the shadow—and we'll see what that can mean. My sense is that true struggles are always struggles with the shadow. There are no other struggles than the struggle with the shadow. Clichés abound. They are everywhere, in my head, within me. When Fromanger causes them to emerge in order to project them on his canvas, he does so in order to destroy them and to bring forth a pictorial fact. And this is already his way of dispelling them. Clichés already abound on the blank canvas, to such a great extent that I will once again list all the risks and dangers that painters must confront.

If you, as the painter, can't traverse the chaos-catastrophe and come out the other side, you will remain a prisoner of clichés, and people might say: oh yes, he has a nice brushstroke. This sort of compliment is completely worthless, and the painter himself will undoubtedly recognize it as worthless. If one doesn't pass through the chaos-catastrophe, that is, if one can't traverse it and conceive some kind of diagram, then it's quite vexing. Why is this vexing? Because it means that the artist has nothing to say or express, that the artist truly has nothing to paint. There are many painters who paint and who have nothing to paint. Fine. But there is also a way of mangling or crushing the cliché. This process seems very close to the diagram, to the chaos-catastrophe, and yet you must sense that it is entirely too deliberate. It's like a premonition of all the practical dangers. Photographers never stop mangling the cliché. That's not a path for them to become painters. While one can always mangle the cliché, crush it, whatever, that doesn't work either.

On the other hand, there's the danger that Klee pointed out: if the catastrophe, if chaos overtakes everything, that's not good either. In other words, we are constantly surrounded by very formidable dangers. I'm thinking of a text. I'm not going to read it because I have trouble reading. It's a text by D. H. Lawrence about which, I think, I've already spoken to you. You'll read it yourselves. It's in the collection of articles that appeared in French under the title *Eros et les chiens* [Eros and Dogs] in which there is a splendid text on Cézanne.[12] Lawrence, as you know, painted with watercolors, especially toward the end of his life. They are not very good, but he understood this, it was a necessity for him. Miller also did watercolors, Churchill as well, but they are even worse. [*Laughter.*]

INTERVENTION: Barthes too.

DELEUZE: Barthes was doing watercolors? Well, maybe they were good. Lawrence said: well, there you go, this is what Cézanne is all about. Never has a painter gone so far in the preliminary struggle against the cliché. Before painting. Lawrence says—and this is where his text interests me greatly—you know, Cézanne had his own clichés.[13] The painter who yields to his own clichés, that's when the true painter creates fakes, as if we were saying: oh, this, of course, is a Cézanne, but it's very close to a fake Cézanne. You get the feeling that he wasn't fully himself. Not long ago, I attended the Modigliani exhibition.[14] Curiously, there really are Modigliani works where you almost feel . . . They are admirable, prodigious, but he's a painter, I don't know . . . Forgive me, I sensed some discomfort, as if he had been too gifted, as if there were Modigliani works that, at the extreme, were an excess of aptitude [*don*] or an excess of ease. Fortunately, Cézanne had no aptitude. Where did his struggle against the cliché lead him? Lawrence's passages are very beautiful. At the end, he asks: What did Cézanne achieve? And Lawrence concludes with a very beautiful reply. He claims: Cézanne finally understood the fact pictorially. What Cézanne captured, what he brought to the painting is the *fact* of the apple. He understood the apple. Nobody had ever understood an apple like that. What does this mean, to *understand* as a painter? Understanding an apple means making it happen as fact, what Lawrence calls the appleyness of the apple.[15] That's what Cézanne was capable of painting, but as the result of what interminable pursuit that never satisfied Cézanne in his endless fight against the cliché? On the other hand, Lawrence also claims: as far as Cézanne's landscapes are concerned—no matter how beautiful they are—he couldn't achieve the same level of the fact. As Lawrence maintains, Cézanne's problem was that if he understood so well the appleyness of the apple, he hadn't really understood, for instance, the feminineness [*le caractère féminesque*] of women. And yes, in this wonderful passage, Lawrence says: Cézanne paints these women like apples, and that's how he resolves matters. [*Laughter.*] Madame Cézanne is a kind of apple.[16] But they are still brilliant paintings. Lawrence says: if at the end of his or her life, a painter can say, as did Cézanne: I understood the apple and one or two pots, that's already tremendous.[17]

You know, it's like everything else: a writer, a philosopher, he or she doesn't understand much, there's no point in exaggerating . . . A painter doesn't just paint anything. What did Michelangelo understand? He understood, for instance, a wide male back. Not a woman's back. A woman's wide back or narrow back, that would be for other painters. To understand a wide male back is quite something. An entire life for a wide male back, okay. That's on a par with Cézanne's apple. As Lawrence says, these are not Platonic ideas.[18] Michelangelo also understood other things, but still, what a painter can understand is always rather limited, that is, the pictorial facts that he or she brings to light. I feel that much of what I'm saying seems mostly to be connected to a particular painter, but these are also things that are valid (or perhaps not) for painting in general. What I'm trying to get at is that this process leading to pictorial acts seems always to have been the painter's task, eternally. Yes, I'm returning to what I've proposed as my three necessary moments in painting that are a bit academic, but let's hope that they will provide us with something: so, first we have the fight against the ghost or shadow, that is, the struggle against the givens. Then, there is the establishment of the diagram or the chaos-catastrophe, and third, what emerges subsequently from it: the pictorial fact.

This has always existed in painting, but in a more or less latent way. I was talking about Michelangelo earlier. For me, Michelangelo's importance in the history of painting comes from the notion that he is (I should nuance all this, one always has to nuance constantly), he is the first painter who brought to light, in its crudest form, what a pictorial fact was. To my mind, if we were to try to give an exact date for when this concept arose, it would date back to Michelangelo. So, now I'll turn my attention to a completely different painter in contrast to the periods and the style of those I had considered in the previous session. I want to emphasize that the pictorial fact establishes itself on the canvas with Michelangelo. Such is Michelangelo's unfathomable contribution to painting. If my impression is correct, this now makes me think: we've arrived at a significant moment in our train of thought regarding painting—it's now or never to attempt to clarify what we could call the pictorial fact as opposed to the pre-pictorial givens. To recall what we've already established, the pre-pictorial givens are the world of clichés, in the broadest sense of the word, or the world of ghosts, or the world of fantasy, or the imaginary world, or however you'd like to qualify it. The painter has to break free from all of this, by creating a necessary rupture. If the painter accepts to reside there, within the world of phantoms and clichés, then all is lost. He or she will be a lovely little painter, and that's all. It seems to me that Michelangelo, in a way, invented the pictorial fact, which doesn't contradict my idea that it has also always existed, eternally.[19] But Michelangelo is the one who makes us see it in a crystal-clear manner. To develop this more fully, I'm going to continue making use of anecdotes because they'll help us make some headway.

First of all, we could say that the status of the painter is truly transformed beginning with Michelangelo. No doubt, this elevation of status required all of his particular personality; it also required his era—the era in which he lived is pertinent—but with Michelangelo, the painter stops simply being a guy who executes orders from others. That doesn't mean that other painters weren't also brilliant and didn't have the freedom to paint what they wanted, but if a pope was ordering a commission, they weren't arguing. What important innovation do we know about Michelangelo based purely on anecdotal evidence? The first anecdote coming to mind is that Julius II told him to complete a specific commission. Julius II had very specific ideas about what he wanted. But it won't happen. Michelangelo does something completely different.[20] And what's more, he actually argued with the pope and was so convincing that, in the end, the pope got fed up and gave Michelangelo carte blanche. This event is truly something new. And so, you might ask me, what does this anecdote imply pictorially? Otherwise, would this anecdote be of any interest?

Let me offer a second anecdote. Michelangelo is one of those painters who exhibited a splendid indifference to the subject.[21] Maybe such an attitude always existed, perhaps it was simply less visible. Perhaps the subject itself is part of the cliché. Maybe all painters understood that the subject or the object represented the equivalent of the cliché. It's certainly what always had to be blurred or erased for the pictorial fact to emerge. In other words, the cliché has always been the object. The cliché was blurred, the object was blurred, so that the pictorial fact, already light and color, might emerge. But it turns out that with Michelangelo, this indifference to the object or the subject appears as a kind of insolence. Knowing which biblical scene a Michelangelo work represents, knowing what the characters in the background are doing—we are almost ashamed to ask these questions, especially with Michelangelo. For instance, the four men in the background of *The Holy Family,* all naked, with an attitude that, from the point of view of figuration, we can only call a pronounced homosexual attitude.[22] What are these four men doing? We feel embarrassed to ask a question like that because it is so stupid. In the scene, they are doing nothing. What is this scene? Here we find a splendid indifference to the subject.

That's where I want to go anecdotally. Someone ordered a commission for him to paint a famous battle. He says: fine, certainly. And what does he do? That's not the painting he'll create. He won't be able to do it. He creates a preparatory drawing [*carton*]. What does the preparatory drawing represent? A group of naked young people in the water, or coming out of the water, and in the background, some soldiers. People say: phew, so there we see soldiers. [*Laughter.*] This is a masterpiece by Michelangelo, these young people naked in the water, splendid, and in the background, some soldiers . . .

Nevertheless, people wonder: Why does he call this "The Battle of Cascina"?[23] Scholars are indeed studying this very question. According to a single commentator from that era, during this battle, a small group of Florentine soldiers went bathing and their commander reminded them of the need for more proper behavior. Michelangelo is not really interested in the subject. He says: Do you want a battle? I'm going to paint naked young people in the water. In a purely fictional episode that he invents, we see these naked young people bathing in the water who would have been surprised by the enemy. While they certainly weren't surprised, we might well consider this gesture a bit like a battle.[24] [*Laughter.*]

What does this mean? How is this more than just an anecdote? I seem to be jumping around, but these are not really leaps. All of this remains quite identical. I'll return to this contemporary painter I was talking about. In his interviews, Bacon constantly says: there are only two dangers in painting—and that's not an original idea because it seems to me that this idea has always been held by all painters—one danger is illustration, and the other, even worse, is narration. A great art critic, Baudelaire, was already discussing these dangers: illustration and narration. What we generally call figuration is the common concept that groups these two things: illustration and narration. What happens when we consider certain paintings? And yes, there's somebody cutting off someone else's head, and so forth. Ah, there we see a battle. One finds a whole figurative aspect as well as a whole narrative aspect. After pursuing this circular process and then always returning to my starting point, I'd say: the struggle against the cliché is the struggle against any narrative and figurative reference. A painting has nothing to show and nothing to relate. That is the basis. If you want to relate something, the narrative disciplines are for you. A painting has nothing to do with a story, it's not a story. At the same time, narrations and figurations do exist; they are the givens even before the painter has started to paint. They reside there on the canvas.

There are a certain number of paintings that could be very beautiful and that we already know are not great paintings, precisely because you can't help saying: Hey, what happened here? Not only: What does this represent? but: What happened? For instance, Greuze is a narrative painter. There is a very beautiful painting by a

Dutch painter whose name I can't recall, which shows a father scolding his daughter.[25] The girl is viewed from behind, her back leaning forward. We can't look at this painting—really, these kind of traps shouldn't be left out in the open—without wondering: What is the daughter's expression? That's not good. I mean, the painting can be quite lovely, it can be amazing; it's just not great painting. This is really a painting that's inseparable from a narrative, right? That just doesn't work. In a contemporary painter who is actually very good like Balthus, we constantly have the feeling that the image is taken, even directly lifted from something that is happening. There is a story in there. I understand that anyone who likes Balthus may find what I'm saying revolting. So I'll eliminate this, I'll cross out this unfortunate example.

Removing narration and illustration would be the role of the diagram and the chaos-catastrophe. Getting rid of all the figurative givens, since figurations and narrations are givens. Making the figurative and narrative givens pass through the chaos-catastrophe, through the germinal catastrophe, so that something completely different emerges, namely, the fact. What is the fact? Bacon defines it quite well, and it really applies to all painting. The pictorial fact is when you have several figures in the painting (the fact can be seen better with several of them) without telling a story. Bacon gives an example that we might appreciate: Cézanne's *The Bathers.*[26] He says: it's amazing, he succeeded in placing twelve or fourteen figures together. Consider all the versions of "The Bathers," and you'll see that he managed to make several figures coexist on the canvas *necessarily,* without telling any story.[27] If the necessity exists for this coexistence, you then sense what the pictorial fact is, this necessity specific to painting. I'll provide a particularly famous example. A well-known nineteenth-century painting shows a female nude in the woods with clothed men, a painting that stirred up a scandal from a figurative point of view.[28] You grasp it pictorially when you eliminate every story. This story could be disgusting only if there were a story. What's this naked woman doing seated in the grass with all these men still dressed? This would be a tale of little perverts. How to remove all narrative givens, all figurative givens in order to bring forth the pictorial fact of this naked body in relation to the dressed bodies, the array of colors or the spectrum of light, and so on?

So, I come back to this famous painting by Michelangelo, *The Holy Family*. It seems that, in this painting, he is more scrupulous. He indeed represents the Holy Family, and, at the same time, the indifference to the subject bursts forth. You understand, the pictorial fact can emerge only through indifference to the subject. The painting generates its own fact. What is the fact? There are three bodies. The baby Jesus is on the shoulders of the Virgin Mary. The three figures are caught up—if you have this in mind, you can see immediately—in a kind of serpentine movement. This treatment of the figures came from Da Vinci, but Michelangelo extended it much farther. It's a serpentine movement as if the three figures were literally cast in a continuous flow. We're not surprised, after all, that this comes from a sculptor who showed everyone what the sculptural and pictorial fact ought to be. Perhaps it was easier for sculpture to cause a sculptural fact to emerge, but as a painter-sculptor, Michelangelo imposes the necessarily pictorial fact.[29] This serpentine movement will, indeed, be prodigious because it gives the baby Jesus an absolutely dominant position, which will then completely set the expression of the figure. The figure of the baby Jesus possesses this expression figuratively only by virtue of its position in the serpentine. The three bodies are thus cast in one and the same figure. And here we have it: the same figure for three bodies. There is no story. No story, no narration, and the figuration itself collapses [*FBLS*, 105 UM; 130–31 C].

At that moment, the serpentine will distribute a whole array of colors. The serpentine plays exactly the role of the diagram, which breaks with the figurative and narrative givens to cause the pictorial fact to emerge. The pictorial fact is three bodies in one figure. That there is a pictorial necessity of the same figure for three bodies—not a figurative necessity, or a narrative necessity—a pictorial necessity that can come only from light and color. As a result, I would say: painters are some fierce atheists who haunt Christianity. The manner in which they tear away Christianity from all figuration and narration as a way of bringing out a pictorial fact. This theme needs to be rediscovered. Why did they experience Christianity as eminently favorable for the emergence of the pictorial fact? This goes back to a distant time. If you will, back to Byzantium. With Byzantium, it's already in its pure state. When I said that Michelangelo represents the birth of the pictorial fact, that was idiotic, requiring that I correct myself. Mosaic painting in Byzantium is fundamentally this founding moment of the pictorial fact.

And what was the name of the movement that coincides with Michelangelo and to which he actually belonged? I've been meaning to say something about this point because it interests me greatly. There is a scholarly term for it, a term to designate the movement into which Michelangelo seems drawn as founder, at least as a co-founder, and which will last long after his death. Of course, I'm referring to the Mannerists. Why were they called Mannerists? Because the bodies they painted display highly contorted postures. To put it most simply, their poses are very artificial. For instance, in *The Holy Family,* the four very artificial characters in the background appear with what might be called either homosexual attitudes or very contorted attitudes. And in my opinion, if you look very closely at the paintings of Francis Bacon, it seems quite clear that he was heavily influenced by Michelangelo.[30] If you want to see what it is like to discover a wide male back . . . There is a triptych by Bacon that represents a man seen from behind, a figure that is shaving.[31] I'll show you an image of it. You won't be able to make out much in this, but you'll be able to get an idea of what I'm trying to describe. I'm turning it slowly. I'm ashamed to show you images, this really should be a course without images. You see the three male backs? The color of the reproduction is awful because it's a difficult color. There is a dominant ocher-red, a dominant blue on the central panel, and to the right, the coexistence of blue and red.

Let's stop for a moment and consider a problem because we'll have to come back to it later on. The question of painting, based on what we've just said but which you already knew, is not to paint visible things; it's obviously to paint invisible things. The painter only reproduces the visible precisely to capture the invisible. And in this light, what does it mean to paint a wide male back? It's not about simply painting a back; it's about painting the very forces that are exerted on a back or forces that a back exerts. Painting is painting forces, not painting forms. The act of painting, the pictorial fact, is when the form is placed into relation with a force. And forces are not visible. To paint forces is, indeed, the fact. Everyone knows Klee's statement: it's not about rendering the visible, it's about making visible.[32] Which implies: to make visible something invisible. Showing the visible is figuration. That would be the pictorial given, which needs to be destroyed by the catastrophe. What is the catastrophe? Here we are able to make some progress in our inquiry. The catastrophe is the locus of forces. Obviously, these are not just any forces.

The pictorial fact is the deformed form. What is a deformed form? Deformation is a Cézannian concept. It's not a matter of transforming. Painters don't transform, they deform. Deformation as a pictorial concept is the form insofar as a force is exerted upon it. Force has no form. So it is through the deformation of the form that the force is rendered visible, force having no form. Without force in a painting, there is no painting. I'm saying this because we often confuse this with another problem that is more visible but much less important, the problem of the decomposition and recomposition of an effect. Take, for example, in Renaissance painting, the decomposition and recomposition of depth. Then, several centuries later, we have Impressionism: the decomposition and recomposition of color. Then, we arrive at Cubism or, in another way, Futurism: the decomposition and recomposition of movement. All these periods of painting and their relation to decomposition and recomposition are very interesting, but they are concerned only with effects. These changes are not the act of painting. Painting itself is not decomposing and recomposing an effect but, rather, capturing a force. And I think that's what Klee means when he says: it's not about rendering the visible but making visible. Form must therefore be sufficiently deformed for a force to be captured. With such a process in painting, we're not talking about a story, it's not a figuration, it's not a narrative. And the diagram's role will be to establish a locus of forces such that the form will emerge from it as a pictorial fact, that is, as a deformed form, in relation to a force. Henceforth, deformation of the pictorial form will make the nonvisible force visible [*FBLS*, 48–49 UM; 56–57 C].

I'll give a very simple example because here, too, Bacon was strangely successful. We're still dealing with the series of questions directed at each painter: What did Bacon understand pictorially? Once again, no painter understands much. [It's] too tiring to understand something. It is not incorrect to say that Cézanne's comprehension of apples would pretty much be the guiding light for his entire life's work. Indeed, Bacon understood, in a triptych, a wide male back. But here, it's not inaccurate to say: this may not be the best Bacon because Michelangelo had understood the same thing and in the same way, including the relationship with forces. What kinds of forces? All sorts of forces. In Michelangelo's case, this even corresponds to these very variations of devices, of style. Sometimes these are inner forces . . .

[*Interruption of the recording,* time stamp: 1:21:57.]

. . . the most natural poses according to the invisible force exerted on the body. Bacon is capable of making the most contorted figures in the world. One has the impression that they are like tortured bodies. But such a claim is merely a first impression that is figurative and narrative because if you take a closer, more pictorial look at his work, you notice that if you manage to vaguely understand the force that is being exerted on the body, in actuality the body retains the most natural position as a function of this force. Perhaps it's good to give some everyday examples, almost restoring a kind of figuration, but the secret figuration of a painting. Take someone who has a mild backache, who has a slightly dislocated vertebra, and who, for some reason, has to remain seated for a very long time. If you look at him outwardly, you'll see that he takes the posture that may seem the most tortured, the most contorted in the world, but which, in fact, and depending on the forces exerted on him, is the most natural and precisely the one that will allow him to endure the longest.

What I mean is this: the pictorial fact is fundamentally and essentially Mannerist. Why? Because Mannerism is exactly the effect that a visible form has on us when we don't see the invisible force exerted on it.[33] If through your pictorial eye, that is, your third eye, you grasp the force exerted on the body—since this is the object of painting: capturing force—at that point, this body ceases to be mannered; it remains Mannerist, since we'll have to define Mannerism as the relation of the visible body with the invisible force. That's what gives it this Mannerist attitude. As a result, I believe that Mannerism is in fact a fundamental dimension, a consubstantial dimension of painting.

Capturing a force is not easy, you know; it's not easy. You are a painter. You want to draw a sleeping man. When you're not a genius, you can draw a sleeping man, even surprisingly well. In what case does this tend toward illustration, and in what case does it stop being illustrative and even narrative? Here's a narration: this man falls asleep, he was tired. The context is indeed narrative: it might be night, it might be day. It's not the same story if I fall asleep during the day or at night, all that . . . The lines you draw are figurative: a character on a bed. All these elements constitute the world of the pre-pictorial givens. It matters very little, after all, that some painters pass through those givens. What does it matter if other painters don't draw them on canvas? This has no importance. In any case, even those who draw them do so in order to blur them, to make them pass through the diagram. And what is the pictorial fact that emerges from the diagram? It would be too easy to say: this is the body insofar as it relates to the force of sleep. The force of sleep doesn't mean anything. It's only a way of reiterating: he is sleeping. The force of sleep is multiple. In Bacon's case, he draws and paints a lot of sleeping characters. And in my opinion, these paintings of sleepers are some of his greatest achievements. Bacon's sleepers are extraordinary.

What is it that is so compelling to us about these works? If you see reproductions or if you have them in mind, what is so striking about them—and I really only see him accomplishing this; there may be others who pulled this off—is that he has completely captured what must be called the *flattening force* within sleep. A truly fatigued body, lying down, we can grasp it visually, but how can one render this body? That's what being a great painter is all about: the body that seems to empty itself completely, to flatten out on the mattress [*FBLS*, 53–54 UM; 62–64 C]. Literally, Bacon's works of the sleepers don't show a body without thickness. If I paint a body without thickness, it's worthless, it's a failure. If I paint a body in the process of losing its thickness, that's an accomplishment because I have placed the form into relation with a force of deformation, namely, the force that flattens it. At that point, we understand why he flanks them with standing attendant figures. And this is what helps us to answer questions such as: What is important, what is secondary in a complex painting?

You see, for instance, Bacon's sleepers lying on a bed, and once again, this seems to be one of his great achievements. This can be in a triptych. The other two panels, left and right, show bulky and very contorted characters. The sleepers can very well be placed on an exterior panel. There are Bacon triptychs in which the essential element is on an outside panel, right or left, not in the middle. So, we ask ourselves: Where is the force, what force is it? What is the force that touches you in the painting? For Bacon, his way of experiencing sleep reveals something quite odd, but you understand, capturing the experience of sleep through its force of flattening the body is no longer a cliché. I could have simply drawn a sleeping man, a painting containing a whole series of wonderful features, a wonder of colors. I could have drawn the bed, a magnificent little bed. But that would be entirely devoid of interest. When something in a painting strikes you, that's because it's the pictorial fact striking you. These paintings I mentioned earlier have no pictorial fact at all.[34] There is a fact that concerns sleep, there is a narrative fact, an illustrative fact. There is everything you want, but no pictorial fact, no advent of a pictorial fact.

What is required for you to be a great painter? [For] Bacon, this is entirely his concern. I'm certain that he's a man who has a special relationship with sleep. I imagine Bacon sleeping a lot, really a lot. He's definitely not an insomniac. An insomniac couldn't paint this. What compels him to sleep so much? I don't even dare think about it, but I'm quite sure that he sleeps a lot. I mean, if he was actually an insomniac, that would be a catastrophe, but it doesn't matter. In any case, Bacon's relation to sleep is clearly a curiosity. Here, too, there is something purely illustrative. There are a lot of sleepers in Bacon, since he has made entire series of male or female sleepers, who sleep with one or even both arms raised, or with their thigh raised. What I'm saying here is figurative. That's what I'm calling the given. I can say to a painter: in fact, this is about a given, this is about the prepictorial. Perhaps Bacon himself sleeps like that, maybe he likes this position, a raised leg, a raised arm. His paintings depict every possible combination of the sleeping body: the pillow can be high, the arm leaning on the pillow . . . I can always say to a painter: so let me tell you, I'd like you to paint a sleeper with an outstretched arm. But what makes Bacon's paintings of sleepers so distinct? As I was saying earlier, look at Bacon's sleepers and see if you have the same feeling as me: that the form is in fact deformed, even if only slightly, by a flattening force. Henceforth, sleep wouldn't simply be defined tautologically as a sleeping force. Rather, it seems to me that in Bacon's experience of sleep, a force that flattens the body is at work. A flattening of the body induced by fatigue, a flattening induced by sleep.

There is something else that also seems odd to me in Bacon's artworks. Bacon also painted—we'll see how a painter's different themes can get short-circuited—an enormous number of haunches of meat. He even calls them by a particularly sophisticated name: "Crucifixions."[35] Few painters have resisted a haunch of meat. A haunch of meat is extraordinary for a painter. It's such a matrix of colors. Certain painters are particularly well known for their haunches of meat. There is at least one large haunch of meat in Rembrandt, which is a truly marvelous carcass.[36] And then, there are the endless, yet so beautiful, series by Soutine.[37] Figuratively we can say: at least three great painters—Rembrandt, Soutine, and Bacon—have depicted haunches of meat and whole carcasses. Figuratively, narratively, there doesn't appear to be any interest to them so far. If I ask myself: What explains Bacon's interest in the haunch of meat? [It's] not necessarily the same thing that interests Soutine, or that interests Rembrandt. You have to see some of these works yourself. It seems to me that there is something very odd in haunches of meat. It's that he experiences the haunch of meat, the carcass, as a movement through which the flesh comes off the bones, as if instead of an organization (in a living body, there is a kind of flesh-bone organization), in Bacon's work, what distinguishes precisely the carcass from the living body is that the flesh comes off the bone. It's not at all that the flesh becomes soft; it's a firm flesh. Literally, I cannot think of a better term, it's flesh that *descends* from the bones [*FBLS*, 20–22 UM; 21–24 C]. I assume that were you to look at a Bacon painting, you wouldn't disagree with me. What interests him in a haunch of meat is that the flesh descends from the bones. How can you paint flesh that descends from the bones? [There is] no formula: it's through a force. There is a force of weight proper to meat—that's what interests Bacon in meat—the force through which the flesh descends from the bones. And here we have something! Descent: crucifixion. The operation through which the flesh descends from the bones: that's what the crucifixion is, or else the way that Bacon experiences the crucifixion. As a result, these kinds of haunches of meat that look like they are dripping, that descend from the bones, he will call them *Crucifixions*. And Bacon's experience opens up new perspectives for us as well. In other words, the crucifixions that interest him are descents.

But the theme of the crucifixion in relation to the descent traverses all painting. Hence the question takes on a new turn: How did the old painters whom we admire represent the descent from the cross? What interested them in the descent from the cross? Certainly not the same thing that interests Bacon. I'm not saying at all that it was the flesh descending from the bones, but it had to be something else. Wasn't it also a matter of force? In any case, you see what I mean. When Bacon paints his sleepers, with an arm raised or a thigh raised—you look at the painting, and what's important here if you're following me is this: it's really a question of looking, not reasoning, it's terrific indeed—it's an entire movement that allows the arm to count as a bone, the raised thigh to count as a bone. Henceforth, the entire body of the sleeper descends from this quasi-bone. This is the very process of descent. We could say that all these sleepers are "crucifixions"; this is the movement of the flesh that descends from the bones. Even if his preference, which is a figurative given, is to sleep like that, the pictorial function of the raised arm is completely different: it is to assign a force of sleep, one of the forces of sleep for Bacon being the movement through which the flesh descends from the bones. It's a bit like when you put your head upside down, and your cheeks go up, that is, they tend to get off-center. This movement of the flesh that descends from the bones, the head upside down, and so forth, the body flowing from the raised arm, the body falling from the raised thigh. Indeed, you cannot view Bacon's sleepers without constituting the body as descending from this thigh, from this arm, and that's what I call the pictorial fact. As a result, I would say that in Bacon's sleepers, there is in fact a deformation of the form.

And this is precisely what I'm suggesting when I speak of the pictorial fact: it's a deformation of the form as a function of two forces—I see only two, but someone else will see others. I don't think these are the only forces, or maybe Bacon experiences sleep as the place where these two forces operate primarily—a flattening force and a descending force. The body descends from the bones.

A sleeping body is a piece of meat because it's a body that descends from the bones. And it's a flattened body. There is no story to be found in these works. When you have finally attained that level, it seems to me that you have arrived at what the painter is trying to show you, that is, what the painter makes visible. In this painting, he made visible two invisible forces. If he needs standing and contorted attendant bodies, these bodies, in turn, have forces. They make forces visible, but in my opinion—everyone may perceive the painting as they wish—it's secondary. The successful rendering of sleep was more important. As a result, the voluminous and contorted bodies serve only as witnesses of sleep and have only a secondary value, but we could say something else.

I'm going to return once again to my conception of the three moments in any painting. You always have figurative and narrative givens. First of all, there are some that are pre-pictorial, that are already there. These are the photos, the clichés, the ideas already present in the painter's mind, and so forth, anything you want. Why are they already there? This is the painter's intention. The intention can only be figurative and narrative, even for the most abstract painter. That's why, once again, there is no basis for any distinction. We'll see at what point we can differentiate between one trend and another. At the point we've reached, there is no basis to make even the slightest distinction. When Mondrian paints a square, all the ready-made squares are already there. He finds himself exactly in the same situation as everybody else. When Pollock draws a line that crosses the entire painting, his canvas is already full of all the lines that fail, of all the clichéd lines, of all the ready-made lines. There is no reason to make even the slightest distinction at this level. So, you have this world of givens, of clichés, and I'm saying: that's the painter's intention. In what sense? In the sense that the cliché, the ready-made, are inseparable from the painter's intention insofar as the painter wants to paint something. Once again, when you are a painter, you want to paint something. I would say: what makes the cliché unavoidable is that the cliché is fundamentally intentional. Every intention is a cliché intention. Every intention is aimed at a cliché. And there is no painting without intention. What do I call intention? If I try to give an abstract definition but also one that remains simple, I say: intention is the difference between an apple and a woman. What I mean is: Cézanne doesn't have the same intention depending on whether he plans to paint an apple and to paint a woman. Mondrian doesn't have the same intention when he wants to paint a big square or a little square. There you have it.

The intention already promotes the cliché. Henceforth, the cliché is necessarily on the canvas before the painter has begun. I'd say: The intentional form in painting is always figurative and narrative. It cannot be otherwise. As a result, the painter's task and the act of painting begin with the struggle against the intentional form. If there was a dialectic in painting, to my mind, it would be this: I can only achieve the intentional form, that is, the form that I intend to produce, precisely by fighting against the cliché that necessarily accompanies it, that is, by blurring it, by making it pass through a catastrophe. I call this catastrophe and this germinal chaos the locus of forces or the diagram. If this succeeds, if the diagram doesn't fall into one of the multiple dangers that we've seen—now that we've said that the dangers are multiple, we'll come back to this—if the diagram is really operative, as a logician would say, what emerges from it? The diagram was the possibility of fact, the fact emerges from it. The fact is the form in relation to a force. What will the painter have made visible? He will have made visible the invisible force.

I'd like to give an example that fascinates me greatly, but its purpose is, rather, for you to find your own examples. There is a painter from the nineteenth–twentieth century who belongs to the great Expressionist tradition: Kupka.[38] If it's true that Cézanne perhaps really understood one or two apples and then Bacon understood a male back and three sleepers, then what was Kupka capable of grasping in his art? He understood something that seems much more important, and yet he's not a greater painter than Cézanne or Bacon. He creates a lot of planets that rotate, with colors that are very . . . it's beautiful Expressionism. For Bacon, I've managed to offer a few remarks. I have the feeling that what I said earlier outlined well the forces that Bacon was able to capture with respect to sleep. I feel infinitely more modest concerning Kupka. He's an absolute mystery to me: How can we explain that, with some kinds of little balls—with indications of rotation, and so on, of course—Kupka managed to capture a force that can only be called a force of rotation and gravitation, a kind of astronomical force? I'd like for someone who understands Kupka better than me, or who loves him . . . I admire this work tremendously because I see it as a very great achievement. It takes a lot to capture a force of this nature. It's true that in a Kupka painting, even in a quick one, even almost a sketch, it's a rather fantastic thing, in the beautiful Kupka works, of course. There, too, you can feel the extent to which he can fail. What is required for the invisible to be captured or not captured, that is, made visible?

I'm coming back to one of Bacon's expressions, and that way, I'll be done with this: at one point, he did numerous series of screaming people. Popes in particular. There is a marvelous series of screaming popes. It's in Bacon's *Popes* series.[39] He uses an expression that I find quite beautiful. In his interviews, he says, quite modestly: what I'd like is to paint the scream more than the horror.[40] That truly sounds to me like something a painter would say. Yet, he's one of the painters who most prolifically painted horrors, something he's well aware of. He's relentless; it's frightful. His crucifixions, they're frightful! There is a crucifixion that represents a haunch of meat with a screaming mouth, caught in the haunch of meat, and at the top of the cross, a dog is waiting. And the dog is very disturbing. This is a horror, he painted a horror here. Why does he tell us: What interests me is painting the scream rather than the horror? Painters are very harsh when they judge themselves. He says: yes, in all my beginnings, I never knew how to separate the scream and the horror, I painted the horror. But painting the horror is still figurative, it's still narrative. Horror is easy. That's the lesson of sobriety. Increasingly sober. It's so difficult to achieve sobriety that you must go through these kinds of excesses and childishness. Painting the horror, painting an abominable scene, yes, fine. Maybe he had to go through that. But even when he was already painting the horror, it was certainly so that he could extract something else from it, namely, the scream.

Painting the scream is something else. Why paint the scream? If I compare the scream and sleep, what's the difference between them or, rather, what is the resemblance? There is at least one pictorial resemblance between the scream and sleep: in every case, bodily *figures* occur that exist only to the extent that the body is in relation to forces, either inner forces or external forces. This relation is the only thing that merits interest: when the body is in relation with forces.

That the painter may first tend to put the body in relation to unbearable, insurmountable forces, even Michelangelo fell into this. What does "increasingly sober" imply? Learning that the secret of painting or that the most beautiful pictorial facts occur when the forces are very simple, very rudimentary. These will no longer be forces that torture a body; these will no longer be horrible forces; this will be the flattening force of sleep. We start by creating abominable accident scenes—for instance, someone who is run over by a bus—and then we realize that the real flattening of the body is not at all the bus that crushes you but the everyday fact that you fall asleep, and that in the fact of falling asleep, there is a pictorial fact that may be equal to all the sufferings in the world, to all the accidents. At that moment, you will be able to recover everything, at once the torture of the world and the horrors of the world, just by painting a man asleep. This occurs inevitably. That's what I mean: this sort of search for sobriety, for an ever-greater simplicity, what Beckett has achieved in literature: making something increasingly sober, which is, in a sense, all the more striking, all the more overwhelming.[41] But in Beckett's early works, there is still too much excess, there is still a kind of narrative and figurative abundance. Later, he'll reach this kind of pictorial fact; in his case, that will become the literary fact, a sort of literary fact in its pure state. You understand, that is what capturing forces means.

The scream rather than the horror. The scream, what is it? It's the body in relation to a force that makes it scream. What is this force? If I answer as I did earlier—namely, that the force that makes you sleep is the need for sleep—we wouldn't have learned anything. I would have returned into the figurative and narrative realm. If I say: the force that makes you scream is the spectacle of the world, I find myself fully in the figurative. At that point, I have to paint a scene that accounts for the fact that the figure I'm painting at the same time in the scene is screaming. I will be entirely in the figurative. So this is not what I call a force. A force is one that is invisible, the invisible force. This is the sense in which I told you that the painter's struggle is a struggle only with the shadow. Bodily relations exist only with the invisible forces, or with the insensible forces. The struggle exists only with forces. What is the relationship between the visible and force that is not visible? Ultimately, the body's relation with the force seems to me very simple. It's because the body is visible and will sustain a creative deformation that the body's visibility will allow me to render this invisible force as visible. Only to the extent that the body embraces the invisible force exerted on it—hence the theme of the struggle with the shadow—will the invisible force become visible. In what way? Everything becomes blurry here. Does the body make it [the invisible force] visible as an enemy or as a friend? If the painter manages to compel a dying body to make visible the force of death, at that moment does death perhaps become a true friend for us, and for the represented body? Everything that was facile, figurative, frightful, horrible, becomes quite secondary in relation to a kind of immense vital consolation. In any case, capturing a force is delightful.

What relation does the screaming mouth maintain? Not a relation with a visible spectacle. I'm thinking of Kafka's very beautiful words. In a letter, he says this: what counts in the end is not the visible, it's detecting the diabolical powers of the future that are already knocking at the door, that, in some way, are already there, but are not visible.[42] Consider the example of fascism, the torture States, all that . . . There is something visible, but there is also something that exceeds all visibility. What is terrible is never what one sees, it's still something that is—Underneath?—Not visible? The diabolical powers of the future already knocking at the door. The first stage: I paint a horrible spectacle and a mouth screaming in reaction to this spectacle. As beautiful as this may be, it is still figurative and narrative. Second stage: I erase the spectacle. I paint only the screaming mouth. I had to pass through the diagram, through the catastrophe that dragged away all figuration. Painting only the screaming mouth means, in fact, that I don't just paint the mouth but, at that very moment, I captured the powers that make one scream in such a way that the screaming mouth becomes both the friend and the enemy of these powers. It's as if these powers are transformed [*FBLS*, 51–53 UM; 60–62 C]. All this is very curious.

Bacon has his vanity. Painters always have their affectations. He actually deals with horror, or even sometimes the abject. But he follows this path less and less, he exhausted this avenue. He is very hard on himself for having taken this path. But he paints a great deal of hiccups, vomiting. He has a very beautiful painting: *Character at a*

Washbasin.[43] There is a guy who vomits in a washbasin. We don't see the vomiting, but the entire attitude of the body, a back that vomits, a back subjected to the force of vomiting. This is not easy to paint, after all. What is there in common between vomiting and a scream? That's not difficult. Here as well, we may find one of Bacon's obsessions. These are two movements through which one tends to lose control of the body. This is curious: I've lost control of my body. It's a very strong impression of panic. This is the catastrophe. If the body is to be painted, in Bacon's case, it must pass through this catastrophe of the bodily control getting away: this is Bacon's diagram. This loss of control can occur in very different ways, through vomiting and through the scream. It's not at all the same mouth, the mouth that vomits and the mouth that screams. It's not the same thing.

I don't know if you've ever had surgery, but those who have undergone surgery have this experience that I think helps people understand things, those who've had a serious operation. Creating figuration would be representing an operation. This is obviously not interesting at all. But in an operation, there is something very strange: even when the operation wasn't life-threatening, it suffices to look at the patient afterward to notice that this is exactly as if he had seen death, but seen it without tragedy. I mean, the eyes of a recently operated-on patient are amazing. [*Laughter.*] If you haven't been around one, go visit some clinics. In my view, you have to see this not out of curiosity. I'm not suggesting things out of some deplorable perversion but almost out of tenderness. If you really want to feel something for humankind, go see people who have had surgery. It's as if their eyes are completely washed, as if they had seen something that wasn't horrible, as if they had seen something that can only be death, can only be a kind of limit of life. They come out of it with this kind of very pathetic gaze.

Rendering that gaze would be possible only if the painter managed to capture the force. With what deformation of the gaze? It's not as if he had a stye on the eye. It's something else, it's . . . it's impossible to say. I managed to express this a little in Bacon's case regarding sleep. I didn't manage to say anything about Kupka's astronomical forces. That's what defines a great painter, you know? In the postsurgical experience, there is something quite amazing: it's that your body has a tendency to flee, to escape everywhere at once. It escapes from all ends. This is not at all worrisome, it's even what we call a fine convalescence. When I describe this gaze as people who have seen something, it's a shame that they forget so much. In fact, people would otherwise be wonderful: by not forgetting an operation, they would come out of this fine. One gets the impression that, after an operation, they have understood something. Yet, they're not the ones who are understanding! Their flesh understood something. The body is intelligent all the same. Their body understood something that they will then forget so quickly. It's a pity. A sort of goodness, a sort of generosity emanates from them because this death that they saw, and which becomes visible in their eyes—it is very curious—insofar as it becomes visible, it ceases to be the enemy, it becomes in a way their friend. That is, at the same time, it becomes something other than death. And that's what a great painter renders.

I am saying, in Bacon's case, that the body gets away, an act of vomiting. I'll read you a passage from a great novelist who wrote prior to Bacon's art. Here's the story, the narrative. This is really a novelist whose narrative is excessive. I'll tell you right away, the author I'm referring to is Joseph Conrad, in a very beautiful novel titled *The Nigger of the "Narcissus."* Here's what happens: the ship is sinking, and there is a sailor who is trapped in a cabin. Everything has caved in, everything is blocked, he can't be saved. And his friends want to save him because he's their favorite, a kind of talisman for the crew: on the one hand, he's black, he's the only black man on the ship, and on the other hand, he's sick all the time. They want to save him all the more because he is condemned. And the entire crew gets involved, like madmen, without really knowing why they must save him. They finally get to the cabin after all kinds of efforts and, with a piece of metal, they smash a bulkhead. Here's the text: "We crouched behind him, guarding our heads, and he struck time after time in the joint of planks. They cracked. Suddenly the crowbar went halfway in through a splintered oblong hole" (you see, the crowbar sinks into the wood and the bulkhead suddenly gives way). "Archie" (the sailor who was holding the crowbar) "withdrew it quickly" (this is where the amazing passage starts; the nigger of the "Narcissus" is locked in a cabin), "and that infamous nigger" (why infamous? You'll understand in a moment) "rushed at the hole, put his lips to it, and whispered 'Help' in an almost extinct voice . . ." (You see, there is a tiny hole, a very small hole in the bulkhead, and the guy who is locked up and is in a panic, presses his lips against it, at the risk of getting hurt, and whispers "Help"); "he pressed his head against the wood, trying madly to get out through that opening one inch wide and three inches long."[44]

Why is the character "infamous"? Let's try to define this physically. We're not doing philosophy. What would abjection be? I wonder if abjection isn't the constant or intermittent effort—we are all abject in that case, that would be good—that traverses the body, the effort through which the body tends to escape through an orifice, either an orifice that belongs to it, that is, belonging to its organism, or an external orifice. Why would that be abjection? I have no idea. Someone might tell me suddenly: oh, I'd like to pass through a mousehole. That's abject. Why? I don't know. There is something abject about it. Why does someone want to pass through a mousehole? Because he's ashamed. "Being ashamed, I would like to become smaller than a mouse." Forget the ready-made formula: passing through the mousehole is abject.[45] How can a person be reduced to wanting to pass through a mousehole? It's grotesque. The one who vomits is doubly abject because, on the one hand, his body is reduced to this . . .

[*Interruption of the recording,* time stamp: 2:08:43.]

. . . it's not serious. That's what vomiting is about, my whole body trying to escape through one of my orifices. And the scream? It's the same with the scream. With no pejorative meaning, I call abjection the effort of the body to escape like this. But when I attempt to escape through one of my orifices, in fact, the effort is always ramped up: I also try to escape through an external orifice, like the guy of the "Narcissus." Bacon's spasmodic guy vomiting, clinging to the washbasin, is manifestly trying to escape through the drain. His entire body is attempting to escape down the drain. Does the painting acknowledge that? At the extreme, Bacon could have called this painting *Abjection.* He's very conservative with his titles because this would have been too figurative a title. He calls it: *Figure [Standing] at a Washbasin.* This belongs to a series, and we see the relationship with the scream. Here, too, it's in terms of the body/force relation [*FBLS*, 16–17 UM and C]. All figuration—even if it continues to be present, and it can continue to be present—will be neutralized, nullified. In Michelangelo's work, in Bacon's work, it continues to be present. In a so-called informal painter, in a so-called abstract painter, it will no longer be present. But, whether currently present or not, even when it's no longer there, it is virtually present. Obviously. Once again, it is simply unified with the intentional form. Any intentional form is figurative and narrative. But in painting, intentional form is the first moment of the act of painting. The second moment, as we've seen, is to introduce the germinal chaos, or the diagram, which will define the possibility of the pictorial fact. And the third moment is the pictorial fact itself.

There is this very beautiful text by Bacon. Yes, I know, I'm once again obliged to show you a little bit of painting. But you won't be able to see anything, so this will serve no purpose. [*Laughter.*] You see, there is an umbrella, for those who cannot see. There is a man under the umbrella, but let's be fair, I hope you are not going to contradict me. And anyway, since you cannot see anything, I can say whatever I want. [*Laughter.*] Regarding the man's head under the umbrella, we can see only the lower half of the man's face, with a rather disturbing, jagged mouth. This mouth and this entire lower half of the face are rising up, in my opinion. There's no possibility to draw him descending from the umbrella. It's as if he were grasped by the umbrella. He rises up into the umbrella as if to escape through a point. At the top, [there is] a large haunch of meat, see. Additionally, [there are] the colors of fields that we constantly find in Bacon's work. In his interviews, referring to the painting titled *Painting* from 1946, Bacon says: it's very simple, I had an intention to paint (here we'll rediscover our three stages, and after, we'll be done), I intended to paint a bird alighting on a field.[46] Do you follow what I'm saying? This can arise in the mind of a painter. It's a good subject, a bird alighting on a field. He says: I started, and, little by little, something else became apparent, and I painted this figure underneath the umbrella. Fortunately the interviewer, who plays exactly the role of the first reaction, helps us a lot. The first reaction would be to say: oh yes, I understand. Instead of the bird form, he painted the umbrella form. In fact, if you see the umbrella, it's a bit like a big bat, there is a bird theme. But that's not at all how it went. Because, to the interviewer who says: you mean that the bird has become an umbrella?, what interests me here is Bacon's answer to the interviewer: not at all, not at all. In other words: you didn't understand anything; that's not what I mean. What must be related to the bird that I wanted to paint, he says, is the whole that came to me quite suddenly—I'm quoting almost exactly, with a bit of summary to go faster—or the series that I created progressively.[47]

That really interests me for understanding how a painter works. The text is already very bizarre. Bacon's answer is extremely confusing because he says finally: you mustn't connect my intention to paint a bird with the umbrella. You have to connect my intention to paint a bird with the whole all at once, that is, the gradual series. It's one or the other, at first glance. A gradual series and a whole in one go seem entirely contradictory. So, if Bacon wants to express something—and we have every reason to believe that he does—it's that he embraces a point of view that eliminates the importance of any difference between "a gradual series" or "a whole given all at once." He means: in any case, the entirety of the painting, considered spatially or temporally. Considered from a temporal point of view, it's the gradual series. Considered from a spatial point of view, it's the painting as it appears to us: the whole all at once. He says: what you have to connect with the intentional bird form is the entire series or the undivided whole. What is the entire series or the undivided whole, if we understand what he is saying? I can define the series from top to bottom: meat, haunch of meat, at the top; umbrella, man with the face eaten by the umbrella and open mouth. That makes my series. What Bacon refuses is any simple relation of analogy between bird-form and umbrella-form. He says: that's not how I work. In fact, that would simply be a transformation: how a bird turns into an umbrella. It wouldn't be that interesting. At the extreme, it would be like a kind of vague Surrealism. That's not it, he says.

And yet, there is an analogy between the bird-form and the painting's undivided whole. In other words, this is the first time that we encounter the following idea, even if we'll confirm it only later: Wouldn't there be two very different forms of analogy? I can speak about a first form of analogy if there is an analogy between the bird-form and the umbrella-form. At that point, I'd say: there is a conveyance of relations. The same relations exist between elements of the bird in form 1 and elements of the umbrella in form 2. There is an identity of relations. Certain given relations are conveyed from one form to the other. Is there perhaps an aesthetic analogy that has nothing to do with that, that is completely different? What would the aesthetic analogy be? Let's go back to the painting, as we vaguely recall it. The meat exists as if it had two arms by which it hangs from something like butcher's hooks. The meat will descend from the two arms I mentioned. In other words, the specific relation to the bird "with spreading wings" has been transformed. The relation itself has changed into a completely different relation. The relation bone/meat: the meat descends from the bones; the tiny arms of the meat are like bones from which the meat falls, descends. We are reminded of the bird very vaguely by this movement of the arms from which the meat will fall, which evokes very vaguely a kind of spreading of wings. Consequently, the meat that falls from these tiny arms, let's call it something like a kind of flow of meat, literally falling from the bones. Here, I'm speaking in terms of the pictorial fact. The meat descending from the bones is the first connotation with the bird that spreads its wings. There's a second connotation with the bird: the meat falls on the umbrella. This time, the umbrella is like the wings that are closing. Then, a third connotation: only the bottom of the face of the figure is visible. A strange, drooping, and jagged mouth, this mouth like a jagged beak. In other words, the bird is completely dispersed across the whole or in the series to the extent that it no longer exists figuratively at all. We could say at most that the painting contains—what can we call this?—traits of birdness. First trait of birdness: the small, raised arms of the meat. Second trait of birdness: the sections of the umbrella. Third trait of birdness: the jagged beak of the figure. Completely scattered all over the painting. The constitutive relations of the painting are: the relation of the falling meat with the umbrella over which it falls, and of the figure that is grabbed by the umbrella. In other words, the pictorial fact is produced by numerous different relations [*FBLS*, 125–27 UM; 155–58 C]. Wouldn't there be two types of analogy? One that proceeds by resemblances that are conveyed—I think we won't be able to see that until later—and another that proceeds quite differently, by rupture of resemblances.[48]

If I sum up everything, there are two important things here: this world of pre-pictorial givens made of narration and illustration; the establishment, the truly fundamental establishment of germinal chaos, that is, the drawing of the diagram. The diagram is located in this painting. If you manage to see a reproduction, you'll see that a little to the left, at the level of the body of the smiling man with the jagged beak who is grabbed by the umbrella, there is a zone that we can properly call diagrammatical, which is precisely made of a kind of very tormented grey. The whole ascending series—man, umbrella that grabs him, and meat above—emerges from this kind of grey diagram. And then [there is] the pictorial fact that comes out of it. What I'd like to remove first and foremost is the impression of an applied formula. This is not an applied formula. Consider that, in fact, everything I am saying strictly loses all meaning if you standardize this notion of diagram. You have to see, for instance, that diagrams of painters of light have absolutely nothing to do with diagrams of colorists, if there are diagrams in all painters. I'm not even sure that there are diagrams in all painters. Once again, a Cézanne diagram has absolutely nothing to do with a Van Gogh diagram. The diagram is not at all a general idea. It's something operative in every painting. It's an operative category.

I'd like to arrive at a conception of the diagram that clearly shows the difference between a diagram and a code—that's what we'll do after Easter break, and that way, we'll get a little closer to problems of pure logic or philosophy. If it were a code, it's disastrous; there would be no grounds to connect it to painting. But precisely, it has nothing to do with a code. Once again, at every instant, there is the possibility all the way to the end that the diagram might fail. At that point, the painting becomes a mess. If you don't see in a painting how close it came to turning into a mess, how it almost failed, you cannot have enough admiration for the painter. Courbet, or anyone really, I'm making references as they come to mind. Looking at Courbet's paintings, people say: it's a miracle. It really emerges as a miracle. It really came so close to turning into some kind of failure. And then, no, he pulls through. Prodigious. All the great painters give this impression. It would take next to nothing for a work by Michelangelo to become a bundle of muscles. Regarding Cézanne's works, it's not even a question of the true and the false, it's a question of the disciples and masters. What for Cézanne's work was a struggle against the cliché will inevitably become a cliché for those artists who will imitate his work. Each time, painting must yet again tear itself away from its state of cliché.

One thing that has always struck me in this regard is the work of Rauschenberg, who, in my opinion, is a very great painter. At one point in his periods of provocation, he took a sketch by a painter who preceded him, and he simply erased it and called it *Painting Erased by Rauschenberg.*[49] [*Laughter.*] It's silly, but it's the very illustration of this erased or cleaned zone. It's not that the other's painting was mediocre; on the contrary, it was remarkable. It was a very beautiful drawing. But it's true that when the painter has excelled, the painting becomes a cliché extremely fast. When a great painter does sketches, that is, copies the painting of another great painter, or when he simply erases it, it comes down to the same thing. There is a kind of will to pass through the diagram so that a new pictorial fact may emerge. What interests me now is how the diagram is entirely different from a code of painting. Well, then, have a great break! Thank you.

SESSION 3

CHARACTERISTICS AND DANGERS OF THE DIAGRAM

28 April 1981

So, let's begin by recalling our current focus: I'd like for us to accomplish two things at once. First, obviously, we're talking about painting. Personally, I find it very difficult to talk about painting. Everything is difficult in any event. I'm not talking about painting in general. Whatever might be general in what I have to say—and it's uncertain that there's anything general whatsoever *on painting*—we'll be able to discern what's generally applicable only by addressing a particular painter or another within a particular period. But along the way and at the same time, I'm equally interested in trying to build—this being a technical point—a concept proper to philosophy. You certainly sense what concept I'm trying to establish because it's the very one I've discussed in each of the past sessions with regard to painting, namely, a philosophical concept of the *diagram* that, in the end, might be uniquely tied to painting, but in any case, it would be coherent as a concept. As a result, this series of reflections about painting is just as much a series on the diagram and the possibility of fleshing out a philosophical or logical concept of the diagram. What logic might this notion of the diagram belong to? That's why I am starting by partially summarizing and partially tracking the primary characteristics of what I called the diagram in the context of painting, since everything I've said thus far boils down to something extremely simple: is there in a painting. . . . So already, a prior question: What do I mean by "a painting"? Do I mean any painting in general, or a certain type of painting? In a particular period? Or are there examples in every period? We can't answer all of these questions up front. But I assume that, within a given painting—I have to leave my reservations on hold—one could uncover a diagram, whether actually or virtually. We don't know what a diagram is, so that doesn't get us anywhere.

Nevertheless, before arriving at a philosophical understanding of this potential philosophical concept, what I'll try to define are the pictorial characteristics of what I'm calling a diagram. Are there diagrams in music? I don't know, that would be a different inquiry. Are there diagrams in literature? What sort of connection is there between a diagram and a language? All these are things that unfold for us as objects for reflection. For the moment, all I'd like to do is just enumerate certain characteristics of the pictorial diagram. Based on what we discussed before Easter break, I can come up with five characteristics.

The first characteristic: when it comes to the pictorial diagram, there appear to be two fundamentally linked ideas, situated in a necessary relationship. The diagram would be the necessary intersection between these two ideas. These two ideas are those of chaos and germ, and as a result, the diagram would be a germinal chaos [*chaos-germe*]. You might ask, why call this a diagram? As always, I'll ask for your patience; please bear with me. If needed, maybe one of you thinks—it's a particular detail—that there's another, more suitable word that would work better. Obviously, more disastrous for me would be if someone were to think: no, painting isn't like that, there's no chaos on the canvas. That would be a fundamental objection. Right now, I'd be much more interested in a formal objection, where somebody says: sure, there's something like a germinal chaos on the canvas, but *diagram* isn't the best word for it. That's possible too. Our inquiry isn't predetermined. For the moment, I'll call it a diagram. This is the first characteristic: a germinal chaos and the establishment of a necessary relationship between the two, chaos-germ. As we discussed in previous sessions, I've selected some texts from writings by Cézanne and Klee where these two painters seem to have truly elaborated this notion of a germinal chaos.[1] But from Cézanne to Klee, that's a rather narrow time frame to focus on this notion. I won't make any broad claims; we'll just have to see. This notion should be able to stand on its own. What does "germinal chaos" mean? It's chaos, but the sort of chaos from which something ought to emerge. This chaos must be present on the canvas in such a way that something emerges on the canvas.

There was an exhibition of Michaux's paintings in 1967. And Jean Grenier wrote a piece about these paintings. The title of Jean Grenier's rather brief text, in which he doesn't say anything major, is "An Orderly Abyss."[2] This expression itself is what interests me. A painting that doesn't include an abyss, its own abyss, that doesn't establish an abyss onto the canvas, for me, this isn't a painting. In a way, it's very easy to create an abyss; it's very easy to create chaos. Well, after all, perhaps I'm wrong; I don't know. Is it actually so easy to create such an abyss or chaos on the canvas? Let's suppose that a bit of schizophrenia is enough to create chaos. Hence, this expression: an orderly abyss. That doesn't mean that there's an order that defies the abyss and replaces it; it means that there's an actual order to the abyss itself such that something emerges from the abyss, but something that isn't ordinary. An "orderly abyss"—I could replace Jean Grenier's expression with my use of germinal chaos. We're speaking about the same thing.

The second characteristic: If the diagram is this so-called orderly abyss or germinal chaos in the painting, how do we describe the characteristics of this germinal chaos? Here, I would suggest that, in essence, the diagram—and this is crucial—is fundamentally *manual*. Only an unfettered hand can trace it. What do I mean by an unfettered hand? Let's break it down. What constraints does the hand have? When it comes to painting, the hand is tied down to the eye, of course. The hand is in shackles insofar as it follows the eye. The unfettered hand is one that is freed from subordination to visual coordinates. And the germinal chaos, the diagram there on the canvas, is fundamentally manual. As a way to make progress with this notion, we must push ahead and see how this approach resonates with classical problems, bearing in mind some of the small things about which we're relatively certain. After all, wouldn't this be another way of returning to the classical problem in painting: How are the eye and hand related in painting? Is painting a visual art or a manual art? If we say it's both, that's no help. And again, keeping in mind the same reservations I bring up every time, is this relation of the unfettered hand to the eye something that concerns painting in general, or does it vary from painter to painter? Or are there at least some broad tendencies that we can distinguish? Instead of basing these categories—abstract, Expressionist, figurative, and so on—on juvenile details like whether or not it represents something, isn't there a case to be made for reworking these major categories—if they're well-founded—by linking them to totally different criteria? For example: Are the hand–eye relationships the same with a so-called abstract painter or with a painter we would characterize as Expressionist or with a painter we would characterize as figurative? How broadly can these eye–hand relationships vary?

This is a sort of indirect way of approaching the classical issue of how the eye and hand are related in painting, all the while understanding that this indirect approach might change the nature of the problem. It always comes down to the diagram at the level of the second characteristic I'm trying to flesh out, namely: this chaos on the canvas—if it exists—which is like the foundational act of painting, is fundamentally *manual*. Even if it isn't true of every aspect of the painting, I must say of the diagram itself that it is manual. The expression *manual* itself reflects a hand freed from all submission to the eye. It's a bit like if I just scribbled stuff down with my eyes closed, as if the hand were no longer guided by visual input. That's what makes it chaotic. In what sense is it chaotic? By involving *this* diagram; I'm not talking about the whole painting as chaotic or composed of the diagram, since, yet again, the diagram exists there so that something might emerge. For now, I'm not talking about what will emerge from the diagram; for now, I'm talking about the action of the diagram itself. I'm saying that it's a manual action, and one carried out by a hand liberated from the eye. That's the potential [*puissance*] of the painter's hand.[3] A hand liberated from the eye is a blind hand. Does that mean that its action is random and that it just scribbles around? Of course not. Maybe there are rules that the painter's hand must follow, a manual sense of direction, manual vectors.

In what way is the diagram a kind of chaos? It's because the diagram implies the breakdown of all visual coordinates. You know, Cézanne's bloodshot eyes.[4] I can't see anything. But that doesn't mean I can't do anything. Doing without seeing. The hand's liberation. Actually, I would say: when it comes to the diagram—as diagram—a painting is not visual; it's strictly manual. We have the revolt of the hand, a hand sick of taking orders from the eye, a hand getting its shot at independence. Only, this is not just independence;

it's turning the tables on dependency. Instead of the hand following the eye, the hand imposes itself with something like a slap to the eye. It commits violence against the eye. The eye will have a hard time following the diagram. For me, not being able to find the diagram would only prove my point, because the eye cannot find it, so everything is fine. Is the eye capable of seeing what's done by a hand freed from the eye? That's complicated. This really twists around the relationship between two organs.

In paintings, there's indeed a point where you get the feeling that the eye can barely keep up, as if the hand were animated by a foreign will.[5] Hold on, what does this mean, as if the hand were animated by a foreign will? This "will" forces us to search for resonances as a way to justify ourselves. For me, this resonates with a truly lovely expression, much lovelier than my paraphrase of it: the hand animated by a foreign will, and henceforth, the terrorized eye wonders, where am I being taken? This expression is from Worringer to refer to what he calls the Gothic line.[6] We'll see much later what he means exactly by Gothic. It's the northern or Gothic line that Worringer will analyze in the context of architecture, painting, and sculpture. We'll see what this is later on, but precisely to define what he calls the Gothic line, he'll tell us: quite literally, this is an unfettered line. It is no longer a visual line, but a manual line that forces itself to be visible, of course, as if the hand drawing it were animated by a will foreign to sight itself. I'd claim, in fact, that there are two ways of defining painting. They may sound identical, but they are far from it. You could call painting a system of lines and colors [*système ligne-couleur*], or you could call painting a system of strokes and patches [*système trait-tache*].[7] I think both formulas have different connotations. When you call painting a system of lines and colors, you're already defining it as a visual art. And it certainly is, of course. When you call it a system of strokes and patches, that has a rather different connotation. It's not by chance that there is a school or movement that goes by the name "tachism."[8] The expression "strokes and patches" has a manual connotation.

There's a major problem: If I try to describe painting as a veritable assemblage [*agencement*],[9] what would that amount to? Assemblage involves or has involved or can involve the following: a canvas, an easel, paints, brushes. The canvas on an easel, that's totally visual.

Why? You know that a great problem of edges has troubled painting throughout its history. The canvas on the easel plays the role of a veritable *window*. The window is a funny thing. There's a really great article—a rather stunning text—that just came out in *Cahiers du Cinéma* on the topic of the audiovisual.[10] It's Paul Virilio at his best. He says: there were two basic developments associated with the house. The first is the door-window. Everything started with the door-window as one of the house's fundamental components. I go in, I go out, and light goes in and goes out. He has us appreciate the window's abstraction, since even if you physically *can,* you're not supposed to go in or out through the window. The window is an orifice for air and light to come in and go out. So, this is a wild sort of abstraction. Having the idea of making windows that aren't door-windows involves a high degree of abstraction. According to Virilio in his brilliant text, this constitutes the first major abstraction that might be called anthropocosmic, namely, the isolation of light.

In fact, sense how putting the canvas on an easel carries out this sort of visual abstraction. Door-windows, on the contrary, are both manual and visual. The window is visual. I would say that the canvas on the easel is the painting's visual determination, its optics. The brush in one's hand is the hand subordinated to the eye. Hence the grotesque classic image—which no one ever took seriously—of the painter closing one eye and stepping back, the hand tracing the visual givens. We can all tell that the relations between the eye and the hand aren't so simple in painting. There's a text that's been very influential by Henri Focillon, a really great art critic, called *In Praise of Hands.*[11] Sometimes, even just on principle, one disagrees; I really try to find what's good in texts. But I can't get behind this one at all because it's a little overdone. It basically explains why the hand is necessary for painting. The hand executes this sort of pictorial idea dictated by the eye. He praises the hand for being fundamentally subservient.

That doesn't sit right with me! If a painting doesn't involve a kind of rebellion of the hand against the eye, it isn't a good painting. While nothing has been as essential to painting as the easel-and-brush, once again, for me, the easel expresses what's yet to be painted as visual reality, like a window, and the brush expresses the subordination of the hand to visual requirements. But a painter has never been satisfied with that. To the point where the question isn't even: Which painters do without easels? There are many who've given up on easels today. There are some who've kept the easel. You can always keep the easel and use it in such a secondary way that it no longer fully functions as intended. So it's not a de facto question: Does a painter still have a use for an easel? It's a de jure question, of possibility.[12]

To take a well-known example: Mondrian used an easel, I believe. [But] you certainly couldn't or wouldn't call his work "easel painting." That is, the canvas isn't treated like a window. I insist on this: the visual reality of the easel means that, when you paint on an easel, it's like you approach the canvas in process as if you were looking through a window, or as if the canvas itself were the window. The theme of windows in painting was fundamental throughout classical painting. But consider this: with Impressionism, when they leave the studio, when they move toward the motif, when they paint out in nature, they also lug around their easel. Van Gogh, Cézanne, they go out for a stroll . . .

[*Interruption of the recording,* time stamp: 26:19.]

. . . In Cézanne's texts, throughout Van Gogh's letters, [we find] many comments like: cannot go out today because it's windy, and the easel will blow away. Why not put down some stones on the easel to hold it down? No, that won't work either, maybe because, in the outdoors, the easel no longer functions as an easel. Once again, the proof is that Gauguin and Van Gogh paint on their knees in order to get a low horizon line.

Even those painters who painted with brush-on-easel, everyone knows that they're always taking the canvas off the easel, just as the brush can always act as something other than a brush. What instruments does the painter have besides the brush? It could be anything, as we've seen throughout history. Modern painters weren't the first to use other materials or tools to paint, and maybe they've propelled it toward a kind of raw form of expression. We would have to figure out why. It's obvious that Rembrandt didn't paint only with a brush. Historically speaking, what have painters painted with? They paint with scrub-brushes, with sponges, with rags. What else? Pollock famously painted with bulb basters. Now that's something, a bulb baster. Sticks. Sticks have always been important in painting. Rembrandt used sticks. Why am I bringing this up? I'm still working out my second characteristic, which comes down to saying: there's a pictorial tension between the eye and the hand. Don't mistake it for a question of harmony, where the hand both obeys the eye and renders something ultimately visual—that's not it. While I don't know what's going to emerge from this, I'm saying: if you aren't sensing a certain opposition, a certain tension, a certain antagonism in painting between the eye and the hand, it's because at that point, one isn't seeing clearly what the concrete problems are.

But if the easel-and-brush pair represents painting as a visual art, what pair do we have when we move away from the easel [*FBLS*, 87–88 UM; 107–9 C]? I am saying: beyond the easel. I'm determining it negatively because there are so many things this "beyond" could be. It could mean painting on walls, but it could just as easily mean painting on the ground. Are those the same thing? In Mondrian's case, for example, it's very clear. He uses an easel, but it's no longer significant, since his painting is fundamentally wall-painting as opposed to easel-painting. There are certainly writings by Mondrian in which, if he said anything about the easel, he would say the easel [still functions because] the time has not yet come for true wall-painting such as he conceptualized it. And it's true that his idea of wall-painting implied an architecture that perhaps was under development at the time, but it was in its infancy, just like Mondrian thought he was at the beginning of something else. Understand how wall-painting is opposed to easel-painting: the canvas no longer functions at all as a window.

And Pollock? He doesn't paint on an easel. He has to have an unstretched canvas on the ground. An unstretched canvas on the ground is a bit of a departure: it's a totally different solution; it's not like Mondrian, who can still use an easel. For Pollock, at least some of his paintings eliminate the easel completely. In short, there's a wide variety of ways that painters forgo the easel. I would say that, beyond the easel, the two tendencies are toward Mondrian's wall-painting, on the one hand, and on the other, Pollock's Expressionist painting on the floor. Then there are brooms, brushes, bulb basters, sponges, rags, that is, painting as a manual reality. I'm not saying that these other modes of painting are opposed to older forms.

I'm just saying that they're very different things. Just as I was saying earlier, if painting is defined as a system of lines and colors, this definition is perfectly legitimate, but it's a visual definition. If you define painting as strokes and patches, that's a manual definition. Similarly, if you define painting with easel-and-brush, that's a possible material definition. Of course, you already know that any such definition doesn't account for every painting, but it gives you an idea. It's a nominal, material definition. But what I'm getting at is that there's also another manual definition, beyond the easel: stick, scrub-brush, bulb baster. This mode of painting will also give you a definition of the material elements of painting, only this time, they're manual elements. And both aspects can be reconciled.

You know how you say "painting" in German? It's *Mal*; "painter" is *Maler*. That alone is noteworthy for those with a knack for languages because the German word—this will come up later, by the way[13]—is absolutely unrelated to the French. There's no connection. *Mal* is a word whose etymology is from Latin, from *macula* (which is the name of a great journal on painting, unfortunately out of print, I believe).[14] *Macula* is the color-patch [*la tache*]. So, for Germans, it's almost like the language itself implies that a painter is tachist. I think this is important because it's so entirely different from the French word *peinture*. The German word veers painting toward the stroke-and-patch pair, that is, toward the manual reality of painting, whereas the French word, derived from *pingere*, draws painting toward its visual reality.[15] Let me add: whatever agreement between the eye and the hand may be possible in painting, we can't assume that there isn't a fundamental problem with their tension and their virtual opposition. Even virtual—I'm reintroducing the vague word *virtual*, which was why I found Focillon's piece so interesting but so unsatisfying. What I find interesting is precisely the history and possible variations of the struggle of the eye–hand antagonism. I'm not at all saying that painting doesn't resolve the eye–hand tension. I'm saying that there's always a point in painting or an aspect of a particular painting where the hand and the eye lock horns like enemies. It might be among the more interesting moments in painting.

The first characteristic of the diagram was simply a germinal chaos. As for the second characteristic, I'd say the diagram is wholly made up of a set of strokes and patches [*un ensemble trait-tache*] and not lines and colors, and that this set is manual. Notice that this second characteristic is an extension of the first because I can explain how there is chaos here. If the diagram is fundamentally manual and reflects a hand freed from its subordination to the eye, if only provisionally—once again, this doesn't apply to what emerges from the diagram—it's easy to see why the diagram is chaotic, since, once again, it entails the breakdown of visual coordinates, courtesy of the act liberating the hand. In other words, it's a set of strokes [*traits*], ones that do not constitute a visual form. We ought to call these strokes literally "nonsignifying." What are patches [*la tache*]? The patch or stain might be a color, but it's like an undifferentiated color. A set of nonsignifying strokes and undifferentiated colors, that's chaos, the collapse.

Leading us to the third characteristic. We've already covered it previously, so I can be brief. If the diagram is the manual stroke-patch that emerges onto the canvas and defies optical coordinates, visual coordinates, that draws them into a kind of collapse, how do we define this stroke-patch? Now we can consider it from the other end and try to define it based on what's supposed to emerge from the diagram. What results from the diagram are pictorial colors and pictorial lines. We don't yet know what a pictorial line or a pictorial color is. The diagram is not yet line and color. So what is it? Klee provided the answer: it's grey. The patch is grey, and that's what the diagram is: it's grey. In what way is this the diagram? Because it's a double grey. It is simultaneously the grey of black-white, and this grey is where all the visual coordinates fall apart; and it's also the grey of green-red from which the whole spectrum of colors emerges. I would also say that the whole light spectrum comes out of the black-white grey. What comes out of the diagram is the twofold pictorial spectrum: light-color. That's what Klee said in some of his texts about grey, which I think are wonderful. "The grey point leaps over itself . . ."[16] It's double, the two sides of grey: the grey of black-and-white and grey as the matrix of color. But it's not yet a color, so something needs to emerge from it. Now, you can tell that the tension is no longer between the eye and the hand; the tension is within the patch itself. In the greyness of the patch, there are two aspects, insofar as this grey is the grey of black-white or insofar as it is the grey of green-red, the color matrix.

Then the same goes for the stroke: strokes aren't pictorial lines, but pictorial lines emerge from them. I maintain that strokes are not yet lines; lines are made up of strokes. Or else: strokes are the manual elements of composition of the visual line. The visual line is composed neither of points nor even of segments; visual lines are composed of manual strokes. Heterogeneity exists between the component and the composite because strokes are strictly manual while lines produced by strokes are visual. As a result, the stroke must be defined, in order to convey its originality, as a line that at no moment bears a constant direction. Thus, this line has no visual reality. A line that almost constantly changes direction, that's what a stroke is. I'm distinguishing the diagram nonetheless from two things irrevocably bound up with it: its before and its after. The relation to a before occurs because the diagram leads this before into catastrophe: the visual world. The relation to an after occurs, since something will emerge from the diagram, the painting itself. As a manual pictorial unit, the stroke-patch will draw the visual catastrophe along in such a way that something new emerges as a result. What do we call it? What about "the third eye"? The eyes had to be annihilated for the third eye to emerge, but where does the third eye come from? It comes from the hand, from the manual diagram.

Now, on to the fourth characteristic. I'll just sum up what we saw at the beginning. What is the function of the diagram? Looking at what was there before it, the function is precisely to get rid of any resemblance. This is obvious. Everyone knows there's never been such a thing as figurative painting, if by figuration we mean the act of making a likeness. That goes without saying. Getting rid of resemblance has always been something that happened not only in the painter's head but in the painting as such. Even if some resemblance remains, it's so secondary that even the painters who feel the need for it, do so as something that regulates rather than defines the painting. In this sense, there's never been such a thing as figurative painting. Unmaking resemblance has always been inherent to the act of painting. And it's the diagram that unmakes resemblance for the sake of a deeper resemblance as some painters put it, for example, as Cézanne often noted.[17] Or else the diagram unmakes resemblance to cause the image to emerge. What does this mean, then? Let's take that literally and make use of all the ready-made expressions from which they're derived: resemblance is undone in order to cause the image to emerge. Let's try to change up the vocabulary solely with the idea that this might help us move forward. I could also put it this way: getting rid of representation to cause presence to emerge. Representation is the before-painting. Presence is what emerges from the diagram. Or else, to say this in another way: getting rid of resemblance to cause the image to emerge, but at that point, what emerges from the diagram is the image without resemblance.

Very early on and very quickly, Christian theology fleshed out a wonderful concept that already prefigures all the fraught relationships between art and religion: the idea of an image without resemblance. If you went through catechism class growing up, you'll remember—this is covered in catechism class, you get it straight from the church fathers; catechism texts had these great expressions: God created man in Its own image and likeness, and through sin, man preserved this image—not even God could take that away from man—but lost the likeness. Sin is the act whereby man is constituted as an image without resemblance. How is that possible? How can an image be an image if it doesn't resemble anything? An image with no resemblance, that's where painting comes in. It gives us an image with no resemblance. Still within our search for a cleaner vocabulary, isn't that what we call an "icon"? Indeed, an icon isn't representation, it is presence, and yet it's an image, an image qua presence. The weight of the image's presence is iconic. I'm saying that the diagram is the instance whereby I get rid of resemblance in order to produce the presence-image. That's why I'm bringing up diagrams: breaking down resemblance and producing the image. There's the aspect before and the aspect afterward, with the diagram in between.

Let's distinguish three terms: given features [*les données*], the possibility of fact, and fact itself. The visual givens are what falls apart in the diagram so that the pictorial fact can emerge. And what is the diagram? According to the painter Bacon's formulation, it's the possibility of fact. As I'm always trying to squeeze in an example wherever I can, who is the painter who really pushed, established the raw presence of the pictorial fact? One of the first—no one was first because really, that's always been the case, but to us, from our modern or pseudo-modern perspective, one artist is synonymous with the affirmation, the imposition of the pictorial fact—it's Michelangelo. There's no denying that he's a sculptor, a sculptor-painter. He brusquely confronts you with a pictorial fact where there's nothing left to be justified, where painting has achieved its own justification. But what form does that take? I really do think that our main artistic categories are well-founded. A lot of people say, Romanticism, Classicism, Baroque: they're just words! Or even the abstract, Expressionism. I don't think they're just words. I think they're well-founded terms; I just think we need to find better definitions than, say, the abstract is the opposite of figurative, because that misses the mark. To the contrary, they're perfectly fine categories, and besides, philosophy functions via categories, so philosophy benefits all the more.

And I am saying that the contemporaneity of Michelangelo and Mannerism is crucial. I think the category of Mannerism neatly sets us up to understand what the pictorial fact is, in the most general sense of the term: something is "mannered" in the painting's figure in the way it emerges from the diagram.[18] It emerges from the diagram with a sort of Mannerism that we can still interpret anecdotally. Take Michelangelo's figures, Tintoretto's figures, Velázquez's figures. Speaking anecdotally, you have a first impression that this is a mix of extraordinary effeminacy, of Mannerism in the attitude, in the pose, almost a muscular exuberance, as if the body were both too strong and singularly effeminate. Michelangelo's characters are unbelievable. The school known as Mannerism, with some intense masterpieces, the manner in which they depict the figure of Christ, it's unbelievable, given what you could call the artificial character of attitudes and postures. This is what our eye sees initially.

Obviously, in a certain way, the affirmation of the pictorial fact is the most beautiful sort of painting. Compared with the visual given, it's quite necessary for the pictorial fact to present the figure in forms that our eye finds extraordinarily stylized, extraordinarily artificial. Within this, while it's not anything profound, there is something, a kind of tiny provocation from the painter. The manner serves precisely to say: this is not what you think. As a result, when people quickly point to anecdotal accounts of painters' homosexuality, they've missed the mark. These painters are working in Mannerism, necessarily, insofar as they're painters. All pretty trivial. You see, getting rid of the visual givens through the diagram establishes a possibility of fact. But the fact itself is not a given; it's something to be produced. What is produced is the pictorial fact, that is, the set of lines and colors, that is, the new eye. Passing through the diagram's manual catastrophe was required in order to produce the pictorial fact, that is, to produce the third eye.

Here's the last characteristic of the diagram, the fifth characteristic. If you're following me so far, it's clear that the diagram must be in place. I no longer even think that it can only be virtual. It can be covered over, but it's in place. It has to be in place in a painting. It cannot just be in the painter's head before starting to paint. The painting must bear witness to this encounter with chaos, "an orderly abyss," as someone said.[19] A painting that might be an abyss, this is nothing; a painting that might be well-ordered, this is nothing. But the painter's main concern is establishing an order proper to the abyss. You notice that at that point, there are huge risks, even in terms of technique. And I'm starting over because that's how I'll eventually rearrange, reclassify everything we've done up to now. I'd like for you to grasp this as concretely as possible. Once again, what I'm trying to do is chart the painting's journey through time. I don't think of a painting as a spatial reality; I really look at it temporally via the synthesis of time proper to painting: the before, the diagram, and the after.

What are the risks? We've already seen them, so I'll recap. The first danger is that the diagram takes over, that it scrambles everything. Perhaps now that makes more sense. Maybe there are paintings that come close. Because the paths get quite narrow now, at the point that we've reached. Maybe that will allow us to refresh our main categories. What does it mean to be abstract, or to be Expressionist? At what point can I say about a painting, "ah, là, là, [this one's a failure]."[20] You can tell that, even though it's a matter of taste, after a while there's nothing to be said. All you can do is wait for everyone to have their own reactions, which isn't easy. It's already difficult managing to grasp what I am feeling from viewing a painting, whereas so many things cause me to feel predictable things. At what point can I say: This one's a failure? It came so very close; it could have been great, were it not for a bit of greyness or some stray and ultimately arbitrary brushstrokes. I ask myself: Why not? This is alright, but he could have just as well done something else; there's nothing strictly required in this one. You know, the enemy of any form of expression is gratuitousness, [as when somebody says], there's no wrong answer [or] you can't make a mistake.[21] But when you say something, why are you saying it? Is it worth the trouble of doing so? Likewise for a painting: Is it worth the trouble of making it? Maybe not . . . even for the one who made it. Plenty of painters make paintings, and it wasn't worth the effort to do so, even for them. But who decides that? I don't know, it's too complicated. Anyway, one senses that something could have emerged from that painting. At that point when the diagram has taken over, nothing can emerge from the diagram.

When the diagram takes over, I can certainly say just as well: this is pure chaos; the germ has died. Klee's turn of phrase is great: if the grey point takes over, overwhelms everything visible, the egg dies.[22] So, it's up to you. What does it mean when a painter judges other painters? He's not actually judging them because, once again, out of all artists, painters might be the proudest but also appear to be the most modest. They don't pass judgment, but they express preferences. It's always interesting to hear why a painter says they aren't attracted to this or that form of painting. When Bacon is looking at a Pollock, he says, "This is sloppy," no offense to Pollock. It takes nothing away from him. At what level does this matter? Not because it tells us anything about Pollock. Bacon gives us more to understand when he speaks about a painter he likes and admires. What exactly does it mean: Pollock's work, it's sloppy? Bacon goes so far as to say about Expressionism (in an almost racist way): I dislike that sloppiness from Central Europe.[23] You can tell what he means; he's Anglo-Irish. How is that relevant for us? It's relevant because when Bacon sees a work by Pollock, he ought to flip it around; he ought to say, "This is chaotic." Indeed, when you see one of Pollock's paintings, it can genuinely come across as a chaos-painting. Putting Pollock aside, some canvases affect us this way: The diagram leans so far into this first aspect—which is chaos—that it has descended into chaos, so that nothing can emerge from the diagram. Everything is blurred. It's all greyed out, or else there's too much color so that everything's grey: a ruined canvas. It happens. That's the first danger.

I'll spell this out: the danger from the diagram—without using the word *diagram*—has been very well articulated by Cézanne. There are letters in which Cézanne writes, with some apprehension: instead of assuring their intersection, the planes [fall one atop the other].[24] Understand that this isn't a question of perspective because painting has nothing to do with perspective, it's a meaningless concept.[25] Perspective is only one possible response to the sole pictorial problem that can be posed pictorially—in paintings where there is a reason for distinguishing planes, since there are paintings in which there is no reason for distinguishing planes—in the form: How will the painter produce and how does the painter bring different planes together?[26] Perspective is nothing if not a case of conjoined planes.[27] The real pictorial problem is that when there are several planes, by what method will they be connected? Cézanne says: when it comes to the abyss of chaos, instead of coming together, the different planes fall one atop the other.[28] Instead of falling into a sequence, the colors mix together, and this mixture is nothing but greyness. The painted object that has lost its resemblance in the chaos is fundamentally off-kilter. The planes falling onto each other, colors mixing into greyness, the object all wrong and off balance, this is the extreme case of the canvas so bound up with the diagram that there's nothing left but chaos. Failed canvases just have no interest.

What is of interest, on the other hand, are the ones that come perilously close to this first danger, but does this occur because it's a great painter (or because these are all great painters), that they manage masterfully to avoid falling into it? Here we might have grounds to establish our first aesthetic category: I think it's specifically what has been named Abstract Expressionism, that is, the whole school that dominated American painting. It's the generation that's now some sixty years old. They're the ones who really flirt with chaos. The diagram takes over, but still manages to produce something fantastic. I think that's what Pollock is about. It's Morris Louis. It's Kenneth Noland, anyway, all the ones familiar to many of you. In particular, I'd refer to Pollock in terms of lines and to Morris Louis when it comes to color-patches [*tache-couleur*]. We'll have a look at this later. If you will, this is Abstract Expressionism's tendency, to push the diagram toward a maximum level of chaos, but contrary to what Bacon says, I think it's obvious that they don't descend into chaos, that their paintings are neither greyness nor sloppiness. So, the first tension is for the diagram to take over. At that point, it all just looks like chaos. So, once again, we could call this Abstract Expressionism.

Let's look into the other tendency. See, now I'm defining these aesthetic categories depending on privileged positions related to the diagram, and without any regard at all for positions related to figuration, which is not relevant. What would the diagram's second tendency be? That's where it gets minimized. How do you minimize "a shallow stream"?[29] By retaining nothing but the bare minimum? Just as I was saying earlier: when you maximize the diagram's potential [*puissance*], it tends to become bound to chaos, so when you minimize it, it tends to become bound maximally to a pictorial order. That is, you tend to reduce the diagram, even to replace it. With what? This is the first time we've run into this idea, a term that may be useful for us. You tend to replace the diagram with something rather remarkable: a sort of *code*. If this term opens things up for me, it's insofar as I am asking: Aren't we finding a new diagram/code tension such that the difference between diagram and code may help us make a lot of progress about what a diagram is, in terms of the philosophical concept that we're after?

What gives me that impression? Obviously, a code can mean something grotesque. I'm thinking of botched paintings. The attempt to reduce the diagram to its minimum and to replace it with a code is an obvious way to define so-called abstract painting. We'll see if that's true. But when it goes wrong, and God, abstract painting has some awful painters, just as many as other kinds of painting, it's catastrophic. The guys who make squares or whatever, it's horrible. I mean, it's so pretentious; a square can be pretentious, a square can be crap. There are some hideous squares in bad abstract art. All these types of abstract painting, at the most basic level, tend toward a sort of geometrism. You get the feeling that what they tend to do is replace the diagram with a code. When that fails, what happens? That's when the canvas merely applies an external code. To put the question another way, what is the difference between one of Kandinsky's triangles and a triangle from geometrist? What makes Kandinsky's triangle an aesthetic triangle? Bringing up non-Euclidean geometry and the possibility of painting by using non-Euclidean codes do not change anything in terms of this problem. It's obvious that when a great abstract painter, in my view, is actually moving toward replacing the diagram with a code, that's not the issue because, at that point, abstract painting in its turn and in its own way would just be another sort of catastrophe for painting.

If abstract painters are great, it's because ultimately, they have an idea. They are ascetic, spiritualistic. There's no problem with that, with the spiritual life. They have a fundamentally religious soul. What do they create? The code they have in mind to inaugurate or what they think will be possible in the future—if you look at all the abstract painters' major declarations, what they are doing is always addressed to a future world for which they herald the new codes—it goes without saying that it's a properly pictorial code. But this is nonetheless a funny thing. The abstract project emerges alongside all sorts of paradoxes therein: establishing a pictorial code, that is, sorting out elements of codification that are at the same time completely pictorial. As I was saying earlier, Pollock's paintings verge on becoming too sloppy and letting chaos reign, but then he pulls it off. I would say that abstract painters verge on a sort of code-painting in which painting would be obliterated as well. But here's the thing: the great abstract painters know how to create and indeed how to forge the elements of a uniquely pictorial code. They turn code into pictorial reality instead of applying a code onto painting. They're Kantians, in my view. With Kandinsky, it's obvious that he's a disciple of Kant to some extent. They create an Analytic of elements, for those who have already read some Kant. Kandinsky offers us a stupendous Analytic of elements.[30] Here, too, it would take very little for this work to fail. I would at least try to define abstract painting by saying: this is the other side of the diagram. They reduce the diagram to a minimum. At the extreme, they replace the diagram with a code. But be careful: this is a properly pictorial code, inherent to painting. Kandinsky and Mondrian converge on one point that I find fascinating, namely, that ideally, genuine code is binary.

What exactly is binarity, painting's specific form of binarity? This form has nothing to do with a binary calculation that would churn out paintings. You can always do that with a computer although . . . A computer can be programmed to make paintings. At that point, code is external to painting. You've encoded your input in such a way that the computer can render a portrait. There's a famous portrait of Einstein made with binary signals o/+.[31] That's obviously not what Kandinsky or Mondrian is doing. What sort of binarity do abstract painters use? The main binary relationship is, as everyone knows, between horizontal and vertical. Mondrian's well-known formula: the horizontal and the vertical are the two elements. That's what the Analytic of elements is, to reach the horizontal and the vertical, and that's it. Because you can make anything with this binary code, not in the sense of applying a code from outside. In every direction, you can develop the code within painting. So, that gives us the second path along which painting also brushes up against danger.

And the abstract painter who I think probably went farther than any other abstract painter in forming a pictorial code—he's on my mind because not long ago he had an exhibit in Paris—it's Auguste Herbin. For those who know this painter, I think he's one of the only abstract painters who at heart is truly a colorist. If you ask me, he's the greatest or one of the greatest colorists. I'll show you an example, for your viewing pleasure. You should be able to see it from back there. He had an exhibit in a small gallery, rue de Seine, but it's over now.[32] In Paris museums, there are pieces by Herbin, but in my opinion, there aren't any that are very good, except maybe at the Centre Pompidou.

In a vague sort of way, I have two actual categories. These two categories—abstract painting and Expressionism—what makes them modern? I think that speaks to a problem which is actually rather modern and motivates a lot of painters. But the less they think about it, the better it is. This problem can be summed up as: Why painting today? There are many who think writing is outdated, and maybe painting is outdated, and so on. There are painters on whom such matters have a strong impact, something quite obvious for abstract painters. Why can the problem "Why painting today?" lead to a renunciation of painting for the benefit of new forms of art, or quasi-new forms of art? But otherwise, when it comes to how today's major painters have answered the question, notice how concrete their answers have become, for example, when it's with a Mondrian sort of response. In fact, doing wall-painting that breaks away from easel-painting clearly means something. That entails—ostensibly at least—a whole new understanding of what a painting is. The painting no longer even pretends to represent anything. Why? Because the painting's task has become to divide up its own surface. Hence the squares: see how it's a pictorial code and not merely the application of a geometrical code. The painting ceases to be a window. The painting has to split up its own surface in relation, I would say almost in an isomorphism, with architectural division, with the division of walls and the divisions on each wall. At that point, the painting is no longer attached to the easel as a mobile reality; it's bound to the wall. And that indeed was Mondrian's idea. He viewed his own paintings as abstract (the wrong sort of abstract) insofar as they lacked their corresponding walls. In fact, by dividing up its own surface, the canvas ought to resonate with divisions on the surface of the walls because here, painting becomes mural. Hence, the necessity for a code.

Why painting today? What's the answer? It can emerge only from what we've called the diagram. I think every painter says, whether they admit it or not, that painting is still worth the trouble precisely because it has a certain relationship to chaos—sometimes philosophically, sometimes poetically—that everyone recognizes in modern humanity. Our world has descended into chaos. Our world is tumult and chaos. Kandinsky is always talking about it. So, why painting today? You can insert whatever chaos you like, all the stereotypical examples of modernity, the atomic bomb, difficulties of city life, pollution, and so on . . . Tumult and chaos. So, why painting today? Because painting would no doubt be justified to the extent that it manages not just to ward off chaos, to confront chaos up close in order to extract from it—let's risk calling it this—a possible modern order. Only, how is this possible modern order going to emerge from chaos without dispelling it? Here we find various responses.

I'd suggest that abstract painters might reply: by limiting chaos to a minimum, and chaos is life outside. A constant theme in Kandinsky's work is that modern humanity needs a renewed spiritual life and that painting becomes the principal agent of humanity's spiritual life. He's always talking about it: spiritual life has become empty. For Kandinsky, painting's mission is to form a spiritual life, to draw it out of chaos, that is, precisely how painting operates [*FBLS*, 84–85 UM; 103–4 C]. All that might sound like a figure of speech, but it ceases to be so. Abstract painters are indeed spiritualists. They are the heralds of the spiritual life to come. That's their charge. But why? If their claim to spirituality is indeed justified—the title of Kandinsky's famous book, *Concerning the Spiritual in Art*[33]—it's precisely because painting cannot do without its confrontation with chaos. Saying that might not be enough on its own, but if it's true that the conditions of modern life give rise to chaos, it's specifically because painting offers the most close-up confrontation, there on the canvas, and has to pass through chaos for something to be extracted from it, that the painter thinks he or she has a response to the question: "Why painting today?" That is, to construct modern humanity's third eye, our inner eye. That might well extend into a sort of mysticism. Herbin's work is fascinating; it's where you get a sort of mystic materialism. The answer from abstract painters is bizarre, since it amounts to saying: you'll extract the germ of chaos by keeping chaos to a minimum. Kandinsky puts it formally: by turning your back on the tumult and inventing the future's code.[34]

At the other pole, what would an Expressionist reply? I think that Abstract Expressionism would provide a very similar response to the question: "Why painting today?" Again, it's because painting engages in a close encounter with chaos. However, for an Abstract Expressionist, for an American, for Pollock and his following, you obviously won't manage to get out of chaos by establishing a pictorial code. On the contrary, it's by fully confronting it, stopping just at the point where chaos would overwhelm the painting. They'll extend it to the maximum because for them, it's another way of experiencing rhythm; because for them, for the Expressionists, rhythm is as close as one gets to chaos. The closer you get to chaos, to the tumult of matter, to molecular tumult, the more likely it is that you'll grasp hold of the germ and the rhythm. In this sense, the abstract painter's formula would be: let's limit chaos as much as possible so that a modern order can emerge, an order that would be a code for the future. Expressionism's formula would be: let's keep adding to chaos precisely this particle almost exceeding its limit in order for something to emerge from it. These two approaches might very well misunderstand each other, but both are paths that flirt each time with catastrophe. Expressionism's flirtation with catastrophe is to fall into chaos, pure and simple. Abstract painting's flirtation with catastrophe is the external application of a code. That's what happens with bad Expressionists—it's just sloppy! Or what you get with bad abstract painters—too much order, orderly enough to be fascist!

What about the third path? We might be tempted to call the third approach moderate, if that wouldn't be an insult to the painters who adopt this approach. Because you sense that this moderate, temperate approach is temperate only because it's not one of the others we've just seen. So, what is the third pole? It's the bizarre act of *measuring* chaos. Using the diagram but preventing it from contracting or expanding too much. Maintaining chaos by imposing a kind of limitation to its dimensions. That's hard to do. So, we might call it temperate, but at the same time, in trying to localize chaos, trying to hold it off, this is a terrible undertaking. In any case, your eyes get tired, your hand starts shaking. Your hand shakes because it no longer follows the diagram's visual givens; your eyes get tired because visual coordinates in the diagram collapse. This is the third path, in fact. We cannot call it figurative. It does indeed come down to establishing chaos, but so that something might emerge from the chaos, which would be the Figure.[35]

The Figure is not a reproduction; it's an image without resemblance. It's Cézanne, it's Van Gogh, it's Gauguin, the so-called figural, rather than figurative, painters.[36] This third position is very awkward, the diagram for itself. Neither extending the diagram so far that it descends into chaos, nor limiting it so that it gets replaced with a code. The diagram, and nothing but a diagram. That lends the diagram some dramatic weight. It would be wrong to call it a temperate path, and yet that fits because, at the same time, it's what drives Van Gogh mad: preventing the diagram from giving into chaos, and yet, chaos still remains. Consider the two contemporary painters, Van Gogh and Gauguin. They both belong to what I'm describing as a temperate third line, but it's obvious that Van Gogh verges on a sort of Expressionist adventure. The encroachment of chaos is fully present, so this third path doesn't avoid any danger. With Gauguin, this is the opposite. If we can call Van Gogh a major precursor to Abstract Expressionism, we can equally call Gauguin a major precursor to abstract painting. He flirts with the other aspect.

We could start to arrange our categories. For the moment, I'd like to start off with three categories that I can call: abstract painting, figural painting, Expressionist painting. We've defined them strictly according to three scenarios regarding the diagram. By no means did we define them in terms of figuration, which we did away with outright. These are three diagrammatic positions. The first scenario: the diagram verges on chaos. The second scenario: the diagram leans toward code and, at the extreme, is even replaced by a code. The third diagrammatic scenario: the diagram acts like a diagram.[37] I'll try to elaborate. Let's bring back the eye–hand dynamic and apply our three categories.

Maybe you all are tired; do you want a break? What time is it? Noon? Let's take a break.

[*Interruption of the recording,* time stamp: 1:38:08.]

We're making some progress because now we're not satisfied simply with the notion of a diagram on its own. We've introduced the idea of different diagrammatic positions. The diagram can take different positions, three such positions that we've identified, and I'd like to follow up on these in concrete terms. How do they work? It's not simply a question of the effect on us; rather, we must ask: How can such effects come about? For painters, it's really a matter of a very slow, very dangerous confrontation with chaos itself, not an abstract chaos but the chaos on the canvas, with these diagrammatic positions that each painter can experience in his or her own way, obviously. If I try to interpret the major pictorial categories based on the diagrammatic positions, we'll have to see what new definitions [are the result] for these categories. What is the diagrammatic position for Expressionism? What is most striking when we view a so-called Expressionist painting? What are they tending toward? I think the answer has already been spelled out, particularly by certain American critics. If you take a painting by Pollock (not from just a single period of his work, but from many periods of Pollock's work), what strikes you immediately is this: a total rejection of the canvas's organic existence on the easel.

What do I mean by the canvas's organic existence on the easel? It's an organic existence because nothing is the same on the canvas, before it even gets touched. There's the problem of centers, focal points, and edges. The problem of edges is made all the more pressing with the addition of the frame or bounds of the painting. What do you do with the frame? If you think of a painter like Seurat (who isn't at all Expressionist), how he looked for a way to keep the frame from being a fixed boundary, turning to a wide range of scientific and artistic techniques to make the frame a part of the painting, that's one problem that arises. Why is it that, when we're looking at a Pollock painting, we immediately know that this wasn't a problem for him? It's a particular American expression (which I'm going to butcher with my deplorable accent), these are so-called *all-over* paintings. American Abstract Expressionism consists of *all-over.* It means that lines do not start at the edge but begin virtually, they start long beforehand. The painting captures as much as it can of a line with no end or beginning. At the extreme, borders and the center are strictly treated as equally probable. What is this *all-over* line running from one end to the other, doubling back on itself, almost covering the entire painting? See, I've begun with an example taken from a line; let's call it the Pollock-line for now.

There's an American critic who published a long article titled "Three American Painters," translated in the *Revue d'esthétique,* which was reprinted in a 10/18 volume titled "Painting." The article is by a very good contemporary art critic, a guy named Michael Fried.[38] Well actually, I've heard that he's recently gone downhill. It's an in-depth look into today's American painters—actually, it's an older generation—and the article is quite good. Because he explains rather well why, in looking at one of Pollock's lines, there's no mistaking that it's genuinely from Pollock because it's a line with no contour. A closed shape [*figure*] traces a contour.[39] You can say, this is a triangle, this is a flat circle, this is a circle, this is a half-circle, and so on. Notice what can be said in contrast regarding this line without contour: it loops from one end of the painting to the other; it circles back on itself without ever closing. It doesn't mark an inside or outside. It's a moving line that never stops moving.[40] Likewise, just as the line started before the left side and continues far beyond the right side, it has no beginning or end. So, no inside or outside, no beginning or end. It's obvious if you're able to imagine a Pollock painting. This kind of line, as line, never ceases being a line and yet verges on becoming equal to the surface. A line that builds up power [*puissance*] through which it tends to become equal to the surface, this means: 1 that builds its power of 1 closer to becoming 2. Surfaces are two-dimensional, lines are one-dimensional. Here you have Pollock's line verging on becoming equal to the surface. This is the line's attempt to overcome its power of one, its one-dimensionality, while remaining a line. Thus, there's a perfect adequation in the painter's intention between what is on the painting and the painting itself. The line inhabiting the painting is equal to the painting. The line will be a surface. It will be adequate to the surface. This is a line without contour. So, the line achieves a dimensional power that, properly speaking, is power to infinity. In a way, chaos will be averted by itself.

What I'm saying might appear very abstract for those who can't picture a Pollock painting. When you look at his paintings with the line inhabiting the entirety, really tending to equal the whole surface, it becomes clear. I should probably mention here, because we talked about it in another seminar and someone here knew this author well, that there's a mathematical logician who wrote a really interesting text on what he calls "fractal" objects. I'm citing this from memory to encourage you to develop encounters of this sort. His name is Mandelbrot. His book, *Les Objets fractals,* was published by Flammarion.[41] What are these fractal objects? They're specifically these objects that turn out to have a fractional number of dimensions. It's fascinating. He proposes a form of mathematics and logic for fractal objects. What does he have in mind? He's proposing a line that's more than one-dimensional and less than two-dimensional.[42] A surface is something that has two dimensions. A volume [has] three. Suppose there's a line with a fractional number of dimensions. As a line and remaining a line, it tends toward becoming a surface. Mandelbrot's example is straightforward and compelling: take a straight line. Split it into thirds. Swap out the middle part for an equilateral triangle. You end up with this shape:[43]

At that point, take all four-line segments remaining [see next page] and split them into thirds. And then put an equilateral triangle onto each of those middle sections. Ad infinitum. At the extreme, you're still working with line's domain and power, and at the extreme, your line is enough to cover the surface. That's what is called

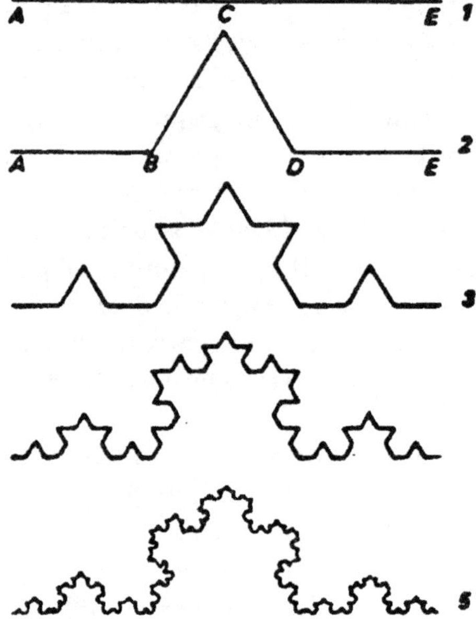

Constructing the von Koch curve, from Mandelbrot's *Fractals*.

a fractal object. You see that it's fully engaged in becoming. It has a fractional number of dimensions. There are all kinds of other examples, it's really interesting.

My point is very simple. A line that appears to change direction at any given moment has a dimension greater than one. At each given moment, you make it change direction. You wind up with a line that acts as a surface. There's a similar example provided by Mandelbrot: Brownian motion. Brownian motion is of this type. It's such that the line's direction is never the same from one point to the other, a line that changes direction at each given moment, no matter how close the points are to each other. It's very interesting to look for mathematical formulas to describe this as one thing, but it's also interesting to express it aesthetically. We're already within a domain where there's no question of reducing one to the other, but where they act as two different expressions: a potential mathematical expression and an independent aesthetic expression. This is exactly what Pollock's line is. Of course, he doesn't just use equilateral triangles, which would amount to a mathematical formula: forming equilateral triangles in the middle of each line segment ad infinitum is a mathematical construction.[44] Pollock clearly takes an artistic route: a line that will inhabit the entire canvas without tracing any contour. Death to the contour.

So, you can see how Expressionists can claim to be much more abstract than abstract painters. Pollock, for one, could say, just as Bacon says about him: personally, I'm not interested in Mondrian, or I'm not interested in Kandinsky. I don't know what he said about this exactly, since Pollock said so little. He didn't talk much, that didn't interest him. Why? Because for him, whether a shape [*figure*] is abstract or concrete hardly matters; that's not where the difference is. Moreover, he'll even claim that abstract painters are doing purely figurative painting. The difference is not at the abstract or concrete level, since, again, you can form abstract shapes [*figures*], which are still figurative. We'll see how an abstract painter might respond to this. Kandinsky paints triangles, or he paints tubes, or he paints circles instead of painting ladies and gents [*des dames et des messieurs*], but what makes that abstract? Whenever you have a contour, you have a shape [*figure*]. Pollock doesn't find this very interesting. The fact that contour entails shape explains why Pollock cannot be slotted into the category of abstract painting, and why, once again, I consider these categories to be well-founded.

For Pollock, real abstraction begins with the line without contour and not with the abstract characteristics of what's depicted by a contour. As a result, as soon as a line reveals contour, it isn't abstract. Expressionism is about achieving real abstraction, and it can rightly lay claim to genuine pictorial abstraction. The others are abstract in a way that has nothing to do with painting because, pictorially, they remain figurative. They're only abstract through what they depict. They say their work doesn't depict anything, but that isn't true. It's still representational, simply they represent abstractly.[45] It's an extra-pictorial abstraction, outside painting. In terms of being painters, they are perfectly figurative, since they create contours. They use lines.[46] They could not detach lines from contours. At the extreme, you can already distinguish the Expressionist pole from the abstract pole. We'll see in a short while what the true problem of abstraction is, but for the moment, I'd say: the problem of Expressionism is really how to draw lines without contour.

And the same goes for color; color doesn't form contour. It's quite difficult to obtain colors that don't form a contour, since, in the end, there are two ways of creating contours: through lines, but also through color. Colors form contours no less than a closed line does. And just as I referred to Pollock's work involving lines without contour, which in my opinion is a fantastic pictorial breakthrough, there is yet another painter, namely, the artwork of Morris Louis, whose work is what I'd refer to as color without contour. This is what's thought of as one side of Expressionism, so-called tachism. How do you keep a color-patch [*tache*] from suggesting a contour? In terms of technique, the required methods are very simple. Morris Louis turns to soaking or to picking up pigment with a roller. As we see, we can add the roller to our list of tools other than paintbrushes. Pollock did a lot more with his bulb baster. Morris Louis's roller is interesting because by letting pigment seep onto the canvas, you get these amazing halo effects.

So there are two modes possible for looking at one of Morris Louis's tachist paintings: either a mode, despite everything, in which a contour of the color-patch is reestablished—but this effort is already quite interesting because effort is required—or else a wandering perception that precisely creates no contour. If an effort is required to pin down the kind of contour of the color-patch in Morris Louis's work, that's because something on the canvas counteracts any suggestion of contour. In the end, it gives off halo effects that are technically quite beautiful. (It's relatively easy to obtain a halo effect on canvas; bad painters can do it. There's a difference.) So, this definition of Expressionism, the line without contour or color without contour, applies to both aspects. I'd say: these are a chaos-line and a chaos-color. They placed their bet on chaos. They planted chaos onto the canvas with the idea that the more chaos manages to get captured on the canvas, the better the result will be. By drawing infinitely close to chaos, this one-dimensional line, that suddenly becomes two-dimensional or becomes a greater-than-one-dimensional power, a fractional power, this is where they'll focus their energy.

The word *Expressionism* is interesting. It's all well and good to define Expressionism as a diagrammatic position and not by what it depicts. But how is it Expressionism exactly? It's interesting to consider these critics who manage to propose a category—doing so at their own risk and peril, once again—if we believe in well-founded categories, that is, if we believe in a philosophy of art. I think people are fully justified in saying, "to hell with philosophy of art!," who prefer talking about painting as little as possible. For them, the less we talk about it, the better. And in the end, I wonder if it's not for the best . . . Yes, it's surely better, but even so, in the absence of anything better, in the absence of such a uniquely lofty stance, if we'll go ahead and use categories, they had better be well-founded. The term *Expressionism* was precisely coined by Worringer, which is interesting because he coined it in a context where there were a lot of complaints about German museums buying too many French paintings.[47] They bought some by Cézanne . . .

[*Interruption of the recording,* time stamp: 1:59:53.]

. . . he took a side and called the painters in this movement Expressionist. What did he mean by that? If you want to understand the word's origin, we have to consider what Worringer had himself written on Gothic art in particular because he tried to define this northern, so-called Gothic line.[48] The way he defined it ought to interest us given what we've been discussing. He defined it this way: the Gothic line, or northern line, is an abstract line, that is, an inorganic line. That alone is intriguing. Worringer was no fool: he didn't see abstract as the opposite of figurative. He didn't even bring that up, it didn't interest him. For him, the abstract was the opposite of the organic, and indeed, according to Worringer's classification, the so-called classical world is not defined by figurative painting but by organic painting.[49] The line is an organic line that doesn't refer back to a portrayed object; it speaks to the faculties of the subject looking at the painting. By looking at the line used in classical painting, the subject feels the harmony of their faculties within themselves, the organic harmony of their faculties. What does that mean? It's a line that is subject to the principles of regularity, symmetry, enclosure.[50] In other words, the organic line is one that creates contour and whose harmony resides in the contour it traces. See, that is not at all a figurative definition, but he thinks concrete lines are organic lines. Consequently, they are figurative; the lines will depict something because in themselves, they will primarily be organic lines. For example, they will depict the higher organism: the human body.

Meanwhile, that's not how it is with the Gothic line. It's an abstract line. It's an inorganic line. He goes so far as to say that it's a mechanical line that substitutes the power of repetition for organic symmetry. He adds: unleashed, the unleashed potential [*puissance*] of repetition. Why? Symmetry is, rather, a repetition that is limited, that's capped off, that creates contour, that, for example, gets boiled down to two terms. It's a repetition where the repeated element counters itself, right and left, such that a closure prevents repetition from carrying on. With the Gothic line, on the other hand, repetition breaks loose. He puts it beautifully: it's a mechanical line, but notice that it's a line that makes us intuit the mechanical forces. Once more, he brings up Kant.[51] The Germans owe so much to Kant. He brings up Kant in order to avoid our misunderstanding what he just said. If you hear "mechanical line," then you might imagine it's a line that could be drawn by a machine. Not at all. It's a line where the mechanical becomes an object of intuition, right, instead of the organic. Thus, it's an inorganic line. All of the figures of this line are possible: as Worringer says, either the line gets endlessly lost in a chaotic upheaval; or it turns back on itself and expires like that, in upheaval; or it keeps pitting itself against an obstacle and receives force and liberation from this obstacle. The line confronts an obstacle that it only overcomes by changing direction, and it constantly changes direction. There are two books by Worringer translated into French: one through Klincksieck editions, called *Abstraction and Empathy,* and another at Gallimard titled *Gothic Art.*[52] There's a lot that he repeats in both books, but you'll notice that what he calls the Gothic line comes close to defining or reaching the idea of the line without contour—not in those words, but it's there in his definition of the Gothic line.[53] That's what abstraction really is. Why does that fall under Expressionism? That's abstract because it's inorganic. It's a line with no beginning or end, with no contour, and so forth. So, it's abstract, but Worringer goes on to say that this abstract is brimming with life, that is, we aren't dealing with geometrical abstract art. There's nothing organic or concrete. The Goths, or the barbarians, the northerners come up with something unusual: the line without contour, that is, nongeometrical abstraction. Classical art was organic; the quintessential example of geometrical abstraction would be Egyptian art.

But the Goth, the barbarian, is different. Like the path they themselves follow, the line without contour they invent has no end. It begins with Scythian art. What actually happens? It's an abstract brimming with vitality, Worringer says. To me, this is a beautiful idea, an abstract brimming with vitality, which is enough to set it apart from the geometrically abstract. But beware: vitality knocks it back over into the organic. And we saw that the line without contour was opposed to the organic line forming a contour. So Worringer is quick to add—something that runs throughout his understanding—a radical distinction between vital elements and organic elements. The life of the abstract Gothic line is a nonorganic life. It's a life beyond the capacities of the organism and the organic. It's the violence of nonorganic life that counters and punctures the classical world of representation, that is, the world of organic life. Organisms crumble under the rift caused by such powerful, inorganic life. The abstract Gothic line is a vital line. It's nongeometrical. It's a vital abstraction.

This is a very particular sort of abstraction. It's life that's been abstracted from organisms rather than essence abstracted from appearances, as is the case with geometry. Notice the foundation and the appearance of the word *Expressionist*. This abstract line, this line without contour, is fundamentally *expressive* because it is the vector for a nonorganic life. There's not much to change in shifting from Worringer's understanding of the Gothic line to one of Pollock's paintings. I'm not one to shy away from any superficial effect, so we should make use in any event of whatever is at hand. Is it a coincidence that several of Pollock's works are specifically titled "Gothic," which involve this line without contour, which ultimately produce a sort of stained-glass effect?[54] American critics quite naturally then used the term *Abstract Expressionism* to describe Pollock and his influence. Notice the lineage that leads us to define Expressionism as the presence of this use of colors or lines without contour, which are endowed with a nonorganic life. This same movement is sometimes called informalism [*art informel*]. There has been a lot of discussion about informal art in Paulhan's circle, and so forth.[55] Consider what makes it informal art.[56] It's because there isn't any form insofar as the line doesn't create a contour. But being informal is a consequence rather than a precondition. It's necessarily informal because the line doesn't create a contour. The line does not determine or delineate any form. And yet it is a kind of pictorial materialism at its purest; it comes together as if it were molecular. I think these are the first painters who managed to bring pictorial matter to a sort of molecular state.

The act of painting doesn't consist in conveying anything. It's about inventing painting's molecular matter. This is what the colorless line creates with the points of color that Pollock puts down, where the line always runs between things, between points. You can never pin down a point on the line. Rather, the points are distributed over the entire painting such that the line without contour constantly moves between points and goes back between them again in another way. The line without contour is actually the line not designating anything but instead perpetually passing between things. Accordingly, once an artistic expression comes to the fore and reaches self-awareness, you can always look back and say: yes, of course, it's always been the case . . .—here, the categories are quaking, but in a good way—it's always been the case that throughout whatever painting that has emerged, you'll find the more or less secondary attempt to have lines no longer determine things but instead to have them move between things. What Élie Faure said of Velázquez is well known—because Godard made such good use of it.[57] Velázquez no longer painted things, was no longer interested in contours, according to Élie Faure, who nonetheless had no stomach for Expressionist art. He painted what happened *between* things, air currents, everything without contour, light between one thing and another. For a lot of painters, everything that happens between things is crucial.[58]

I'm bringing up Velázquez through this incredible, well-known text by Élie Faure, but consider a painter like Turner. In Turner's work, there is a sort of coordinated dissolution of things in order to move the lines and color-patches between things, with all this occurring against the backdrop of the chaos-diagram. Using the diagram means stretching chaos until things cease to exist, and so on. By stretching chaos over the whole canvas, its secret for a new order will be ripped forth. The new order is the course of the line or the color-patch without contour. You might be wondering what makes this a new order. It's an order of molecular movement.

Humanity is led toward ordering itself molecularly within a space of materialism. Accounts are being squared. Abstract spiritualism has no appeal for them at all. I mean, it's a human being, by his or her nature, who undertakes the work of painting. An Informalist or an Expressionist is certainly capable of leading a deeply spiritual life. I'm attempting to avoid idiotic remarks, but I do think that [the painter's] pictorial tendency is a deeply materialist one, not a materialism external to painting—that's how the artist can be extremely spiritualist—but concerning an order born from drawing molecular pathways.[59] It's like a pictorial micro-material, necessarily so. In this regard, all the connections drawn between modern physics and informal art are justified—I don't see anything incompatible, that's fine—based on this idea: their abstraction is a very special sort of vital abstraction.

To return to a very simple point, Worringer said of Gothic art: it's abstract, but what sort of abstract is this that doesn't trace any contours? There are coiling lines, snail shells, that either reset or run out in a sort of swirling hole. That's the Gothic line. From one perspective, it could equally be understood as a ribbon and as an animal, but a nonorganic animal. Hence the penchant for monsters in barbaric art, these strangely contorted animals; hence as well (I can't think of another way to put it) this uniquely barbarian Mannerism, since all I'm trying to say is that this is an attempt to sing the glory of Gothic Mannerism in painting, these coiling beards that could just as well be abstract ribbons.[60] Or else the folds of cloth in Gothic art, which play this quite astonishing role of abstraction of the line without contour, only to pulse eventually with vitality, exploding onto the scene, causing us to wonder: What it this? Again, is it a ribbon? Is it a spiral? Is it a beard? Or else these weird, overly convoluted animals? This aspect had already shown up in this kind of barbarian art. My last question is just this: How are we to characterize this Expressionism?

Getting back to my consideration of the eye and the hand, this should help move us along more quickly, but we'll be done very soon. I'd say: yes, that's exactly what the manual line is, the hand freed from the eye. Insofar as the hand remains subject to the eye, it forms contours. The lines are still organic or geometric depending on whether it's the mind's eye or the seeing eye. When the eyes fail, when they are beset with chaos, the hand's power is unleashed. That's when the hand is animated by a foreign will that imposes itself on the eye instead of serving it.[61] The eye is struck with this line it can no longer control; the eye can no longer grasp the rule or law whereby it constantly changes direction. The eye doesn't get a moment's rest—the tragedy of the eye. The eyes might as well shut down immediately. The eye will be terrorized by the hand and the hand's product, the manual line. Given the manual character of the Expressionist line, is it any wonder that it doesn't require an easel? Is it any wonder that Pollock laid his canvas out on the floor, that he needed tactile contact with the floor, and that it's not just an affectation? Is it any wonder that, by all accounts and on video—since he was one of the first painters to be filmed while working—his work is a frenetic dance?[62]

The first American critic to have labeled Pollock and his school "Action Painting" was a really talented guy, Harold Rosenberg.[63] According to him—and you can immediately see the stereotypes this can lead to—the act of painting itself in a way becomes the true object of painting. The expression *Action Painting* has the advantage of highlighting the manual nature of this form of painting. It no longer uses easels or brushes but involves bulb basters and putting the canvas on the floor, sticks, scrub-brushes, sponges, whatever you like. The painter whirls into a kind of tactile frenzy, a manual frenzy above all. The eyes can't keep up, which is why the films of Pollock painting are significant, since, in fact, the eyes really can't follow what he's doing. Once the paint is thrown—Pollock's famous stream of paint—the eyes are no longer in charge, it's the hand. The hand has found its expression: lines that the eyes can no longer follow. The painting should become a transgression against the eyes. In what sense? It should liberate modern humanity. You see in what sense we're trying to draw a metaphysics from all this. Modern humanity will fundamentally be a manual one, but we don't even know yet what the hand can do once it is freed from the eye. There's a sort of, dare I say, revolutionary message here. I'll just ask you to hold that thought because abstract painters will take a completely opposite stance [*FBLS*, 85–86 UM; 104–6 C].

What bothers me, and this is where we'll pick up next time, is that American critics, who are very good, not just Fried, whom I talked about earlier, but Greenberg, also a wonderful critic who was closely associated with Pollock and was even crucial as a critic in kick-starting Pollock's career, he put out a book—unfortunately yet to be translated, but fascinating—on art and culture where he talks a lot about this period of American painting.[64] And Greenberg emphatically defines the Abstract Expressionism of Pollock, of Morris Louis, as the inauguration of a purely optical world. So here, I find this point annoying given how important Greenberg is. He produces all the commentary: how Abstract Expressionism for him is modern precisely because it manifests a world that is now purely optical. In other words, Pollock would be like the founder of a breakaway movement leading to so-called optical arts. Greenberg is unambiguous as to what he means by a purely optical world, that it's cut off from any tactile reference. Fried takes up the same idea in that excellent article on three American painters, that Pollock and painters that he inspired establish and bring about a purely optical world in painting.[65] Why does this annoy me personally, since my view is the exact opposite? My sense is that it's absolutely not an optical world but, rather, that it's a manual world. The only thing I would agree with is that it's an innovative undertaking. But I'd describe its innovation in exactly the opposite way, namely, that it's a purely manual world, it's a manual line. This is the first time that a manual line is absolutely free of any subordination to visual givens [*FBLS*, 87–88 UM; 106–7 C]. Something isn't right. That's where we'll begin next time. I believe that this is simply a misunderstanding, but obviously, I'm right.

SESSION 4

DIAGRAM, CODE, ANALOGY

5 May 1981

We've tried to categorize paintings based on the position of what we have been calling a diagram. We were looking to flesh out our understanding of this notion. We said that a diagram could assume several positions and that, after all, some pictorial categories could be defined as so many positions of the diagram and that the necessity of thinking through these pictorial categories was not at all motivated by a concern over figuration, but rather based on the positions of the diagram. We delineated three diagrammatic positions, each as distinct tendencies. On the one hand, the diagram can tend to take up the entire painting, spreading over the whole painting. Broadly speaking, this seemed to be the so-called Expressionist tendency. Or else, in the second diagrammatic position, while the diagram is indeed there, it's kept to a minimum. It tends to be replaced or overlaid, dominated by a genuine code. This gets complicated, but we're playing loosely with our wording because we haven't said anything yet about what a diagram is, or what a code is. We're just trying to lay out our categories. In this second tendency, keeping the diagram to a minimum—the diagram is and continues to be the real germinal element of the painting—and the substitution or application of a code: that might be the tendency of what is called "abstraction" in painting.

And then the third diagrammatic position: the diagram neither takes up the entire painting nor is it minimized. It's like a path that, in a rather exterior way, might be called temperate or restrained. While it is present, acting like a diagram, it doesn't take up the whole painting for the simple reason that the diagram then realizes its full effect, namely, to cause something to emerge from the diagram. And this something that emerges from the diagram isn't a resemblance or figuration, no more so than with the two other cases. It isn't something figurative. Rather, it's what we can call a nonfigurative *Figure*, that is, one that doesn't resemble anything. A Figure emerges from the diagram. What I examined last time—and we were nearly there, I almost finished—was the first tendency or the Expressionist position. At best, it's as if the diagram were developed amid a kind of overwhelming process of blurring or scrambling [*brouillage*]. Why am I referring to this sudden interest in the concept of scrambling? Because our three diagrammatic positions somehow seem to include it: recall the first position—the diagram that stretches out until it becomes a kind of genuine scrambling; then, the second position where the diagram is overlaid or determined by a code; and finally, the third position where the diagram begins to function as a diagram. But if we're going to attain a logic of the diagram, we still have a lot of work left to do.

So, in order to wrap up the first position: Do you remember what this diagram is that eats up the whole painting? As I was saying, take your pick: either line-strokes [*le trait-ligne*] or color-patches [*la tache-couleur*]—the two main pictorial elements that don't trace contours, either lines without contour or patches without contour. I was saying that Expressionism necessarily achieves a level of abstraction far beyond that of so-called abstract painting. Because obviously, all painting is abstract, but where things get interesting is when we look for definitions of abstraction corresponding to each tendency. It's obvious that, for an Expressionist (again, I'm not about to say that one is better than the other; I'm just trying to figure out our categories), so-called abstract painting doesn't suffer from being too abstract, but from not being abstract enough. How so? Because however abstract the abstract painters might be, their lines still trace a contour. You can easily make out circles, half-circles, triangles, and so forth. And in the most abstract works of Kandinsky, you can still make out triangles, that is, a particular contour. Maybe not always, in Kandinsky's case. But perhaps he's not just an abstract painter. In any of Mondrian's works, you'll find his famous squares, and so on. These are all lines creating contours.

So, in a way, Expressionists might say, "We are the true abstract painters." Why? And in fact, this is a problem—a problem in painting as a whole—that I believe they were the first to pose in a conscious and deliberate way. In making such a claim, I'm protecting myself against the obvious objection of this practice already having existed in painting. Painting has actually always used and drawn lines without contour. What is a Pollock-line? All we can say about it is that it's a line that constantly changes direction and doesn't follow a contour. Or Morris Louis's stain painting without contours.[1] These are all painters specifically known as "Abstract Expressionists." These stains or lines are lines without contours, that is, they delineate neither an interior nor an exterior. The lines are neither concave nor convex. They don't go from one point to the other, even virtually; rather, the lines move between color-points thrown down by Pollock. It's a snaking, breaking, convulsing line that constantly changes direction at every turn. As I was saying, it's an odd sort of line because, ultimately, it's a line that's more than one-dimensional. In other words, it's a line that's almost commensurate to a plane. Consequently, this leads the plane itself to stretch and become commensurate with volume. In other words, it's a line whose dimension could be mathematically expressed only as a fraction, between one and two, whereas ordinary lines, which outline contours, are one-dimensional. Flat figures are two-dimensional. Volume is three-dimensional. It's clear that Abstract Expressionism resolves the problem of depth in a totally new way. If you end up with fractional measurements, you end up with characteristically intermediate measurements between one and two, that is, between line and surface, and consequently between surface and volume. At the extreme, the line takes up the entire painting, hence Abstract Expressionism being famously known as "all-over" painting, that is, from one edge of the canvas to the other. There is a sort of probabilistic approach to painting that refuses any privileged particular positions. Every part of the painting is equally weighted, whereas with classical approaches to painting, there was always the center, the edges, and so on.

That's the point I had reached. As I was saying, when it comes to the problem that's troubling us and which we're still discussing, since there are all kinds of things at stake in the concept of the diagram, [we're] trying to figure out the relationships between the eye and the hand in painting. I said, we have to assess these relationships in keeping with our diagrammatic positions. At the very least, let's discover what's worthwhile in these positions since, as I said, critical texts on the eye and the hand don't seem to have fully accounted for the tension existing, at any rate, between the eye and the hand in painting, whether painting is understood as a certain resolution of this tension and requires the tension between the eye and the hand. And you'll recall that I really emphasized the fact that the diagram in painting is fundamentally *manual.* It's an arrangement of manual strokes [*traits*] and patches.[2] Obviously it produces something visual, but that's not the point.

When the diagram starts to take over, when it seizes and takes charge of the entirety of the painting, the prevailing order is clearly a manual one. I think this is obvious for Abstract Expressionism. This more-than-one-dimensional line—one that doesn't outline a contour, with neither inside nor outside, which is neither concave nor convex—this line is a manual line. It's a line that the eye literally has trouble following. It's a line that the hand can trace only to the extent that it shakes off its subordination to the eye. It's a line expressing the hand's rebellion against the eye. How does this kind of conversion from eye to hand figure into Abstract Expressionism? The triumph of manual lines and manual patches. While this is far from always being the case, I was saying that it's reflected in the way that Abstract Expressionists have abandoned the easel. There are many ways to abandon the easel. After all, the canvas is never reducible to its place on the easel.

You see why I keep emphasizing positions or placement. Even when a painter paints with an easel exclusively, it's obvious that the canvas is a lot better when it's off the easel. Concretely, for so-called Abstract Expressionism—for Pollock, for Morris Louis, for Noland, for all these painters—what is it that's technically essential? There's a necessity driving them—especially Pollock—to abandon the easel in order to paint on the ground with an unstretched canvas. I think that's really important to note. When an American critic baptized this whole movement as "Action Painting," he was referring to what was considered a kind of frenetic action, where painters fling paint, using sticks, bulb basters, while walking around with the canvas at their feet.[3] What's the significance of having the canvas unstretched on the ground instead of having the canvas on an easel? It amounts to a fundamental conversion: converting the horizon into the ground. It means passing from an optical horizon to the ground under one's feet. In this case, hands and feet are the same. The manual line actually is expressed by this kind of conversion of the horizon into the ground. The horizon is fundamentally optical. The ground is fundamentally tactile [*FBLS*, 87–88 UM; 106–8 C].

This is where we left off last time. I was saying that one annoying thing is that [while] American critics are excellent, especially those writing on Pollock and his followers—notably two I cited, Greenberg and Fried—they've written really very beautiful pieces on this movement, on so-called Abstract Expressionism. But when they define it, they say, it's wonderful, and it's modern because it involves developing a pure optical space. To be very candid, this sort of description bothers me because I have exactly the opposite impression of their art. I agree that Pollock is great; he's really something special because, for the first time, a purely manual line is freed from any visual subordination. For the first time, the hand is completely liberated from any visual directive. But the way these critics describe Abstract Expressionist work is to say the exact opposite, so this just doesn't work. We therefore find ourselves with one last problem.

GEORGES COMTESSE:[4] Perhaps, if you can't see that there's no contradiction between the manual line and pure optical space, it might be because of your concept of the pictorial diagram. Since you define the pictorial diagram as a hand detached from the eye, one the eye can't keep up with, a rebellious hand. But in painting's process of experimentation, the hand's diagrammatic detachment from the eye might contain something else that precisely you aren't expressing: it's specifically an optical machine of detachment that has nothing to do with the eye, the optical machine of the gaze. The painter's gaze is perhaps neither the eye of perception, the sensitive eye, nor is it any possible eye whatsoever. The painter's hand is certainly still framed by this machine that's irreducible to the eye, and which would certainly shift to some extent your concept of the pictorial diagram. I don't mean that the painter turns into this gaze machine while painting. But there's like a sort of constant shifting when it comes to this gaze machine, which itself is primarily geared toward the task at hand.

DELEUZE: All right! We have our first possible response to this problem.

ANNE QUERRIEN: Everything that you are saying is perfectly correct from the painter's point of view, about Action Painting, about the action of painting. There is a kind of pure optical space that occurs from the point of view of the passive affect of looking at painting that you don't mention at all. You talk about the act of painting. And throughout the entire Kantian period, the Romantic period, the Impressionist period, and so on, and from everything we're taught in school, we're directed to look at painting by putting ourselves in the painter's shoes. Thus, we had to have a tactile relation in how we view painting, to see how the layers were put down, and so forth. Furthermore, we were taught to paint in order to appreciate aesthetically the paintings created by others, following Kant's model of universal humanity. But here, there is a gap separating the positions exactly as in mathematical spaces, where the painter and the viewer are no longer in the same position—and what's more, regarding canvases painted on the ground with the painter turning around them, they aren't displayed on the ground. They're displayed in an optical space. They're viewed vertically.

[*Interruption of the recording,* time stamp: 20:28.]

DELEUZE: Excellent! That's perfect. So now we have a second response. That's good because I have a third response. But they don't cancel each other out, on the contrary. There are even fewer problems. What I'm wondering is: Why do Greenberg, Fried, and so on, call space in Pollock, in Morris Louis, and so on, a purely optical space? We have to follow their texts carefully. Here's the reason why this space is opposed to so-called classical pictorial space. This space is classically defined as a tactile-optical space, meaning that it's an [optical] space with tactile referents on the canvas.[5] What are these tactile referents? One example of a tactile referent: the contour. Do things have a visual contour just as they have a tactile contour? Yes and no. There is indeed a tactile referent whenever the contour remains self-identical, no matter the degree of luminosity. You have so many remarkable paintings that develop a tactile space. You will recognize the presence of a tactile referent when, for example, a contour still remains intact, as we say—the reference is indeed tactile—under a bright light or in shadow. I think it's obvious that perspective does involve tactile referents. It's clear what we mean by visual space with tactile referents, and such a space would be called tactile-optical.

It's clear that the line without contour in this sense breaks with any tactile reference. There is no more form; there is no more tactile form. The tactile–optical form is thus decomposed into a line without contour. So, I think that when American critics define Abstract Expressionist space as an optical space, they mean that it's a space which has cast aside all of its tactile referents. Let's take this literally. Does that settle the matter? Is this what a purely optical space is then? You can see why I'm emphasizing this despite the two analyses just given. I almost feel like it's the other way around. There is indeed a pictorial direction or vector that achieves a purely optical space, but this isn't Expressionism at all. It's abstract painting. In abstract painting, you get something that could actually be called a pure optical space, but this wouldn't work at all in Expressionism. Why not? It's true that with Expressionism, all tactile referents are eliminated, not because space has become optical, but because the hand has succeeded in becoming independent from the eye. Now it's the hand that imposes itself on the eye like a foreign power that, once again, the eye struggles to follow. Consequently, the tactile referents that expressed the hand's dependence on the eye are effectively suppressed. That's because it's a pure manual space where tactile referents, which expressed the hand's subordination to the eye, are clearly driven out and cast outside the canvas. That's fine. I am fine with this logic as long as there aren't any contradictions.

ANNE QUERRIEN: Is it possible there are both at the same time?

DELEUZE: Yes, of course.

ANNE QUERRIEN: A pure optical and pure manual . . .

DELEUZE: Yes, you're saying that the painting becomes purely optical, but that raises a different question. It becomes purely optical from the viewer's perspective. Sure. At any rate, that's an issue I can't get into yet, because we'd have to figure out what sort of optics come from the hand. Namely, what optics are produced by a purely manual gesture.

ANNE QUERRIEN: It's the idea that there's no longer any communication anywhere. There are no longer any directives implying that one should be situated in the painter's position to look at painting. This change seems really important! There's a liberation of the viewer's eye from the position of painting whereas in all the education we've received at school, we're always told that you can appreciate painting only if you yourself are some kind of amateur painter [*peintre du dimanche*].

DELEUZE: For the viewers themselves, I'm not sure much is changed in regard to this optical conquest, since the violence done to the eye remains. So there is some kind of a need for a learning process through which the eye comes to accept this violence committed against it.

ANNE QUERRIEN: I don't think it's necessarily a violence. I find that we are emerging from a kind of Hegelian dialectic in which there is only the active that is positive or negative, and we have an active affect of painting, which is to paint, and a passive affect, which is that of viewing . . . [*Inaudible comments at the end.*]

ANOTHER STUDENT: I think we have to approach it in terms of contemporary physics because there's a transformation in optics that perhaps results in it becoming manual. I don't know.

DELEUZE: For those who can't hear, she's suggesting we'd have to include a type of contemporary physics. And, in fact, some so-called informal Expressionist painters already find such an alignment compelling, that is, with a contemporary physics—for example, the whole physics of signals—that takes into account, oddly enough, some novel relationships between the optical and the manual. That seems fine.

GEORGES COMTESSE: We shouldn't forget that, in Pollock's first major periods, the main problem in his relations with Robert Motherwell wasn't just the paintings-to-be-created, nor was it new painting techniques. What was important was the pictorial line, pictorial creation, and they directly posed the question in their relations with the unconscious. It's a crucial problem for Pollock and in Motherwell's writings on Pollock. There's the whole issue with

Pollock over his botched Jungian analyses and how painting would be a certain way of revealing the unconscious. So this raises the problem of the relationship between the pictorial diagram and the unconscious, since the artists themselves, in their own artistic processes, repeatedly raised the problem of this relationship precisely by use of their lines.

DELEUZE: Yes, Comtesse, that's an apt description of the diagram, but it isn't unique to Expressionism because some will say, the diagram, or its equivalent, is an instance of randomness. Others will say, it's an instance of the involuntary. Still others will say, it's an instance of the unconscious. Ultimately, all perspectives can agree that indeed, the diagram—the kind we first loosely defined as a germinal chaos—is sort of the unconscious of the painter. Yes, I agree with this. You see, this has so many ramifications, it's perfect.

I'm moving on to the second diagrammatic position. This time, it isn't the extended diagram, what Klee calls the grey point, that takes up the whole painting. On the contrary, the diagram is totally constricted, as if the painter wanted somehow to suppress everything obscure about the diagram, everything, let's say, that's unconscious, involuntary, and so forth. What about this tendency to reduce the diagram? This will certainly get us tangled up and off track. For viewers like us, you get a strange feeling, the feeling that once again we've reached painting's liminal edge—but all painting is at the very limit itself of painting—because we're dealing with a sort of code we don't know how to decipher. And how do we recognize this form of painting tending to verge on code? Once again, my immediate thought, once and for all: these painters are painters. They wouldn't be painters if they applied a code or painted based on a code. That's not what I mean. But the liminal edge may perhaps be quite thin.

When a painting tends toward applying a code, what do you say? Any computer can turn out paintings using code; that's easy. Anyway, that sort of nonsense is not what I have in mind with abstract painters. This movement toward Abstract Expressionism unfolds as if we're being shown what was to serve as an *internal* code for painting, a uniquely pictorial code. To quote a nineteenth-century painter who, incidentally, isn't an abstract painter, strictly speaking, but I don't think he's far off, I'll read the quote: "Synthesis [. . .] consists of making all perceived shapes conform to the small number of shapes that we are capable of imagining: straight lines, a few angles, arcs of circles and of ellipse."[6] Isn't that a sort of geometric code? But geometry has a code. Once again, it's not about applying geometric figures.

Kandinsky clearly distinguishes between so-called abstract figures and geometric figures. What Kandinsky calls an abstract figure is a figure representing nothing other than itself. In that case, abstract pictorial figures and geometric figures appear to be the same thing. The triangles that Kandinsky paints and triangles delineated geometrically both seem to qualify as figures that only represent themselves, as opposed to concrete figures. Only here, he adds: this is a figure that has internalized its own tension.[7] Tension is the movement that characterizes [the figure]. It has internalized its own tension, something that geometric figures do not do. As we go step by step, you see why an abstract painter can say: It's abstract even though the line forms a contour, even though it has a contour. The problem is very different from that of Expressionism: There is a contour, and yet the contour no longer determines a concrete figure or an object; the contour only determines a tension. For Kandinsky, that's the pictorial definition of abstraction. The idea of tension will be crucial throughout everything Kandinsky says about painting. What do we make of this tension? Once again, in Kandinsky's writings, you constantly run into passages that allude to the invention of a code. These are celebrated writings by Kandinsky (based on a lengthy inquiry and extensive commentary; I'm limiting myself to his results, so this may necessarily seem a little arbitrary) in which he informs us, for example: "Vertical, white, active. Horizontal, black, passive or inert. Acute angle, yellow, building tension. Obtuse angle, blue, weakness."[8] There are long lists in Kandinsky's work. You get the sense that it's not just a table of categories. These are the elements the other guy mentioned:[9] "Synthesis [. . .] consists of making all perceived shapes conform to the small number of shapes" that are well determined. What is this small number of shapes? I'm trying to clarify this idea of a pictorial code.

It must be said that there isn't just *one* code. Nearly every abstract painter invents a code. Just as in language, where there are all sorts of possible spoken versions, there are all sorts of codes in a virtual pictorial code, meaning that perhaps every abstract painter is the inventor of a code. What would a code immanent to painting be and that doesn't exist in advance, waiting to be invented by one painter or another? I'll use Kandinsky's terms. Notice that he always has three criteria: vertical lines, horizontal lines, obtuse angles, acute angles, right angles, and so on. And then he'll use that to form squares, rectangles, circles, half-circles. So, there is line or form: the first category. The second category: an active, passive dynamic. We could add to that. We could imagine a code with more than two values [*FBLS*, 84–85 UM; 102–4 C]. There wouldn't just be active and passive dynamics at work. There could be active, passive, and a baseline. I know of some painters who describe three fundamental rhythms: an active rhythm that tends to grow; a passive rhythm that tends to diminish; and a baseline, constant rhythm. And these rhythms are at work on the canvas: you have elements functioning at a constant baseline, you have elements that function in a descending manner, you have elements that rise or ascend. So, there is the first category referring to lines or figures, a second category referring to the dynamics—referring to activity/passivity—and you have a third category of which Kandinsky never loses sight, referring to a kind of affective disposition, what we could call a kind of a category of affect. And then there is also a category referring to color. So the categories could be understood like this, as a kind of code, for example: vertical, white, activity, joy.

Just what is a code? It seems like one of the criteria for a code is, on the one hand, whether you can identify a finite number of discrete meaningful units. I'm putting it in abstract terms for now. The second condition is that these meaningful units ought to bear out a certain number of binary relations. Actually, it isn't just for the sake of convenience, I believe, that codes are binary. There's something crucial about binarity and codes that binds them together. I'll take a familiar example, that of language. How might there be a code in language [*langage*]? What might justify saying that language involves a code? Linguists have been making this claim for a long time. First of all, language breaks down into so-called meaningful units known, for instance, as "morphemes." But these meaningful units can be broken down into smaller elements. These morphemes are broken down into smaller elements called "phonemes." Phonemes do not exist outside binary relationships. You know, there are well-known ubiquitous examples in phonology. Let's say the meaningful unit is "vent." You mishear it. So I clarify: I said *vent*, not "dent." A relation between V/D. It's a binary relationship, a phonemic relationship. It's not "bent"—a relation between V/B. It's not "meant"—V/M, and so on.[10] These binary relationships are what are called "distinctive features" [*traits distinctifs*] in linguistics. As a result, phonemes strictly depend on the set of their binary relationships to other phonemes. There's indeed a linguistic code because there are meaningful units that have the possibility of being broken down into elements caught up in binary relationships.

What have I just described? This might help us move forward later on, so I'd like us to keep this in mind as we move along. It's a detour I can't avoid. In a way, what I've just described is the concept of articulation. As Martinet tells us, there's even a double articulation.[11] Language is articulated. That doesn't just mean that there are glottal movements that articulate language. It's not solely a question of articulatory physical movements. Language is actualized via articulatory physical movements because it is in itself articulated. What does it mean to be articulated? It means being composed of discrete units that themselves refer to elements tied up in binary relationships. That seems to me like the best way to define code.

But how does that move me forward? What does that do for me? I'll be able to elaborate a bit more on this topic later on, but for now, I'll just give you my conclusion. That is, we tend to associate the two concepts of code and articulation. Are they entirely interchangeable or not? That's beyond me; that's not what interests me. In any case, I can suggest that there is some overlap between the two concepts, code and articulation. There is no unarticulated code. The idea of code has two basic components: a finite number of discrete units, and these discrete units are selected according to a series of binary choices. Why bring up the idea of choice? In order to account for the relationship between meaningful units and elements caught up in binary relations. To take a common example from computer science: how do you select six out of the eight first numbers?[12] You select six based on three successive binary choices. You take your set: 1, 2, 3, 4, 5, 6, 7, 8. The first binary choice: you divide your set in half. You select the right half, greater than 4. You take that set, or subset—5, 6, 7, 8—and divide it in half. You select the part that includes 6. That gives you a subset with two terms. The third binary choice: you select 6. So, it's always possible to reduce a code-based decision to a sequence of binary choices. I don't need any more, I won't go any farther. Code = articulation. Articulation = units determined by a series of binary choices. So, what do I think is crucial about that?

Now, let me bring this discussion back to painting. In what manner would abstract painting be something like the elaboration of a code to which the diagram itself is subjected? In the case of abstract painting, it actually works like this: you have a certain number of discrete units. That doesn't mean that it's easy to paint or anything. But this is a kind of painting by code. It's the invention of a properly pictorial code that exists only in painting, and that exists only insofar as it is invented. If this is the case, then painting would mean inventing a uniquely optical code. The idea of an optical code seems to reside at the most basic level, at the very core of abstract painting. That would be the modern sense of painting as understood by abstract painters. You're presented with an internal, optical code. In light of my brief mention of Kandinsky's writings, how does that show up there? Meaningful units are definitely there. White, active, vertical, for example, are all meaningful units. These meaningful units cannot be broken down into smaller units, but they can easily be broken down into elements subject to binary choices. What sort of binary choices? They're choices about figure, about color, about affective disposition. Active/passive: here, you have a binary choice. You might tell me, that doesn't work for color. Yes, it does; with color, there is a series of binary choices, exactly like my computing example. And the entire color wheel itself is a kind of binarization of color relationships. The complementary relationships between colors, and so on, intermediate colors, and so on, everything about the chromatic circle and its opposing relationships gives you a system of binary choices between colors.

That's why I can say that literally, for Kandinsky, there are two clear levels of pictorial articulation: on the one hand, meaningful units bundling a whole series of binary choices; [on the other hand], what do we call these binary choices that allow us to establish meaningful units? They're called "digits." *Binary digits.* What a great word for us. What is the "digit," or finger? What role does the finger play here? It's the finger pressing a keyboard. The finger as a runaway simplification of the hand. The finger is what remains once humanity loses its hands. A finger pressing keys, it's a handless humanity. The digit is the manual state of handless humanity. I'm thinking about a passage from Leroi-Gourhan where he talks about future humans; he says it's a form of humanity that lies prone. It doesn't need to move. It's kind of a science fiction portrait.[13] Humanity is more and more infantilized, and then it loses its hands. Humans still have one finger left to type with. You see, in our future evolution, we won't have hands anymore [*FBLS*, 84–85 UM; 103–4 C]. [*Laughter.*]

This already leads me to make a slight modification in what I'm saying. With the problems surrounding the eye–hand relationship that I brought up before, things get complicated because the hand alone can take so many forms. I could develop a list of categories of the hand, make a start at it, give it a try. It's pure conjecture at this point, but we'll see whether this is confirmed later on. For starters, I'd like to make a distinction between the manual, the tactile, and the digital. Please allow me to offer a few definitions that suit me, just some standard definitions. That way, there won't be any objections. "Tactile" is what I'd call the hand subordinated to the eye. When the hand follows the eye's commands, then the hand becomes tactile. When the hand shakes off its subordination to the eye, when it imposes itself on the eye, when it does violence to the eye, when it strikes back against the eye, that's what I'd call properly "manual." And, in contrast, the "digital" is the hand's absolute subordination to the eye. It's not even that the hand's tactile qualities are enlisted in the eye's service. Rather, the hand has dissolved; only a finger remains for picking between visual binaries. The hand is reduced to a finger pressing on a keyboard. It's the computerized hand. It's the handless finger. In a way, isn't that the ideal—in a very qualified sort of way—of abstract painting: a pure optical space such that the hand is undetectable?[14] The hand is undetectable; it's an expression you run into everywhere in painting. Painters say to each other: What a beautiful painting! You can't detect the hand. Not being able to detect the hand may well be a flaw. Is it possible for the hand to be undetectable? Isn't abstract painting the painting of a handless humanity [*FBLS*, 84–85 UM; 103–4 C]?

Clearly not; that's not right. What makes us certain that it isn't? When it comes to distinguishing a fake Mondrian from a real

Mondrian, what do they do? There's a famous passage from a critic on this. What do you look for in order to tell if it's fake or not? Critics say: it's not very hard, it just takes a little practice. You get up close to the square: you're told that this is a Mondrian. You look at where the square's two sides overlap, and you see what's going on with the painting's layers, with their overlap. There's a good chance you'll notice whether or not it's a forgery, especially if the square is colored, when the layers of color overlap.[15] In other words, you can detect the hand. But with Mondrian's work, it's worse—or even better, depending how you look at it—than with Kandinsky's work. Because in some of his theoretical writings, Mondrian really has a sort of fantasy of boiling everything down to two binary units. This is a kind of code that exaggerates the horizontal and vertical.[16] On multiple occasions, with the utmost austerity, in all his spiritual asceticism, Mondrian professes: to reach the point where everything is depicted via horizontal or vertical lines. Nothing else is required. From the perspective of code, that is code's ideal. As I was saying, normally, a code is a finite number of meaningful units, that is, more than two, that are determined following a series of binary choices. The supreme ideal for code is for it to have only two meaningful units and therefore only one binary choice. Then you'd have a code of code. The code of code is when instead of a set number of meaningful units determinable by a series of binary choices, you have only one binary choice between two meaningful units. And that's never what Kandinsky tried to do. But Mondrian goes a long way with horizontal/vertical as all that's needed. With a horizontal line and a vertical line, I can give you the world in its abstraction. It's all there.

Just to give you a sense—but you see it already—that, ultimately, while aesthetic categories are well-founded, everything gets mixed together. Among the finest writings on Mondrian are those by Michel Butor. Butor wonderfully demonstrated that Mondrian's squares do not have the same thickness in length or breadth.[17] That's obvious, actually. He didn't need much to demonstrate that. However, this difference in thickness has a very peculiar optical effect: it's why the intersection between the thinnest length and the thickest breadth, for example, becomes increasingly crucial, and this intersection will determine a virtual line. Just as one talks of a virtual line in music, here we can speak of a virtual line in painting.

The fact that both sides of the square don't have the same thickness makes the viewer's eye follow a diagonal line that Mondrian doesn't need to draw himself.[18] What can I say about this virtual diagonal? If pressed, I might call it an abstract version of a line without contour, since it isn't traced by the painter. Likewise, what makes Kandinsky so complicated is that he has some wonderful paintings where you get these meaningful units, but they are strangely traversed by lines that, in Kandinsky, have a truly Gothic source, by nomadic lines, without contour, by lines that pass between figures, that pass between points, that have neither beginning nor end, and that are characteristically "expressionist" lines, and that nevertheless do not manage to disrupt the painting's harmony or rhythm. This is to tell you, I think, that it's not because things overlap that the categories aren't well established.

When it comes to abstract painting, the one who went the furthest, I think, is the painter I told you about, Auguste Herbin, who I think is a truly great abstract painter. He goes a long way. He just invents his code. One just doesn't borrow a code from someone else. He calls his painting a "plastic alphabet."[19] It takes four basic forms, four meaningful units that, for him, are: the triangle, the sphere, the hemisphere, the quadrangle. He has four forms for units that he puts through binary relationships, a bit like Kandinsky, this time with regard to color, with regard to affective disposition, and then he adds—is this just affectation or is something more profound happening here?—letters of the alphabet. As a result, he'll compose or attribute a painting's title according to the letters determined by his pictorial units. For example, he titles a painting "Nu," and you have to break down "Nu" into *N—U,* then see what plastic form corresponds to *N,* what plastic form corresponds to *U,* what color, and so forth, a bit like how Bach played with the word "Bach" in music. So, he takes the idea of a "plastic alphabet" pretty far, which results in masterpieces. He's a great colorist. Is that idea just tacked on? No. I have a hard time imagining how one could view abstract painting without viewing it as the invention of an optical code, rather than as applying a preexisting code, this optical code being based on double articulation: first, pictorially meaningful units; second, the elementary binary choices that determine these units. So, we get a definition of a sort of pure coded optical space where the hand ultimately tends—but it's only a tension[20]—where the hand is cast out for the finger's benefit. A digital space.

As I was saying, there's a third path. My two diagrammatic positions are opposed to each other, point-for-point . . .

[*Interruption of the recording,* time stamp: 1:07:13.]

. . . scrambling and code, hence the response in fact of these painters who appear to take the third path, that is, this kind of moderate, middle-of-the-road path, but once again, only ostensibly moderate and middle-of-the-road, only nominally so. Just who are these painters? I'm borrowing terminology from Lyotard that I think is very fitting when he contrasts the "figurative" with what he calls the "figural."[21] It's not figurative painting because, in fact, there is no figurative painting. It's a "figural" painting. I'm endowing diagram with its the full sense—that is, I don't at all intend for it to be a code—and at the same time, I'm preventing it from overwhelming the painting, from scrambling the painting. I'm using the diagram in order to produce the pure "figural" or the Figure.

You understand, the hand/eye relationships that I'm going obtain are completely new. The hand will no longer be opposed to the eye or impose itself on the eye as with Expressionism, broadly speaking. The eye will no longer reduce the hand to the extent that only a finger remains. What will this be? It's a hand/eye tension such that the manual diagram gives the eye a new function, such that the hand forces a third eye to emerge. This tells you that this path isn't at all moderate. It's only moderate compared with the other two, meaning that it doesn't stretch the diagram over the entire painting, nor, on the other hand, does it submit the diagram to a specifically pictorial code. But [it comes with all its] dangers, including the double risk of verging into the abstract or into Expressionism instead of forging its own path. But that would be a third path, the purely diagrammatic position.

Today we have a lengthy inquiry ahead of us, a long detour. I'd like to get to the point where we can propose a definition of painting. Everyone has the right to do so. There are so many possible definitions, so everyone can give their own. That's a game one might play . . . At the very point we've reached, we have to forget painting a bit. I told you that my goal was twofold: to talk about painting, but [also] to sketch out a kind of theory of the diagram. Now it's time to attempt to work out an answer: Well, what is a diagram? What is the difference between a diagram and a code? From this inquiry, I'd like to derive a sort of definition of painting. If it's true that painting is the diagram, what are the relations between a diagram and a code? These are certainly some very complicated relations, since, once again, painting absolutely includes the endeavor of inventing optical codes that I believe define abstract painting.

So, we're back to square one, and that's perfectly fine. We're now back in a purely logical element that will then get us back into painting.[22] After all, there is another pair than the code/diagram pair; we have to use everything. A code is digital in the sense I worked out before: what we call "digital" is the binary choice determining the unit. A code is digital; you'll grant me that much. Typically, in every theory of information and even linguistics, what is the opposite of digital? Analog. Analog and digital. Synthesizers today, for example, are either analog synthesizers or digital synthesizers. The processes of retransmitting signals are either analog processes or digital processes. Technologically, it isn't anything complicated. It's a distinction that concerns us today, regarding my two pairs: code/diagram, digital/analog. What does this have to do with painting? Why do I sound like I'm talking about something else, and yet I'm not talking about something else?

Is painting a language [*langage*], or is it not a language? Is this matter at all of interest? For me, yes, it is. What I'd also ask is: What is an analogical language? Not so easy to define an analogical language. Is there an analogical language? Is painting an analogical language? Is painting *the* analogical language par excellence? Or else, cinema? Is cinema an analogical language? We ought to consider the ideal setting: Does this apply to cinema in the silent era? Or when film had sound but no talking, was that an analogical language? After all, everyone in silent film thought they had invented what they themselves constantly referred to as a universal language. And silent film is a universal language, hence their frustration—at that moment—when talkies came onto the scene. All of cinema's pretensions as a universal language were called into question. Are there connections between painting and silent film? Maybe so, but never where you think. We all know that film is at its worst when a director thinks he or she can make a scene or a shot as beautiful as a painting. It's a disaster. Everyone cracks up, everyone falls asleep, or else it only works when it's funny, when it's Buñuel. With Italian cinema, for example, you get scenes that make you think, what a disaster! You think: this is a straight up Raphael. It doesn't get any cheesier in cinema than that. So, if film and painting have anything to do with each other, it's not in that regard.

Analogical language, what is it? We already know a bit about what makes a code digital and what the expression "digital code" means. Code is the basis for a digital language. As the Americans often say: language is digital.[23] It doesn't mean that it's done with fingers or that it's like a sign language for the hearing impaired. It means something very specific: language is constituted by meaningful units determinable through a sequence of binary choices. That's what it means to say that language is digital. Are there analogical languages? How should we understand "analog" in that case? Do the two ever mix? If there are analogical languages, how do we define them? Would painting be an example? Would painting be *the* analogical language par excellence? Why not pantomime? Why not all of the visual arts? How would painting stand out from the rest? On the other hand, will it suffice to draw a crude distinction between digital code and analog language? We really have no choice but to see our hypothesis through to the end: it's the diagram that would be analogical and code would be digital. But would this be a simple opposition, or would there be some code grafted onto analog diagrams?

Here we have a whole series of confusing problems surrounding the logic of the diagram. I'll try to be brief because I want to get back to painting. I'm starting with an initial approximation. Digital code would imply convention; the diagram or analogical language would be a language of similitude. My two concepts would be distinguished with reference to the following procedure: similitude for analogy or for the diagram; a conventional rule for digital code. See, that doesn't take us very far. The notion of the diagram and its extension, its eruption into logic and into philosophy, resulted from the general approximation laid out by an incredible author whom I've already discussed with you in past years, named C. S. Peirce, an English logician who invented a discipline that went on to enjoy great success, semiology.[24] His departure point—I'll stick to what's relevant for our concerns here and now—was a very simple distinction between what he called icons and symbols. He was saying that icons have to do with similitude, generally speaking. An icon is determined by its similarity to something.[25] A symbol, on the other hand, he said, is inseparable from a conventional rule. You might say we don't need to refer to Peirce because this doesn't add all that much. But this is Peirce's starting point, and he takes it even further. And he takes it further only in order to put this validity into question [*FBLS*, 94–95 UM; 115–16 C].

I'm starting from this simple problem: Can I define analogical language by similitude and coded or digital language by convention? You'll recall the many Saussurean points: language is conventional, the linguistic symbol is conventional . . . Immediately it's obvious that is not the case, but these reasons explaining why this first dualism is inadequate should interest us. Here you need to sense their order, since we're tentatively dipping into an area of logic. This similitude/convention duality isn't at all satisfactory because, on the one hand, there are phenomena of similitude in codes, and on the other hand, similitude isn't sufficient for defining analogy. Those are the two points that I'd like to examine.

The first point is that we can't simply oppose convention and similitude because a code necessarily includes—I'd almost say that it necessarily produces—phenomena of similitude. Here's what Peirce was doing; his thought is very complex, gorgeous, really, but I'll only paraphrase. Basically, Peirce says that there are two sorts of icons based on similitude: there's a similitude of like qualities—for example, you paint with blue because the sky is blue. That's a qualitative similitude. You look for the blue that's closest to the blue of the sky. And then, there's a similitude of relation, so there are particular icons that are icons of relation. What he calls "diagrams" in his analysis are icons of relations. This is of interest for us, but he maintains a definition of the diagram that depends on similitude. That's why, for our purposes, we won't be able to follow his lead. All of the Americans afterward who developed a theory of the diagram have hung on to Peirce's iconic principle, that is, the diagram as primarily defined by a similitude of relation. What for Peirce is the exemplary diagram or diagrammatic process? It's algebra. He says that algebra isn't actually a language because it is an icon, so it's within the domain of similitudes of relation. The algebraic diagram extracts similitudes of relation. He adds that, on the other hand, algebra as such is not separable from certain conventional symbols that belong to the other pole, which implies a code. This shows the extent to which Peirce is aware of mixtures of code/analogy or code/similitude. At the same time, I stated why we won't be able to follow Peirce too closely.

Coming back to my first question, that the diagram cannot be defined by similitude, it's for a first reason, namely: I cannot imagine a code that doesn't involve or produce phenomena of similitude inseparable from it. In fact, what can you do with a code? As I see it, there are three things done with code: you can tell stories; you can make illustrations; you can make subsystems. Keeping things simple, how do you make an illustration with a binary code? A distinctly digital exercise (not a pictorial code). Once again, a computer can give you a portrait. All you have to do is encode the model's data according to a purely binary code consisting of 0/+ or 1/0, the binary system. Your computer can be programmed to render the portrait. The code as such (the simplest binary code) can give you a huge range of illustrations. For example, computers at this moment. All you need is to encode the data. And what does encoding data imply? Binarization. If you binarize a figure, you can very easily render it by computer. In this case, there is a resemblance produced by way of a code and encoding.

Code more commonly—especially when it comes to language—results in stories rather than illustrations. In my first example (the computer generating a portrait once it was programmed to do so), you have a direct connection between the encoded program and the end result. What differentiates language from a computational function? It's that with language, you necessarily have a third term. As linguists say, you have the signifier, you have the state of affairs. In an illustration, you have a signifier that produces a state of affairs, the coded signifier. It doesn't work that way in language. What characterizes language is precisely a third entity, namely, the signified. The signified is not the same thing as the designated state of affairs. And what do we make of the well-known principle, linguistic symbols are conventional? It means that there is no relation of similarity between the signifying unit and the designated state of affairs, between the word *ox* and the ox state of affairs. Their relation is purely one of convention, that is, it's by convention that this morpheme designates the thing with horns, and so on.

On the other hand, the word, the signifying unit, has a signified. What is the signified? It's the way in which the state of affairs appears in correspondence with the word. Consider languages where there are two words for designating "dead ox" and "living ox." Each of these words correspond to a different signified. When it's said that language is a conventional system, that means that the relationship between a word and the external state of affairs it designates is arbitrary. If it's true that the relationship between words and what they designate is always arbitrary in language, by contrast, the relationship between the signifying word and the signified is not arbitrary. Why? Because, as people say, these are two sides of the same phonological or sonorous reality. In other words, there are necessarily relations of similitude between the signified and signifier. This is what linguists call "isomorphism." Consequently, linguists have been obliged to amend Saussure's principle (that linguistic symbols are conventional) by adding: yes, insofar as you hold them up to designated states of affairs and insofar as you determine them in relation to these states of affairs. However, there is a perfect isomorphism—that is, a similitude of relation—between the signified and the signifier. The signified and signifier necessarily have similarly formed relations. Isomorphism is the principle stressed by all linguists. So, I'll stop there because that's all deadly boring. What I'm after is something very straightforward: a digital code implies similitude in two ways. It implies illustrative similitudes and narrative similitudes, that is, similitudes of quality and similitudes of relation.

Counterexample: Can analogy be defined by similitude? Of course not. Why? For one very simple reason: for starters, that wouldn't sufficiently distinguish it from code. Once again, if code necessarily implies and encompasses phenomena of similitude, there's no question about opposing them directly while also tying similitude back to analogy. But I also need a reason inherent to analogy. Just as I was asking earlier what one can do with code, now I ask: What can one do with analogical language, as obscure [as this notion may be] for the time being? You can do two things, I think: you can reproduce, and you can produce. I'd claim that it's reproduction when what's conveyed is a resemblance or a similitude of relation. When you convey a similitude of relation, you produce a resemblance. Analogy is thus the production principle behind resemblance. I'd call this type "figuration." I'd call this first form analogy or common analogy—*analogia communis* (because we have to squeeze in a little scholarship)—the conveyance of relations of resemblance. That is: you produce a resembling image; you make it "resembling."

Painting is never like that. However, notwithstanding its pretensions and ambitions, I wonder whether photography isn't necessarily and always like that. What makes photography different from painting? Well, photography very generally—I'm putting this in really rudimentary terms—is about capturing and conveying relations of lighting [*rapports de lumière*]. That opens up all kinds of possibilities. Your strategy can be to adjust the mode of conveyance for sufficient margins to obtain the deepest variations, the most extreme degrees in resemblance, vast variations of similitude. You could obtain fainter and fainter effects of resemblance. That doesn't change the fact that there is no photograph if it doesn't convey relations of lighting. As a result, I can't see how photography could overcome what we might call the figurative aspect. By figurative, I don't mean the extent to which it resembles something, but the extent to which the image is produced by conveying similar relations, by a similitude of relations, however faint the similitude might be.

One might say the photo possesses its condition of possibility and "lives" in common analogy. But analogy isn't bound to that. We can do something else with analogy, this time producing—rather than reproducing—resemblance. What does it mean for a resemblance to be produced? Notice that code could also produce resemblance. It could make us a portrait, but at that point, resemblance was produced through the detour of a code and a binarization of its givens. Whereas I have something else in mind: an analogy that would be capable of producing a resemblance independent from any mode of conveying similitude. Now things are coming to a head for us because if we manage to define this sort of analogy, we'll have a possible definition for painting.

Indeed, painting does produce resemblance or the Figure. I am reintroducing the word *resemblance,* but there's no difficulty about doing so if I add: painting produces resemblance through nonresembling means. It produces resemblance through means that are completely different from conveying a similitude, from conveying similar relations. You approach a painting—a Van Gogh, a Gauguin—you see a Figure: you don't need to see the model to be convinced that you're looking at an icon. But this icon is produced via nonresembling means. You reproduce resemblances through nonresembling means. That's what analogy means.

What are these nonresembling means? I'm already getting ahead of myself because, in a qualified way, I've characterized code through articulation, or through the common sphere. I said there is a common sphere between digital code and articulation. Articulate, and you get a code. Which committed us to an at least determined path. I'm committed to defining analogy—and as a result, the diagram—as the analogical principle. I can't avoid it. You see, it's great when your hands are tied when it comes to concepts. We'll either be forced to give up (that would be perfect, everything is perfect) or we'll have to manage to define analogy (and the diagram on which the analogy depends) by something as straightforward as articulation; and this "something" would be to the diagram what articulation is to code. I already know that it won't involve any resemblance, won't convey any similitude, nor any code. What does the diagram do that's distinct from articulation and that can be defined neither by its conveying similitude, nor by code, nor by encoding? At least the conditions of our problem are well-defined.

So, we have to press on. For now, I'll just say that, just as code doesn't rule out similitude but rather implicates it, likewise analogy cannot really be defined by similitude. Only common analogy is defined by similitude. *Aesthetic* analogy isn't defined by similitude, since it produces resemblance through wholly different means. If similitude isn't able to define analogy, what is able to define it? Let's take a look. We'll take a second step. Our second hypothesis is that we might be able to define analogy, or analogical language, by—or as—simply a language of *relations.* That's Bateson's hypothesis, who is really such an interesting writer. Analogical language would be one of relations as opposed to conventional language, that of codes.

Keeping things simple in order to demonstrate something very peculiar, Bateson says a language of code would be a language of states-of-affairs. Our coded language, our digital language, would be one suited for designating, determining, or translating states-of-affairs, whereas analogical language would express and would be used for relations.

What does Bateson mean? He elaborates on how we ought to understand relations. This will lead us back to painting via some odd twists and turns. Bateson famously wrote on the language of dolphins.[26] Bateson has led an extremely eventful life, having done all sorts of things—and he's still alive![27] He was the husband of ethnologist Margaret Mead. He started in ethnology, but in my view, he was even better than Margaret Mead. His ethnological studies were so intriguing, so profound, so important. He really had an American-style career, quite amazing. It was a perfect example of an American hero, always on the move, a kind of hippy in philosophy. He divorced Margaret Mead, and then he divorced the tribes he studied. Then he stumbled upon schizophrenics, and he developed a whole theory of schizophrenia, one of the finest there is, a theory now known in France as the theory of the [double-bind].[28] He did all that by using logic, applying the theory of logical types to schizophrenia—he's quite familiar with [Bertrand] Russell's logic. And then he threw himself into dolphin language, which was even better. The schizophrenic still seemed too human for him, too monotonous. Obviously, he gets a lot of funding from the U.S. military, who are very interested in dolphins, but Bateson's results are hilarious, because they're totally useless for the army.[29] [*Laughter.*] So, it's wonderful, it's excellent work, and you'll definitely see why I'm going through his career.[30]

He starts by going over very basic things, because that's the American style. They aren't familiar with our European-style process. They start with extremely simple terms, whereas we make deductions. They take simple bits and pieces from which they build a sort of hornet's nest and draw out a paradox—and they always come up with such lovely paradoxes—then they use logic to unravel them. All this is completely different from our way of thinking. I'm talking about when Americans do it well. That's why they invent so many concepts; they invent a lot more concepts than we do because, for us, the invention of concepts is a very deductive process.

They make theirs by bundling stuff together, drawing on a wide range of things. Bateson brings together a schizophrenic, a savage [*un sauvage*], and a dolphin, and he'll then draw something out of this. I think it's some of the greatest philosophy, and it involves as much rigor as ours, since it'll all come down to the logic of the paradox. This is what makes them logicians in the end; they're open to everything. It's wide-open, outdoor logic, whereas ours is deduction occurring in confinement. For us, we do philosophy on an easel, in the end. Our easel is the history of philosophy, whereas for the Americans, they don't do that. But then again, it's rare for them to be at Bateson's level.

Bateson says conventional language is the left side of the brain, which controls the right side of the body. Analogical language is the [right] side.[31] What do we usually put under analogical language, by comparison [to digital language]? Let's go back to one of our reference points: conventional or digital language is fundamentally articulated. Analogical language is thus the right hemisphere rather than the left hemisphere of the brain. It's not articulated. We're circling around to the heart of it. If we found out what it is—since [analogical language] isn't articulated—then we might get our definition of painting. What is it made of then? It's made of nonlinguistic, even nonsonorous things, of movements—of kinetic movements, so to speak—of emotional expression, of inarticulate sonorous input: murmurs, cries.

If we were talking about music, we'd find a similar problem, because is singing articulated or nonarticulated, analogical or digital? We don't know. So we won't throw music on the pile. This analogical language is in a way an animal language, but it's made out of very heterogeneous sources. For example: hairs standing on end, a grimace, a yelp. All of that is analogical language. We're already making progress: a scream doesn't resemble anything. Similitude isn't what defines analogical language. What does it resemble when your hair stands on end? It's not a language of similitude. A scream doesn't resemble the horror that causes it, not in the least. What is it that defines analogical language? Bateson says that it's a language of relations. What does he mean by relation? He doesn't mean just any relation. There are some writings in which he seems to mean just any old relation. At that point, we wind up with similitude again, namely, analogical language would be one that functions by conveying relations. For example, in a diagram, your task is to represent one quantity that's big and one quantity that's relatively small, and you make two levels, one level smaller than the other. That's similitude; that is a language of relations, in fact. But that's not what he means, because the similitude hypothesis has been ruled out. He means, it's a language that's supposed to express the relations between the transmitter and the receiver, between what emits it and its intended destination. In other words, analogical language primarily expresses dependency relations in all their possible forms. You see that this is very different from similitude.

Whenever he makes any headway, Bateson feels the need to joke around, but they're always good jokes. He calls this the μ-function. Mu (μ) is the Greek letter equivalent to our *m*. Whenever he needs an example for something, it's always cats. Cats meow in the morning, meow . . . The μ-function is the "meow" function.[32] The English and the Americans have never gotten past Lewis Carroll. [*Laughter.*] What is the μ-function, or meow-function? Bateson says that when cats meow in the morning, as you're getting up—which is analogical language—they aren't saying *milk, milk*; they're saying *Dependency! Dependency!, I depend on you,* with all kinds of variations: there are angry meows, that is, *I depend on you and I'm sick of it.* It's a very rich language, but it always expresses the relation between transmitter and addressee, with all sorts of reversals imaginable.

Bateson says it's a language requiring a lot of deduction, since if you look at the language's structure, it directly expresses μ-functions, that is, functions of dependency from which one deduces the state of affairs. I ought to deduce: hey, my kitty wants some milk. If it's one animal talking to another using analogical language, there are also grounds to deduct something. For example, he refers to the famous ritual among wolves or dogs, where an individual shows its inferiority by exposing its neck, demonstrating its dependency vis-à-vis the leader or the stronger animal. You have a dependency relation from which one deduces a state of affairs. In our language, it might be "I won't do it again." States-of-affairs are fundamentally deduced from relations, from dependency relations. That's how Bateson defines analogical language. On the other hand, what is our coded language, our digital language? Bateson says it's a language that primarily concerns states-of-affairs, a language essentially intended to designate states-of-affairs, but that doesn't mean there isn't any analogy behind the scenes. That takes us a great distance, and I'd like for you to hang on to it for later. Anyway, I think codes are practically steeped in analogy, analogically glued together.

[*Interruption of the recording,* time stamp: 1:54:00.]

In our coded, conventional language, Bateson would claim that language designates states-of-affairs by convention, from which one *induces* analogical functions, whereas, in analogical language, it's almost reversed; language directly expresses analogical dependency relations, from which one *deduces* states-of-affairs.

And yet, dolphins have a language, and no one can understand any of it. Bateson says that no one understands it because it's likely that there's not much in their language to understand, other than one very strange aspect. Consider the following really crazy process. One wonders who'd be capable of it. For the moment, I have my two languages: an analogical language for relations, a coded language for states-of-affairs. Let's say I get a bit of a wild idea: to encode analogical relations as such. To encode μ-functions. This is a language that remains analogical, but which is fed through a code. It's a very odd sort of language: a code grafted onto analogical flows. At first glance, it's impossible; it's contradictory. However, it's sort of what we saw earlier with the computer. Endowed with binary code, computers encode something to be reproduced, a design or drawing to be reproduced. Now suppose that dependency relations, μ-functions, and so forth, are likewise encoded. We considered what "encoded" might mean: being caught up in a system of binary choices. Then again, why would an analogical language get encoded? Why would you ever need to encode an analogical language? That is, to graft code onto analogy?

On only one occasion, Bateson says: in the case of large mammals who've abandoned the life on land and have fled to the sea. Why? Because large mammals are the land animals that have taken analogical language the farthest. They're screwed once they take to the water because unlike fish, they're not capable of having their own analogical language, one particular to a marine environment.

And they no longer have the means to use terrestrial analogical language. In fact, terrestrial analogical language implies a clear distinction between the head and the body, implies hair, expressive movements, all things that water's parameters not only limit, but what's more, even if they had these, their message wouldn't be received, since the conditions of visibility underwater are such that terrestrial analogical language doesn't work.[33] Bateson says that we think that dolphins have a mysterious language. Not at all. We think that dolphins have a conventional language, and he warns the American military that they're setting themselves up for serious disappointment. Is he right? I have no idea. The paradox with dolphins is simply that the maritime conditions to which they had to adapt are such that they had to encode the analogical as such. They didn't develop a digital language, nor a language of codes; they've had to encode analogical language. He says he's personally convinced that if we manage to decipher a bit of dolphin language, we won't find a linguistic language. What we'll find in this language is strictly analogical content that simply expresses dependency relations and that expresses nothing about states-of-affairs.

Why do I insist on going over Bateson's thesis on dolphin language? It's because he opens us up to something that really intrigues me: the possibility of grafting binary code onto purely analogical language. This allows us to overcome somewhat the duality that was our starting point. What I mean by that is: just think about the formula I would end up with; it no longer appears so simple. I sort of get the feeling that an abstract painter is no different from a dolphin. They're dolphins; they're painter-dolphins. That's what makes them abstract; their real method is inventing a code for a specifically analogical matter and content. They graft code onto the pictorial material. With this, they manage to achieve something awesome. In other words, they aren't abstract painters; they're actually marine mammals. It's exactly the same problem as with the dolphins, it seems to me [*FBLS*, 95–95 UM; 117 C]. But that's not important. We just need to keep moving forward.

Analogical language is no longer defined by similitude but is defined by dependency relations. Does that offer us anything new? Maybe, but not on its own. I think it still needs development. What needs to be changed? How are dependency relations expressed?

At this point, I need a third determination for analogical language. Because strictly speaking, dependency relations are the content of such language. But if analogical language has its own specific form, what will this form be? Suppose it's painting. What then? It needs a form. How are dependency relations expressed? Then we'd be able to define analogical language. We've got it, it's in hand. Suspense. What were you going to say, Anne?

ANNE QUERRIEN: That reminds me of a passage from *A Thousand Plateaus*, where you talked about order-words and transformations of bodies by incorporeals.[34]

DELEUZE: Fair enough—me too, but that's even more complicated. Since things are complicated enough as is, that won't make it any easier.

ANNE QUERRIEN: And then it reminded me of something else, the vocabulary of masons for cathedrals, and so on, particularly, for example, there was a study done by a guy named Scobeltzine, where he analyzes Roman and Gothic sculpture and demonstrates that they all have a code for capitals that directly express dependency relations by how they're positioned, in the way . . .

DELEUZE: Oh, that's interesting!

ANNE QUERRIEN: It's called *Feudal Art and Its Social Significance*, by Scobeltzine, an architect. He shows how sculpture is an expression of dependency relations and that you can interpret all Gothic art in this way.[35]

DELEUZE: That's wonderful! Did you all hear what she said? Would you mind standing up and saying that again quickly? Because they might be interested.

ANNE QUERRIEN: There's an architect named Scobeltzine who wrote a book titled *Feudal Art and Its Social Significance*, and he says that all cathedral sculpture and architecture is the expression of social dependency relations, using both an architectural code for raising the vaults and sculptural code essentially relating to capitals.[36] He goes into detail about this whole Gothic line, outlining the different forms of capitals.

DELEUZE: I have to read this book. Write down a note with his name for me because I didn't jot it down earlier.

ANNE QUERRIEN: I ought to have my notes at home.

DELEUZE: Send them my way—that way I don't have to read it myself. [*Laughter.*] This is very important. See, there are tons of things I haven't considered.

Let's consider the example of sound: analogical language exceeds the voice, fine, but there is also analogical language in the voice. And, precisely, linguists don't hide the fact that language, what they call conventional language, is made up of so-called internal distinctive features. What are these? They're precisely the binary phonological relationships between phonemes. A binary relation between phonemes is an internal distinctive feature of language.[37] But they've always claimed that there were other linguistic features. What are these linguistic features? They're tones, intonations, accents, or, to put it more precisely, pitch, loudness, and length. Pitch, loudness, and length form three kinds of stress [*trois espèces d'accents*]. Just what are linguists doing? That's what bothers me. And actually, these noninternal features, you might even say nondistinctive features, they acknowledge them. For example, [this is how] Jakobson defines what he calls poetics in its relation to linguistics.[38] What I find strange is that, despite everything, they acknowledge the specificity of this domain, but they still try to encode it exhaustively. That is, they apply their binary rules to it. It's very apparent in Jakobson. As we continue this inquiry into analogical language, I'm working instead under the assumption that we must not apply rules of code, that is, we must not binarize this realm of so-called prosodic or poetic features.

Then what is it? I would say as well: it's the nonarticulated voice. It has pitch, loudness, length, and it has stress. Stress and articulation present an even bigger problem when it comes to music. Fortunately, we're not concerning ourselves with music. Also, what role does code play in music? What is the role of the nonarticulated? What is the opposite of musical code in music itself? That would be a problem. Everyone knows the opposite of code in music, ultimately. But anyway, we'll come back to all that later. What's on the table when it comes to the analogical? There's a convenient term, but it won't fix anything because it'll be hard to develop a concept for it: *modulation*. In what way is it modulation? I'm not claiming that there's a simple opposition (although in some ways, there is a simple opposition) between articulation and modulation. I can say that modulation refers to the values of a nonarticulated voice. I can start there. That being said, and this will help, modulation and articulation can combine in all sorts of ways. Now I can expand the point so you can see what's at stake in all this. I'm saying that analogical language would be defined by modulation. Where there's modulation, there's analogical language, and thus, there's a diagram.

In other words, the diagram is a modulator. Notice how that does a good job of meeting my requirements: the diagram and analogical language are defined independently of any reference to similitude. We must not reintroduce any givens of similitude into modulation. Analogical language is about modulation. Digital, or coded, language is about articulation. All sorts of combinations are possible such that you can articulate a modulation's flow. At that point, you're grafting a code, which might be important. Maybe code has to be involved to allow analogy its full development. How can this hypothesis help us with painting?

Let's just try applying it as best we can, since painting is indeed an analogical language, maybe the highest form of analogical language to date. Why? Because when you say "to paint," you *are* saying "to modulate." Mind you, you modulate something on the basis of something else. Let's clarify this. What will this concept of modulating involve? At its most basic, you modulate something using what's called a carrier or medium according to a signal. You're as much of an expert as I am on this topic. It's TV, or whatever you want; we exist within this, within modes of modulation. A carrier, or a medium, is modulated based on a signal to be conveyed. Modulation does not convey similitude. What is it? We don't know yet. When it comes to painting, can I apply this very broad definition in a way that isn't merely an application, in such a way that what we get is undeniably a definition of painting?

What is the signal? Let's stick to worn-out categories. The more worn-out, the better. The signal is the model. In more complex terms, the signal would be what we called the motif, based on our discussion of Cézanne, which isn't the same thing as the model, but no matter. Or else, I'd say—and these aren't mutually exclusive—it's the surface of the canvas. That's also the signal. The model is a signal, but so too is the surface of the canvas. No doubt, it all depends on my perspective; I can come at it from all sorts of angles. What do I modulate on the canvas? I can see only two alternatives for what would provide material for modulation. Either I modulate light, or I modulate color—or I modulate both. In fact, light and color really are the carrier waves of painting. As a result, once again—I insisted on this at the last session—I'm not so sure we can define painting as just line and color. I'd claim that to paint is to modulate light or color—light *and* color—depending on the flat surface and (these aren't exclusive) depending on the motif or the model that plays the role of signal.

What result do we get from modulation? The figure on my canvas. Whether it's Pollock's line with no figure, or Kandinsky's abstract figure, or Cézanne or Van Gogh's figural figure: that's what I get from modulation, what I might call Resemblance with a capital *R*. However, I produced it via nonresembling means, hence the painter's motto: I'll achieve a resemblance deeper than one from a camera, deeper than any resemblance—since I produced it through wholly different means: the modulation of light and of color. With all of the countless definitions for painting, starting from: it's an arrangement of colors assembled on a flat surface; or else, it's carved out of the surface; or else, it's this or that, in the end, we've achieved something by coming up with one more, which obviously isn't a big deal. But at least we now have a precise problem: How are light and color the objects of modulation? What exactly is the modulation on a flat surface of light and color? There you have it.

So now we can't get around defining a concept of modulation, one both clearly distinct from the concept of articulation and, at the same time, one that makes no reference to similitude and the relation of similitude. I might say: the diagram is the matrix of modulation. It's the modulator just as code is the matrix of articulation. It's not at all impossible that we'll end up involving a *phase* of code if it gets us closer to the diagram, to analogical language, to modulation. It may very well be that modulation has a lot to gain from a code phase. In other words, it may very well be that abstract painting constitutes a fundamental step forward for all painting from the twofold perspective of the modulation of color and the modulation of light. Not from the viewpoint of the invention of a code, but from the point of view of progress of an analogical language, that is, from the paradoxical perspective. What would it mean to modulate color, to modulate light?

We'll go back to square one. Modulate, modulate, modulate, not articulate. I'll try to draw from wherever I can, left and right, to construct a concept. I'd like to refer us to two sorts of information domains [*données*]: the literary domain and the technological domain. Regarding the literary domain, that's easy. There's a great text that has already been covered from every angle, but I'd like to discuss it in light of our analysis. It's Rousseau's *On the Origin of Languages.*[39] Why? Because, in this extraordinary text, Rousseau's core premise is that language cannot have originated in articulation.[40] Articulation can at most be the second stage of language. That's a bit of an overstatement—for Rousseau, all language is articulated, but articulation can only be the second stage of the voice's development. The melodic voice existed prior to articulated language. Rousseau defines it in a very precise way. It's the intonated, accented voice. Not just intonated or accented—because you might think that all language has intonation [*accents*]—but in fact, for Rousseau, languages have lost all intonation.[41] Some intonation still remains more or less, but the key to understanding intonation lies in extinct languages. The Greeks still had an accented language [*langue à accent*]. English might also be one somewhat, but it's not Rousseau who says it. Why is he insisting that our languages are no longer accented? They have accents, yes, but they're no longer "accented," he says.[42] When there are accents, intonation [*l'accent*] is gone.[43] He means that differences in accent, as he sees it, ought to correspond to tonal differences. And, in our case, differences in accent don't correspond to tonal differences. Our accents have deteriorated so much in our spoken languages [*langues*].

Why has our language ceased to be melodic whereas real language is melodic? As soon as languages became articulated, they ceased to be melodic. Why did they turn into articulated languages?

Rousseau's idea is wonderful but quite strange. He says languages became articulated once they left their birthplace, because in his view, language was born in the South. That's where you'll find the conditions for a language to emerge. Languages are originally southern. But that doesn't stop them from prevailing in the North. Tough northerners are the articulate ones because they are industrial.[44] I hope you peruse this; *On the Origin of Languages* is a very short essay. He goes so far as to state explicitly several times: articulation is conventional by its nature. What that means in modern terms is that articulations are determined by choice. Making choices puts it unquestionably in the realm of binary choices. Articulation is a matter of the conventional. The northern man, with his industrial needs, is forced to articulate because he no longer knows how to say, "love me," Rousseau claims. He no longer knows how to say, "help me," and for him, the proof of one's love is helping with work.[45] The language of work, the language of industry, is one that's thoroughly articulated. There are still nonarticulated sounds among northern men. This text is beautiful. They articulate, they articulate, but they retain some nonarticulated sounds. Only, they've turned into fearsome cries. They happen in tandem: when articulation begins to rule language, nonarticulated sounds turn into paroxysm, a fearsome noise.

What does he have in mind? The sad situation of Rameau's opera. In music, what's the equivalent? What is musical code? Articulation is akin to what Rameau described as the matrix of all music. What was the matrix of all music for Rameau? It was "harmony," with its vertical sections of melodic lines and how they establish chords. Rousseau touches on this—his essay is quite scholarly—when he says that harmony is to music precisely what articulation is to language. It's the conventional aspect.[46] Melody alone is natural. Harmony is convention; you make music purely by convention. This conventional music broke so far away from melody that everything nonarticulated, nonharmonic turns into awful shouting. At that point, for Rousseau, our whole relationship with the voice and music is fundamentally distorted. The voice reverts to awful shouting while the melodic flow winds up depending on purely conventional harmonics. As a result, in his struggle against Rameau, what does Rousseau counter in response? He counters Rameau with a purely melodic music, with very little harmony, in which the voice is nonarticulated but doesn't resort to shouting, [that is,] the pleasant voice of pure melody. Hence, the double or triple voice, point and counterpoint, and so on, but without conceding to harmony's demands. Melody as opposed to harmony will define the modulation of the voice, which will provide a positive definition for the nonarticulated voice. Whereas, from the point of view of harmony, the nonarticulated voice can be defined only negatively, in the form of awful shouting. What would a present-day Rousseau say about Italian opera, Wagnerian opera? Obviously, that's unfair because it is obvious, but I'm trying to resituate his schema. You see what he's thinking: language has two basic stages. First, language couldn't have been born from interest or from need. That's an interesting idea. Here, he runs counter to the entire eighteenth century in this regard.

ANNE QUERRIEN: There's another extraordinary text by Brisset, *La Grammaire logique* et *la Science de Dieu* [Logical Grammar *and* God's Science], which has been reedited by Foucault, in which he says humans descend from frogs, emerge from the water and discover their sex, that is, the fundamental binarism and, based on this sexual matter, little by little they start talking.[47] The code is created based on the frog's croaking.

DELEUZE: Yeah, but that's no good for me, as opposed to the example from earlier because it's purely sonorous similitude. It's just a play of similitude.

ANNE QUERRIEN: Afterward, if you will, he gradually builds everything back up . . . [*Inaudible words.*]

DELEUZE: Yeah, but unlike your earlier text, we have to force things in order to bring in Brisset. I feel like Brisset is a whole other problem.

Interest and need—and even industry at the extreme—gesture would suffice. A pure gestural language would do. I find that interesting because gestural language is a language of similitude. It just mimes things. A soldier draws his sword and then points it in a direction. Even the most boneheaded cavalryman knows to head *that way.* [*Laughter.*] A language of gestures is enough.

[*A student intervenes to discuss the anthropologist Marcel Jousse, a discussion that Deleuze does not pursue,* 2:30:48.][48]

Rousseau's idea is very straightforward. It's that language can have but one source: passion. This puts us into an almost aesthetic element. It's precisely what some art critics call the pathic moment, *pathos* as opposed to *logos*.[49] You could say that *logos* is code, but there's an element that is the pathic element of passion. So this is how language has a southern origin. The young boys and young girls gather around the fountain, says Rousseau. Then they begin to dance, and so on. That's the origin of modulation.[50] You get a sense of Rousseau's schema: you exclude gestural language because it works via similitude. It's common analogy. The second step is modulation of the voice. Yes, that's the second analogy, the great aesthetic analogy. It's no longer defined by similitude but by modulation, the melodic voice. Third, language heads north: the people of the North get their hands on it and, as a function of industrial development, introduce laws of articulation and apply them to all melodic language, just as music will be subject to the laws of harmony. It's not a bad idea. So, here's what I draw from this: Rousseau himself will define this modulation by melody. All right, so what will become of this melodic voice?

Whew! Anyway, until next time.

SESSION 5

TYPES OF ANALOGY, SIGNAL-SPACES, AND MODULATION

12 May 1981

Our objective was to come up with a definition for analogical language. Once again, the terms of our problem are clear, since it's relatively easy for us to imagine the opposite of analogical language, namely, digital language: the language of code. In fact, we ended up defining the language of code, or digital language, with the concept of articulation. Let's recall that this is indeed a concept in the sense that it isn't reducible to its associated physical or physiological aspects. It isn't reducible to the movements of so-called articulations that accompany digital language or that cause it to rise to the level of speech acts. We tried to pin down the logical concept of articulation in the simplest terms possible, so we said that articulation consists in the position of meaningful units as these are determinable through series of binary choices. And we concluded that such a finite set of meaningful units determinable by successive binary choices corresponded to the characteristics of code.

But then, how might we define analogical language, as opposed to digital language or code? I'll remind you of our first hypothesis: analogical language is the language of similitude and is defined by similitude. That's insufficient, right, but similitude allows us at least to define our first type of analogy that we called common analogy, or at the extreme, photographic analogy. Analogy is indeed defined by conveying similitude, whether a similitude of relations or a similitude of qualities. We shouldn't be too hasty in giving up this approach because it'll be really important for us quite soon. If I define the language of analogical language as similitude, what is the model in that case for analogical language? What will the model be for common analogy? The model would be the *mold*, casting a mold, imposing a likeness.

Do operations of molding essentially belong to analogical language? Perhaps. But even if one dimension of analogical language is well defined, what led us to say that this doesn't cover everything about analogical language? It seemed to us that, naturally, there's always a sort of similitude at work in analogical language. But that doesn't explain or it doesn't prove that analogical language can be *defined* by similitude. In what case can analogical language be defined by similitude? Solely in the case where similitude is what produces an image. And that's exactly what happens with a process of molding.

But there seemed to be many cases where analogy didn't make use of resemblance or a productive similitude; on the contrary, similitude or resemblance was produced as the end product of analogy—and this is precisely what happens in painting. Whenever resemblance is the end product of a process, the analogical process cannot be defined by what it produces. Hence the necessity—even if we keep similitude-as-molding as the first pole of analogical language—the necessity of moving beyond this criterion of similitude based on other forms of analogy. We briefly considered a second criterion: the possibility of defining analogical language by and as a language of relations, a particular sort of relations, that is, dependency relationships between a transmitter and a receiver, between a speaker and a recipient. We saw that this was a different definition. What model did that refer to? We'll look at that later on. And there, we also noticed that even if a form of analogy corresponded to this model, the pole of analogy still was not exhausted.

And finally, we reached a third analogical layer. Actually, it seemed like these dependency relationships, inscribed into analogy, had to refer to a particular form of expression. And what was the form of expression for these dependency relationships? We proposed a third option for analogy—and here Rousseau came to the rescue—namely, something more along the lines of *modulation*. It's up to us obviously to develop a concept of modulation as rigorous as the ones for code or for articulation. What bearing does that have on our main problem? When it comes to aesthetic analogy, modulation is the rule. The rule is at work whenever resemblance or similitude isn't what produces but what is produced by other means. These nonresembling means that produce resemblance—means that bear no resemblance to the model and that produce a resemblance—that's precisely what modulation is. Producing resemblance is what it means to modulate.

We have something like three forms of analogy: analogy via similitude; analogy via internal relation; analogy via modulation. Our concern is twofold: at once to maintain a coherent concept for all of these cases and also to keep all three fundamentally distinct. I'd like to come up with some identifiers, but we'll drop them if we don't find them useful. With the first form of analogy—as similitude or as conveying a similitude, as productive resemblance—I'll call it a common or physical analogy. While these terms do not quite suffice, they'll work tentatively as a point of reference, for the time being. I'll call the second form of analogy—as internal relations of dependency—organic analogy. You'll see why I call it that. And for now, let's call analogy as modulation—resemblance produced through completely different means—aesthetic analogy.[1]

Let's add even more terms. The model for the first form of analogy would be molding, mold-casting. Casting a mold basically means having a resemblance, a similitude imposed from the exterior. I might define it as a surface operation. For example, I put a mold down onto some clay and wait for the clay to even out under the mold's impression. Then I lift the mold away. It conveys a similitude. That precisely demonstrates common analogy, crude analogy. It's a surface or border operation. I emphasize this point because I'm getting our concepts in order for later on. You could also call this type of analogy a superficial or skin-deep analogy. I'm making it a point to find a real-world example that would correspond to this. Since I'm going to need this, I'm purposely searching by going all over the place. I would say: this is the crystal stage. As they say, crystals are individuated in layers. They grow on the edges. What matters isn't the internal substance. The crystal is fundamentally a superficial development that grows on the edges.[2]

If I move into the organic domain, what distinguishes organic individuality from crystalline individuality? How are organic laws and crystalline laws distinct? This might be really important for our aesthetic categories later on. At the risk of confusing things, what led certain critics to define Egyptian art by crystalline laws as opposed to Greek art, defined by organic laws?[3] This line of inquiry should show you that we haven't left our essential problem.

While we may seem to have drifted away from our main themes, we may well be doing the opposite, namely, laying the very conceptual groundwork, in fact, for returning to them. How does organic conveyance differ from molding? [The Count de] Buffon, the great Buffon, developed a particularly daring concept, for his time, a concept so daring because it was so philosophical. This notion falls under the heading of one of the world's injustices because he was mocked for it, even in the eighteenth century. Actually, it's so beautiful that, like all beautiful ideas, it invites both criticism and irony. In *L'Histoire naturelle des animaux* [Natural History of Animals], Buffon says: you understand how odd a problem the reproduction of the living is. The problem is so odd that, to understand what sort of problem this is, it requires a contradictory concept. The wonderful, contradictory concept that Buffon develops is what he baptizes an internal mold. A living thing reproduces not by molding externally (however imprecise that might be, I could say roughly "by crystallizing"), but via an internal mold.[4]

What makes the idea of an internal mold so strange? In effect, it's a mold that doesn't apply to the surface, a mold that molds the inside, which sounds absolutely contradictory. What does it mean "to mold the inside"? The only way a mold can reach inside is by making the interior into a surface. Buffon goes so far as to say: an internal mold is as contradictory as if I referred to a "massive (or thick) surface."[5] Wonderful. So, beyond the extrinsic mold, can we begin to grasp the notion and the operation of an intrinsic mold, an internal mold? Buffon clarifies this: it would be a form of measure, but a measure that subsumes or contains diverse relationships between the parts, a measure that in itself incorporates a variety of relationships, internal relationships. Here I've come back entirely to the second analogy. What might we call a measure with variable times, a measure occurring over different times? Let's try out another term. Isn't that what you might call a module? We're just getting our terms in order.

There is the mold and then there is the module, entirely distinct. Wouldn't a module be something like an internal mold? And then there would be modulation.[6] Now I've got a series of concepts. We can categorize analogy along three lines: mold, module, modulation. That's great because our concept of modulation is starting to come into focus. We have something like a progressive series: molding, modeling, modulation. Looking at either end of the series: What is the difference between a mold and a modulation? Between molding and modulating? In his book on individuation, Simondon explains the difference rather clearly.[7] He says they're like two ends of a chain.[8] To mold is to modulate permanently, definitively, imposing a form onto material. In molding, it takes a certain amount of time for the material to achieve the equilibrium imposed by the mold. Once it reaches this equilibrium, you turn out the mold. So, you've modulated once and for all. If molding means to modulate it once and for all, on the flip side, at the other end of the chain, modulating is to mold continuously. It's a variable, temporary, and continuous mold. A modulation is like a mold that never stops changing. It reaches equilibrium immediately, or almost immediately. Only it's the mold that's variable. Simondon's text—the book is *Individuation in Light of Notions of Form and Information*[9]—page 30, reads: "The difference between the two cases" (molding and modulating) "resides in the fact that the operation of form-taking is finite in time for the clay" (the molding operation for clay). "It tends very slowly (in a few seconds) toward a state of equilibrium, and then the brick is removed from the mold; the state of equilibrium is utilized in the unmolding when this state is attained. In the electronic tube" (now we're dealing with modulation) "we utilize a support of energy" (a field of electrons) "such that the state of equilibrium [. . .] is attained in an extremely short time [. . .] (several milliseconds in a large tube [. . .]). Under these conditions, the potential of the control grid is utilized as a *variable mold*; the distribution of the support of energy in proportion to this mold is so rapid that it is carried out without an appreciable delay [. . .]: the variable mold then serves to differentiate in time the actualization of a source's potential energy. We do not stop when equilibrium is attained" (in fact, it reaches it immediately) "but continue by modifying the mold, i.e., the tension of the grid. The actualization is almost instantaneous and there is never a halting for the unmolding, since the circulation of the support of energy is equivalent to a *perpetual unmolding*; a modulator is a *continuous temporal mold.*"[10] Wonderful! That's exactly what we needed.

We're figuring out our concept of analogy insofar as it has to satisfy a twofold requirement that is nearly contradictory. First requirement: that we cannot be content to define analogy as similitude or as conveying similitude, since, in fact, analogy's finest moment, such as royal or aesthetic analogy, is when similitude is what is produced and not what produces. But on the other hand, at the same time, we must group all these instances of analogy under a single concept, including analogies of mere similitude. And I'm inclined to satisfy both of these requirements by saying: on the one hand, similitude is not what defines analogy and analogical language, it's modulation. Rousseau was absolutely right: analogical language is a language of modulation. On the other hand, I can regroup the different instances of analogy—including that of mere similitude or vulgar analogy—by saying: be careful, modulation is only the end of a sequence of subconcepts, a sequence of operations: one that I'll call molding, another that I'll call internal molding, the third that I'll call modulation, in the strict sense.

Simondon concludes the page I was just on by saying that there is indeed a sequence. Here's what he says: "The mold and the modulator are the extreme cases, but the essential operation of form-taking is accomplished in the same way for both; it consists in the establishment of an energetic regime, whether or not it persists. To mold is to modulate in a definitive way; to modulate is to mold in a continuously and perpetually variable way." There's something in between them that he calls "modeling."[11] It's clear that modeling is the intermediary between molding and modulation. It already hints at a continuous, temporary mold. Modeling for us would not be, perhaps, quite precise enough a determination. We saw that it worked better for our purposes to have the three forms of analogy as: external mold, Buffon's internal mold, and modulation.

In order to set our terms, I'll add: as first case, we have molding, which I'll link to a type of law that for now we'll call crystalline law; as second [case], the internal mold, organic law; and for the third [case] . . . Here, our wording continues to vary for the moment. I'd like to call it either aesthetic law or, drawing literally from Simondon, energetic law. I can simply conclude this first point. Modulation is a concept just as coherent, consistent as its counterpart concept of articulation. It allows us both to define what is particular about analogy or about the aesthetic act, but also what there is about analogy that's general. What is particular is modulation insofar as it is distinct from any sort of molding. The general description is how there is the series running from molding to modulation and from modulation to molding. So, that's the first point.

GEORGES COMTESSE: I wanted to bring up digital language and analogical language, for example, what you find in information theory, communication theory, pragmatism—Watzlawick or Bateson, for example. It's that the distinction they draw, Bateson in particular in his first book, *Naven* . . . ,[12] between digital language and analogical language, could not be totally covered or explained by a simple linguistic channel. For example, the speech that you put out presupposes a linguistic channel where, precisely, there's a binary choice at work at the level of the elements or at the level of articulation within the molar units of language, the meaningful units. That's a linguistic channel. But the linguistic channel is a channel corresponding to spoken language [*la langue*].[13] Obviously, if we define morphemes and phonemes, meaningful units and distinctive traits, we're working with the structure of spoken language. And we're on a linguistic channel. And precisely, the digital/analogic distinction doesn't reside at the level of the linguistic channel, thus at the level of spoken language, but at the level of language's sense, in information and communication theory, in pragmatist behavior theory. It's the difference between language and spoken language. For example, someone like Watzlawick says: the real difference between analogical and digital language is that digital language does have a binary, but it doesn't address the elements of spoken language. Not just the elements of spoken language. The binarity assumes that language, in order for the language's syntax to be homogeneous with its semantics, has to recognize—in that identity—it necessarily has to recognize two elements as mutually exclusive: "and" and "or." That's crucial. If we recognize that when we talk, whatever the status of our linguistic channel, what we say in a language—according to or through spoken language—presupposes that "and" and "or" are exclusive, regardless of the content of what we say. At that point, we're dealing with digital, unambiguously digital, language. Whereas, as they argue, analogical language is when the exclusive difference between "and" and "or" fades away and is replaced by a mirror-image resemblance, a reversibility between "and" and "or." They give a celebrated example. They say: analogical language might be not simply an animal's cry, but in terms of humans, it might be a smile. And they say that when someone smiles, you cannot tell if their smile comes from joy, or sadness, or love, or hate. In other words, in real life, "and" and "or" aren't mutually exclusive. Such that analogical language, far from being a language with univocal meaning, where syntax and semantics are homogeneous, is rather a language with equivocal meaning. It's the profound equivocity of analogical language, that is, that the difference between analogical language and digital language only scrambles—only a little, not too much—the fundamental structure of the voice, only it isn't linguistic. The voice, that is, the difference between difference and identity, the difference between "and" and "or" being different, and of "and" equals "or" being identical; [the difference of] "and" over "or" [and of] "and" equals "or." What pragmatic theory does not at all explain is how this voice's structure is imposed on them, and where such a structure comes from, one where afterward the difference between digital language and analogical language only produces a slight scrambling effect and certainly something very misleading on the level of difference, of the very subdivision of language.

DELEUZE: Excellent. Excellent. That all sounds like confirming comments. It's not an objection?[14] I'm fine with everything you just added. This definition of digital language makes significant progress, but in my view, it remains essentially binary, the binary being that between "and" and "or." However, what bothers me more is that this is still a primarily negative definition of analogy; it still doesn't offer a positive definition as what we've attempted with modulation. But I think that everything you said is really very good; it needs to be added to our work. We'll add it.

ANNE QUERRIEN: I've read the texts that Comtesse mentions, and I believe that we would have to put this differently to have it better correspond to what you are doing. That is, instead of opposing "and" and "or," we should oppose two uses of "and." There is the exclusive "and," which really means "or"—that's the digital. And then there is the "and" in the sense of [conjunctive] synthesis, that is, it's "and, and, and," and so forth.[15] And analogical might just be the domain of disjunctive synthesis [*Inaudible words.*] . . .

DELEUZE: Ah, yes, but now things get complicated.

ANNE QUERRIEN: And then the other thing I wanted to bring up concerned the last “aesthetic law,” which I’ll call machinic rather than energetic, because in fact, I believe that law, the three molds, and so on, will correspond to the three states of energy [*Inaudible words.*] . . .

DELEUZE: You’re right; energy is everywhere.

ANNE QUERRIEN: . . . the first law of thermodynamics; organic legality, is the second law; and modulation is the third law that we are in the process of . . .

DELEUZE: Yeah, okay. That’s not bad.

RICHARD PINHAS:[16] I just want to cut in here. From a simple practical, “scientific” or functional point of view, whatever language you use—and you learn this in first year in computer science, and all the way to the most recent developments—the “and” doesn’t exist. So, your question is resolved: there is no “and.” The “and” is excluded from all possible computer language, from the most modern to the most rudimentary. The “or” functions wholly digitally, but at no point would it be acceptable to use the term *and* in the linguistic sense of the term or in the semiotic sense with which we’ve become familiar in recent years. It doesn’t exist.

DELEUZE: Unless we agree that, in the conditions with which Comtesse is operating, we agree that the binary is between “and” and “or,” rather than between 1 and 0.[17]

PINHAS: It doesn’t work like that. It works via “or.”

DELEUZE: Yes, but the “or” is between two terms.

PINHAS: No, no. All of the most primary computers, from the very simple early microprocessors to the most complex, the most complicated computers using the most complicated military language, they work as grounded in exclusions, with these exclusions forming integrative modules on a higher level, if you will. You could always rebuild something else and say that in an advanced computer language, you'll be able to form strings of characters that necessarily lead to conjunctions, but they'll be in separate chunks. In very simple terms, the mode of digital operation precludes "and." I'm absolutely formal about that. If we use "and" to try and locate the criteria differentiating analog and digital . . .

DELEUZE: Right, I see what you mean. Yes, that's all good.

ANOTHER STUDENT: I would like to recall a text by Thom that might be useful for us. There's a recent text by René Thom in which he explains that there are two sorts of analogy. The first form of analogy, he says, has been around since Aristotle, an example of which might be like: "Old age is to youth what night is to day." He says that there would first be this form of analogy that doesn't produce anything new, and it's based on [substantives]. There is a second unfamiliar or less familiar form of analogy, which Bergson studied and which would instead be based on the verb and would be, for example, dependence.[18] We can say that the first analogy is founded in the substantive and it doesn't tell us anything new.

DELEUZE: That's the mold, right.

THE STUDENT: While on the other hand, the second would be based on a verb, an open-ended verb, right, so you don't know where it's going.

DELEUZE: We need a third one.

THE STUDENT: I have an objection about your first form of analogy . . .

DELEUZE: An objection? Ah, right . . . [*Laughter.*]

THE STUDENT: Because when you speak of conveying similitude, whether a similitude of relation or similitude of quality, which we'd think of normally, we'd think of a semantic analogy, which would be a conveyance of quality, as opposed to what would be relation-based analogy, which would therefore be syntactical. And the idea we end up with is that there's a kind of analogy that's structural. If it is structural . . .

DELEUZE: You're the one drawing that conclusion. Not me, not me.

THE STUDENT: Everyone does.

DELEUZE: Oh, okay, everyone . . . [*Laughter.*]

THE STUDENT: If the analogy is structural, it's internal structure. It isn't external. Besides, when you refer to crystals by using analogy, you say that crystals grow on the edges, but that's not what defines them. What defines them is their internal structure, so that has to change.

DELEUZE: No. I don't think so.

THE STUDENT: It doesn't work.

DELEUZE: No, one would simply need to say that such a definition of the crystal bleeds over into being a module, that it isn't a matter of molding. And in fact, when crystallographers talk about the process of crystallization, they speak of "seeding," which is a perfect example of a module's process. No, that would work out fine without us needing to adjust anything. Rather than an "internal mold"—again, I think it's a fantastic, wonderful concept—and modulation, we now have mold, module, modulation. These are the three forms of analogy.

ANOTHER STUDENT: [*Inaudible remark,* 45:05.]

DELEUZE: As I see it, energy was what defined the external mold, but that, we'll see later, when it comes to art, we'll see that energy is strictly subordinate to form. While elsewhere, energy isn't subordinate to form. Those are the stages. You can distinguish them in terms of the three states of energy . . . Yes?

GEORGES COMTESSE: I find myself in deep disagreement with you:[19] it's impossible to get around the particular problem of the voice in communication theory by directly translating it into the terms of *Anti-Oedipus*—except through a drastic oversimplification—to the extent that in Watzlawick's or Bateson's own work, what they fundamentally rule out is matter, energy, the unconscious, accepting instead an idea that strikes me as a complete ideology, namely, making symptoms depend on a circular causality of interpersonal interactions.

[*Brief inaudible intervention by Anne Querrien disagreeing with Georges Comtesse.*]

DELEUZE: Well, it looks like we're all on the same page! [*Laughter.*] But in fact, Richard's comment is very important.

[*Interruption of the recording,* time stamp: 46:44.]

PINHAS: It's [computer programming] bound to functional requirements, the ones that work. This is not a theoretical model. What has to be understood is that the theoretical model results from practical givens. Even when early computers began working, you find models by Pascal, and so on, but they were rediscovered afterward. It started to get theorized afterward. Computer metalanguages, including the advanced kinds like COBOL, and so forth, that are being used today, are derived from these laws. I mean, it was at a later moment that they came to appreciate that, effectively, computers function—computers broadly speaking, at least—function via a method of exclusion. This does not mean that that's good or bad . . .

DELEUZE: That idea is crucial for our definition of articulation. Yes. It's fundamental.

PINHAS: Hence the necessity of articulation's definition, which we don't necessarily see with analog.

DELEUZE: Well, you don't get articulation at all with analog.

PINHAS: Systematically you find, in every metalanguage, that is, in every operational computer language, whether for medical use or for military use, or whatever it might be, you'll run into articulation.

DELEUZE: This is perfect. Let's keep moving forward. We still have to come back to our concerns with painting, but I think that we're going to be much better prepared when we do return to it. At the simplest technological level—but it'll be your job to expand on it, as always—what is the act of modulation as the limit, if you like, of every instance of molding or modeling? I'll go over two areas very briefly in really fundamental terms, since I want to play it safe. In the first area (refer to Richard Pinhas for any further comments or corrections), we're distinguishing two sorts of synthesizers: analog synthesizers and digital synthesizers.[20] What is the basic difference, or what seems to be the basic difference between these two sorts of audio synthesizers? I'm just looking for some technological applications to see if our concept of modulation is off to a good start. Analog synthesizers are called "modular." Digital synthesizers are called "integrated."

What does it mean to be modular or integrated, in concrete terms? It means that in an analog or modular synthesizer, there is a connection between disparate sounds. This connection is forged on a genuinely immanent plane. When reproducing sound by connecting elements, producing a new sound is achieved by means of a plane where everything is responsive. In other words, the constitutive production is no less responsive than the product itself. In other words, every step of the process in an analog synthesizer is active and responsive. That's why the plane is truly immanent, since the process of production is no less responsive than the product itself. At that point, we can say there's genuinely a modulation. It's a modular synthesizer.

On the other hand, what characterizes the digital, or integrated, synthesizer? This time, the principle behind making the product—the produced audio—involves what's called an integrated plane, integrated specifically because it's distinct. In fact, this distinct plane entails homogenization and binarization of so-called data. Homogenization and binarization of givens occur on a distinct, integrated plane such that the product's production entails a distinction between levels. The principle behind the production won't be discernible for a discernible product. It goes through an integrated plane and the binary code that constitutes this plane. And this allows us to make a little bit of progress. This is because digital synthesizers have an infinitely greater productive potential [*puissance*] than analog synthesizers, as if, on this level, something were already telling us to stop thinking of the analog/digital distinction in terms of opposition. Somehow, it's possible and desirable to transplant encoding into analog in order to magnify analog's capacity.

[*To Richard Pinhas.*] Do you see something to add here? I'm sticking to the basics in this.

PINHAS: Just one small thing. It's that digital methods only authorize mathematical, countable, deferred time, and so forth, whereas analog methods authorize what is one of their innate characteristics, in addition to the ones you described: real time.

DELEUZE: It's not the same thing, you're correct, but that follows directly from the idea of a principle of production that's just as discernible as the product. Henceforth, time is necessarily real-time, whereas indeed, in the case of the integrated plane where the plane is distinct by rights, you necessarily get deferred time, since you have a jump. You can arrive at the product only through an act of translation-conversion.

RICHARD PINHAS: Building on that point, I don't know if it was a goal, but transplanting a digital control system into something primarily analog, that would be the ideal result in today's top-end systems. That is, the only existing systems that operate efficiently in real-time are so-called hybrid systems, analog-based systems fitted with digital controls.

DELEUZE: Yes, that's what is known as a code transfer into analog. And what transfers code when it comes to painting? It's the abstract painter who pulls it off wonderfully. That's why all of painting's potential [*puissance*] involves abstraction. Fine; that doesn't make painting abstract or mean that it ought to be abstract. It means that abstract painting's process indeed consists in transferring code into the analog pictorial flow, and this is what gives painting potential [*puissance*], so much so that, in a way, every painter makes use of abstraction in a painting. That's what the diagram is. Something new is taking shape for us. We'd manage no longer to think of diagram and code as particularly opposed to each other but to consider the possibility of transferring code into diagrams. That is—for those already familiar with this—of doing the complete opposite of Peirce. Peirce instead imagined analog operations, that is, diagram operations within codes.

There's an even simpler second technological example that we haven't mentioned yet: What do you call a modulation when it comes to TV? What's the definition of modulation, if we're just looking it up in the dictionary? It says that modulation is an operation related to waves. It's the state a wave takes on, precisely called a "carrier wave" depending on what signal is transmitted. The carrier wave is modulated according to the transmitted signal. To modulate means that you modify either the frequency or the amplitude of the carrier wave according to the signal. Meanwhile, the receiver demodulates, that is, it recovers the signal. What I'm saying is quite rudimentary, so why do I find this interesting? Because it gives me a kind of rough example of what I call "produced resemblance." Demodulation is the production of resemblance. You recover the signal not by conveying a similitude [but] through modulation, that is, by employing entirely different means, by altering the carrier wave's amplitude or frequency. But in this case, I'm going with the easiest example: a continuous signal.

What happens when the signal is discontinuous or discrete, or when a signal consists in a series of discrete pulses? At any rate, you'll translate the carrier wave—which will give you something new—into a sequence of periodic pulses. And then there are two outcomes. First case: with this sequence of periodic pulses, you either modify the amplitude (amplitude of a pulse), or the duration (the length of one pulse relative to that of another pulse), or the position (which is actually more interesting: you offset its timing). That's what modulation is. Consider what problem that's meant to address. It's a matter of understanding in which case modulation can grasp the discontinuous as such. Second case, something even more important for us, an even more modern process which was invented around 19 . . .[21]

[*Interruption of the recording,* time stamp: 1:03:29.]

. . . binary code, defined by 0/1. "0" when there's no pulse, "1" when there is a pulse. And that's the best system. What do you get by grouping pulses in binary code? You get exactly the same result as what we just looked at, namely: a transplant of code into analogical material or flux. So far, so good. I'm trying to draw some conclusions before you cut in.

So, here's the point of this long tangent on the concept of modulation. As I see it, what we get from this is a concept of modulation that goes from mold to modulation proper, via the module, and that starts to take shape for us. The second point: from one point of view, we think of modulation and articulation, analog and digital, as two completely opposite determinations. But from another point of view, we could say that every digital language and every code is deeply embedded in an analogical flux. In other words, every code is in truth grafted onto an analog ground or an analogical flux. Third point: analogy, in the strictest sense or in an aesthetic sense, can be defined precisely as modulation. In what way? Precisely because there's no conveyance of qualitative similitude in an aesthetic operation or an operation of the molding type—apparently at least—because there isn't simply a module, namely, one conveying internal relations, but there's a modulation proper, that is, one producing similitudes through nonresembling means. And that's what we called the presence of the Figure.

Consequently, I'm returning to my definition of painting—even if, once again, we're going to add yet another. At least ours is built on our problem's framework, so it's sure to suit our purposes. We can't be sure that it's right, but at any rate, it's no worse than any other definition. And besides, it's necessary because we formed it based on everything we covered before. To paint is to modulate to plan, on the plane,[22] that is, on a surface, the canvas. What is the "wave" in painting? The wave is quite straightforward. The carrier wave is light or color, light and color. To paint is to modulate light; it's to modulate color. Now we're echoing Cézanne: "modulate."[23] And the word *modulate,* the way he uses it, is all the more interesting given that, in certain texts, he contrasts it with something that was well-established in painting: modeling. We're back in the sequence: molding, modeling, modulating. Mold, module, modulation. Cézanne makes a claim on modulation (does that mean he's better than someone who came before? No, that's not how to understand this). In his case, what is this? It's enough to look at a Cézanne painting [to see] it's not a modulation of light, [but] a modulation of color. It's precisely because he invents a new regime of color that he invokes the concept of modulation.

And everyone else? Weren't they already undertaking the modulation of color? Or of light? These are questions we must consider. Does modulating light follow the same rules as when you modulate color? I'm not so sure. Of all the great painters, Bonnard is among those who had the least to say. It's a pity because his notes are all little gems. We find this in Bonnard's notes; I'm citing nearly verbatim: with a single drop of oil, Titian would make an entire arm. Cézanne, on the other hand, wanted his choice of every color to be deliberate.[24] It's a lovely turn of phrase, but, what exactly is Bonnard trying to say? Painters take one dollop of oil and paint an entire arm with a single color. That's not how Cézanne does things. Sense that we're already dealing fully with the continuous and the discontinuous.[25] Cézanne proceeded by juxtaposing colors according to a law of modulation. Let's recall the technical terms that I used earlier: it's a modulation via discrete pulses. As for the other method, however, it's not a color modulation (which presupposes using discrete pulses); it's a modulation in the continuity type that presupposes values, all values of a single color. Our problem of the continuous and discontinuous in terms of modulation is perfectly illustrated by Bonnard's comment on two approaches to painting an arm. If it's true that painting is the modulation of light or the modulation of color—or both at once—there will be extremely diverse kinds of modulation. We're left with a major problem: painting would mean modulating, okay. But do we mean modulating broadly speaking that encompasses as well a kind of molding or a kind of modeling? Or else is it a strict sense of modulating that is distinct from any molding or modeling? We'll leave both options on the table.

Finally, the last question: to modulate is to modulate something—light or color—but on what basis? What's the "signal" to be transmitted? What is the signal of painting? It's not the model. The model is already an instance in which the modulation leans toward the mold. The model is simply a form of modulation in the broad sense. The signal is *space*. A painter paints nothing but space—and maybe time as well, space-time. A painter paints nothing but space-time. What space? Perhaps the grand styles of painting differ according to—and at the same time as—the nature of their space-times. Thus, I'm tending toward my complete definition: to paint is to modulate light or color—or light *and* color—based on a signal-space. It's still missing something. What does that produce? It produces the Figure. It produces this resemblance more profound than photographic resemblance, this resemblance to the thing that is more profound than the thing itself, this nonsimilar resemblance, produced through different means. The act of modulation is composed precisely of these different means. Modulating light or color based on a signal-space will give us the thing in its presence. Hence the theme: that painting isn't itself when it resembles something. Painting clearly is not figurative, since what's on the canvas is the thing, in its presence. With that, I have all the parts of my definition.

As a result, there are only two problems left to consider, which is perfect, since we're reaching the end of the year. What are these two problems? First problem: What are the major signal-spaces in painting? Second problem: How does modulation work based on these signal-spaces? There is something quite obvious: the Egyptian signal-space is not the same as the Byzantine signal-space. If there is such a thing as a sociology of painting, you can see what it would mean for us. It's the identification of painting's signal-spaces based on groups, civilizations, or collectivities. You could refer to them like people normally would: a Renaissance space, an Egyptian space, and so on. Each time, you'd have to determine a correspondence and find the laws governing these correspondences, between the signal-space of a period of art and the processes of modulation in the broad sense, whether mold, module, or modulation proper. You understand?

ANNE QUERRIEN: Current research into television technology is working on liquid crystal displays, where color will be displayed discretely point by point, and there won't be any grain like there is with TVs today, which make tiny black holes . . . [*Inaudible words.*] On the liquid crystal screens, there will be an entirely different image, without black holes.

DELEUZE: Won't that involve transplanted code?

ANNE QUERRIEN: Absolutely—then the screen becomes responsive and is grafted onto an analogical flux. The signal is still digitally coded, but the screen corresponds to what you've defined analogically.

DELEUZE: Wonderful! Wonderful!

ANOTHER STUDENT: Wouldn't this be like in fiction, in Philip K. Dick, who describes advertisements coming in a future era, which would be messages grafted onto kinds of amoebas, crystals, and that work like that, by moving and entering your home and constantly repeating their same message?

DELEUZE: What a time to be alive!

RICHARD PINHAS: Just to support something important you were saying about research discoveries. You brought up reorganizing discrete, I mean encoded, information, and that's so central to the theories surrounding reforming communication technology, that they have a name for these bundles of pulses: they're called packets [*paquets*]. This is all the more important, since networks have been created, both private and national, for transmitting these packets. These consist of transmitting data, transmitting discrete pulses, and the national French network is called Transpac.[26] It's a national network. Private groups aren't allowed to undertake this. It's not an obscure network, but it's not widely available yet, which would allow you to send a packet of information from Paris to Lyon, or from Paris to Los Angeles. Transpac is the contraction of "transmission" and "packet"; quite simply because the information is bundled into packets, of course, this constitutes the accumulation you were talking about, and it's become a key concept for communication technology.

DELEUZE: Great! So can we steal a packet? [*Laughter.*]

[*Interruption of the recording, apparently following a break,* time stamp: 1:21:45.]

Since there are only two things left to cover, let's start with the first: the nature of signal-spaces. I'd like to start things off, arbitrarily, with one type of space so that we think about this: for this study of spaces, our touchstone is still the central problem, that of modulation. Therefore, I'm selecting these signal-spaces based on what we need regarding the category of modulation. I'd like to come back to something I mentioned in a previous seminar and under different circumstances.[27] What is this space from which, to some extent, Western art emerged? First off, what is Egyptian space as an example of a signal-space that inspires forms of painting and sculpture? Here I'm relying on an author who's gaining some prominence in France but who still doesn't get his due, a very important Viennese author from the late nineteenth, early twentieth century named Aloïs Riegl. His contribution to aesthetics is indisputable, and, in particular, some of his analyses focused on Egyptian space. Among his main books is an incredible work titled *Problems of Style,* where among other things, he discusses the evolution of certain decorative elements when they move from Egypt into Greece. We'll see how this will be useful for us. Another really great book: *The Group Portraiture of Holland.* Finally, there's what's thought to be his main work, *Late Roman Art Industry,*[28] and finally, to my knowledge the only book translated into French: *Historical Grammar of the Visual Arts.*[29] I'd like to draw from *Historical Grammar of the Visual Arts* and *Late Roman Art Industry* to work out a few characteristics that will pave the way for what's to come and how Riegl attempts to describe what Egyptian space is. You'll see that it works well with the idea of a signal. I'll delineate a few characteristics, [all of which] I am borrowing from Riegl. One of Riegl's basic ideas is that art is never defined by what one can do but by what one wants to do.[30] At art's core there is a will. From a certain perspective, he holds on to a sort of idealist standard. It's the idea that material always bends to a will, and that this is not a question of saying, at a particular moment, the artist didn't know how to do that. The know-how [*savoir-faire*] is fundamentally subordinate to what Riegl calls a will-to-do [*vouloir-faire*]. This approach works for us, more or less. It raises enormous problems. What is this will-to-do about? Just what exactly is this will-to-art?

If we accept this point of departure, what does the Egyptian artist want? The response [that Riegl provides] is very precise:[31] the

Egyptian artist, as an Egyptian man, wants to extract essence. That Riegl tells us this is in itself already noteworthy because here we have somebody who isn't a philosopher and who is telling us that the Egyptian artist extracts essence from appearance. Why would they want to do that? Because appearance is what changes; it's the variable phenomenon. The phenomenon is appearance: appearance is tumultuous, appearance is dangerous, appearance is in flux, from which eternal essence is extracted. Simply put: essence, eternal essence, is individual essence. It's about preserving the individual in its essence, subtracting it from the world of appearance.[32] Insofar as we're doing philosophy, what should we take away from that? There's an odd discrepancy here: we're usually told that this is a Greek gesture. This seems like a minor detail, but it'll be important for us later on. One might think of Nietzsche's writing, when he defines metaphysics and Plato. We're told that the fundamental act of Greek metaphysics was the opposition between two worlds: the position of a world of calm and eternal essences, a world abstracted from appearances. Thus, there would be this other world that would serve as a refuge beyond appearances. Nietzsche defines Greek metaphysics as this distinction between essence and appearance, and the extraction of essence out of appearances. Nietzsche's insight is later taken up by Heidegger.

Why is this relevant for us? After all, on the subject of art, Riegl used these terms not so much to define Greek art as to define Egyptian art. This is an Egyptian approach. It's reminiscent of the *Timaeus*, where Plato has the Egyptian say: you Greeks will be never anything but children compared with us.[33] And what if we were wrong to define the Greek world by the distinction between essence and appearance? What if this definition was actually more apt for describing how Egyptians perceived the world? In fact, if we follow Riegl's logic, what does the Egyptian say? He identifies the [Egyptian] double known as the *kâ*, and the double is to be understood as individual essence subtracted from appearance, from death, and so on.[34] It's the subtracted double. Freeing individual essence from randomness and from change. What is this individual essence? Its law is that of closure. It's closed off, shielded from accident, shielded from the flow of phenomena, shielded from variation. It's the closed-off unity of the individual. Closure is the contour.[35]

Individual essence is established by the contour that closes it off. Riegl tells us that this is geometric abstraction. Closure is the abstract geometric line that surrounds the individual essence and subtracts it from becoming. Every figure, every individual essence's contour will be isolated. This would be the will to extract essence from nature, which Riegl calls: improving nature.[36] This is an art that presumes to improve on nature. Riegl maintains that art was never meant to imitate nature; however, there are several things it can undertake.[37] According to Riegl, it can even undertake three things: either improve nature, or spiritualize it, or re-create it.[38] Egyptian art improves nature by extracting isolated essence from the phenomenal, from becoming.

Second characteristic: If the Egyptian will-to-art is to extract essence, by what means will it do so? Riegl says it's via surface-level transcription. The tool Egyptian art uses to reveal individual essences is the flat surface. Warding off the accidental, the changeable, or becoming means suppressing spatial relations by transforming them into planimetric relations, that is, pinning them down onto a plane. Egyptian art uses the contour to isolate the form onto a plane. Let's take that literally. You sense that it all comes down to space. What is this planned space [*espace planifié*]? Indeed, variations emerge, becoming emerges through depth, through spatial relationships. Open spatial relationships are suppressed to give way to a planning [*planification*] of the surface. The aesthetic relationship is the one on the plane [*sur le plan*].[39] On the plane, the contour isolates the form or the individual essence. Contour is the geometric line. The figure is the individual essence, and the contour isolates the individual figure onto the plane. How is it translated? All the relations are planned, meaning that, for the Egyptian artist, form and ground absolutely, positively must be on the same plane; they must be equally close to each other and equally close to ourselves, the viewers. The Egyptian approach fortifies itself. We grasp both form and ground on the same plane.

What does that mean concretely? In concrete terms, it is already the bas-relief. Egyptian art is essentially bas-relief or things amounting to bas-relief. What's the opposite of bas-relief? Its opposite is high relief. Bas-relief is when the relief is barely distinct from the ground. You take in form and ground on the same plane.[40]

So no shadow or very little shadow, no modeling. No overlapping figures. This agrees with the Egyptian will-to-art. As an example, no overlapping figures, almost a law in Egyptian art. Indeed, if figures are individual essences set off by a contour, having figures overlap would be a fundamental flaw. If form and ground are on the same plane, there are no overlapping figures. The figures overlap insofar as there are distinct planes. Having overlapping figures already implies an art capable of distinguishing between different planes. Is it because the Egyptians didn't know how to make figures overlap? Was it a lack of know-how? Not at all. It went so far that sometimes, although in fact, in very rare instances, figures did overlap. In what cases? Among other things, in battle scenes and with rows of prisoners in particular, as if having figures overlap referred us to a world of variation and becoming suitable only for those who have lost their essence.[41]

High relief is when the relief is much more distinctive, with a contrast between ground and foreground, as a result of which you can almost imagine them turning. Anyway, there is a new breakthrough, to circulate around a statue, but is this a new breakthrough or a shift in artistic will? Bas-relief is characteristically Egyptian. You might object that there are many Egyptian statues one can walk around. Sure. But consider the circumstances. Just as there are figures that overlap, fine, but shouldn't we note that it's mainly with rows of prisoners as if they'd been relegated to the world of phenomena? So, strictly speaking, they possessed the know-how for this, but it ran counter to their will-to-art. Bas-relief implies rejecting shadow, rejecting modeling, rejecting overlap, rejecting depth. Form and ground belong on the same plane. These rejections do not stem from a lack of know-how [*savoir-faire*] but from the positive efforts of the will-to-create [*vouloir-faire*].

What would prove this? Riegl is brilliant as always. For example, he analyzes the evolution of the folds in clothing. He says, look at the folds in Egyptian bas-relief. It's enough to compare Egyptian and Greek folds. Riegl has some great passages on this. He writes: notice how the fold truly falls, as if it were pasted down [*figé*]. "Pasted down" isn't a reproach. The fold of Egyptian clothing is completely pasted down, and its rule is not to pile on layers. Riegl also provides reproductions and analyzes the lining, that is, tucked up at the bottom of a dress, forming a double layer, how all of that is essentially flattened out on the same plane. There is no grooving deep enough to cast a shadow. It's a flattened fold, as if the fold were treated by a process of ironing.[42]

Riegl starts to wax lyrical: compare this with the Greek fold. Ah, the Greek fold is something quite different. The dancer leaps, and how is she draped? Ah, such a different sense of the fold's harmony! Now, along the chest, the fold is curved, following a kind of a law of proportion. Let's say immediately: following a module containing internal, variable relations. Observe the suppleness of the Greek fold. Does that mean the Greeks knew how to do something the Egyptians didn't? By no means. Not that saying so would be wrong, just that it would be meaningless. What could we say quite simply? They certainly didn't interpret clothing in the same way. What could we say about two opposite types of clothing? Here I'm getting away from Riegl, but as this is totally his idea, I'm not really away from him at all. What is [Egyptian] clothing,[43] this clothing where an edge is folded back onto another, the fold is flattened out as if it were ironed? We should call it crystalline clothing. It's as if [Egyptian] bodies are clothed in crystal. What about Greek drapery or clothing? It's organic clothing. The laws have changed. Egyptian folds obey a crystalline law. The Greek fold obeys organic law.[44]

Then there are still other kinds of folds. If we went through the history of the fold, we'd have to go through all of the Middle Ages. The fold has an important role to play in Christian painting. At a certain point, we'd see that clothing changes in nature; it's no longer organic, for example, in the seventeenth century. I won't get into it here—we're just flagging things for later—but we can say that clothing ceases to be organic in order to become purely optical. It's as if random folds in seventeenth-century painting, as if the fold-marks [*pli-trait*] are no long fold-lines [*pli-ligne*]. With the Greeks, it's still a harmonious line. There'd be a long history and all sorts of variations in clothing or in the fold in painting.

Is it a coincidence that Riegl specifically says that all Egyptian laws are crystalline, geometric laws? Our first characteristic was the closed-off individual essence. Our second characteristic is that form and ground are henceforth necessarily on the same plane. Form is apprehended on the same plane as the ground. Then what is the contour? Insofar as form and ground are taken up on the same plane, contour is independent of form. Contour is autonomous. It's the geometric contour; it's independent from organic form. In other words, it stands on its own. Why? Because it's the boundary shared by form and ground on the same plane. It doesn't depend directly on the form, nor on the ground. It separates and reunites form and ground, the two indissolubly. It unites by separating; it separates by reuniting. Where does it reunite them and where does it separate them? On the very same plane. The contour's autonomy. The contour is crystalline-geometric. As a result, Egyptian bas-relief or painting has three distinct elements: the calm ground, since it's empty, devoid of any phenomenal matter; the individual form, stable, eternal essence; the geometric contour that both separates the one from the other and joins them together on the same plane. This is the crystalline-geometric world.

What makes us Egyptian? We're all Egyptian because, in a way, the Egyptians established three fundamental elements of painting that we can call: ground, figure, and contour. You'll tell me, but that's too simplistic. No, not really. What allows us to rediscover Egypt in our paintings? Perhaps this effort that is no less important than its inverse (we don't even know where its inverse comes from; I'm looking for what's Egyptian), this effort that endeavors through all painting to minimize the difference between planes. It's a pretty recent development or innovation in painting, a delightful development known as shallow depth.[45]

[*Interruption of the recording, then some inaudible interventions that Deleuze does not pursue,* time stamp: 1:52:28–1:53:35.]

DELEUZE: I'm coming back to a painter I talked about the last time, Bacon, because for me, he's a particularly striking example. What impresses me immediately in his paintings? Granted it's not Egyptian art, but what allows us to claim that Bacon is an Egyptian?[46] Consider a large majority of Bacon's paintings. You see three distinct elements, much more distinct—in my view—than with any other painter today. To recognize a Bacon painting or Bacon's approach, you'll find right away that he's a painter for whom the ground is made up of fields [*aplats*]. Straight off, you can see fields and sections of fields. The field is more or less varied. Sometimes it's a completely uniform field, which renders the ground figure, [sometimes with distinctions?][47] in the field that are very fine, but no longer simply monotone or monochrome, a monochrome field. Then you have a Figure, one that's always quite athletic, contorted. Obviously, it isn't Egyptian, but it's just as clear as an Egyptian essence [*FBLS*, 99–100 UM; 122–24 C]. And then you have a third element.

For an example, I'll use the cover of this book.[48] So, you have the region of the fields, for instance, this purple field, a yellow field, and then there's the third element, which is this strange round area, this lovely round area here on the door. Generally speaking, Bacon is much more classical: he puts round areas around the Figure's feet. Now that should tell us something about this history regarding the enduring persistence of Egyptian elements. If there's something more important still, even as far as color regimes are concerned, [it's the halo]. After all, it wasn't out of piety that Christian painters focused so much on the halo. You can distinguish between a pictorial halo and a religious halo, even if it's the same. It's clear that they took great pleasure in their halos.[49] The Byzantines were no strangers to halos—a halo really is something! It can be a fantastic burst of color, it can be a fantastical light source. Halos have to do with modulation.

But primarily what are they? A halo is a certain state of a thing that begins with Egypt, namely, the contour that's independent of form. What comes to occupy it is what's left of a contour independent of form. The form of the head is lodged in the halo-contour. The halo distinguishes between form and ground, though it might be on the same plane, or sometimes there are different planes. At that point, while that's changed, the independent contour that relates form to ground and ground to form will live on in the halo. It's as if, in this age of atheism, the halo for Bacon serves to encircle a foot, an unbearable insult to any pious soul: a halo around the feet instead of around the head, but that carries out the same principle of the independent contour. And in what sense is it modern in Bacon's work? All modern painting went through this. On close inspection of this Figure, you see that normally it would be a case—we'll come back to this later—of so-called shallow depth, achieved by something other than perspective.[50] But here, that isn't what matters; it's really the separation of three elements. To my knowledge, I think no living painter goes as far as Bacon does in keeping three pictorial elements separated: Figure, contour, ground. By transforming the entire ground into a field [*aplat*], by isolating the Figure and the contour as relating field-to-Figure and Figure-to-field onto what's presumably the same plane, or nearly the same plane. If this is modern painting, it's because you can easily see that what ultimately interests him by means of these three elements are the regimes of color. What matters here is a certain way of modulating color. There will be one modulation when it comes to the field, a very different modulation with the Figure, and finally, the halo's role, the contour's role in allowing for a sort of exchange between colors.

That obviously wasn't the point for the Egyptians. But you could say that a painter like Bacon revives the three elements of bas-relief, such that when reading Bacon's interviews, you'll happen upon a rather curious passage where Bacon says, I'd really like to do sculpture. But each time I want to do it, I would hardly get started when I'd get the feeling that the ideas I had in sculpture were precisely what I did better in painting. As a result, I gave up sculpture and lost any desire to pursue it. This is odd. He's telling us textually, I wanted to do sculpture, but my conception of sculpture, in fact, is my painting in which my sculpting had already been addressed in such a way that I cannot sculpt.[51]

Let's go back to the Egyptians. A bas-relief is actually the transition between painting and sculpture. Is colored bas-relief sculpture? Is it painting? It's not paint on canvas, okay, but it is wall painting. It's really at the boundary between sculpture and painting. Indeed, there are problems that painting and sculpture share in common. And some of their commonality is guaranteed through bas-relief. As Bacon continues, he says, here is the sculpture I dream about. He says, there would be three elements. That's not me messing with the text; that's textually what he says.[52] The first element would be "armature," and then there would be the "Figure." Furthermore, I'd be able to move the Figure around on top of the armature.[53] By all accounts, the sort of sculpture he's describing as his wish in sculpture, in fact, works like a movable bas-relief, where the figures would be mobile on the wall. He says, my figures would look like they're rising out of pools.[54] Indeed, there's a painting by Bacon that contains these three elements; it's incredible. There's a sidewalk as the field [*aplat*], a sort of really stocky, mean bulldog coming out of a pool.[55] There are three elements: Figure, ground/field, and contour: the pool. The contour [has] become independent, and the Figure comes out of the pool onto the same plane as the field, and the pool relates the Figure to the field, the field to the Figure.

How is he not Egyptian? It's interesting that he tells us, I couldn't do sculpture because I had already achieved what I wanted to do in painting. I won't get anything else from sculpture. Sculpture is how he wanted to achieve it, but it's through painting that he pulled it off. In other words: he can no longer be Egyptian because no one can be Egyptian anymore. You have to make do with what you've got. Of course, there are painters who've returned to bas-relief. Does that reflect a present-day will-to-art? I don't know. But it's clear what it means. In what sense is Bacon Egyptian? I think he's truly the modern painter who maintains the greatest independence and, how to say it, "equiplanarity" of the three Egyptian pictorial elements: the ground/field, the figure/essence, and the independent contour. Let me come back to Riegl. You see why, in the authentically Egyptian world, that's fully realized in bas-relief that, in fact, minimizes shadows, modeling, depth, overlapping figures, or even does away with them altogether, and all that related in such a way that form and ground are on the same plane. That's what we're calling geometric-crystalline law. You'll grant me that this works for bas-relief.

At this point, here's an objection: What about the statues you can walk around? And their houses? Were they ultimately intending to suppress volume? Yes, they were constantly trying to avoid volume because volume belongs to space, it's the matrix of becoming, the matrix of that which changes. It's shadow, it's relief, it's high relief, it's modeling, and so on. It runs counter to the world flattened out [*mis à plat*]; that's Egypt's accomplishment. How do you get away from volume outside bas-relief? Riegl's answer is great. He says: the pyramid is an ingenious effort to exorcise the cube, everything that's in there, everything about the cube: shadow, and maybe also light, modeling, the inside, and so on—everything that can't belong in a flat world.[56] The cube is like the primary expression of relations in space to translate them onto a single plane. This is the pyramid's process for doing away with the cube. In what sense does the pyramid do away with the cube? As religious monuments, the pyramids house the pharaoh's burial chamber. But when you look at a pyramid, not only would you not know that this fantastic armature was made for a cube, you could not know this. Furthermore, it wouldn't make sense to say that was its purpose. The pyramid is the process whereby the burial cube, that is, the cube of death, is hidden, subtracted. It's replaced, improved upon by the pyramid (here, the Rieglian concept of "correction" as improvement fully applies). In fact, what exactly is a pyramid? Instead of a cube, it presents you with one side unifying three well-defined isosceles triangles, with this movement, this kind of slope, which is just the plane's tribute to space, a way of transcribing spatial relationships into planimetric relationships.[57] This is what the pyramid is all about: translating volume relationships into surface relationships. Isn't that beautiful? Lovely, it's a lovely thought.

By comparison, what is Greek architecture? Greek architecture will be the explosion, the emancipation of the cube. You already sense that this opens up quite a few possibilities. Since you've been doing this so well up to this point, I'd like for these reflections to continue within you. I'll add a famous phrase from Cézanne: "Treat nature in terms of the cylinder, the sphere, and the cone, with everything put in perspective."[58] Many scholars have commented on how mysterious it is that Cézanne left cubes off his list. Why did he leave cubes out? Because, when you consider Greek art, the cubic form is the foundation for spatial relations.[59] Think about someone like Michelangelo, for example. The figure's spatial coordinates form a cube. It's been that way ever since the Greeks. The Greek temple is fundamentally cubic.[60] If Cézanne comes along and excludes the cube, it's because his primary concern lies elsewhere. Not with the Egyptians, nor the Greeks, nor with the Renaissance, and so on. So we have to appreciate how important that is. But what is an Egyptian house? Their houses aren't pyramids, right, but they're like the bases of pyramids, that is, it's a house made of slanted trapezoids.[61] And what is the decorative motif? It's the famous concave palmette. Really, the concave palmette is minimally raised, as raised as it's allowed to be. The plane will be on a slant. The pyramidal plane was a slanted plane and one that called for, or had a decorative correlate in, palmettes or half-palms.

And again Riegl, in a particularly brilliant moment, tries to demonstrate how the palmette undergoes a series of transformations in the Greek world to yield something totally different: the famous acanthus leaves on Greek temples. While from the perspective of reproducing nature, you see why acanthus is very important. The acanthus is a weed. What the hell is a weed doing in temples? If the goal was imitation of something, obviously the Greeks wouldn't have chosen a weed as tribute to the gods.[62] What Riegl demonstrates beautifully is that, qualms with figuration aside, the acanthus leaf is like a three-dimensional projection of the palmette. This is from *Problems of Style.*[63] It's really beautiful. This is where I'll wrap things up: it's not restricted to bas-relief; pyramids and Egyptian houses are equally motivated by what Riegl characterizes as the Egyptian will-to-art, namely: form and ground are presented and are perceived on one and the same plane. As a result, the space that beckons to the Egyptians is one where form and ground are on the same plane.

Hence, our final point: What does this signal-space look like? What does it evoke in us? What in us corresponds to this signal-space? We'll see next time.

THE HAPTIC AND THE THIRD EYE

SESSION 6

19 May 1981

You'll recall that we were in the middle of our analysis of Egyptian space, but I'll pursue a brief aside on these color illustrations [*schémas*] [drawn on the board] that I will need next time, and that we'll already have considered.[1] By explaining them to you, we'll have these details in mind, and I won't have to draw them again. You'll see it in these two figures: one is an equilateral triangle, the other is a circle. The former is known as Goethe's color triangle, the other is the so-called chromatic circle.[2] I'll try to work through Goethe's great propositions to make sure you can learn something from this.[3] Apologies to those who already know all this.[4]

The first proposition: Goethe starts with a very important theme. By understanding this, perhaps we'll grasp the entire development and the problems tied to color. He emphasizes the dark nature of color. That doesn't mean that he privileges dark colors; that would miss the point severely. Dark colors exist, but when he talks about the dark nature of color, he clearly has something else in mind. Color *in general*—and not a particular one—can be said to have a dark nature, since it is the darkening of light. No doubt, it's also the illumination of black. It is the darkening of white as well as the illumination of black.[5] Darkened white is yellow; illuminated black is blue. There we have our two so-called primitive or primary colors, yellow and blue. See, here are yellow and blue in the color triangle—an equilateral triangle that itself breaks down into other equilateral triangles. Say I want to form a color triangle out of equilateral triangles; if I put them in order, I'd have my two equilateral triangles at both ends of the base, yellow and blue.[6]

Due to its dark aspect—darkened light—color is inseparable from movement. You can sense that these things are really quite rudimentary, but this is genuinely Goethe. It's not surprising that this book

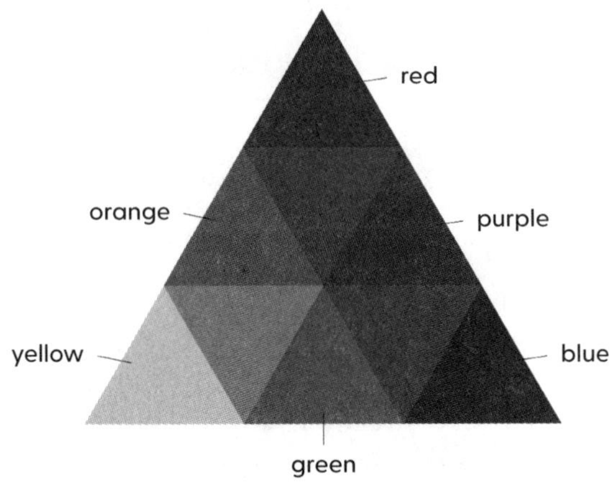

Goethe's triangle, or a genesis of color.

is still a basic treatise on colors. [Color is inseparable from a movement], yet it must still be determined.[7] You see that what he did is already extraordinary: he started with white and black, but he sort of changes direction. If you layer a ray of light in depth and if you layer white and black in depth, you find the whole field of colors sort of spreads out, gaining independence. I think that Goethe's deep concern is how color spreads out and becomes independent in relation to light, in relation to white and black.

And from this dark stage—darkened light, which implies an illuminated black—all color will extend, initially in the form of yellow and blue, but here's what I'm saying: this entails movement, already being dynamic. With yellow as darkened light, blue as illuminated black, there's already a whole dynamic here. What do we call this nascent dynamism, this time not in terms of white and black, since we already have two colors here, but in terms of yellow and blue? This is the dynamism of emergent color. Goethe has several names for it: intensification, saturation, darkening. Why darkening? Due to the dark nature of color. The intensification of yellow or its darkening tends toward red. It's a simple experiment: you apply several layers of yellow. In overlaying color on color, you obtain and you can discern yellow's dynamic tendency toward red. Thus, you darken yellow.

On the other hand—I think there's something quite devilish going on here in Goethe's text—you also tend toward red when you soften blue. What do I mean by softening blue? Blue is illuminated black. If you say: I'm softening blue, you mean: I'm softening the illumination. In other words, blue softened into black releases this same tendency toward red. What's really important is how he doesn't view darkening and illuminating as contradictory. Color has a dark nature that is at work when you darken yellow no less than when you illuminate blue, since you're illuminating an illumination when you illuminate blue. Thus, yellow tends toward red as it intensifies; blue tends toward red as it intensifies. The pure red, what we would call magenta [*pourpre*],[8] will be—and pay close attention to Goethe's terminology here—*fusion,* the point of fusion between yellow and blue at the point of maximum intensification. This leads him to say that magenta or pure red is the ideal satisfaction.[9] I mix yellow and blue, and I have green. See the extent to which red and green aren't symmetrical. Goethe says that green is the point of real satisfaction. Red is the point of ideal satisfaction or the point of fusion; green is the point of real satisfaction, or mixture.[10]

So, I can make the apex of my little triangle red, as the point of maximum intensification, and for my intermediate triangle, between yellow and blue, I can make it green. With green, I start over again. The triangle is genetic. I insist that the first main point is this: there's a genesis of colors in Goethe's triangle. Green gave me an idea. Green emerged as the combination of yellow and blue. Now I just have to mix yellow and red, which gives me orange, [above, in the upper triangle].[11] Then I just have to mix red and blue, which yields purple. And there, I've generated my six basic colors—I'm emphasizing this because often, when you read Goethe, they're listed as a function of the image of the color triangle. It's not just that there are colors—three primary colors (yellow, blue, red) and three binary colors (orange, purple, green). I'm sensing that, in Goethe's text, the color triangle expresses this genesis.

Listed in order, you have: the emergence of yellow, the emergence of blue, the twofold emergence of red via the intensification of both yellow and blue, the emergence of green via mixing, carrying on mixing through [*indistinct word*].—Imagine if I had colored chalk, that'd be lovely.—So, what's left? I still have combinations, but that will be complicated. That's the reason why we will need the chromatic circle later. The yellow-green combination, here;

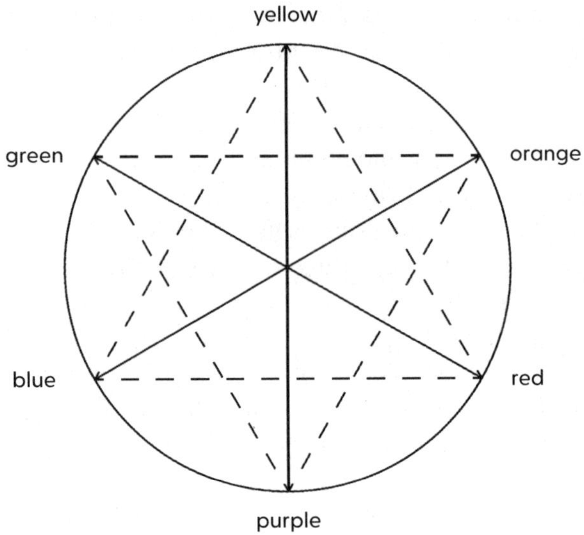

Goethe's chromatic circle, or a structural deduction of color.

the green–blue combination; the orange–purple combination. And that's how the color triangle is completed. It's simple but elegant. Once again, I think [one must not read it] as a fully complete triangle. It's a genetic triangle. Moreover, you can't build it up gradually; I think you're led to construct it in order. [*Deleuze indicates the schema's order with a numbered list.*] That's what the color triangle is.

[*Following an inaudible intervention.*] You could add this: color's exterior—light-dark, white-black—and notice the strength here: how color blooms out of its exterior. That's the emergence of the different colors' independence. This is a genesis. The triangle is genetic. Any issues?

As for the chromatic circle, it is structural. I am starting off from yellow. There's a reason I'm starting with yellow. I'll put it at the top of my circle, and from there, I'll establish the first diametric opposition. What is the diametric opposite of yellow? Yellow is one of the three primitive or primary colors: yellow, blue, red.[12] The opposite of yellow is the combination of the two other primitive colors. A diametric opposition would be between one of these primitive colors and the combination of the other two. This diametric opposition is well known as the relationship between complementary colors. What are two complementary colors? Two complementary colors are such that one is a primitive color, and the other is made by combining the other two. So yellow is diametrically opposed to the combination of blue and red, that is, purple. Notice that this circle is no longer genetic at all. It begins with the problem of diametric opposition; it begins by drawing a structure.

This is why I think it's obvious that, listed in order, the chromatic circle is lifeless if you haven't first worked through the color triangle (without adding that I have a great preference for the color triangle). [*Laughter.*] So you've got your first diametric opposition, yellow and purple. Purple as the combination of blue and red forces us to situate on our circle—since you know already, having seen the triangle, that there are six sections, the three primary colors and the three binary colors—[*An inaudible passage about the distribution of colors in the circle drawn on the board,* time stamp: 22:07–22:33]. It's no longer at all a genesis; it's a structural deduction whereby you situate your two other sections along the periphery: blue-yellow with green as the intermediary, yellow-red with orange [as intermediary]. Henceforth, you can read your diametric opposition: just as yellow is diametrically opposed to purple according to the law of complementary colors, red is diametrically opposed to green, since red is a primitive color diametrically opposed to the combination of the other two: the combination of the other two (the combination between yellow and blue, or green). So, the diametric opposition between red and green, the diametric opposition between blue and orange (since orange is yellow-and-red diametrically opposed with the third primitive color). I'm almost done.

A first type of relationship between colors is provided by the chromatic circle via diametric oppositions. It's the theme of complementary colors. Goethe's dotted lines suggest that there are other relationships,[13] when the relations between colors follow along chords and no longer across the diameter.[14] Diametric oppositions, [in Goethe's terminology, which will have considerable influence],[15] are harmonious combinations between yellow and purple, orange and blue, red and green. They're complementary relationships. We are leaving behind the diameters in order to consider chords, two types of chords. You select two colors by passing over an intermediary. These must be called the big chords. These are what Goethe will call "characteristic combinations."[16] That's what I've written with dots; the list of characteristic combinations will be: green–orange, orange–purple. You've drawn a chord in the chromatic circle such that you've brought together green and orange by skipping yellow. That's the big chord.

We then move on to the second characteristic combination: orange–purple, skipping over red. Third combination: purple and green, skipping blue. In the other direction: combining blue–red, skipping purple; red–yellow, skipping orange; blue–yellow, skipping green. And you have your network of so-called characteristic combinations. And lastly, what I didn't include there to keep it from getting too complicated, but Goethe does include it, are what he'll call noncharacteristic combinations.[17] These are the small chords where you don't skip colors; you just skip the intermediary between two colors. And the noncharacteristic combinations include yellow–orange, orange–red, red–purple, purple–blue, blue–green, green–yellow. You have your structural set. The triangle expresses in genetic fashion what the chromatic circle expresses structurally. My feeling is, and it's just a feeling: the circle is dead. Although you might make it spin . . . Why is this important? It's not just theory; it's the basis for all theory. It's not entirely certain that this is adequate; we'll see that it's not adequate. Was it necessary to wait for Goethe? We'll see the extent to which this topic is complicated. Why was it created at that point in time, and so forth?

Delacroix made his palette into a chromatic timer, that is, a clock. You might say that he wanted to assign hours to the chromatic circle.[18] It is already symbolic. Being necessarily structural, it is symbolic. [*A brief inaudible passage*, time stamp: 30:09–30:15.] But anyway, you could say the reverse. [*A brief student intervention*, time stamp: 30:18–30:27.] What was Delacroix up to with this? For painters, it's very important to put things in order; they were all very orderly. Sometimes, they get photographed in disorderly studios, but that's something else. He situated his diametrical colors, and then he surrounded that with derived or blended colors, and then that really created a chromatic timer [*chronomètre*]. That's a first anecdote. This might be like exercises. If I were a painter, I'm sure that I'd necessarily find that interesting . . . [*Long inaudible passage, an interchange with students near the board*, time stamp: 31:21–32:18.]

A painter who hates a color is a great painter. So, based on these schemas, how might a painter arrange colors on the palette? That's a first practical problem.

A second practical problem: What does it mean when a painter hates a color? For example: Mondrian and green. Abomination. A painter who detests green. That's one of his main reasons for leaving New York because New York is the only city in the world where there are no trees . . . [*Inaudible passage,* time stamp: 33:03–34:04.][19] There are colors missing from a painter's palette. It's just as interesting to ask a painter about the colors that are missing as about the colors they use. You could have all sorts of practical exercises. When a color is named after a painter . . . This isn't [based on] laws or norms, especially with the genetic element of colors. It's in this way that you make your basic choices. What's more, it's so genetic that this triangle has thickness. It has strata; it's completely stratified. It has to be read perpendicularly. If the genetic color triangle had a structure, it would be a perpendicular structure.

The first stratum: it bursts forth from light and from darkness. That's the theme with color's dark nature. What evidence is available that color has a dark nature? You'll find this nature at the level of this kind of emergence from white and from black. If you rotate your chromatic circle, you get the famous grey from white and black. Here you have the deepest stratum: color is emerging from light and darkness. What you must sense is that the space of light and the space of color are not the same. There isn't just any color given; that's what "chromatic color" implies. What is the principle of the relativity of colors? A color is only determined in relation to neighboring colors, the color of context. In this way, color is created. This first stratum emerges from darkness and light, emerges from grey, grey being understood as white and black.

The second stratum. It starts taking on its independence from this ground [*fond*]. Light and darkness, black and white, are color's *ground.* Color emerges from this ground in the form of yellow, blue, and their shared intensification: red. At this point, relationships between colors are formed, irreducible to the light-dark relationship. While still affecting color in the form of light and dark colors, the light-darkness relations by no means exhaust color relations. This is what is called "value relations" [*rapports de valeur*] in color itself, the relationship between light and darkness. But color exists only through independent relationships, not between value relations but between *colors* [*tons*], relations of colors with each other at the same level of saturation. A typical example is the relationship between complements [*FBLS*, 106–7 UM; 131–33 C].[20]

Let's go over a brief history of colorism.[21] What is colorism? These are useful terms. Riegl proposed a distinction between polychromy and colorism.[22] Polychromy refers to any detail or any use of color (which will be extraordinarily complex and extraordinarily rich) where color is still subordinate to something else. It can be subordinate to form. You arrange your colors organically according to the form. Egyptian art and Greek art are classic examples of polychromy. Color can also be subordinate to light. With any painting, you actually had to distinguish, if only vaguely, between a luminist tendency and a colorist tendency. Luminists are those who achieve color *through* light, and colorists are those who achieve light *through* a treatment of color. Rembrandt, for example, whose works are marvelous, is rightly hailed as among the greatest luminists to the extent that already it's no longer polychromy; it's something else. But it isn't colorism either because it isn't color for its own sake. It can develop all of its value relations; it cannot develop the full extent of its tonality relations.

And regarding the chromatic circle, Goethe indeed strongly emphasizes the following theme: based on the chromatic circle—and this accounts for why there's a movement, a dynamism to color—each color tends to evoke the totality of the chromatic circle.[23] More or less. Here, coefficients of speed or slowness might occur. Each color suggests the chromatic circle's totality, first, via its diametric opposition. Red will suggest green, and it's only in your eye. One complement suggests the other. Recall that famous experiment in every introduction to color: you stare at a color, and then, once the color is taken away, your eye suggests the complementary color. For example, red suggests green.

If I were to attempt a brief overview of the history of colorism, I think that the first colorism is a moment in which it resides at the border of luminism. Light-color, the problems are still combined. And colors emerge from the ground. The ground becomes captivating; it's like overlaying two greys. Colors emerge from a dark ground—which goes through so many developments in the history of philosophy. And this dark color is now meant to manifest the dark nature of all colors. These colors emerge from this dark ground, which is ultimately grey on grey. However, it's not a grey grey, since there is a luminist grey from black–white and a chromatic grey from green–red, two sets of complementary colors.

So, in an early colorism, colors indeed emerge from this dark ground, which expresses the overlay of both greys. As vivid as they are, they attest to their dark nature. Starting from there, all of colorism's movement, all of colorism's dynamism, will increasingly assert itself for itself. What will that entail?

[*Interruption of the recording,* time stamp: 46:32.]

How does one reach this vivacity that expresses the relationship between colors? How does one achieve bright colors, since only bright colors express the relationship between colors? It will occur in stages. Just looking at French painting, I'll use my little sequence of three stages. There's the great moment that is Delacroix. What do we see in Delacroix's technique, because these are technical problems? We find something rather strange. The ground's dark color often lingers and for quite some time. It's already fully color, but dark color. Only, with Delacroix, we do get bright colors. How do the most vibrant colors get drawn out from this dark color? That's a crucial moment. Each time, it's always colorism that is born, that is reborn. [This is a problem.][24] Delacroix invents a technique that will be recognized even in his lifetime, whether people mocked him for it or instead used it themselves: it's the process of using something called "crosshatching" [*hachures*]. He will literally chop up [*hacher*] his dark color—there's no other word for it—green crosshatching, red crosshatching. It's with crosshatching that color will realize its bright aspects, in bright colors. One of Delacroix's greatest moments: give me a heap of mud, and I will bring out an exquisite color.[25] This is not a literary formula, it's what he does on the canvas. Thanks to him, what becomes possible? The unfolding of bright colors and the relationships between bright colors that, in a way, no longer depend on the dark ground from which color emerged.

It's as though Delacroix had kept [the dark ground]—well, I'm extending the dialectic a bit far; things didn't happen like this—to reach the moment when he'd no longer need it. Which takes nothing away from his masterpieces built around dark color. By isolating and heightening the relationship between bright colors without passing into dark color, the dark ground, who does that remind us of? Of course, the Impressionists. This is perhaps the first time that colorism appears in its pure form: light completely subordinate to color. This is perhaps the second time since Turner's work, Turner with his yellows. There's a really beautiful, remarkable painting by Turner called *Homage to Goethe* that is like the pictorial version of the chromatic circle.[26] For the Impressionists, there lies the problem. By the same token, what will become of Delacroix's crosshatching, which merited its name as crosshatching, since it was used to chop up the dark color? It became the well-known Impressionist element, the comma-stroke, the juxtaposition of commas. No longer crosshatching chopping up the dark color but little commas on their own. Throughout all Impressionism, there are various styles when it comes to commas: Monet's commas. That's how an expert recognizes [him]. Sometimes you're hard-pressed to [distinguish] a Pissarro from a Monet—that can happen—a little bit less for a Renoir, although there are cases. [*An inaudible passage on experts and on Van Gogh's comma,* time stamp: 52:29–52:51.] Understand that in the end, with colorism and the development of color relations and of vivacity of colors for themselves, it's as if the basic unit of painting gained its balance from a smaller unit, a kind of atomism. Delacroix's crosshatching turns into the Impressionist comma; the Impressionist comma turns into Cézanne's little dabs. [*An inaudible sequence in which Deleuze mentions Seurat's points,* time stamp: 53:25–54:06.]

[*Interruption of the course, for an apparent break,* time stamp: 54:30.]

That section is a long parenthesis we could put before or after. It serves as something to take home with you. You can read more about this in Goethe. I'd rather you read it. Well, are there any comments or additions?

A STUDENT: I read Goethe's text. It seems to be an even more complicated problem, because on the one hand, black and white are colors. He says that white is the initial genesis of darkness and that black is the extreme of darkness. So, they are colors, but at the same time, he's opposed to Newton entirely on the question of white, which is born from the chromatic circle. Goethe says: not at all. White cannot be generated from the chromatic circle; that's grey. We find this ambiguity.

DELEUZE: Absolutely. I think that the ambiguity is easily accounted for. It's what I was getting at when I said that the triangle must be interpreted genetically. In that case, color doesn't actually have an absolute beginning; rather, at the same time, white and black are both the milieu for the exteriority of color, the form of color's exteriority, which doesn't yet have any color inside, and that will be the emergence of the inside. Especially since what he reproaches Newton for, among other things—here, this would get complicated. In fact, everything in Goethe is developed against Newton.

ANNE QUERRIEN: I have the feeling about Newton that he was using the laws of optics, decomposing light through the prism. Indeed, on this very topic, you'll find in some pop science books on color the idea that the eye's three primary colors [are]—and it's what was used in television—red, green, and blue. As for television, I have the equation here for its wavelengths: it's just about 51 percent red, 39 percent green, and 10 percent blue. So, according to the color triangle, that puts television completely onto the black side. On the other hand, in an article in the Sunday *Le Monde,* there's a fascinating piece on how color images in television are coded to ensure that color broadcasts are compatible with black-and-white receivers. Instead of adding colors, these colors are subtracted, drawing them even further toward black so that black-and-white receivers can pick up color broadcasts. One would have to juxtapose techniques because it seems that the development of chiaroscuro emerges at the same time as color printing and the additive composition of colors in printing, and Delacroix and company are completely parallel to the research on color photography.

DELEUZE: Or Seurat's method, right, in pointillism, would be another technical comparison to draw with a coding of points . . .

[*A student's intervention on the impossibility of finding the number 9 in the numbering proposed by Deleuze for the chromatic circle, comments that he does not pursue,* time stamp: 59:10–1:00:45.][27]

DELEUZE: Fine, let's continue. Do you remember the point we reached? We had just defined our first Egyptian signal-space. And at the same time, this Egyptian signal-space wasn't made for painting, or, at any rate, it certainly wasn't exclusive to painting. It's even expressed formally, infinitely more directly in bas-relief. Won't this establish something long-term that's essential about painting, namely, the idea of flatness?[28] Take Greenberg, for example, whom I've already talked about. He says that painting consists in two things: flatness and the determination of flatness.[29] Maybe, but it's not entirely obvious that painting is defined by flatness. Isn't there a thickness or depth [*épaisseur*] to the canvas? There are some painters (not all) who even stake a claim on the canvas having thickness. Wouldn't his idea of painting—as flatness and the determination of flatness—in part come from a very old horizon in painting, the Egyptian horizon, an Egyptian achievement?

If we try to define Egypt's signal-space, according to Riegl, we more or less get the following formula: form and ground are taken on the same plane, flatness, that is, an equal flatness of form and ground. Form and ground are taken on the same plane, both equally close to each other and equally close to us. If I try to sum up, this provides us with Egypt's mode of presentation, as Riegl maintains. That's Egyptian bas-relief, and we saw how it could be equally true for pyramids—in a more complicated way—and this is Egyptian painting. We'll have to hang on to this idea of flatness. Was it perhaps Egypt that accomplished painting as flatness? And it doesn't go without saying that a canvas is flat. The proof, after all, lies in the many painters today who paint backward.[30] What does painting backward mean, if not that the canvas has thickness or depth? There are painters who problematize the idea of surface. There's a very important group, the Supports/Surfaces group,[31] and even various other groups. Numerous Americans continue problematizing it. But we'll leave all that aside.

Flatness won't so much be the necessary outcome of painting as it will be painting's external Egyptian horizon. Is this the expression of a will-to-art, as Riegl puts it, or is it tied to—it's all fair game, we can always dream—to certain conditions both of civilization and of nature: bas-relief's relationship to the desert, the pyramid's relationship to the desert, the eye's relationship to the desert? Doesn't this relationship specifically imply a kind of flattening of space?[32] I'm reaching something I didn't get to say last time. When Riegel tries to say what sort of vision corresponds to Egyptian space (and I'm just summarizing here), on the side of the object, there's indeed an operation of flattening. The relationships in space are transformed into planimetric relationships. Form and ground are on the same plane; this is linearity. And, as [Greenberg] asks, that is, from the fact that form and ground are taken in the same plane, what determination of linearity will emerge from this?

Coming back to what we covered at the last session: The determination of linearity that emerges from this fact about form and ground corresponds to the three elements of painting. This is precisely because form and ground are taken on the same plane, inhabit the same plane, that painting will have three elements: ground, form, and what relates ground to form and form to ground, namely, the geometrical crystalline contour. This is the geometrical crystalline law [*légalité*]. And I told you: when we happen to look at a modern canvas and are in a situation such that we're forced, subjected, led to distinguish three elements, form, ground, and contour, then we can say, "An Egyptian's been here!" [*Laughter.*]

I'm thinking of a very beautiful painting by Gauguin: *La Belle Angèle.*[33] Maybe some of you can see it in your mind's eye. What a painting! It's a very fine example (and in my opinion, it might be one of the first examples in modern painting) of what's called (I tried to state this in broad strokes) shallow depth.[34] There is indeed depth, but it's very limited. Form and ground are quite close to the same plane. What is the form? It's the head of a Breton woman named Angèle and that Gauguin was fond of, a real Breton woman! [*Laughter.*] She's depicted with her headdress. She's perfect. The ground is a field [*aplat*].[35] It isn't clear who invented this idea. Things are quite confused in the correspondence. Is it Van Gogh? Is it Gauguin? It doesn't really matter who. Or was it yet a third member of their group? They created fields [*aplats*], but to liven them up a bit, they included bouquets of flowers, like on wallpaper. Van Gogh created several portraits of a postman from Arles to whom he was quite close. There's a very fine one, among others, where the ground consists of a field that is like wallpaper. If memory serves, it's green with charming little bouquets of flowers that weave a decorative motif onto the field.[36] So the field is present. The form is the head of the Breton woman that is clearly not treated as a field.

You'll notice that there will still be one problem that runs throughout the history of painting: When someone is a colorist, what do you do about flesh? Here is the point, bizarrely, at which painting and phenomenologists really come together because both are so animated by the question of flesh, by embodiment.[37] It was the problem of flesh that led Merleau-Ponty to painting.[38] What do you do about flesh? I tracked down a very nice quote from Goethe, just to mix everything together: for flesh, the color should be totally liberated from its elementary state.[39] Flesh poses an odd problem for painting. How do you make flesh without winding up with greyness? In the case of an Impressionist's work, flesh is even more of a problem. How to treat flesh? For objects, this is no big deal, but flesh doesn't exactly give off much light. How do you prevent flesh from getting muddy? It's a tough problem. You need to treat color in a particular way. So, in *La Belle Angèle,* what's incredible is that you have two color treatments corresponding to your first two pictorial elements. Naturally, it wasn't like that with the Egyptians. That's why this is a great modern painting. I'm getting ahead of myself. One major solution to treating flesh pictorially is using what's called broken colors. What is broken color? We'll see later on. It doesn't matter. Here we're introducing a term, a new category in color. Broken color is how, for example, Van Gogh and Gauguin treat flesh.

Gauguin uses a method that a minor painter in Gauguin's day tried to bring back, and this painter called it "cloisonné."[40] You'll see that in *La Belle Angèle,* the figure is surrounded by a sort of yellow circle that'll be very important. For starters, this yellow circle unquestionably has a comic effect. Gauguin had a real sense of humor visually. He's one of the most lighthearted, yes, most comic of painters. When it's bracketed off in cloisonné, *La Belle Angèle* starts to look like a head on a cheese container. It's cropped like she's a Breton mascot for Camembert. This yellow line is great because that's what brings out the figure's broken color and the ground's color field [*ton aplat*]. At the same time, that'll also be a crucial component of shallow depth that will situate the form and ground *almost* on the same plane. When you see a painting like this—or even in the large majority of Bacon's paintings—you'll find three elements that stand out, which are: a field for the ground; the Figure, always treated in broken colors; and the autonomous contour referring the form to the ground and the ground to the form. In Bacon's work, contour is no longer mere cloisonné, but takes on something like traits of volume, of surface or even of volume, namely, a kind of mat [*tapis*] that is in a color relationship with the grounding field's color. There are indeed three colors in Bacon's work. There is a kind of mat or ring in the middle of which—or inside, at least—the Figure is contained or propped up. As a result, you get three regimes of color: a contour-regime, secured by the mat or ring; a ground-regime, secured by the field; a Figure-regime, secured by the broken colors, and these three regimes work together. You can declare: homage to Egypt.

This kind of return to Egypt clearly means returning to Egypt by thoroughly non-Egyptian means, since now we rediscover the three Egyptian elements through different approaches to color. You see what Greenberg meant by linearity and the determination of linearity: in fact, the Egyptians provide for linearity, that is, the identical plane shared by both form and ground, and thereby determine this linearity with three elements: form, ground, and autonomous contour. If you've understood that, and that this matter wasn't settled by the Egyptians, that it can live on if a modern painter can recover and resurrect Egypt via non-Egyptian means, then you've understood generally what happens constantly in art.

There's one last thing to be done to wrap up this topic of Egypt. We've defined the objective elements: the same plane for the form and ground; the three elements constituting the determination of flatness: the ground field, the form, the bas-relief figure and the geometrical crystalline contour that carries the form to the ground, and vice versa. What remains of your Egyptian eye? It goes without saying that Egyptians have lost this eye. Today's Egyptians no longer have this eye, unless they do have it. I don't know, after all. Here's how Riegl defines the Egyptian eye, but you'll see that the Egyptian eye can be defined only according to its correlate, that is, according to Egypt's signal-space. What will the Egyptian eye be? And so, in Riegl's crucial text, *Late Roman Art Industry*,[41] in the first edition we find something very simple but which comes across as difficult. The first edition tells us, this Egyptian space is a closed-in space. It's a space that invites a nearsighted vision. We might want to respond:

that does not really stem from a will-to-art. This is a factor coming from the desert and from light. One's view is fundamentally closed in; in Egypt, you look from close up.

[*A student from outside intervenes to announce a forthcoming general assembly, after which the recording is interrupted,* time stamp: 1:19:30–1:20:50.]

DELEUZE: I'd like there to be a newsletter with updates on the [government's] "late-stage proposals" [*projets très avancés*]. Everyone in their respective fields is up to speed with proposals that are already in a "late-stage." For example, the university project was catastrophic. It's not hard to understand. The university project consisted in bypassing university councils. Our knee-jerk reaction is always that no one gives a shit about the university council. But hold on, that depends: What will you replace it with? Credits would have been distributed directly to the UERS.[42] Which, quite obviously, placed the UERS—which in fact are complacent about this—into the ministry's hands because there was no longer any university structure.[43] Now that was a terrible proposal. Any time I talk to somebody in a given field, oddly enough, they confirm this. Not long ago I met with a banker. Nothing he told me came as a surprise. He said, you know, there was a "late-stage proposal" to blow up collective bargaining agreements in the banks. It'd be interesting to get a rundown so that we might know the "late-stage proposals" going into effect one or two years from now. And, for me, that's what the election is about.[44] What were they plotting? This is no joke!

[*An exchange occurs between Deleuze and students regarding the upcoming general assembly, followed by a return to the session,* time stamp: 1:22:21–1:24:36.]

DELEUZE: Riegl is trying to describe what sort of eye corresponds to Egyptian space. In the first edition, he says, it's a nearsighted vision. How does a nearsighted eye behave? He says, form and ground both occupy the same plane, and I—the viewer, with my eye—I'm just as close. It's an eye that literally acts like a kind of *touch* [*tact*]. It's a tactile eye. What we get from this passage in Riegl is that this is not a metaphor. Moreover, Riegl is pointing out two of the eye's functions. You have optical vision and tactile vision. The tactile eye isn't an eye that's supplemented by actually touching [*le toucher*], like when I use my hands to confirm something I've seen, when I touch a face, for example. It's the eye insofar as it acts as touch. This passage from Riegl is still ambiguous. It's only in the second edition that he comes out and uses a particular term.[45] He has to coin a complicated term to avoid confusion. He says there are two kinds of vision. There's optical vision and there's vision that he calls *haptic*. He borrows the word from the Greeks, *háptô*, which means to touch. The eye's touch, a haptic sense of sight.[46] The haptic sense of sight would be a use of sight that's no longer an optical use, that is, no longer distanced vision. However, the haptic vision is a close-up sight that grasps form and ground on the same plane, equally close to each other.[47] Before we take a break, I'm thinking: There are a lot of problems here!

We'll make use of this word, *haptic*. After all, this might be a really interesting category because painting is intended for the eye, right? But which eye? I might suggest that painting perhaps causes an eye within the eye to develop. Painting might have something to do with what we'd literally have to call "the third eye." Is it possible that we have two eyes for optical vision, and then a third haptic eye? In that case, is it painting that produces the haptic eye? I'm jumping ahead here; we're no longer dealing with the Egyptians, you understand. What would this haptic eye be?[48] Let's link this up with everything we've covered today. Light is the optical eye; light solicits an optical eye. Perhaps. I don't know really. But color? Doesn't color solicit a haptic eye? Wasn't the topic of our entire earlier discussion: how a haptic eye is reconstituted out of optical eyes?

In a spirited letter, Gauguin says, the painter's eye is in heat.[49] I don't remember what page, but when it comes up, it's pretty funny. What is this painter's eye—this eye that Cézanne himself claimed turns all red? I come back home, and my eyes are red, I can't see anymore.[50] Eyes so red they can't see anything: isn't the painter's eye, Gauguin's eye in heat, a really very strange use of vision? Isn't it the reconstitution of a haptic eye, the Egyptian eye, the third eye? I'm saying "third eye" not because it's in the brain. It isn't in the brain; it's in the nervous system, but it's there in the middle between the two other eyes. That's where the painter is located. Wouldn't color be a totally independent and original way of reconstituting haptic sight that the Egyptians had achieved in an entirely different way? The Egyptians achieved haptic vision by placing form and ground on the same plane and by producing three elements: form, ground, and geometrical crystalline contours. But, for us, haven't we recovered an Egyptian eye through non-Egyptian means, namely, through colorism? Isn't the haptic eye the eye that draws the inherent relationships of color from an optical external milieu—light, white, and black? All these sorts of questions we leave hanging because we now stumble upon the question: the Egyptian world appears to be dead. It can only be resurrected by totally independent means. What made the Egyptian world die off?

[*Interruption of the session for a break,* time stamp: 1:33:02.]

During our break, a lot of you were saying that you've been feeling unwell and worn down by this weather, so I should just cave in and shorten class. [*Cheers and applause.*] I continue to hold on to the expression "linearity" and the "determination of linearity." Once again, we situated it in Egyptian space. Linearity is the plane. Determination of linearity is the plane's three elements: ground, form, and contour. What takes place for this space somehow to be overturned? Once again, this space will be so thoroughly overturned that you'll be able to find traces of Egypt only through completely [different] means. This will be a resurrected Egypt. We're putting Riegl aside. We'll come back to him, but here we're asking a question for ourselves, and as I'm always trying to demonstrate, there's a sense in which we have no choice. What can occur concerning this flat space in which form and ground are taken on the same plane, with three elements? What is the accident? Accidents are accidents. Events are events. What is the accident or the event? You have your Egyptian space. Bas-relief. However slight this may be, an earthquake occurs. Imagine that the plane is splintered, but with such an aftermath, it's insane! The plane is splintered: a foreground draws closer, a background pulls back, even if only slightly. What occurs is the disjunction of planes [*FBLS*, 101–2 UM; 125–26 C]. From this point forward—with all this open to correction ultimately—there will be a foreground and a background. This is not something huge, as slight as it is. The disjunction of planes is what causes us to shift into other signal-spaces.

If I have the disjunction between planes—to move along quickly—what can come of it? I'm trying to think through the possibilities. A space in which planes are disjointed, and which is essentially organized based on the foreground, that's a first possibility. This becomes the signature of this space, namely, a distinction between planes, but it's the foreground that is *determinant.* I'm still using the concept of determination. So that'll be great, this foreground-determined space. Then why not the other way around? Let's try to imagine this, a background-determined space. Well, our reply is: no, really, *that's* the one we want—each time, there's something new, it's *that* one we want—because a background-determined space ought to be great. Just consider this for a second: everything emerges from the ground, comes from the ground. What a burst of power compared with the foreground-space! Form *emerges* from the ground in the most energetic sense of the word *emerge,* whereas in the opposite case, when the foreground is predominant, the form sinks into the ground. It is form that will determine its own relation to the ground, whereas when the background becomes determinant, form spurts from the ground. Before we've even grasped this, I'm looking for logical positions for my spaces. What also might occur when the planes are dislocated? In fact, a third thing might occur, something very devious [*tortueuse*]. As the planes are dislocated, they no longer remain much of a concern in themselves, neither the foreground nor the background. Everything located between the two planes will get drawn forth. What is it that's located between the two planes, and what might there be between them that's not dependent on either the foreground or the background? I see only these three positions. Logically, there are only these three.

Let's try to pin down some specifics. What about this artistic space where the foreground is determinant? Volume occurs, since the planes are dislocated. In any case, this is the death of the Egyptian world, since volumetric relations have been liberated from planimetric relations. Volume occurs, but what's determinant is the foreground because it's the foreground that contains the form. The relations to the background are determined by the form and by how the background takes shape in the foreground. Here, we'll all recognize this as Greek art.[51] Take a Greek sculpture, but I prefer starting with a purely abstract schema, not in order to apply it, but because I'd like to demonstrate to you something right away. The Greeks had words for a sculpture's highs and lows [*temps forts, temps faibles*]. The highs are the brilliant reliefs. The lows are the hollows and the shadows.[52] All the sculpture has different levels, and, in this way, this art is *measure,* the variable distribution of highs and lows in equal measure. Such is Greek harmony. It's the highs of the reliefs that are determinant in Greek sculpture, that is, form is worked out in the foreground, and working out the form determines the relations with the background. This is an aesthetic space of the foreground where it's the form that is determinant. And Maldiney puts it well when discussing this in his book, *Regard Parole Espace*: it's wrong—oh so wrong—to say that the Greek world is the world of light.[53] It's not the world of light because light is strictly subject to form's requirements. Sure, it's the world of light, but nonliberated light, light subject to form. Light must reveal form and submit to the requirements of form. All Greek sculpture consists in this wonderful way of handling light in the service of form. We're no longer in the haptic world of the Egyptians—it's an optical world. Only it's an optical world where light is in the service of form, that is, it's an optical world that still refers back to tactile form: it's a tactile-optical world.

This is the way in which Riegl defines Greek art as tactile-optical art with a corresponding space: the primacy of the foreground over the background. From this arises what's likely the most profound conception of art as rhythm or harmony—in the Greek sense and not in the modern sense. We'll get to that. If you see a Greek sculpture, I hope you'll be convinced, but the same also holds for all of Greek art. Light, not at all. Light is subordinate to the cube's requirements, and the cube precisely constitutes the primacy of the foreground. It is form on two planes. There is a depth, there are shadows, there are lights, and all of that must be subordinate to the rhythm of the form, since the rhythm is form. This will really force us next time to reconsider the conventional definitions of the Greek world.

Moving on to yet another revolution, what could have possibly happened to reverse the Greek relationship such that, on the contrary, the background becomes the determinant ground and the form, the figure, emerges from the ground? It's a very different sort of figure when it emerges out of the ground. The Copernican revolution always gets mentioned, but these revolutions we're discussing are even more important, or at least just as important as the Copernican revolution. To say that Egyptian space gives way to a space determined by the foreground is just as consequential as saying: the Earth revolves around the Sun or else the Sun revolves around the Earth. Here we witness the complete reversal of spatial structure, and all the more so with a second reversal when everything comes from the ground. How do you expect form to have the same bearing when it's determined by the foreground—even as it responds to the background—or else, on the other hand, if it's literally projected by the background? This is by no means the same conception of form. I would say that when the background becomes determinant, the figure emerges directly out of light and darkness.

In other words, the space of the background is a space where light and darkness are liberated from form. It's form now that depends on the distribution of light and darkness. This is a radical reversal of Greek space. Who is responsible for this? It concerns Byzantium.[54] That's why it's so sad—because it seems to me that today, no one understands anything anymore—to see books on this that start off by associating this [reversal] with Greek space. It's the opposite of Greek space. While there are similarities, obviously, Byzantine art's grandeur in art history is inexhaustible, but its hallmark is precisely to have caused the figure to emerge from the background instead of determining the figure as a form in the foreground. In this case, light is in fact unleashed, darkness is unleashed. Moreover, the Byzantines are the first colorists because when light is liberated from form, we're also not too far from liberating color.[55] The Byzantines are the first in art, I think, to manipulate both color scales, the luminous scale in values, and the chromatic scale in color [*tons*].

The Byzantines even had three primary colors: gold, blue, red, the three well-known mosaic colors, with complex relationships to white (as in marble) and black (as so-called smalt), which grow and form a kind of framework through the relationships between colors.[56] The first luminists, just like the first colorists, will occur in Byzantium, that is, giving up polychromy for colorism and luminism.

That warranted numerous persecutions, as the emperor will end up persecuting these artists.[57]

If you consider the opposition between Greek space and Byzantine space, this same history isn't a linear historical development. If I'm looking for another sequence, this time in painting, just picture a Byzantine figure. Everything necessarily emerges from the ground, since the mosaic is in a niche. It's a distanced vision, if only from the viewer's perspective.[58] You get these figures eaten up by eyes. It isn't form that defines the figure. What is it? Form answers to darkness and light. The eyes of a Byzantine figure are everywhere that this gaze from the ground circulates. It's the very antithesis to the Greek world. No doubt, this might be one of the most beautiful spaces. Well, really, there's no better or worse. If you compare it with Greek space, it's the exact opposite of Greek space.

I'm seeking to establish a sequence in painting. Just as I singled out Riegl, there's a major figure in the history of painting named Wölfflin, with a very good book.[59] He considers the sixteenth-seventeenth centuries. His analyses are very thorough, very detailed. He obviously read Riegl because, among other things, we learn that, moving from the sixteenth to the seventeenth century, we shift away from tactile-optical vision that still corresponds to Dürer or Leonardo da Vinci—so, that vision involves a lot of variants; I don't mean to say that it's the same space—to the seventeenth century where a kind of key or major revolution takes shape, which will be the discovery of a purely optical space, a discovery that culminates with Rembrandt, but with plenty of others besides.[60] And with these two spaces, sixteenth-century space and seventeenth-century space, what comes first, as the first determination? The primacy of the foreground. If you can recall something by Leonardo da Vinci or Raphael, you'll see it right away, with some remarkable innovations. In Raphael's work, for example, the foreground is curved, a wonderful curve and a wonderful discovery only possible thanks to the primacy of the foreground.

Let me clarify, since there are some things that I'm taking from Wölfflin given how great they are, and then there are some things I raise by association of ideas. I'm saying that around the sixteenth century, there's a wonderful discovery, and it was the same, I think, as what the Greeks discovered. What was this discovery? I don't have a better expression, but I don't like it: it's the existence of "the *collective line.*" You can really see the contrast with the Egyptian line. The Egyptian line is fundamentally individual; it's the contour of individual form.[61] That the collective is able to take on form is an idea that didn't occur to Egyptians. In other words, for an Egyptian, an individuality can get stronger and stronger, but it's always structured as an individuality. That a collectivity as such might exist, that only starts with the Greeks. And in Greek art, you get the invention of a line that no longer coincides with a particular individual, a line that encompasses several individuals. Moreover, the true line is the contour of the aggregate [*ensemble*]. The invention of the collective line means that the line becomes the contour of an aggregate. The Apostles, for example: of course, they're still individualized, but what matters is the enveloping line that goes from the left-most Apostle to the right-most Apostle. Take *The Miraculous Draught of Fishes,* by Raphael.[62] In my opinion, the collective line is the line of the foreground. It can be identified only via the foreground, as if the fact that the foreground has become determinant allows us to overcome the individual limits of form. As a result, from a Greek perspective, what acquires form in Greek statuary is an aggregate, even if it's only the couple—and that's insane from an Egyptian perspective. The line is the contour shared by two individualities. Immediately I can imagine the objection: there are plenty of solitary figures. Sure! But we shall see.

And what does sixteenth-century painting discover? Leonardo da Vinci's collective line, or Raphael's collective line, they aren't the same. You can tell painters apart by their style of collective line. Something remarkable emerges with sixteenth-century painting: a tree has a collective line that doesn't depend on its leaves, and the painter has to relocate the collective line in the foreground. A flock of sheep or a group of Apostles has a collective line. Group-painting literally moves downstage, that is, moves into the foreground. That appears to be just as true for Greek art as for sixteenth-century art, but in entirely different conditions. In Leonardo da Vinci's writings, there's something that stands out when he says, form must not be surrounded by lines.[63] Reading this, we risk falling into a huge contradiction because the sentence can be understood in two different ways, one of which Leonardo did not intend. One might think that it means that form should be free of lines. That's not at all what he means because the line's primacy is indisputable for him. Besides, a form free of lines is a form subordinate to light and to color. And that's obviously not what da Vinci means. I think his writings and context make it clear that he means form shouldn't be contained by lines. This means that form exceeds the line of individuality. But form will be determined by the line of the foreground. Hence we see the importance of Raphael managing to bend the foreground like some kind of balcony where the foreground itself is curved. That's one of the brilliant achievements of this period. When it comes to the technique of their spaces, both sixteenth-century art and Greek art share a kind of signal (the primacy of the foreground and the discovery of the collective line), just as Byzantium and the seventeenth century share a signal (the primacy of background, unleashing light and even color).

Everything comes from the ground. And that's what seventeenth-century painting is all about. It's so obvious. I have something really simple in mind, a theme in the sixteenth century: Adam and Eve. It's also one of Wölfflin's examples.[64] Adam and Eve, standing side by side. This could be very complicated, since the foreground might be a curved space. What perspective is famous in the seventeenth century? The diagonal. There's really no more foreground. Of course, a foreground does exist, but it's not what counts. It's as if the foreground were perforated by a depth that drags the left toward the ground or emerges from the ground, while the right is pulled from the ground. There's no more foreground; there's a differentiation based on the ground. This is clear, for example, in a great painting by Rubens that depicts the meeting of two people.[65] In the sixteenth century, they'd meet in the foreground, and the foreground is where meetings occur. Not at all with Rubens. Between the two people meeting, something like an alleyway has been excavated made up of other people on other planes. As a result, each of the two people meeting in the foreground emerges from the ground through their difference, with the highlighted alleyway separating them. They meet in the foreground, but only insofar as each emerges from the ground. It's no longer the foreground that determines things; it's the background that's determinant.

So, there we have two new spaces: Greek space *or* sixteenth-century space, and Byzantine space *or* seventeenth-century space.

I was saying there's still one more. Let's say we're no longer interested in planes, neither background nor foreground, but what's between the two. Who could be sufficiently barbarian to reject the plane and be interested in the in-between? What would the in-between planes be? By what term can we call this thing that is neither ground nor form? For convenience, let's call it barbarian art. Perhaps this might be barbarian art. It has to be barbarian art; that would be fine. We have our three positions: primacy of the foreground; primacy of the background; the in-between. The barbarians arrive: they always arrive via the in-between.

What has occurred? As I was saying, somehow the Egyptian way of achieving unity shifted. I suggested that it's either an accident or an event. That's the formula: accidents or events. Because once the planes have shifted, once there's a disjunction between planes, what do you expect form to do? There's only one thing that form can do: fall. It falls between the two planes. Or else, if push comes to shove, if form is animated by some miraculous energy, it will rise. We now enter this history of Western art in which everything comes down to rising and falling. The figure is constantly falling and rising. Imbalance is always on the verge of emerging. In other words, either accident or event—accident: the fall of the figure; event: the rise, the figure's ascension—both never stop enlivening . . . I would say that fall and ascension are the two vertical movements corresponding to the expansion of planes. For example, it's the aesthetic sensibility of Christianity, this rising and falling that sweeps up the Figure. The Deposition of the Cross and the Ascension. At this level, we're no longer talking about religious categories; these are aesthetic categories. The endless series of the Depositions of the Cross or the Ascensions of Christ, these never end. The Figure is surrounded. It's no longer determined as an essence; the Figure becomes fundamentally swept up by accidents or events. The Egyptian was the painter of essences. Here we have accidents and events truly taking and receiving their place artistically. Always something just a little bit off balance [*FBLS*, 100–102 UM; 123–26 C].

In a great text specifically on Dutch painting, *The Eye Listens*, Claudel analyzes in detail what he calls this kind of imbalance of bodies. There will be no curtain painted that doesn't just seem to fall back down. Or in Rembrandt's works, the lemons from which some peel dangles or these glasses that are on the brink of tipping over.[66] In this regard, however forcefully Cézanne invents, this isn't what prompts his invention when he's also looking essentially for the point of imbalance of form. It couldn't be otherwise. In several great passages, Claudel asks, what is a composition? The painting becomes the composition. In what way? In the celebrated form of still life, for example. He explains it all in one beautiful sentence; he says, composition is organization in the process of coming undone. He doesn't say it like that, but almost. This is an organization in the process of coming undone, taken at the point of imbalance. Claudel also talks about disintegration by light. Disintegration by light will be the motif running throughout his entire commentary on Rembrandt's *The Night Watch*.[67] That's something we'll consider later.

So, I'm just stating what we've established: you get into all kinds of adventures once you discern a disjunction between the two planes. I'm not at all saying that everything henceforth gets mixed up, only that all these adventures fall under the heading: the fall or rise of accidents. These accidents can be all sorts of things. They could be the collective line of a temporary group, flocks of sheep, leaves rustling on trees in the wind, and so on. They might be light that no longer coincides with the form of the object. They might be color's eruption. Painting discovered its essence in what was accident in relation to the Egyptian plane.

You can see what's left for us to cover. We still have two more sessions. What we have left to consider is all this business with spaces, if I have time, and then color. There you have it.

SESSION 7

MODULATING COLOR

26 May 1981

I'll remind you that all we have left is today and next week, and as of today, we must at last reach the problem of color and discuss only that next time. I'd like you to bear in mind the overall problem that we've been trying to consider, so let me recall this problem. It concerns reflecting on painting as the act through which—no matter which term you use—a signal-space is transmitted or reproduced onto the canvas. In fact, painting never concerns some object; a painter always paints a space. He or she paints a space-time, but a space.

How does one transmit or reproduce a signal-space onto the canvas? Thanks to an attempt at logical analysis, our answer was: this occurs through analogy. But what does analogy mean? As a result of our analysis, we arrived at least at a strong hypothesis, to wit: analogy does not at all mean similitude or resemblance. It indicates a very special operation concerning different aspects that must be called *modulation*. And we tried to analyze this concept of modulation. By modulating some highly variable thing = *x*, the painter transmits the signal-space.

Given that we were not engaged in a thorough history, we felt the need to consider arbitrarily certain signal-spaces and the corresponding types of modulation. The first signal-space considered was Egyptian space, a space in which form and ground are grasped on the same plane. This is a definition of space. Directly linked to this was our question: What type of modulation was suited to transmit this space, be it on a surface or on a slightly deepened surface of the bas-relief type? Our answer was quite simple (if you recall, this is why everything we did nonetheless forms a kind of whole): it's a type of modulation that could possibly be specified in the form of a mold, a mold-modulation, this mold defined as the geometric crystalline contour.

Then we jumped to another type of space. Quite a lot must have occurred between the two. But this truly supports the divisions we're proposing, given the other examples we'll select. This succession is neither ordered nor total. We have seen this event that no doubt marks a kind of emergence of the Greek world or space; we could define it by a quite momentous event, namely: the distinction between planes. The plane of ground and the plane of form become distinct and separate. Between them, what occurs? A new form of light. Thanks to Maldiney, we once again observed that it seemed entirely false to call the Greek world a world of light.[1] It's not a world of light. If pressed, we could say the Egyptian world would be much more of the world of light. Perhaps what we're learning about painting should be of use to us for philosophy. Indeed, the Greek world is sometimes defined philosophically as the world of essences, and that's not true. The Egyptian world would be much more of the world of essences in which, in fact, the individual figure surrounded by the geometric crystalline contour defines the stable essence separated from the world of phenomena, accidents, and becoming. But the Greeks are much closer to us.

It's very odd: it seems to me that what's attributed to the Greeks should have been said about the Egyptians. All that should be rolled back a notch because what is striking is that already with the Greeks, essence can no longer be separated from its manifestation in the world of phenomena. Indeed, notice that it's the same thing, light is subject to form. We could say something quite simple: essence is no longer essential; it has become organic. This is obviously true about Aristotle, but it was already true for Plato. Over the entire Greek world reverberates for me what Plato attributed to an Egyptian, saying: you Greeks, you're only children,[2] that is, literally, you have lost the secret of stable individual essences, now isolated and separated. In a sense, you've lost the secret of light, that is, of this space in which form and ground are on the same plane.

This is why the Greeks invent *philosophy*. Indeed, any comprehension, even a confused one, of philosophy truly suffers by allying it even the slightest to wisdom. In philosophy, there is indeed *philo* and *sophia*, and *sophia* is wisdom. But *philo* means precisely that the philosopher is no longer a sage. The sage is Egyptian. The "philo-*sopher*" (*philo*-sophe) is someone whose diminished status is no longer to be the friend of wisdom, with all the complexity inherent to the meaning of *philos* in Greek. Grasp the kind of fall that occurred from the *sophos* all the way to the *philo-sophos*. What could the "friend of wisdom" mean? He no longer even claims to be a sage. You can translate this: you Greeks, you will only ever be children.[3] We could say just as well: you Greeks, you will only ever be *philoï*. You are no longer sages, you are philosophers. You may no longer achieve stable and separate essences; you may achieve essences insofar as they are already embodied in the movement of phenomena, in becoming, insofar as they are in some way subject to the rhythm of becoming.

So this is a change of space, of time, of elements, of the entire conception of art: essence having become organic, that is, essence grasped at the moment that it is embodied in the flow of phenomena. If I am pursuing this philosophical digression, it is for those who define the Platonist world as the world of Ideas with a capital I, of separate Ideas. That is no longer valid at all. It is indeed true that this aspect exists in Plato's thought, ideas separated from the sensible, but this is an homage to an ancient tradition that he no longer possesses and that he knows has slipped away. Plato's problem is not at all the world of separate Ideas; on the contrary, his problem is the world of participation, namely, Ideas participating in the flow of the sensible or the flow of the sensible participating in Ideas. This is therefore the world of essences having become organic.

And I had begun to define this space in the previous session; from the perspective of our concerns with painting, I was seeking some kinds of correlates between Greek sculpture and painting, and—once again, since all this is not about chronological periods—and something that had been reintroduced into so-called classical painting in the sixteenth century, as if there were an echo effect between this space and the Greek world, on the one hand, and [on the other, between] this space and the Renaissance world. This Greek space or this Renaissance space will be defined by the distinction of planes, which suffices to distinguish each from Egyptian space. This will be a signal-space operating in an entirely different manner. But saying that there are distinct planes would not adequately define Greek space. That would not distinguish it from subsequent spaces, from Byzantine space, from twentieth- or nineteenth-century spaces in any case. What must be added is that, yes, it's a space in which the planes have become distinct, in which form and ground are not on the same plane, but this is also a space in which the foreground is the primary determinant. The foreground becomes determinant. Why? Because the foreground receives the form.

Of course, exceptions always occur in Renaissance painting or in Greek art. I am simply asking: Is it a coincidence that when you find an exception in Greek art (in my view, you will always find late-stage exceptions), you can already say and you sense immediately that this is the birth of a new world that will no longer be Greek, and that what will explode with Byzantium, for example, with Alexandrine art, is already in preparation? All I am saying today and especially at the next session is that nuances are required in this. I don't have time for nuances, [but] that does not mean always, nor for all cases. As a general rule, you have this space both in the high-Greek and in the Renaissance where planes are distinct with the foreground's primacy; this foreground can be extraordinarily complicated. I made reference to Raphael's curved foregrounds, his admirable foregrounds with the foreground's curvature. The foreground is the site where form is determined, and form is determined in the foreground.

So, as this relates to Egypt, you'll sense that a fundamental change will occur, for example, in the contour's status. That's a direct result of such change. If you consider a given space, no longer planimetric but a volume-space determined by the foreground—the Greek cube as opposed to the Egyptian pyramid—you are simultaneously considering the primacy of form. Form is determined in the foreground, and you change the status of contour. Do you recall something quite marvelous that occurred under the Egyptians? Well, all their spaces are marvels, none can be surpassed. You will recall that among the marvels of Egyptian space, there was contour's independence. Contour gained autonomy in relation to form and ground, through which contour's nature is crystalline, a geometric crystalline contour. In fact, contour necessarily gained independence, since it was what linked form to ground and ground to form on the same plane. Henceforth, this space was compelled to grant autonomy to contour on the plane. Contour was therefore geometric and crystalline. Then we leap into the Greek space: the distinction of planes with primacy of the foreground.

What happened, then, to contour? It becomes the self-determination of form in the foreground. Contour directly depends on form. All of these notions are begotten thanks to their relations with each other. Here we have what can be called organic contour. When contour depends on form, its Egyptian independence is lost; it becomes organic contour. Henceforth, essence is itself organic, no longer separate essence, isolated by the Egyptians' autonomous contour. Henceforth, it's no longer even individual essence. What does Greek art invent? It invents something like, I don't know, like the group, group harmony. What does Renaissance painting invent? At the previous session, I needed a rather special term in order to name this invention, the "collective line." Once again, I'm not claiming that the entire Renaissance is reduced to this invention. It's up to you to make corrections each time. That a herd of sheep has a line constitutes a magnificent discovery—there we have the organic contour. None of that works in the least for an Egyptian, necessarily so, since his line is geometric crystalline. No, for the herd to have a line, it must be organic.

At that point, we enter an entirely new domain, one of rhythm. What relation will the collective line of the sheep herd have with another type of collective line, a cloud's collective line? What sort of resonance will these two kinds of lines have? These collective lines enter into harmonic relations. Essence for the Greeks is no longer individual essence precisely because it's no longer separate essence. I'd like for you to grasp that everything is linked. The line has become organic, it has become collective. You'll tell me: in Greek statuary, for example, there are plenty of gents or ladies all by themselves. Yes, yes . . . And so what? That doesn't bother us in the least. Even before the objection is raised, thank God, we have our answer. So, there is no objection, ever. What are these isolated or apparently isolated figures? They are *organisms.* What does it mean, an organism all alone? It's a collective line. Why a collective line? When the lovely Greek individuality gets discussed, for example, in all of Schopenhauer's texts, and by others, that's not what is proposed, I believe. All that they are proposing, once again, is valid much more for the Egyptians than for the Greeks. What they are proposing is valid for the Egyptian ground, which is still vibrant for the Greeks. But to the extent that the Greeks speak on their own behalf, their concerns are different. The Greek world is not one of essence; it is a world of the *organon*. I am saying it in Greek since there's a series of famous texts by Aristotle collected under the title *Organon*. For Aristotle, there are many separate forms, a final homage to the Egyptian world. In the world known by the lovely word *sublunar*, forms are strictly inseparable from a random matter to which they give form, and the entire hierarchy of the Aristotelian world will be the types of forms correlated to the types of matter given form. That's a truly Greek conception; it's not Egyptian.

Of course, an organism is a unit. I don't at all mean to suggest that this is a world of dispersion, but it's a world for which there is no isolated unit. Each unit is a unit of a diversity. The unit is quite strong in the Greek world, but it's always the One among the diverse. There is never an absolute unit. Once again, although the One is discussed, with a capital O, the One in Plato's work, this One in Plato's work is finally pure transcendence, that is, an homage to the Egyptian world. But the Greeks' spatial assemblage [*faisceau*] grasps a kind of intermediate region between the pure and separate One and pure multiplicity. They grasp all the variable degrees of the One, this whole gradation through which the One or the form plunge more and more into a matter, or all these upper regions along which matter tends more and more toward form. So, when they create an organism, it's a unit, fine, but a unit of differentiated parts.

Here I'm really saying some extremely basic things. If you take a typical Renaissance canvas and a typical seventeenth-century canvas, these paintings give us the impression, even a somewhat imprecise one, that they do not exactly belong to the same world, that is, to the same space. We can choose all sorts of things, a female nude. It's obvious that you find the same things in Renaissance nudes or in Greek sculptures: namely, the organism affirmed as a unit in a distinct multiplicity; the organic parts, of course, are caught in an echo chamber, but are entirely distinct. When you go home, pick up a Venus by Titian and a Venus by Velázquez. The body's volume is not at all rendered in the same way. In fact, that's what makes it so beautiful. In Titian's case, it's very clear how much the organic is truly the unit of a multiplicity of differentiated parts. We'll see that, in the seventeenth century, with Velázquez among others, this unit is developed in an entirely different way. The body ceases to be an organism; it becomes something else. I would say that even when a solo individual is represented, it's an organic individual, that is, a unit of a multiplicity. So this is still a collective line, simply a strongly unified collective line, whereas a herd of sheep is a less strongly unified collective line. It's not by chance that the contemporary philosophers spend their time creating a hierarchy of degrees of unity, asking, for example—which is quite interesting, something you'll discover in Leibniz's philosophy—what is the hierarchy of the degrees in unity? In what way do a pile of pebbles or a sheaf of wooden branches, a herd of sheep, or an army, an animal colony, an organism, a consciousness, and so forth, represent increasingly stronger degrees of unity on a hierarchical scale?

On this basis, what I will be saying is quite fundamental, but we will complicate it afterward. You notice that I am not yet introducing color. I cannot do so yet, but it will be coming. I am just saying that far from being a space of light, Greek space, while strongly lit, is one in which light is completely subordinate to the requirements of form. In other words, it isn't an optical space but, as we've stated concisely, it's a tactile-optical space. You recall that we followed the Austrian author, Riegl, in defining Egyptian space as a haptic space and the eye as having a haptic function.[4] I won't go back over this. Given all that we have just considered, Greek space is not haptic; it is tactile-optical. What does tactile mean? What is it that refers to contact [*tact*]? Precisely that all the optical effects are subordinated to a certain extent to the integrity of form, and the integrity of form is tactile within the form of the organic contour. In other words, this is an optical space with a tactile referent. Yes, there's light, but it must not compromise the clarity of form. And clarity of form is tactile clarity. In the book I've cited several times in the previous session, Wölfflin calls this absolute clarity.[5] Even in the shadows, contour will retain its rights, since contour is tactile whereas shadows are optical. In Renaissance paintings, you see this marvelous effect that derives not from their clumsiness but, on the contrary, from an astonishing amount of skill: contour, that is, tactile allusion, subsists forthrightly through the play of shadows.

So this optical space with tactile referent is a very odd space, and we'd almost have to say it possesses a double tactile referent. It seems to me that the tactile reference is double. [There is] indeed subordination of light to form or, amounting to the same thing, self-determination of form through an organic contour that is necessarily tactile. Why a double reference? Because everything occurs as if the eye dominated on the plane of the real. While this is an optical space, it obtains confirmation of things through contact [*le tact*]. It's as if the hand followed the eye and confirmed contour through the play of shadows. But on the plane of the ideal, almost the reverse occurs: the eye refers to an ideal contact. Why? What is going to regulate what's optical in this Greek world? The same thing that will regulate this collective line. What is regulating the organic line? I'd say measure and number, that is, rhythm. Why will they regulate the collective line or determine the form? Perhaps you sense why: precisely because form must be grasped at the moment when it is embodied in a matter, because form is always the unit of a multiplicity. Measure and number, that is, rhythm, will determine the collective line of the foreground, constituting form. What does that mean concretely? This is why, during the entire sixteenth century, you have so many painting treatises titled *Treatise on number and measure*, as much in Italy as in texts by Dürer. What does that mean for us?

Let's return to Greek statuary. I'll select an example: a female couple, two figures side by side, a stele representing two women.[6] What does the optical eye immediately notice? What makes this Greek art? It's Greek art because the two figures have a common measure, that is, the two lateral planes—I'm not saying it's always like that. But in this common measure, there is a division of beats [*temps*]. Variations of beats for a same measure: that's what rhythm is. What are the beats within Greek rhythm? If the Greek Idea is no longer Egyptian essence, if it is truly rhythm, that is, essence in the process of embodiment within a matter in movement, you sense that essence is fundamentally rhythm. According to an article by Benveniste, the Greeks had two words to designate form: *schema* and *ruthmos*.[7] *Ruthmos* means form. How does this occur? In his linguistic study of the word *ruthmos* in Greek, Benveniste shows quite well that it's not by chance that this means form. It's just that *schema* (from which we have our word *scheme*) is either isolated essence (here again is a reference to the Egyptian world), or essence actualized in a matter once and for all. But *ruthmos* is essence that never stops being actualized and modified according to the levels of its actualization. This form that is actualized and modified according to the levels of its actualization becomes a same measure but with variable beats: that's what *ruthmos* is. The Greeks speak of dance having a form. It has no *schema,* but it has *ruthmos.* We settle typically into the idea of a collective form, which has a measure but as measure with variable beats. Dance is a state of essence for the Greeks. Even on the level of dance, this would need comparison; notably, it's quite different from the so-called hieratic Egyptian position.

I'm returning to my stele, the two women side by side, a same measure with the two lateral planes. Let's suppose that your eye starts from the bottom. As your eye rises, you'll see within this measure the beats varying and passing through thresholds marked by strong beats [*temps forts*], namely, the luminous reliefs. The strong beats of a rhythm [and] a sculpture's luminous reliefs are the same thing. Luminous reliefs are what emerge in the foreground. This time, I'm no longer speaking of lateral planes; I'm speaking of the foreground, the plane from the frontal perspective. The luminous reliefs graze the foreground. They are what define a sculpture's strong beats. And the shadows? The Greeks have an entire theory on this topic, both for music and sculpture. Shadows are precisely rhythm's weak beats [*temps faibles*]. Moreover, they have terms, marvelous ones, for this. Shadows are the weak beats of the second plane or the background. This is a space that gains rhythm from the strong beats of the foreground and the weak beats of the background. If you want to understand Byzantium's contribution and what revolution Byzantium initiates . . . your eye does this all by itself when looking at a Greek sculpture. Moving from bottom to top, the eye indeed gathers in the variation of beats, not only the strong beats and weak beats, but the strong beats of the foreground in variation. With thresholds marked by organic articulations: the knees, the groin, the waist, the shoulders, the face. These effects are still greatly subdivided. As a result, within the same measure, you have a double variation: variation of strong beats in the foreground from bottom to top, while also a corresponding variation of weak beats in the background.

What does that mean? I'm trying to summarize this tactile-optical space. I'll return to my question because we must never lose sight of it if we want to move forward. You recall that for any signal-space, I vaguely committed myself to uncovering some sort of principle of modulation. We are no longer at all at the level of the Egyptian modulation of signal-space through the geometric crystalline mold. Here we have a second great type of modulation: modulation of the line or, more precisely, what has been called rhythmic modulation through the interior mold. You recall this notion that I borrowed from Buffon because it seemed quite illuminating, this strange kind of notion that seems richer in other domains than those to which Buffon applied it, although there is indeed a reason for us to use it, since Buffon used it and developed this paradoxical notion to help us understand the organism's reproduction, that is, a modulation through interior mold.[8] The interior mold is the unit of measure whose beats [*temps*] are variable. In other words, this is a *module.* Although the expression as such has no meaning but I'll use it to summarize this segment, I would say that Greek space is modulated altogether differently than Egyptian space. It is modulated via a module, that is, through an interior mold. This is the means for transmitting, if you will, or for reproducing the tactile-optical space. This is the great organic world.

When a great art critic like Worringer defines the classical world, the Greek world, he says that it's the world of organic representation, and when he clarifies what he means by organic representation, we tend to understand this as an art having chosen the organism above all as its object. I'd like to add a digression if it won't bother you? This is very important: [this art] chose the organism as its object. That's certainly true. Art will need lengthy development for painting to cease being organic—and it has not always been organic. But simply saying this is not adequate. If I make a timid step forward in what we have left to do, this matter will cause us enormous problems from the viewpoint of colors. How do we translate or reproduce the organism's colors pictorially? It's an awful European problem, a typically European problem. Notably with Michelangelo's nudes. With the advent of the nude in painting, what occurred? A frightening technical problem. We'll see how it will be resolved, but we could say that it is one manner of expressing the total problem of painting. *One* manner only, but everything is there. How to reproduce the colors of an organic body? A very difficult problem. Why? Because whatever method you use in the West, given the nature of the Western organism . . .

[*Interruption of the recording,* time stamp: 46:38.]

. . . the way in which the problem of the organism and the problem of color collide with each other. This is an intense problem. The color problem is: How does one manage color without producing a kind of greyness, a kind of earthy mud? The organism problem is: How does one render the organism without sliding into the same earthy mud? In fact, why does the organism—alas, above all, the Western organism—present this problem? In other words, we are pale and, worse than pale, we are pale and red, and if you mix these up, earthiness [*du terreux*] is the result. It's awful! There is a text that I really like in Goethe's *Theory of Colors.* He is only taking note of a pictorial problem; it's not a paradoxical opinion for him. He says: "The nobler a being is and the more the being's material nature is revealed, the more the being's external envelope will accord essentially with the interior."[9] What does this mean? It means that the nobler a being is, that is, the more the being rises in the array of animals, the more it represents a differentiated organism. I insisted on reading this so that you'd see I wasn't making this up. Why does he say this? The more perfect a being is, there are more so-called topological relations between the exterior envelope and interior differentiation. Oh really? Is this the status of a complex being within the organic array? Let's reread this: "The more the being's external envelope will accord essentially with the interior": this is exactly Buffon's account of the internal mold. The more a being is noble in the array of animals, that is, complex, and the less you'll be able to reproduce it and the less it can reproduce itself through the exterior mold, the more an interior mold will be needed for it to reproduce and "the less will we see any isolatable elementary colors." There you have the organism's problem in its evolution. Painters know this problem so well that they have an expression for it that echoes strangely with Christianity in Western painting: the problem of the *flesh.*

How does one render flesh? For a colorist, this is the problem of problems. Why? Because at each moment, a supreme danger looms close at hand: producing earthiness, producing earthy color. Here I am introducing matters that will become clear only later.[10] Western painting is permeated by this task: How to leave earthiness behind? No doubt, this same task needed to be undertaken anew each time. Consider our Western painters. It's fascinating, as if each of them had to start this kind of lengthy task all over again. It's what I called the two dangers of the diagram. The diagram wavers between a blurring-danger (instead of a diagram, you are left with mush, something entirely blurred) and a coding danger (instead of a diagram, you get pure code). And an effective, fertile diagram is neither a blurring process, nor a coding process.

Here we slip fully into the blurring-danger. How can one prevent colors from getting blurry when colors restore the organism? Consider how striking it is with painters, even over a short time span. I'm starting my history over again. Everything occurs as if fate dictated that painters should first wallow through blackish colors—and at the same time, I'm stepping back. You provide the nuances and corrections yourself. There are some painters who remain in this state but precisely without wallowing anymore. Black for them gets turned into something so extraordinary that it has become a color. These would be very special cases. They're not wallowing. But how do so many of them traverse this experience in which it really seems to us that their reason wavers? And this experience that sometimes turns out quite badly for painters [occurs] at the very moment that they discover and triumph over what they were always seeking, namely, color. [It occurs] at the moment when we viewers, like idiots, once again tell ourselves: He's got it! It's going great! It's wonderful! He's found life—at that very moment, he kills himself. This truly is strange. I don't mean that suicides are exclusively pictorial, but in any case, they are pictorial as well and not psychoanalytical in nature.

So what happened? I'll choose references at random: once again, the greatest colorists of the seventeenth century. For years, Van Gogh wallowed in his artistic pursuits with chalk and charcoal while employing the pretense: Color? Oh no, not that! Not that! That's for later! It's always for later. In Van Gogh's entire correspondence, his appeals to his brother are fascinating: go on, send me some chalk. Color? No, no! When he starts working with color, it's earthy, as if by chance. For those who know his work, you see what I mean. You see some potatoes, the pure state of earthiness. What's going to unfold so that this triumph over color might occur? He rips color out of the earthy depth of all color. We might say: he's found salvation. That's the very moment that he kills himself. There's the very recent exhibition that I beg you to go see: Nicolas de Staël, at the Grand Palais.[11] You enter, and what do you see? I'm not saying that the initial paintings aren't admirable. They are quite extraordinary. They reveal a kind of science of brownish, blackish colors with arabesques. Then what happens? You see marvelous canvases where something absolutely new is revealed, hues [*teintes*] that must be called—we'll see later if the term is justified—pale hues. An entirely extraordinary pale regime of color. All the colors are there but according to a pale regime. You move into another hall: a frightening triumph over color. One almost has difficulty not concluding or not insisting: yes, that's what he was seeking the entire time. One wants to say: these are such joyful canvases. You'll see, *The Football Players*, for example, which is superb.[12] What happens? Once again, it's at this very moment that he kills himself. I can't begin to grasp this. Lacan's statement often gets quoted, making one shiver: it's when things are going well that one kills oneself. [*Laughter.*] In the case of the pictorial experience, it's when things are going so well on the canvas that the guy falls apart. It's the same story for Cézanne. Each time, one would have to show (and I almost regret [not having] slides)[13] the purple period, these utterly strange canvases of scenes of strangling, these purple colors—and the triumph over color.[14] When Manet reaches Impressionism, he leaves behind so-called earthy hues.

So, now that I've developed my digression, let's return to Goethe's text. The problem is that the more an organism is elaborated—and the human organism is the most elaborated of organisms for the entire theory and practice in Renaissance painting—the more the organism is elaborated, the more it needs an internal mold, in which elementary isolatable colors will not be visible. Hence the problem: How is flesh painted if flesh precisely is not nor should be constituted by elementary isolatable colors? What did painters do? Here's one way of posing the problem of color. Mixtures are created, fine, but what can be done so that the mixture isn't completely earthy and doesn't produce a perfectly dull whole? Goethe's text is quite interesting because he says: there is only one case in which the mammal, on the contrary, possesses fully brilliant colors. In fact, elementary isolatable colors are found in the lower organisms. Fish and birds display elementary isolatable colors. Goethe is indeed annoyed because there is *one* higher-level mammal that displays lovely isolated elementary colors, but he gets around this by saying there is only one such mammal, the ape. And while the ape may well be a complex mammal, it is almost the caricature of the human. This mammal isn't noble, he says. In fact, this is the problem of baboons. Baboons display the lovely colors for which they are renowned, reds and blues in a pure state, lovely colors on the nose and buttocks. While these are wonderful animals, Goethe condemns them precisely because they display elementary isolatable colors. He goes so far as to say that the cow is better than the baboon. [*Laughter.*] He no longer even knows what he is saying given how firmly he believes in the superiority of white Western man, because the cow, precisely, is entirely dull in relation to baboons, fish, and birds. Here we see the organism's problem from the viewpoint of color.

Classical Greek or Renaissance representation is defined as organic representation. That does not only mean that their object is the organism, but also that classical representation provides for the subject, that is, the viewer, an exercise integrated with his or her faculties. Worringer avoids any misunderstanding in saying quite well: the organic doesn't only mean that the painter's preferred object is the human organism. It means that whatever the painter's object may be, the viewer gazing at a particular work will experience a harmonious exercise of his or her distinct faculties, starting with contact [*tact*] and sight [*oeil*].[15] The eye will refer to contact and contact to the eye by means of this tactile–optical space or this rhythmic modulation.

For the moment, I have two signal-spaces and two types of modulation. I'm going to consider the third very quickly. This time, an optical vector space comes to life. One of the large topics in Wölfflin's book, *Principles of Art History,* focuses on the passage from sixteenth-century painting to the seventeenth century with analysis of important examples. Wölfflin shows the spatial conversion, and as a distant disciple of Riegl, he establishes the law of his topic: the passage from the sixteenth to the seventeenth century is typically the passage from a tactile-optical space to a purely optical space. At this level of well-established generalities, my impression is that while it would not mean the same thing, one could say precisely the same thing about the passage from Greek to Byzantine art, since in this passage, with other materials, problems, and techniques—whatever you'd like, keeping in mind all the differences—there was also the passage from a tactile-optical space to a purely optical space.[16] How would this purely optical space be defined? By very strict major oppositions to tactile-optical space. Just as in Greek space, the planes are entirely distinct, but now *everything comes from the background.* There is a primacy of the background, with form emerging from the ground. In saying "from the background," it is no longer clear where it begins or ends. Henceforth, we no longer know where the form begins or where it ends either. Why? Because space from the background is a space full of light—for example, think of many of Vermeer's famous paintings in which the foreground is darkened and light comes from the background—or else [in which] the background is very dark, but light on other planes emerges from this dark ground. In any case, the variants are infinite. Form will emerge from the background, no longer being determined in the foreground, as if thrust forward from the background. This is a revelation [*manifestation*], an epiphany. This is no longer as it was with the Greeks. At the extreme, essence no longer develops a relation with this revelation; this revelation now creates essence in a kind of epiphany that is the Byzantine epiphany. This is the moment to say: yes, light has become independent. In other words, form depends on light, with light no longer depending on form.[17]

A STUDENT: And what if the form is light?

DELEUZE: Who said that to contradict me? [*Laughter, including Deleuze.*] That doesn't seem to make much sense to me because one of them must be derived from the other. Technically, given the result, one can say form is light, but one can say that of everything and anything.

THE STUDENT: Well, no, it's not just anything because colors, in fact, . . .

DELEUZE: Ah, colors. I haven't spoken about them yet.

THE STUDENT: Substance is always obscure and unknowable matter. As a result, form necessarily is light, as the logical opposite of substance and as color.

DELEUZE: That's correct, quite right . . .

THE STUDENT: There you have it, monsieur!

DELEUZE: Thank you. [*Laughter.*] Well then, there we have it. I need a moment to recover a bit. [*Laughter.*]

[*Interruption of the session,* time stamp: 1:08:30; *upon their return, the previous speaker proposes an explanation, partially inaudible, that Deleuze does not pursue,* time stamp: 1:08:35–1:11:50.][18]

GEORGES COMTESSE: Can we say about Byzantine painting, and I'm not familiar with all seventeenth-century painting, but in preceding seminars, you made a connection, so can we say that this is a painting of the event, of accidents? I'm thinking of these figures on a luminous background. Can we say that this is a painting of the encounter, within a space, with a figure on a luminous background? [*Inaudible sentence,* time stamp: 1:12:14–1:12:25.] Given what you said earlier, can we conclude that Stoic thought would be another Greek effort at distancing themselves even more from Egypt?

DELEUZE: Yes and no. There's no basis for thinking that Egypt remains such an important reference point that everything is oriented in relation to it. In the comments you've just made, there is indeed a parallel that has been noted, in fact, by one of the best critics on Byzantine painting, Georges Duthuit.[19] He greatly emphasized the resemblances between, on the one hand, neo-Alexandrine texts that did depend on Stoic texts, that is, a neo-Platonic Stoic tradition and, on the other hand, the Byzantine enterprise. Such resemblances would occur at a very precise level. While reflecting Oriental influences, Stoicism is the start, in fact, of a radically new conception of limit. In discussing Spinoza during the first half of the year, I believe that we've seen the Greek limit truly being defined by contour, with all of contour's complexities. This is a very complicated notion especially because, once again, for the Greeks, it no longer exactly concerns geometric contour, but really an organic contour, even for geometric figures. With the Stoics, a conception of limit arises that breaks with contour. It's like a kind of fact.[20]

A text by an ancient Stoic summarized this very well by stating: the limit is not geometric contour but, rather, it is the zone in which potential [*puissance*] is exerted, is no longer exerted, and so on. He says: the sculptor does not provide us with the model of limit, in the sense of a contour or even of a modeling. We receive it instead from the plant's seed.[21] This is a radical change of the verb "to be." I "am" up to the point where I exert my potential. I "am no longer" within the contour of my limit. My limit has stopped being a contour. My sole limit is when my potential is no longer exerted. Here we have something fundamental, which is the discovery of light. This is not at all a matter of misrepresenting the texts. In all of Plotinus's texts on light, he discovers a purely optical light. He explicitly causes light to say: Where do I begin? Where do I end?[22] This is the negation of contour on behalf of a limit that will be precisely defined in painting by chiaroscuro, and which implies this dispersion of an optical space that is completely different from the Greeks' tactile–optical space.

I'll choose another example analyzed quite well by Wölfflin.[23] Let's go back to the example of the two nudes but, this time, not at all from the viewpoint of color. He asks: What is a Renaissance nude, for example, one by Dürer? How is it treated? Here you'll find what I called the collective line or the organic line, namely: the body's limit is really traced by a curved line, very nearly a continuous curve. Even if it's interrupted at some point, it continues virtually. A complex continuous curve is what defines the contour. The body limited in this way by the organic line disconnects from the ground but quite obviously does not emerge from the ground nor does it have any intention of doing so. If you consider a nude by Rembrandt, you even see something entirely new from the material perspective, something that will be very important for the entire history of painting. I'd say the same thing about portraits, if you consider a sixteenth-century or seventeenth-century portrait.

If you consider a nude by Rembrandt, you see that it isn't at all composed by a curved line. You'll tell me: there is indeed a contour. Yes, a contour is still present. We'll see that this new kind of contour can no longer be determinant. It's no longer the self-determination of form. What proves this? It's no longer even a curve that's complex and virtually continuous. It's a very fine succession of flat traits [*traits plats*].[24] You can supply some nuances: for a long time, you had Rembrandt paintings that developed with curves. Each time that I say Rembrandt, we're not discussing a formula that he applied in his works. I'm simply saying that certain Rembrandt paintings would seem to us particularly representative of seventeenth-century painting. This kind of flat trait or broken line no longer has the same function. It no longer creates a contour at all. Everything is distributed based on the background. This kind of flat trait indicates the way in which the body emerges from the ground within a kind of perpendicular structure of the painting. In this case, a contour is nonetheless present because there are continuous flat traits. But once again, these are no longer curved traits; these are really a succession of flat traits that constantly change direction. The result is the body truly emerging from the ground. The body is no longer on the ground, but rather emerges from the ground.[25]

If you consider examples of portraits, this effect becomes even clearer. During the Renaissance, the contour gains importance: the line of the nose, the eyes, the mouth, and so on, truly form traits of contour. In a seventeenth-century portrait, what is striking is this: just as I was saying earlier, contour is transformed into a succession of flat traits—for example, in certain Rembrandt paintings—in many seventeenth-century portraits, you simply could not restore a face's line of contour and lines that would still be modular, in the sense I was using module earlier. This time, on the contrary, the whole portrait—which obviously takes on an intense vivacity at this point—is organized by discontinuous traits drawn from the mass. The dual formula of the portrait or the body in the seventeenth century is, on the one hand, the curvilinear contour replaced by a succession of flat traits changing direction; [on the other hand, it's] modular interior lines on the face replaced by discontinuous traits drawn from the mass, which then typically indicate the play of shadows and lights.

As a result, in fact, everything in this space is reoriented based on the form necessarily emerging from the ground. With this emergence from the ground, form can no longer be defined by a contour, as Wölfflin says, by absolute clarity. It can be defined only in terms of relative clarity: discontinuous traits drawn from the mass of the face, the flat trait causing form to emerge from the ground. This is a space of values, a space of chiaroscuro. In fact, light has ceased depending on form. So, that and only that, in other words, as much in this Byzantine space as in this [seventeenth-century] space, this is hallucinating . . . Here we even find the hallucinating characteristic of these figures: that they emerge precisely from the ground, and that this ground contains the whiteness of brilliant light as well as the obscurity of blacks. Everything emerges from there. The triumph for art at that moment is truly a perpendicular structure.

Notice the theme of the encounter in the seventeenth century: How do characters encounter each other? As much as in the sixteenth century, two characters who meet—this lies entirely at the heart of a sixteenth-century problem concerning the collective line—they meet in the foreground, and one aspect of sixteenth-century art is the beauty of the foregrounds. These foregrounds are not flat. Once again, the example of Raphael always comes to mind as one of the painters who pushed farthest the effects of twisting the foreground. But they obviously meet one another in the foreground because the foreground is what distributes forms. These are determined in the foreground; hence the collective line that is really the line of the foreground, however twisting and complex it may be. On the other hand, the encounter in the seventeenth century is organized differently. While characters have access to the foreground, this encounter happens through the background. Each character has his or her manner of belonging to the background. For example, when two characters arrive in the same foreground, they don't arrive there in the same way because they do not emerge from the background in the same way. If they meet in the foreground, it's because their way of emerging has been harmonized, and the foreground itself remains full of holes, punctured by the perpendicular structure of their emergence from the background. In this regard, I believe that Rubens is one of the painters who goes the farthest with this kind of perpendicular structure.

In concluding this, I'll say that I should have spent much more time on all this, but this suffices for you to grant me the principle: this optical space is a third type of modulation. Transmission of a pure optical space refers to a third type of modulation, the modulation of light. You indeed see, in the other cases, that when I defined Egyptian modulation through the crystalline mold [and] Greek modulation through the rhythmic module, I obviously did not mean that in Greek art, there is no light, and so on. Light has not yet gained the status as an independent factor from the viewpoint of the operative modulation, but it's already there. Light is already obtained, produced through the operative modulation.

So, at this point, I think we are coming to our last remaining problem that I'd just like to start today, and which will be our topic for the next session. So, here's what we have: we find ourselves with three spaces and three types of modulation. The fact is that I haven't had much opportunity to speak about color. I must indeed explain why this opportunity hasn't arisen. An initial, rapid outline is possible, and while clearly inaccurate, it might be useful for organizing our inquiry. I'll admit that, after all, a modulation of color is quite different not only from a modulation of line but also from a modulation of light. That's why we haven't discussed this earlier. Perhaps there are grounds to reserve the place for a colored signal-space that would refer to its specific type of modulation. Let's consider this hypothesis. It would consist in saying: even if someone argues that the same painters are great luminists and great colorists (that's possible; it's not entirely certain; people frequently say that they are not the same ones), in fact, these are not the same problems. So, a painter can confront two problems, but it's quite possible that his basic problem is light, not color, and that he reaches the problem of color only to the extent that it involves and touches on light. The reverse is possible as well. So, my first hypothesis would be that we must define a signal-space proper to color corresponding to a very special type of modulation, distinct from all the ones we've seen, including the modulation of light.

What does "modulating color" mean? What space does this modulation refer to? This is the first hypothesis. I'm trying to bolster this hypothesis. In the history of Western painting, there have been moments of great colorism, that is, in which the problem of color was truly the basic problem. As I have been selecting examples, I will stick to a famous era: the Impressionists. They present themselves basically as colorists. In what ways does this stance pose other problems than problems of light? Moreover, sometimes they make rather exaggerated or rather simplistic claims, but precisely like the ones we are using, these function as great reference points. There's Van Gogh proclaiming his allegiance to Delacroix, whom he insists is the first great modern colorist, by saying: what Rembrandt is to light, Delacroix is to color.

That's a simple claim. He made it in passing, in a letter.[26] Is this true? Is it not true? It hardly matters; it's a reference point. What does that even mean? At the extreme, it strongly suggests that there is a space of color that isn't the same as the space of light and a modulation of color that isn't the same as the modulation of light. It goes without saying that luminists reach color, but do so through the intermediary of light. It goes without saying that colorists reach light, but do so through the intermediary of color, and by color. Here is a text about Cézanne that seems curious to me. It's a text by some of Cézanne's contemporaries. They say: "It's through the opposition of warm and cool tones" (as we've seen, warm and cool function as determinations of color as color, that is, warm yellow and cool blue) "that the colors used by the painter" (that is, Cézanne) "without any absolute luminous quality in themselves, come to represent light and shadow."[27]

This text interests me because, at the point we've reached, I consider it a very precise definition of Cézanne's painting, at least in his late career: to reach light and all the relations of light and shadow through relations of colors without including their luminous quality, which would belong solely within colors themselves. Cézanne helps us move forward a bit. For the more he proceeds, the more he discovers his colorist method, and the more he calls it modulation. There are some admirable texts by Cézanne: to modulate, to modulate colors. He goes so far as to say (which works perfectly for us): one must not say "to model"—and certainly one must not say "to mold." So, one must not say to mold or to model; one must say, "to modulate."[28] This is excellent for us, since our work has led us precisely to take the mold, modeling, the module, and so forth, as cases of modulation. The real mystery of this operation is modulation.

[*Interruption of the recording*, time stamp: 1:33:20.]

[Cézanne] treats the same subject or the same theme through two entirely different techniques. The first case is a double painting, that is, two copies of the same theme with the title *Seated Peasant*.[29] A seated peasant, one in oil, the other watercolor. Second example: here, unfortunately, the two titles are different. The portrait of a lady in a morning jacket.[30] It's obviously the same lady, both rendered in oil. If you read this text by Gowing on this point, it seems to me that he provides a strong piece of evidence, that the technique is not the same because the seated peasant, the one rendered in oil, is entirely rendered through modulation of light, local tint, local color, and chiaroscuro.

The watercolor is treated in an entirely different way, in a colorist manner. If you understand, even only vaguely, what we've just considered about modulating light, this whole play of chiaroscuro and emergence from the ground, what does modulating color mean? In *Seated Peasant* second manner (watercolor), something quite odd is revealed. The modeling [*modelé*] will be obtained through a juxtaposition of colored patches [*taches colorées*]. These examples are not restrictive. Gowing will then show that this invades all of Cézanne's work. What are these colored patches in rather tiny dimensions? That should mean something to you. This is perhaps the essential moment of colorism. Gowing insists on showing that there is indeed a method here, an astonishing method that consists in substituting a third thing for tactile contour and optical modeling through chiaroscuro. This is precisely what Cézanne calls: modulating color. A modulation of or by color will replace the tactile-optical contour—that is, the collective line—as well as the chiaroscuro modeling. It's a matter of a succession, of a juxtaposition of patches, closer and closer, along the spectrum's order.

I'm making a bit more progress; I just want to put this in place because I'll wait until next week to explain in detail these odd sequences from Cézanne that will constitute a kind of revolution in color. He proceeds closer and closer, through the spectrum's order. We'll see what that means based precisely on our drawing from the previous session. A patch of one particular color, a patch of another color, a patch of yet another color, developing all the way to the culminating point, and then the series goes in reverse: a dual progressive and regressive series around Cézanne's famous culminating point. That's how this kind of new modeling will work, no longer a modeling but truly a modulation by color. The same thing for the lady in the morning jacket. And this is very odd. Why? It indeed seems that in terms of watercolor, Cézanne began to find his niche [*son truc*], this new colorist method, and that he'll then extend it to oil. In the case of the lady in the morning jacket, the most minor reproductions, even reproductions in black [and white] are fascinating from this perspective. Gowing's article includes very fascinating reproductions in black [and white] because there is a very clear version:[31] modulation of light, chiaroscuro, and color reduced to local color, simply influenced or modified by light. The other version of the lady in the morning jacket is absolutely different. You get the impression that it's an entirely different style. There, it's a modulation by color in which you find the sequence of juxtaposed patches all the way to the culminating point and then the regressive series. Even when these are the same [themes], it seems to me increasingly obvious that modulation of color and modulation of light are not at all the same thing.

A second comment: henceforth, we might venture to draw the conclusion from this that modulation of color itself has a signal-space. So, we will have to define both this modulation and the signal-space that it transmits or reproduces. This effort will require that, following the seventeenth century, we select examples [from] the nineteenth century. You can create a colorist sequence that's very decisive for painting—and we would rediscover the problem of how to paint a body—that began with Delacroix and a Delacroix technique (which, in fact, was perhaps already one of Turner's) that he'll call, even during his own era, the crosshatching technique. To simplify—and with the same corrections that you'll provide—everything in this sequence would start with Delacroix's crosshatchings.

A second moment: I'm borrowing this after all from a very fine book. So, if you happen to encounter it, do read it. There is a Post-Impressionist painter, a very well-known Neo-Impressionist named Paul Signac, who wrote a very good book, *D'Eugène Delacroix au néo-impressionnisme* [From Eugène Delacroix to Neo-Impressionism].[32]

He develops that same sequence himself: everything starts via Delacroix's crosshatching. Notice the way in which this technique is a magnificent answer to the question: How does one paint the body? Because, in fact, Delacroix maintains his entire personal heritage gleaned from earthy colors, except that he will crosshatch the earthy colors with pure tints [*tons purs*]. He thus creates his famous crosshatchings. Go see a typical example: the decoration of the Saint-Sulpice church where the bodies with earthy shades or muted hues [*teintes rabattues*] are crosshatched with juxtaposed green and pink.[33] Delacroix will face insults for this or, just the opposite, will be greatly admired, even acclaimed, because he creates the impression of pulling color out of a muddy bog. And although I wouldn't say that he was alone, this crosshatching technique is very significant because it will have its subsequent practitioners. It's not by chance that the Impressionists will hail Delacroix as their great figurehead. What happens next? You have the formation of sequences of colored patches at an entirely different scale than Delacroix's. Why? Because, to arrive at these sequences of little colored units, something Delacroix had maintained needed to be rejected: the earthy colors. Or even the muted colors. We will get a better look at all that, but I am introducing this topic here so that we'll have something already on the table. Their unit is no longer crosshatching, but something that develops directly from it. As Signac says quite well, it's the famous Impressionist comma.[34] They paint with little commas. Delacroix's crosshatching became the Impressionist comma because it can be utilized on its own.

The comma is a strange little device if you think about it because, at the time of early Impressionism, this famous comma is quite ambiguous, which, in Van Gogh's work, will then engender something that can no longer be called a comma, transformed into a point or full stop. But he borrows it from the Impressionists as a kind of pictorial technique. [The Impressionists] can do that precisely because they have been freed from the problem of the earthy, from earthy colors and muted colors. They have eliminated [them] from their palette. They necessarily did something amazing: a subtraction, an intense restriction of the palette because that was the cost of causing color to emerge in a form that we still have left to determine. Notably, they eliminated all the so-called earth or earthy colors; they banished muted colors.[35]

However, Signac quite rightly presents himself as a Post-Impressionist, that is, from a third moment, beyond Delacroix and the Impressionists. He says, yes, but there's one gimmick that's not right. Their comma is still very strange because it's either figurative or already abstract, however you'd like to see it. It's figurative because it's wonderful for creating blades of grass. What they learned, notably from English painters, is that grass wasn't created by laying on some green and even by muting it, that is, even by playing with its values. Rather, grass was created with tiny touches of green, of shades, of different hues, and that's how grass was created.[36] Notice the extent to which the collective line has been left behind. This is more about the collective line of an aggregate that would be a grass-aggregate. They immersed themselves deeply *into* grass, within grass's interiority. That's how this tiny comma remained figurative but at the same time completely abstract. It works quite well for creating leaves or grass, but it's already something else entirely. As Signac says rather strangely, these Impressionists absolutely rejected, eliminated the earthy. This choice is indeed the basic Impressionist question: How do we extract vividness [*le vif*]? How do we extract the vivid shades from the earthy mixture, from earthy color, from greyness?

Signac's outline is very academic, but since I find him very lively and philosophical, I'm citing him. The first moment is Delacroix. He maintains earthy colors and extracts vividness from them; he renders them fully vivid through the crosshatching technique. The second moment, the Impressionists who eliminate earthy colors. So, they can develop vividness by means of brief sequences of different shades. But, as Signac says, this development is not random because they use this tremendous way of reconstituting what's earthy. They take the opposite path from Delacroix's. Delacroix started from what's earthy and exalted it through his crosshatching technique, vitalizing it. The others did the opposite: they eliminated the earthy. Their technique included vivid, immediate shades, sequences of vivid shades for reconstituting instead the overall earthy or muted impression. And God knows that it's wonderful then when Signac seems to say, what a shame. For us, this view is delightful. The two great examples of Impressionism's extreme in this regard are Monet's *Cathedrals* in which, in fact, the stone's greyness is reconstituted through the technique of tiny touches of pure shades, and Pissarro's

Boulevards—those of you who were at the recent Pissarro exhibition saw these canvases from his late career, the boulevards[37]—in which his explicit object is: How to reintroduce the sense of muddy streets in a city like Paris using vivid shades?[38] It's wonderful.

But Signac is not happy because, for him, pure colorism should not have been used, that is, this extraction of sequences of pure shades to reintroduce an earthy or muted impression. So what was required instead? According to Signac, the greatest painter arrives, [Seurat]. It's strange that he does not mention Cézanne in all this. But obviously, that's in his interest: Seurat is a close friend. What does Seurat do? There are no more commas. The technique has become the famous tiny point of so-called pointillist painting.

Observe that from crosshatching to the comma to the tiny point, you have successive steps of colorism. The succession of tiny points—but this was already in Cézanne, not in the same way; Cézanne's work did not develop via tiny points—the pure sequence of pure shades along the spectrum's order, with a culminating point, will precisely define this modulation of color. At the same time, this is only one sequence because, in the same period—that's how rich this world of painting was—I would have a hard time situating Gauguin and Van Gogh in this sequence—especially Gauguin for whom pointillism and Seurat seemed comic and devoid of interest. It seems as if my sequence eventually required adjustment to account for a branch, for a differentiation in the Van Gogh / Gauguin direction.

What problem am I trying to reach? I can always isolate a problem of pure colorism in this way. That doesn't prevent colorism from having constantly belonged to my preceding worlds, to my preceding spaces. What I mean is, belonging not only to the Egyptians' signal-space, to the Greeks', but obviously to the signal-space of light. Byzantium has at once a colorist spectrum and a luminous spectrum. I believe that I already said this in the last session: Byzantium invents colorism at the same time as it invents luminism. Certainly it wasn't through the same means, with the result that Byzantium already created a double modulation. Notice how mosaics not only allow a modulation of light but also an amazing modulation of color. Instead of little patches, these are small tesserae. This is wonderful as a possibility. In the seventeenth century, there is no less a whole regime of color than a regime of light.

As a result, my problem is double. As quickly as possible in the next session, we have to return to the precise question: What are the color regimes corresponding, for example, to Renaissance space and to the optical space of the seventeenth century? Or: what are the color regimes corresponding to Greek art and to Byzantine art? I can just argue—this is how the whole discussion gains a bit of coherence—that modulation is not created principally through color. And yet, this is false for Byzantium where I believe there is a double modulation. But in seventeenth-century painting, the principal modulation is not from color, instead remaining from light. On the one hand, we have to establish the color regimes and, on the other hand—without one excluding the other—we have to define a specifically colorist space to which the modulation of color in a pure state would correspond, even if there are already regimes of color before this specifically colorist space.

To close, I'll offer something that I will need to elaborate in our next session about the simple characteristics of colors. To those who are interested in this, I am just asking you to note this for a bit of reflection. These are questions of terminology. Since a great effort is needed to try to unify the terminology on the level of colors, there would be four simple characteristics of color, namely: two that depend on the factor of color's luminance, and these are light/dark; two characteristics that depend on the factor of color's so-called purity, and these are saturated/washed-out [*lavé*]. The result when you combine them two by two—what I just want you to retain so that you can create your own table; otherwise, the terminology cannot be understood—light/saturated [*clair saturé*], that is called a bright hue;[39] light/washed-out [*clair lavé*], that is called a pale hue; dark/saturated [*foncé saturé*], that is called a deep hue; dark/washed-out [*foncé lavé*], that is called a muted hue. You can create your table with arrows, all that. I need these four notions because my hypothesis would be that there are really four regimes of color: a pale regime, a bright regime, a muted regime, and a [deep] regime, and from each of these regimes, all the colors can emerge.

[*Inaudible intervention, end of the session.*]

SESSION 8

REGIMES OF COLOR

2 June 1981

In today's final session, we will wrap up our reflections; well, actually, more simply, we will lay down some final guidelines for continuing our path toward resolving this problem of color. This is a very complicated issue, since—you will recall from our previous session—not only are there colors, but there are also what we can call regimes of color. That gives us two options: regimes of color can accompany the sign-spaces we discussed previously and the modulations characteristic of these spaces. Or else we must pursue an entirely different question concerning color, a whole other aspect: Aren't there regimes of color that themselves constitute a sign-space and that are subject to a modulation of their very own? If this is the case, then we are already starting off on shaky ground, since by introducing something that is, for now, a very vague notion of regimes of color, there would be regimes of color that one could identify practically, historically, theoretically, and scientifically, and all of these regimes would be unequal. Correspondences would exist between the scientific determination of regimes of color, the practical determination, the historical determination. There would only be an interplay of correspondences.

I already see two options as regards my possible regimes of color: either they'll correspond to a signal-space and to a modulation defined by other means, or else they will themselves make up a coloristic space and a chromatic modulation all their own. No doubt, color is capable of both. How could a color-regime be defined, understanding that by "color regime," we don't mean all colors? This means a certain treatment of color, but a treatment with what coherence, one that would cause us to say: This is indeed a color-regime? What would these color-regimes be?

I'd like to define them via four characteristics.

The first characteristic: for a color-regime to exist, the ground must be determined in a certain way. The ground isn't necessarily determined by color. You might sense that a color-regime will imply *its* own coloristic space and *its* own chromatic modulation if the ground itself is colored. But a color-regime might very well adhere to another sort of space and to another sort of modulation. So, I am suggesting that the idea of ground, which is clearly fundamental in painting, will be the first requirement that a color-regime must satisfy.

But what does "a ground" mean, exactly? I find the notion very interesting. A ground is twofold, a twofold concept. On the one hand, the ground refers to a so-called support, that which supports line and color. This provides an initial, well-established definition. In this sense, you talk about a plaster ground, a chalk ground,[1] or a colored ground. Our system must constantly include parallels [*échos*], by which I'm saying: immediate parallels in the history of painting. For example, you have well-known grounds from the fifteenth and the sixteenth century being researched and gradually perfected, formulas for plaster—so-called slaked plaster[2]—which will serve as the painting's ground, that is, which will determine the quality of the color support. But at the same time, the notion of ground also refers to the background, but not in just any regard. On the one hand, the ground is the support's determinate quality; it's the determination of the support. And on the other hand, the ground is not exactly the background, but it's the determination of the background's variable value. This is the very nature of the ground as quality of the support that, in a way, will result in the relative position of the background. What does "the relative position of the background" mean here? We saw it in the sign-spaces we examined previously. Renaissance painting implies (this is too general, but as is our practice, you'll add nuances) a background position such that the background remains subject to the foreground's requirements. Painting of the seventeenth century implies a sort of reversal in values in the sense that everything emerges from the background. Byzantine painting had already undertaken this conversion in favor of the background. So, I'd say that the ground is both the quality of the support and the variable position of the background. With this, we would have the first characteristic of a regime of color.

The second characteristic: What then is the role of color in the operative modulation on the surface supported by the ground? We've already covered the different types of modulation.[3]

The third characteristic of regimes of color: it's the character of the hues.[4] A regime of color implies a certain privilege—provided that we clarify later what I mean by privilege—that is, privileging a type of hue. What is a type of hue? As we've seen, there are two variables in color. I've returned to the schema that I asked you reflect on.[5] A color can be light or dark, on the one hand, and on the other, it can be saturated or washed-out. It's a bit like with alcohol, if you will. It's a bit like the distinction between titration and dilution. Every alcoholic knows this, but even those who aren't alcoholics do. It isn't hard to understand. You have an alcohol of 40 percent. Even if you dilute it greatly, it still remains 40 percent alcohol: it's diluted 40 percent alcohol. If you absorb it undiluted, it's saturated 40 percent alcohol. Saturated/watered-down, saturated/diluted forms a pair consisting of color where purity is the factor.

From there, you combine the two pairs together: a hue might be light or dark, saturated or washed-out, that is, diluted. The possible combinations will give you the types of hue. The first possibility, light/washed-out is "pale." The second possibility: light/saturated is bright, bright hues. [The third possibility]: dark/saturated, these are the deep hues. [The fourth possibility]: dark/washed-out: these are the muted hues.[6] A regime of color implies the dominance of one of these types of hue. We can imagine pale regimes, bright regimes, deep regimes, muted regimes. What does "privilege" or "dominance" mean? It's very simple. It doesn't mean that most of the colors will be, for example, in pale regimes. It doesn't mean that most of the colors will be pale hues, although that might be the case. But I'm thinking of something else entirely. Once again, everything I'm saying, especially today, might be wrong. It's up to you not only to modify it but to correct it for yourselves. When I talk about a "pale" regime, I mean that the pale hues will be the way in which the aggregate of colors, including the bright, including the deep, including the muted, are distributed depending on the ground. So, it's not at all a sign of frequency; it's a sign of importance, the importance of the pale hues, negotiating the interplay between the colors and the ground. A bright regime doesn't mean there won't be any muted hues. Sometimes there aren't muted hues in a bright regime. For example, the Impressionists avoid muted hues. But while some might still be there, it's just that these hues, of the colors in general and the ground, will be negotiated by the bright tones [*tons vifs*]. So I could say, this is a bright regime.

Finally, the last [characteristic] for these regimes of color. This time, I'm looking for a scientific, or quasi-scientific parallel [*écho*]. You haven't forgotten that our problem is always one of analogy. We wanted to define analogy by modulation, and not at all as conveying similitude. What does colorimetry have to say about ways to reproduce a color—which is the problem of analogy? You see a color; you reproduce it. How do you reproduce a color? We're told that there'd be three unequal methods. I'm wondering: Won't these three methods, this time these scientific methods, have a practical parallel and a historical parallel, tying everything together?

The first method. You're looking at a complex beam of light, not monochromatic. How do you reproduce it? One of colorimetry's basic principles is that every complex beam can in principle be reduced to a white beam—to be calculated—accompanied by a monochromatic beam. In truth, I'm getting this from some dictionary. Hence the formula: F (that is, the complex luminous flux, the colored flux, of a given color); $F = F_d + F_w$. What does this formula mean? It's very simple. F is the complex flux of light of a given color; F_w is the flux of white light, with the *w* referring to the English; + F_d is the monochromatic beam whose wavelength is called L_d, namely: the dominant wavelength. At the extreme, the wavelength of the beam F is called L, and then you have the formula $FL = F_w + FL_d$. You've replaced your complex beam with a beam of white light + a monochromatic beam with a wavelength different from the beam you started with. That's the so-called dominant wavelength method. What's more, in some cases, your monochromatic dominant wavelength beam itself might not at all be included in the reconstruction of the original beam. In other words, this first combination is: flux of white light + a monochromatic beam. That combination can, in principle, reconstruct any complex beam. There you have the first method. Hang on to that because we're indeed going to need it.[7]

The second method. Why a second method? Because the first method is very theoretical.

[*Interruption of the recording,* time stamp: 21:29–21:43.]

In the previous case, the color matrix started with the beam of white light. In this one, on the other hand, the matrix starts from a tricolor system, the three primary colors, blue-red-green. You'll recognize these from TV screens. Why blue-red-green when you'd expect it to be blue, red, yellow? It's simply because you cannot reconstruct a complex beam with blue-red-yellow. Why not? This reconstruction requires that the selection of the three primary colors be such that none of them can be counterbalanced by the other two. If you go with yellow-blue-red, you'd have a chance of counterbalancing red with yellow and blue. So, it isn't possible. Your three primary colors, then—in the most practical, simplest terms—will be red-green-blue. There are some remarkable paintings in the de Staël exhibit.[8] There's a remarkable landscape with the title *Agrigente* that is a landscape in only three colors, plus a black and a white. Those three colors: red, green, blue. This method is no longer a dominant wavelength method, which implies privilege given to white; this method is known as "by additive synthesis" [*de synthèse additive*]. It corresponds to the formula: F (any colored flux whatsoever) = F_r (red flux) + F_g (green flux) + F_b (blue flux).

With the third possible method, now we're switching domains. This time, we have to move away from the ray of light and toward colored bodies, whether pigments or even filters. What is the color of a body? A body's color is precisely the color that the body doesn't absorb. It's the color that it reflects, diffuses, or transmits. Why are plants green? The standard answer, as in the Larousse [dictionary], is that plants are green because chlorophyll absorbs red [light] and then they reflect green. So, you can imagine a synthesis of pigments. But what is this synthesis? Either yellow pigments: they absorb blue and send yellow or green back to the eye. Or blue pigments: they absorb yellow and send back green and blue. You mix both types of pigment. The blue is absorbed, the yellow is absorbed, and you're left with a purely green reflection. What do you call this mixture or this synthesis? This time, it's called a *subtractive* synthesis. It can't be created with light rays. Moreover, appreciate that subtractive synthesis can produce whatever you want except white. In what case can it render black? If each body absorbs what the others reflect, then you'll have black. So, black can be produced through subtractive synthesis or subtractive mixing, but you cannot have white. There you have my three scientific formulas from colorimetry.

Let's put these formulas aside, this research from colorimetry. Here's my question—listen carefully so that you can make modifications: Hadn't people working in the pictorial arts already developed such regimes of color? The last criterion for a regime is the means of reproducing color. We'll stop there, since it's getting too abstract. I would therefore define a regime of colors by four characteristics.

First characteristic: by a state of the ground, in both senses of the word *ground,* namely, determination of the support—qualification of the support—and the variable position of the background. Second characteristic: by a corresponding modulation. Third characteristic: by a hue privileged among the four primary hues: bright, pale, muted, deep. [Fourth characteristic]: by one of the three primary means of reproducing color: the dominant wavelength method, referring to a white flux; the method of additive synthesis; the method of subtractive mixing. It's fortunate that I've already reviewed this because, in fact, my second characteristic disappears, since modulation is included in the last characteristic. So, in fact, there are only three characteristics. There you have it! Whew! Time for a short break.

[*Interruption of the recording,* time stamp: 30:32.]

So, I'll come back to my problem. If it's true that we can define regimes of colors, these regimes of color will refer sometimes to previously defined spaces and to previously defined modulations, sometimes to a space specific to color and to a specific chromatic modulation that we haven't yet defined. Let's follow up a bit within the history of painting. For example, I attempt to define a Renaissance regime of color. We'll see how this unfolds—if we can ascertain something a tiny bit technical, but really in the interest of our examination into regimes of color. Would there be a Renaissance regime of color, albeit with many exceptions and problems? But such problematic questions are also what enlivens a history of painting. Yes, it does seem like there is in fact a regime of colors as we've just described it. This is no doubt a long history, but the existence of white grounds in Renaissance painting is what makes it famous.

So, white grounds, let's start from there. This might bring us back to our first colorimetric formula, but we can't push it too far, since they pursued this as painters, as practitioners, not as scientists. They use white grounds. What does that mean? It means that the support is coated with a layer of plaster treated in a special way, or else with a rather thick layer of chalk. With that in place, what happens? An important painter for the history of painting is known for having perfected this system, and well before the Renaissance; that is, the Renaissance was endowed with something long in the making. This particular painter functions as something of a turning point between the Renaissance and what came before. I'm thinking of the great Flemish painter, Van Eyck, to such an extent that Van Eyck's secret formula is a common fixture in the history of painting. This secret starts with the use of so-called slaked plaster as a ground.[9] Van Eyck died around 1440, that is, shortly before the birth of Leonardo da Vinci in 1452. There's a recent book of criticism that greatly emphasizes how Van Eyck was considered a painter among painters—everyone is free to choose their own painter among painters—but this emphasis is based precisely on this mysterious white ground. Because there's a lot at stake in this white ground. Actually, obtaining slaked plaster involved a whole process with plaster and glue. The pharmacy of painting, the chemistry of painting, became a real concern. The author of the book I'm referring to is Xavier de Langlais. He wrote a very interesting book, published by Flammarion, called *The Technique of Oil Painting*.[10] It's terrific; it's a real joy to read. It's really funny because it's a very particular sort of criticism that you can sometimes find in every artistic discipline. I think he's literally what you could call a reactionary, but in a good way. You'll see what I mean by reactionary in a good way.

De Langlais is one of those art historians who proclaims art has stopped evolving at a certain point and says, No, no, that's it, we're done, it's all downhill from here! These kinds of critics are delightful to read, actually. [*Laughter.*] In music, for example, there are many fans like this of Gregorian chant. There's nothing after Gregorian chant; it's a decline, a slow decline. We probably shouldn't joke about this. It happened in philosophy: a happy moment with

Neo-Thomism. Jacques Maritain was great: after St. Thomas, it was hard for him. And Descartes? If there was a little of St. Thomas in Descartes, that worked fine. Sometimes these people who freeze everything at a particular moment and don't want to bother with anything else turn out to be surprisingly modern. And from two perspectives, they are fine. On the one hand, they have a lot to teach us about the cutoff point they develop. That's easily explained: they're so worked up by their thinking "after this, it's all over" that they have a profound technical knowledge of the period where "everything" stops. To understand what's going on with Gregorian chant, you have to ask someone like that. To understand St. Thomas, you obviously have to ask Maritain. Everything else is such decadence that, according to them, you're better off starting from scratch.

Back to our example, because I'm fascinated by it, the example of Xavier de Langlais. He'll say that oil painting reached its apogee with Van Eyck, thanks to the white ground, thanks to slaked plaster. Afterward, everything falls apart. Already in the Renaissance, of course, Van Eyck's secret is maintained, but they understand it less clearly. Things were already on the decline in the Renaissance, but it's awful after that. What's so awful about it? Here we see Xavier de Langlais's personal obsession: it's the process of craquelure. Paintings crack. So Xavier de Langlais loses his bearings. Paintings after Van Eyck crack more and more. De Langlais loses it when it comes to really "cracking" painters. [*Laughter.*] In particular, the punching bag for Xavier de Langlais is an eighteenth-century English portraitist named Reynolds.[11] We'll see why; in terms of the regime of color, there's no avoiding craquelure in the work of Reynolds. But Xavier de Langlais has even greater contempt for Delacroix! He simply doesn't know how to do his job, as his craquelures demonstrate. [De Langlais] bitterly says of the Impressionists that they had good ideas but lacked know-how. They never could solve the problem of ground.[12] Notice that I'm coming back to my question about the regime of color. Xavier de Langlais is someone for whom there is only *one* regime of color: the great regime of the dominant wavelength, that is, the white ground.

There you have this first regime of color: the Renaissance, which holds Van Eyck's secret, which employed it and modified its support as plaster or a thick layer of chalk. What happens after that?

[Two phases:] on the white ground, they make what's called an underpainting [*ébauche*] and, second phase, they wash the underpainting. That's how they worked. Third phase: they spread and place the colors in thin layers.[13] Here I'll make a quick aside: my first two phases, white ground, washed underpainting, of course, offer us the light/washed-out formula [*clair lavé*]. This is what I described as: privilege given to pale hues. This doesn't prevent them from placing the colors in the third phase—maybe bright colors, maybe saturated colors, maybe deep colors—but the principle remains: placing thin layers of color on the white ground such that the white ground peeks through, especially, for example, through a garment.

The white ground will give the colors luminosity. For the shadows, they'll saturate the color placed on the ground; they'll go through several layers. The color placed on the white ground over the underpainting while following the lines of the underpainting provides the first formula of so-called glazing.[14] A thin layer of color on the ground. But although they use the word *glaze* as a technical term, I'd rather insist on saying: this isn't true glazing. It's a glaze in a very general sense. We'll see why I have this reservation. I have every right to my preference, to save the word *glaze* for another regime.

That's the first regime. This is the Renaissance formula: white ground, washed underpainting, glazed colors. I maintain that I'm justified in saying that this is a pale regime even if the pale hues aren't dominant, even if there aren't exclusively pale hues. It's a pale regime because the aggregate of colors, whether they're bright, saturated, deep, what have you, will be obtained through this matrix: white, washed underpainting. And what's going to happen here that truly belongs to the history of the Renaissance? In what way does painting shift? What occurs is that Renaissance painters who borrow Van Eyck's system (you'll see that the Italians get it from Flanders, and then we'll see that through Italy, it comes back to Flanders and to Holland; these pathways are very odd) Renaissance painters—I'm talking about the greats, so this is not a critique; for de Langlais, that's already a critique—will gradually tend more and more to thicken the white ground. A phase in their technical prowess hinges on a thickening of the white ground. The white ground gradually becomes a thicker white or, at least, more and more opaque. This is very important, if you follow me—this is the last sticking point; if you understand this, you'll understand everything that comes after—in particular, in Titian's works.[15] This really bothers de Langlais because, as he says, obviously [Titian] is a genius, among the greatest of painters, and at the same time, his technique is already setting the stage for decadence, since it's no longer the old Van Eyck ground. Titian is the painter known for a visible and considerable thickening of the support's ground. The white ground becomes very thick and very opaque. You can sense that this will already be a nascent form of luminism. This practice will really foreshadow certain aspects of the seventeenth century. The white ground becomes very opaque, even in Leonardo da Vinci's work where, strangely, his plaster seems—as specialists have said—not really thicker than Van Eyck's, but still much more opaque. These strictly technical differences are interesting.

What will develop from making a much thicker white ground? A very thick plaster? This will have two consequences: the first thing is that by washing the ground, diluting it with water or with turpentine, the dilution becomes darker and darker. It's as though color creeps back into the ground. The colors of the underpainting will in themselves affect the whole ground. Instead of a white ground, as it gets thicker and more opaque, the white ground starts to take on color. That's the first major difference. A pale color, but it is colored. The second notable difference: the underpainting stage is under threat. By what? The underpainting will gradually be replaced by working *impasto*—this is particularly clear with Titian's work—as the ground gets thicker.[16] What does it mean to work *impasto*? This is what must be opposed to underpainting. Working *impasto* is the method of the painter's *pentimento* [*repentirs*].[17] Instead of a well-defined underpainting after which all that's left to do is add colors, there will be a perpetual reworking, working *impasto*. Particularly starting with Titian, one finds such appealing things, the painter's *pentimento* in which you see the trace of a *pentimento*, when you look very closely or else when you look at it scientifically—for example, as a fifth leg of a horse, the leg that was covered up in order to reposition its legs.[18]

As far as the regime with white ground is concerned from a technical perspective, the Renaissance's evolution is distinguished by three things: a gradual increase in thickness and opacity; grounds are more and more starkly colored; the substitution of *pentimento* for underpainting. Indeed, for someone like de Langlais, this is all quite sad: this thicker plaster, this ground that absorbs color directly, and abandoning underpainting in favor of working *impasto*. All that leads him to suggest from his particular viewpoint, ah, well, painting has taken a wrong turn. When I suggest that he is nonetheless quite modernist, this becomes quite understandable. He's so convinced that oil painting was already in decline during the Renaissance that he says: hurray for acrylic paints, hurray for oilless paints, hurray for contemporary colors. He gets transformed into quite a modernist all over again. He says: oil painting is screwed, so we'd be better off starting from scratch with [acrylic], vinyl, and so on.

Back to what I was discussing. A Renaissance regime of color indeed existed—you see, that's all bound up with everything we discussed earlier—but by necessity, this regime of color is employed by another sort of sign-space and modulation. As we saw, the sign-space of the Renaissance is the tactile-optical space, defined by the collective line and the primacy of the foreground. But note that the primacy of the foreground is specifically established by way of the white ground. Note that it's precisely the underpainting that establishes the collective line. That doesn't prevent a regime of color from existing to the extent that, whatever your colors might be, you lay them in pseudo-glaze onto this ground acting on the colors. That's what I can call the pale regime of color employed by the Renaissance tactile-optical space and by the collective line's modulation.

That's our first regime of color. Let's move on to another regime of color at the risk of complicating things while also simplifying things—maybe, I don't know—because we're going to consider the *several* seventeenth-century regimes of color. For the sake of convenience, I was calling for a single [regime], even a highly varied one, but there's no way around it—there are so obviously two, two that'll form a sort of pincer around seventeenth-century luminism. Here as well, this regime still won't be a space of pure color; it'll be a regime of color subject to optical space, which is how we defined the seventeenth century, and relative to the corresponding modulation, the modulation of light and no longer the modulation of the collective line. Here as well, the regime of color still doesn't refer to its very own coloristic space; it's dedicated to another kind of space: the optical space of light. However, this represents a drastic change compared with the regime of the Renaissance.

A painter emerged at the end of the sixteenth century, with incredible technical importance, who is predictably abhorred so much by Xavier de Langlais that he doesn't even talk about him. It's Caravaggio. And what does Caravaggio do? What does he invent? The strangest thing—of course, he had predecessors, you'd have to locate them—he invents "dark ground" [*fond noirâtre*], pitch ground [*fond de bitume*], or more precisely, red-brown ground.[19] What difference does that make? Here we have the support modified by this sort of—how can I put this?—of indefinite color. I'm emphasizing this because when Wölfflin talks about certain aspects of luminism in the seventeenth century, that's exactly what he says: the ground is an indefinite color.[20] What I find important is that it's something indefinite. I cannot say, strictly speaking, it's this-or-that color but it is *some* color, whereas with the Renaissance formula, you had a white ground. In other words, color was obtained in a noncolored matrix. Coloring hardly began after the underpainting. Here you have an indefinite color. You get the feeling that all the colors mix together in their dark nature. This fully illustrates what Goethe says: every color is dark, every color is obscure. The color matrix is this kind of dark bath that will make up the painting's ground.

All of our concepts come back into play with this dark ground, with this obscure matrix. There's a good chance of securing the primacy of the background. This time, the ground is responsible for securing the background's primacy. Everything emerges from the background. You already sense that it's no longer about spreading out glazed colors on a white ground. What's in play here is causing every color, every gleam, all the brightness—that is, every kind of lights—to emerge from the dark ground, from this dark matrix. The dark ground will be even darker where shadows are located, causing the bright colors to emerge, and obviously, the painter's primary task develops toward *blending* [*dégradation*]. He or she will blend the bright colors into the shadows—this is an entirely different regime of color—and this will be *one* of the poles of the birth of luminism, these bright lights that burst from a dark ground. A famous example: Caravaggio's *St. Matthew's Vocation*.[21]

A STUDENT: Didn't Leonardo da Vinci do that? Didn't he do shading?

DELEUZE: Why yes, obviously, since he places his shadows . . . I'm not saying he invented shading. Shading at that point turns into something belonging entirely to the second task, since inevitably the ground will be colored in an indefinite way, it'll be the dark ground. The lights and the shadows will be organized in such a way that they emerge from the dark ground instead of being placed upon [it]. Caravaggio's *St. Matthew's Vocation* is a famous example revealing this dark ground, this indefinite color: a version of St. Matthew in a seedy dive, with a pitch-black shadow, and a ray of light shining from a narrow window on Christ's hand pointing at Saint Matthew like: "Hey, you . . . you . . . !" (as in, "you, follow me!"), and this hand is caught in the beam of light. This work already heralds the great turn of the birth of luminism. My point is that Caravaggio had a fundamental influence on the entirety of seventeenth-century painting, which spread everywhere, to everyone. Caravaggio's influence can be seen spreading as far as Spain: it spread to Ribera and El Greco. It was all over France. He also influenced the Flemish. Caravaggio's work itself was kind of a turning point.

And, in terms of technique, if we look for the origin of these dark grounds that Caravaggio perfected, it seems you'll find them already in some of Tintoretto's paintings.[22] As I was saying earlier, this is a pale regime, with a white ground and washed underpainting. Here, however, it's a dark ground and *impasto* color. This time, it corresponds to saturated dark and to washed-out dark. In other words, it's a mixed regime that is at once a regime of deep hues and of muted hues. There, too, all the hues are produced. If I try to find an equivalent for this, I'd say real quickly: this time, the matrix is the mixture of three colors that don't counterbalance each other. The indefinite color is this dark mixture of colors taken in their dark nature, in their obscure nature—that is, the three primary colors no longer counterbalance each other. In other words, it'd be a regime of additive synthesis.

But in the other direction—this is how we see luminism's dual aspect—the legacy of the Renaissance presses on, but precisely in doing so, its meaning will completely change. Picking this back up starting from Titian, you recall, this white ground became thicker and thicker as a result of which it no longer supported an underpainting but was the object of *impasto* work and took on color. That'll be very important; that will be the birth of glazing properly speaking. That is, going back in time, starting from painting's origins, the ground becomes more and more starkly colored, while the painting is done more and more via *impasto*. It's Rubens who goes all the way; as a result, you'll tend to identify a glaze strictly speaking, to wit: colors are applied on a light, colored ground. In other words, glaze in the strict sense is color put on top of bright colors, colors applied to a bright ground. Colors that are sharp, that are translucid, and if necessary, brilliant, applied to a bright ground. Why aren't bright colors applied? Precisely because they are too opaque. The light colors are what will make up the ground, and glazing occurs because color is applied to this bright ground. That's Rubens's formula, for example, colors like ultramarine or pitch will be applied to the bright ground.[23] I believe one of the first to have proceeded like this—in Titian's line, but who represents an evolution, a precipitation in relation to him—is precisely a Spaniard, meaning that Spain would have its two painters, Ribera descending from the Caravaggio formula and Herrera who literally paints on pink-silver grounds (often, not always), silvery pink grounds where there is really a kind of glazing.

As a result, I think the strict definition of glazing is exactly the one provided by Goethe. When I apply colors on a white ground in the Renaissance way, it's not glazing strictly speaking. Goethe distinguishes three grounds in the *Theory of Colors*. In a quick overview,[24] he says: there is the white ground in chalk (he doesn't mention plaster, but in fact, it was especially in plaster). There is the white ground of the Renaissance; there is the dark reddish-brown ground of Caravaggio (he cites very few painters, but here, he indeed cites Caravaggio). He says: glaze must be added. He defines glazing this way: it's what happens when one treats an already applied color like a bright ground.[25] As a result, despite how the word is used, I'd rather not employ the word *glaze* when color is applied on a ground that isn't itself already a color, a necessarily light color. It's only glazing when you place colors in thin, transparent layers on a light ground.

[*Interruption of the recording,* time stamp: 1:08:13.]

The Caravaggio formula, once again, consists of dark, saturated, or washed-out. Dark, saturated as well as washed-out, sometimes saturated from one perspective and washed-out from a different perspective. So, this is a regime I'd call, following our terminology, a deep and muted regime as opposed to the Renaissance's pale regime.

Rubens's regime—colors put down on a light, colored ground—is the other aspect of luminism. This time, the light is not drawn out of a dark ground, nor does it dig up a dark ground. The light is in the background, and it's great stuff. There's no backlighting in Caravaggio's style. The light is always localized, and either it's drawn out of the dark ground, or it digs up the dark ground as in *St. Matthew's Vocation.* But the real formula of glazing is an indeterminate light that bathes the background, with the foreground being dark instead. And it goes without saying that, for example, in Vermeer, you see this constantly, or very often, at least, the light background and the shadow of the foreground. It's an extraordinary formula, but it's also present in a painter who is nevertheless very different, in Rubens. What regime would that be? It's a saturated light regime, that is, a bright regime.

Before we take a break, I'll conclude. You see there are regimes of color that refer to spaces we examined before. In particular, I've returned to two spaces we examined before: the tactile-optical space of the Renaissance with modulation by the collective line. That provides, or that entails, or that corresponds to a pale regime of color. But color presupposes this space and this modulation. [And referring] to the seventeenth century, [we find] optical space: modulation of light or by light. Here again, you have several regimes of color: either the Caravaggio-type of regime or the Rubens-type of regime. As different as they are, they both fall under luminism. They're luminist regimes, that is, regimes made up of color but serving an optical space and a modulation of light.

What does it mean when they say that in Western painting, the true advent of colorism occurs in the nineteenth century? In my opinion, what this means is very simple. All the problems of color were present in the other centuries. Why was the problem with color posed in a new way in the nineteenth century? Because the regime of color was undergoing change in relation to the preceding criteria. At the same time, the regime was not simply undergoing change. Coincidentally, painters at that time no doubt needed something their predecessors didn't need, that is, for colors not only to be a regime that is invented or reinvented—which in itself already implies a supreme colorism—but furthermore, for color to be what determines a new type of space, no longer tactile-optical space, nor the optical space of light, but one that is color's very own space and with a modulation that is color's very own.

All these accounts of color—complementary colors, diametric oppositions between complementary colors—have so much importance in the nineteenth century. Today, their importance is quite limited. In the nineteenth century, the law of so-called simultaneous contrast, that is, the complementary and diametrically opposite relationships between complementary colors, is truly color's highest premise. Today, once again, my sense is that painters aren't concerned with this issue. It ultimately culminates, if you will, with Seurat. I don't mean that Seurat has become outdated. I mean that even when painters take something and borrow something from Seurat, they totally ignore the problem of the contrast of complementary colors, which is so present in his work. Today, that's no longer a problem.

But that's fine, you know. It's the same thing in philosophy, in music, and so on. You can't say that works responding to a given problem have become in any way outdated, but it explains why we see them in a new light. There is a decentering that takes place. Something that was essential for the painter undertaking a painting stopped being essential for us from a practical point of view, as a result of which our evaluation of the painting will emphasize things that were merely unspoken. An entire history lies inside the painting. Such contrasts are very interesting, but today anyway, painters no longer really experience that problem very much, for a very simple reason: they discovered things that are so much more complex in terms of color that this higher law is necessarily unsatisfactory.

And before that? There's no point in exaggerating; the relationship between complementary colors was well known. Following up on someone's comment a second ago, it's already present in Leonardo da Vinci, already there in the Renaissance. They knew all about it, practically, optically. In the seventeenth century, in Rembrandt, you'll find any combination of complementary colors you can imagine. When he renders the dark ground that you'll often find in his works, where light is drawn out, you might have, for example, a bright red foreground, and there's a muted resonance in the background, in the greenish dark ground. I'm thinking of a specific painting, *Susannah Bathing*.[26] They knew all about this problem. What makes us say that it explodes in the nineteenth century? We do so because in the seventeenth century, they were only slightly familiar with it; they didn't really use it. Their knowledge of this problem was such that it was taken for granted. It was taken for granted, since the relations between complementary colors, between contrasts, between oppositions of complementary colors can be deployed in the seventeenth century but based on a totally different sort of ground and treatment of ground, for example, the Caravaggio treatment.

On the other hand, these same problems regarding complementary colors become essential once the treatment of ground brings them to the fore. And, in fact, with the nineteenth century, something occurs such that this problem—despite its secondary status for seventeenth-century luminism—becomes a central concern for a period embracing nineteenth-century colorism, notably in the Impressionist moment. Today, colorists don't take that route anymore. What happens in the nineteenth century? I bet you can already guess. The route they take explains why Xavier de Langlais's despair descends into a bottomless pit. Circumstances can only go from bad to worse. As he says, they didn't know how to paint. Or rather, they knew very well how to paint. He says: they're great painters, but they no longer know how to prepare. So, here we have all the reactionary themes, speed, to hell with speed, all that. They speed up; they don't prepare. What does preparing mean? It's the fundamental act in painting, since it concerns preparing the support. So, in fact, there are some painters who no longer prepare at all.

A STUDENT: [*Inaudible comment that they no longer make use of eggs.*][27]

DELEUZE: Yes, egg was the binding medium, but it was tied to the underpainting. If eggs went away, it's only because concerns about underpainting became obsolete with *impasto* work.

ANOTHER STUDENT: [*Inaudible remark*, time stamp: 1:18:11–1:18:18.]

DELEUZE: There's also the advent of tubed paint, which changes everything. You see, they couldn't paint outside before tubed paint. And tubed paint is very recent: the nineteenth century. How did they do things before? With Rubens, it's very straightforward. He prepared his colors. There were jars of prepared paint. He made his jars, three for each hue: a color, a dark hue, and a light hue. He painted to get gradients into the shadows. And then he had paste color on his palette that he used only at the last moment to make accents. Hey, this really helps me move forward: for making accents. The process had a sort of sequence to it: preparing the thick ground; working *impasto* on already placed colors, potted paints with gradations, with a distribution of shadows and lights, and so on; and then, third, the essential moment: paste colors for making accents.

If I were to describe in very broad strokes the techniques of the nineteenth century—but here, I'm really going too fast—I'd say: the ground becomes less and less important. What happens with the work of support? You even have painters who work directly on the canvas. Paint on paint [*couleur sur couleur*]. I find that great because that's the formula for real glazing. The base is treated by color paint. For example, there are some works by Signac, and while not the greatest, they are intriguing because there isn't any ground. Or in Manet's work, for example, there is the use of raw, unworked plaster, a plaster that's very absorbent. In other words, it's almost the same, from the viewpoint of my quick overview: the ground is colored. The advent of colorism in the nineteenth century, it seems to me, comes down to painters who work with paint on paint [*couleur sur couleur*]. They no longer go through the mediation of an external white matrix, nor through the mediation of an internal dark matrix. And that's great. It means that color begins to exist for itself, on one condition: that painters be capable of constituting a coloristic space and a modulation proper to color. It'll no longer be mediated by light. Light will be derived from color. The line will be derived from color, and so forth.

Everything slips further and further back. We can devise a series of temporal stages going back more and more. You had three calm impulses [*temps*] in the Renaissance: white ground, underpainting, a pseudo-glaze of color. In the seventeenth century and already culminating with Titian, you had a precipitation: a thicker and therefore increasingly colored ground, working *impasto*. The need for underpainting is short-circuited, and finally, the triumph of color with Titian's accents. So, in the seventeenth century, you have this kind of temporal slippage in which things get rushed. If I were to sum up the problem of colorism in the nineteenth century, color is in the accents; there's nothing left but accents. A whole world is created with what would, for others, be final accents. Hence what I said last time: Delacroix's crosshatching, with which Delacroix still uses a Caravaggio ground, only everything is condensed. Right onto the ground, he'll make crosshatches that draw color out of the ground. And then, the comma-stroke, the Impressionist accent where it's a bit like we say in music: the accents are what matter. They discover that with color, it's the accents that matter. Henceforth, it's no surprise that this space's unit becomes either Delacroix's crosshatching, or the Impressionist comma, or Seurat's tiny point.

So de Langlais has a legitimate concern, but he says there's only one guy who emerges from all this, that is, whose work doesn't crack: it's Seurat. His treatment of the ground, his tiny point, and so on, prevents his works from cracking; they hold up. Again this demand for things to endure rises up. As Cézanne puts it: I wanted to make of Impressionism something [solid and] enduring.[28] The sense that a painting endures or doesn't [is] very important for a painter. It's rather a question of time. We'll see, if we have time, why time comes up here.[29] A painting that bites into time. De Langlais isn't totally off. If it cracks after twenty years, this is upsetting in any case. We still don't know how well "petroleum" colors or acrylics, and so forth, will hold up. We'll have to wait.[30] The conditions are already inscribed in the painting, although we can't say in advance: Does it endure? There's weight, time, and so on. Paintings have a way of belonging to time, of being within time, of having weight, and so forth. And Cézanne's idea of making Impressionism something durable and solid came down to problems with technique.

A STUDENT: [*Regarding a court case about an issue of valuable paintings becoming white after several years.*][31]

DELEUZE: There is a lovely novel by Balzac on that.[32] Yes, it's quite possible, like any problem of restoration. De Langlais is so amazing;

he says: there are only a few beautiful works by Delacroix, the ones that were restored by someone other than Delacroix.[33] Then they're not bad, he says, since it was done by people who knew what they were doing.

Here's the point I want to reach before our break. I could suggest: there's yet another new regime of color in the nineteenth century. It's one that I'd also call bright. But how is it different from the bright regime of the seventeenth century? The seventeenth century's bright regime involved a glaze on a light ground, while now they proceed with a painting of accents. There's no longer any glazing. There isn't any ground. The ground tends to disappear or to be neutralized, and so on, truly reaching color for itself. Henceforth, this color will deploy the relationships proper to colors for themselves, namely and foremost, the principal relationships, the princely relationships between complementary colors. Hence the possibility of a modulation of color and of a modulation particular to color, whereas, before, the regimes of color were also skillful but, once again, in the service of colorless spaces, whether tactile-optical space or the optical space of light. And therefore in the service of a modulation that was defined differently: either the modulation of the collective line or the modulation of light. Whereas here, we reach the opening of a space *through* color and *of* color, a space proper to color, the unit for which is in accents. At the extreme, I would say that this is no longer the underpainting nor even working *impasto*. A painting of accents is altogether something different. We're faced with this issue of a regime of color that, finally, for the first time in Western history (well, I'm obviously exaggerating a bit here), develops a space that can be exclusively defined only in terms of color and a modulation that can be defined only in terms of color. So, there's very little left for us to cover, mainly to see what this space and this modulation consist in. Let's take a break.

[*Interruption of the recording,* time stamp: 1:29:35.]

There's not much to cover, then. I'll just lay out some guidelines unless, which would better, you wanted to discuss something. That would be fine as well . . . Yes?

GEORGES COMTESSE: Regarding the question of the white or blackish ground that marks the difference between the Renaissance and the seventeenth century, for example . . . [*brief inaudible passage.*][34] [The issue is] the shift that results from this problem of the ground and of colors, of light and colors, the shift that occurs in contemporary American painting, in particular in works by the painter Sam Francis. It's very interesting to see just where this shift is located because, in his work, there is a white ground and the colors from scratches [*raies*], a bit like Delacroix, scratches that cross the white ground. This particularity stands in contrast to Goethe, for example, in his *Theory of Colors,* where black and white are like the matrices of the color triangle only, black and white basically standing for light and shadow. Whereas in Sam Francis's work, there is another shift insofar as white is in no way shadow or light. White, he says, is the color of all colors, the primitive color. He calls that the dazzling-distracting color, and it's even the dazzling color in which the painter paints the birth of the painter's gaze onto the canvas.[35] This has many implications. Concerning white as a dazzling-distracting color, light becomes black. Or else shadow passes into light, or light returns to the shadow, either way. At any rate, it spills over binaries, and it shatters the color triangle. The color white as simultaneously white and black. And at that point, regarding colors, it's utterly strange to see the sorts of chromatic bands that he spreads across the canvas. It's not a color somehow placed onto a white ground, nor even one torn from a white ground; these are colors that emerge from the dazzling-distracting whiteness while still seeming to disappear at the same time into white. This is a kind of simultaneity, neither presence nor absence, the simultaneity of emergence and disappearance in relation to the event, the dazzling event that can at the same time be a black hole event for the painter. So here, there is a rather extraordinary shift in relation to the ideal division that you've traced in the history of painting or the history of regimes of color.

DELEUZE: Very well expressed. What we especially need to avoid, in fact, is believing that it's a revival of Renaissance spaces, even a modern revival. Because it's in response to colorist demands that all this modern colorism, with the role of white—it's not only Sam

Francis, of course—it's because of that . . . That's all I meant. But then I'm going very fast to give you some guidelines, in fact, and to wrap things up.

If you understand the new requirements of this new bright regime of colors, namely, the deployment of a corresponding space and modulation, I'll outline something like a first stage. I'm dividing this into stages in order to give you some reference points. Within Impressionism, you have a painting of accents. What turns out to be fundamental are the relations between colors as determining a new space. What makes that so fundamental? Once again, relations between colors existed much earlier. Their interplay wasn't in a purified form due to this long history of the ground throughout the Renaissance and the seventeenth century, whereas this interplay now reaches a free state. This amounts to saying that what softens or reinforces color is another color. It's no longer mediated at all by a matrix or by a ground in any manner that these might have been conceived. In the Renaissance no less than in the seventeenth century, there is this mediation by the matrix or by the ground. Not anymore here; there is no longer any need. Even if the ground remains, it no longer serves that purpose. Colors now regulate one another and are deployed for themselves, constituting a space.

So, my first reference point necessarily begins with an Impressionist type of painting via tiny units [*à petites unités*], since, once again, the tiny pictorial unit—the comma-stroke or the point—is specifically what replaces underpainting and *impasto* work. This space will be constituted in punctual fashion, not because it's made unit by unit but rather because the space is thereby conceived as a network. Points are fundamentally linked. However, the first stage that I want to emphasize, corresponding to Impressionism, is really a sort of practical problem of privilege. For the relations of color with the color that now reaches into the foreground have been doubled. Theoretically, you can always say that this works out quite well. Practically, if you are a painter, you are necessarily required to privilege one or the other.

Unfortunately, my circle's been erased. You remember the chromatic circle?[36] You remember that you can conceptualize the fundamental color-color relations either in terms of diametric oppositions—it's the relation between complements (for example, red/green, which defines a diameter of the circle), this is simultaneous contrast, or else [in terms of] the peripheral relation produced by the chords, from one color to another, skipping an intermediary color or even without skipping. So, there are closer and closer peripheral relations and diametrical relations of opposition. Understand that the Impressionists, whether with their comma or with their tiny point, make use of both. That's why, whenever color is discussed, every Impressionist text refers to both laws: the law of contrasts and the law of the analogical. The law of contrasts designates the diametric oppositions between complementary colors. The law of the analogical designates the chords or the peripheral pathway along the chromatic circle. In Cézanne's work, you constantly see this reference to both sacred laws, but it's in works by all the Impressionists.

Why can't they do one without the other? They cannot deny that, for example, even if you proceed along the edge, you'll reach complementary colors by going around the circle. And the complements are singular points on the circle's periphery that you'll cross along the way. So, the periphery's pathway will pass through and will involve the interplay of contrasting colors. Conversely, there's a contrast between two complements. The contrast implies precisely that they're not to be juxtaposed. If you overlap two complements, you wind up with grey.

So long as we handle complements as large, pictorial units, as surfaces, the opposition implied that both complements, for example, your red and green, are quite distinct, otherwise they couldn't be opposed. They aren't juxtaposed, since a problem existed in shading, from one to the other or into the other. When you proceed as Impressionism did—we saw why they worked like that—with little color units and no longer in sections, at most you could juxtapose two color-patches, a red one, a green one. You can't juxtapose two points, since the juxtaposition of tiny units—I won't get into it, we all know this—it's precisely the definition of optical mixture in contrast to chemical mixture. It's the eye that blends them. If you juxtapose little red points with little green points, the eye automatically performs an optical mixture; it creates grey. So, if you make a little red point, your little green point must be at a certain distance for you to blend from red into green and for the blend, or the gradient, from green into red. This shading can be done in light/dark, but it can obviously be done in color. There is a tonal shading in the order of the color spectrum no less than a shading in light/dark.

I'm saying that if you privileged contrasts, or diametric oppositions, you're nevertheless bound to introduce peripheral pathways of color. If you privileged peripheral pathways, you're nevertheless necessarily bound to encounter major contrasts, the diametric oppositions. You might say: "So what? That's all very fine. Here, we're strengthening our position: this is what will define colorist space." Yes and no. In practice, you have a very curious choice to make. Among the Impressionists, you have painters for whom everything is organized around diametric oppositions. And even in Neo-Impressionism, Seurat never stops saying: what matters in the end are complementary relations. The peripheral pathway will be relevant only for shading one complement onto the other. That, indeed, is the method of pointillism.

But there are others who greatly prefer analogy, the peripheral pathway, that is, the relationships between neighboring colors on the circle's periphery, neighbors affecting variable discontinuities depending on the chords you choose. That seems to me very interesting. I see a real extreme in Pissarro. I'm not at all saying that there aren't any contrasts or complements in his work, but he isn't interested in that. What interests him is building a world out of neighboring colors. In other words, what interests him isn't oppositions of tones, it's transitions from one tone to the next, with gradations in half-tones, quarter-tones, and so on. You may wind up with ambiguities, in impasses that are breathtaking because they are creative. Pissarro is the most benevolent painter. He was aged, he taught so much to other painters, he occupied a very respected position in the group. "Ah, good old Pissarro," and so forth. The dignified, perfect, amazing Pissarro. At the same time, he really admired what [the younger painters] were doing. It's so rare in human nature for old guys to admire what the youth are doing that we have to commend him. Pissarro finds that Seurat—who for him is a very young man—he thinks what Seurat's doing is marvelous. So there we find him working with Seurat's little points. And at the same time, he's uneasy. As talented as he is, this old painter says:

well, yeah, Seurat's right; he's seen something. He's seen the necessary link between the little unit—the point, at the extreme—and the world of color that we're all searching for.

He begins using tiny points, since what they have in common is capturing this space of color. There are Pissarro's famous pointillist works. He isn't comfortable with it, which we understand as: he's using a method, but he isn't the one who created it; it doesn't work. Something bothers him. What bothers him, it seems to me, is quite simple. It's that the method of using tiny points was an excellent method for building a space of color grounded in a privileged way on diametric oppositions. What interests [Pissarro][37] is the other aspect of the chromatic circle, the peripheral pathway between neighboring colors. There's little reason to use tiny points. The tiny point even loses its necessity; the tiny point is sort of gratuitous, just like the painters who rendered the tiny point gloomy, a dim point, a noncolored point. There is Henri Martin. At a time when everyone was berating and jeering at Seurat and his bright tiny points, there was one jackass who adopted his method, who used tiny points, but noncolored points, little uncolored points. Entirely uninteresting. Everyone thought it was terrific, but I'm exaggerating. Henri Martin sold a lot of paintings; Seurat didn't. It wasn't working. There was this exercise employing an entirely vacuous method: no reason for making tiny points. He [Martin] made tiny points, [and] everyone said: What lovely little points! [And in Seurat's case:] Ah, that's awful. For Pissarro, this wasn't even his issue. He adopted the method through a sort of love for Seurat, telling himself, there's something here I can make use of. Alas, no, the method didn't really suit him because, once again, his problem was the transition from one tone to another.

With Cézanne, it turns into something inextricable. Cézanne endows this whole colorist space with a kind of absolute perfection. In the previous session, I pointed out the treatment of the same subject using the luminist light/dark approach, local tone regarding color, and so on, shading the local tone through shadow, through light/dark [*clair/foncé*], and so on. And then the other method that he's really the first to pull off, the first one even to systematize it, although it varies with each painting (he isn't using a formula), and that specifically involves: not allowing any light to show, not showing any lines; instead, a creation of modeling through color. And the modeling through color will establish a sequence—only he never uses the same sequence twice, obviously—a sequence of tones, a gradient of neighboring tones in the order of the spectrum around a culminating point.

So, you see that here, too, both aspects are combined because the culminating point will have complementary relations with another point, located elsewhere in the painting. But the thing's entire color-volume will be rendered by this sequence of small color-patches—since he doesn't use points but fairly small color-patches—moving along the neighboring gradient on the order of the spectrum. I referred to the very fine and detailed article on Cézanne by an Englishman, in which he analyzes a dozen different sequences, alongside reproductions of the paintings—unfortunately, in black-and-white, but that doesn't matter.[38] To some extent, Cézanne seems to me closer to Pissarro than having differences. Cézanne's the one who cries out: What matters is the transition from tone to tone! And what he forbids himself from doing—that develops into an extraordinary technique—is to fill in part of a sequence by using a mixture. The shading must be shaded through color, not through light/dark. Every time, he has to find the right tone in the sequence. Otherwise, he leaves it blank. Hence, as the renowned Vollard commented, upon seeing a blank spot: but really, these white spots, they're strange. And [Cézanne] responded: please try to understand. If I use a mixture or roughly guess at the color, I'm screwed, I'd have to begin again, starting with the color that I applied too quickly.[39] It's like he's searching for transitions. When Cézanne railed against Gauguin, he said: Gauguin took everything from me, but he understood nothing.[40] That was completely unfair, since I think that Gauguin didn't take all that much, and he understood perfectly well. He says: Gauguin didn't understand the main problem, the problem of transitioning from tone to tone along the order of the spectrum. Here he is providing us with his method. So, you see, that's the first stage: it's this space of color, made up of tiny pictorial units with a problem that is roused during this first stage, namely: how to establish the coexistence of this space's two paths, the peripheral path and the diametric path? And in each painter, how does all that occur? That would be the first stage.

What happens after that? Please forgive me, these are just some reference points. This account of Cézanne's colored sequences or this colorist space through tiny units is already a micro-space pictorially compared with previous schools. This colorist micro-space is the triumph of brightness. You can see how brightness is achieved through these sequences in a totally different way from the bright regime of the seventeenth century. They're two completely different regimes. If I were to circle back to some things I mentioned much earlier, you'll remember that in my comments about the diagram, I said that what's frustrating about the diagram is that it's continually oscillating between two poles: between a pole of code (and there might be codes grafted onto a diagram; in fact, it's necessary for some grafting to occur) and a pole of blurring or interference, pure interference. We see it quite well in the history of color in the way I've tried to describe it. You'll find the pole of blurring perfectly demonstrated, for example, in Caravaggio's dark grounds, when the ground . . .

[*Interruption of the recording,* time stamp: 1:53:58–1:54:02.]

. . . in terms of the diagram toward the other pole. It doesn't take much for it to be a code. And ultimately, in light of some of Seurat's remarks or even some of his paintings, you think: What is he introducing to painting? A veritable code, a pictorial code of tiny points. This turns into a code. In Cézanne, even in Cézanne, the sequences of the neighboring gradient along the order of the spectrum are like the equivalent of a code particular to color with its two main laws: diametric opposition and the transition of the neighboring gradient.

What happens after that? This coloristic space is wonderful. There's nothing else to say; it's perfect. A thing disappears, I believe, when it produces works as intended, when it's saturated by the very products emerging from it. Then it can disappear and die. We move along to another problem, another way of addressing problems of space. There were two problems with the first stage of using tiny units. The first problem was: What's to be done? You had sequences from point to point, from tiny unit to tiny unit. Wouldn't that destroy the overall architecture of the painting? With little color-patches, tiny points, and so forth, how do you maintain the structure? That is, how do you preserve the structure perpendicular to the colored sequences? Or to the diametric oppositions? How do you maintain the structure? That's a problem.

With Cézanne's work, that doesn't go without saying. There is a whole interplay of diagonals in Cézanne where, in a way, the line is summoned back in. A Cézanne line with the purpose of preserving the structure or of reintroducing the structure into space as colored field. Gowing goes so far as to talk about a virtual architecture in Cézanne's work, based on examples, even if the lines aren't traced, but a sort of structure of planes perpendicular to the colored sequences has to be maintained, or else the painting winds up limp [*mou*], I don't know, just boneless.[41] And Cézanne pulls it off. [There's no longer any code; this is no longer a code from color;][42] it's something else. So that's the first problem: How do you maintain structure? The second problem: the tiny units also compromise the special form of the object, which is in danger of shattering into the dust of these tiny units. For Cézanne, too, it's an extremely vital problem. He works out his whole theory of the culminating point precisely in order to preserve the sort of singular volume of the object.

It seems to me that the clash arises for those who'll break with Impressionism to establish a kind of expressionism, in particular Van Gogh and Gauguin. There are a thousand other things to say. I'm just providing some directions. My impression is that their real problem is: Impressionism gave us everything, did it all. Cézanne is a great man. They don't like Seurat, except Van Gogh. He's very considerate, Van Gogh. He thinks that Seurat's points and his own tiny comma-strokes can be made to work. But Gauguin is a lot harsher. He made up a funny song about Seurat, with the refrain: one tiny point, two tiny points, three tiny points. No, it's not by him, but by one of his friends. I'd love to find someone who could put it to music, because it's a charming song, very cheerful. But anyway, he hated all that stuff.

What did Gauguin want? And what does Van Gogh want as well, although maybe in a less pointed way? I believe they want to save two things, but which will require a new space and a new use of color. Totally new. That causes them to bolt from Impressionism. On the one hand, preserving the architecture, that is, reintroducing solid structures, and on the other hand, reconstituting the special volume of the thing in itself. And how will they do that? I believe that they do find an interesting and elegant solution, but one that will in effect spell the end of Impressionism. So, Impressionism lives on with Signac's or Seurat's Neo-Impressionism, but already with Van Gogh, not to mention Gauguin, they take it in such a different direction that it really isn't Impressionism at all. What is it then? What do they do? I think they restore the architecture, restore the structure, that is, they elevate color. It's not about going back to an Italian Renaissance sort of architecture, which in the Renaissance was called the painting's composition. At the point they'd reached, they couldn't go backward. They had to reinvent an architecture with color and through color. How do they accomplish this? That's their first direction: restoring architecture through color, with color. They rediscover something that had already existed, but for them, it's within an absolutely new context: ultimately, they'll discover color-structure. In this, they're surprisingly modern, that is, something like what Comtesse just said, citing the example of Sam Francis; but there are many American painters who use a color-structure. This is kind of a triumph, I think, for a modern form of painting, more modern than Impressionism.

And what is this? In the simplest terms, color-structure is the return to the field regime [*régime de l'aplat*],[43] that is, a monochromatic color laid flat onto the canvas. And that clearly has nothing to do with a return to the Renaissance. It's truly the use of color-structure, while in the Renaissance, structure is maintained by a type of collective line. This restoration of the field is going to be incredible; it'll lead to all sorts of things. Once again, this is about the same time that Van Gogh and Gauguin enter into the monochromatic field. In relation to what? You see what Cézanne means when he says: Gauguin didn't understand anything about transition. It's true, Gauguin didn't understand anything about transition: that's not his problem. You can't expect people to do everything. On the other hand, Cézanne doesn't understand anything about Gauguin's problem. Gauguin's problem is how to make a structure out of color. The monochromatic field is the simplest form of structure; it's a uniform structure.

You might ask me, "That doesn't work; in what way is a field a structure?" Well, it indeed works fine. Because something starts to take shape, something we're still dealing with, notably something into which American painting immersed itself deeply and conquered a formidable coloristic space, to wit: a kind of band-structure or ribbon-structure. Now here, we can see that color turns into structure. When you combine the field with a band of ribbon, there's something specifically colorist going on. Some of Sam Francis's works are like this. One of the greatest American painters in this direction is [Barnett] Newman, who rightly is called an Abstract Expressionist.

What does that give us? You make a monochromatic field, and in cases of complex structures, you're going to introduce divisions, sectors, either of another color, for example (I'm speaking at random) a red field with a violet sector. You can have a field with several sectors. Or quite simply, you just run a band of a different color across your field: What happens? You get this whole interplay. You can introduce nuances of light and dark shades into your field. There are some painters who did that, but not for long, since the point, on the contrary, is for the field to be monochrome and for the only intervening differences not to be in value (that is, light/dark), but differences in saturation.

At what level do these differences in saturation operate? Of course, it depends on the regions within the field, on whether they're close to the ribbon or far from the ribbon. You'll have relations of proximity between the field and the ribbon that crosses it or bisects it. There's any figure you can think of: a rectangular section in the field, a ribbon cutting across it all the way from top to bottom or from right to left, from left to right, and so forth. Depending on the field's color and its relationship to the ribbon's color, what's going to happen, what kind of saturation? At the point when you've encompassed these complex sorts of ribbon-structures or field-ribbon structures, then you can return to pure monochrome, that is, to a pure field. At that point, you'll see that it obviously makes a structure, that the differences in saturation can themselves introduce a whole framework, a whole structure, that is, they can function simply like nonlocalized sections, or like nonlocalized ribbons. There you have a first detail.

So, here you have a deployment of color-structure. You might ask: What does that change? Understand that at this stage, this is what

I was talking about earlier: complementary relations are unimportant. We're done with that. Why? You've come back to large surface painting—and it's true that currently, there's a very important trend to return to the large unit. Are you going to ask: Do complementary relationships or diametric oppositions motivate your sections of the field? No, that's done with! By "that's done with," I don't mean that it's completely ended. My point is that it's just a dead end. If you think about all this later, for me it's the same thing in philosophy, it's the same thing everywhere. There are some things that haven't lost any of their timeliness so long as we don't repeat them. If we repeat them, it's just crap. It's just a dead end. We have to look elsewhere. After all, if Cézanne did what he did, it wasn't so people would repeat something like Cézanne. It's the same with literature, it's the same with philosophy, it's the same thing everywhere.

These aren't the complementary relationships; they're differences in saturation between hues. What does that mean? At this point, I'll only briefly refer to a great text by Schopenhauer. In an early essay, Schopenhauer had revised Goethe's theory in a really interesting way because he introduced the idea of a space proper to color and a weight proper to color.[44] He said that there's no reason for the chromatic circle to be divided in equal parts. With devilish cunning, he proposed the following division: it was generally accepted that the chromatic circle was abstractly divided into three parts. In fact, there are three complementary relationships: red/green, blue/orange, and so on. You have three complementary relationships. You divide your circle into three equal parts. If you follow me, every complementary pair occupies one third of the circle, but within each third of the circle, the relationship between a color and its complement is not equal. For example, blue and red would be two-to-two: here the third of the circle would be divided in two, but the blue-to-orange relationship isn't even. I don't remember the numbers, but it's like two-thirds and one-third. You see? So, each group of complements has its own area of distribution. I think that's important because we already have a sort of structuration proper to color. Color has a sort of spatializing quantity that varies from color to color. He made a few remarks on weight that I find quite innovative, especially in light of how interested American colorists today are in colors having a kind of weight.

A modern color theorist named [Josef] Albers draws a very concrete conclusion from all that, since he's a practicing painter. This concerns what he calls quantity studies, either color's spatializing quantity or its weighable quantity, the weight of color. He ends his piece [*machin*] by saying: "Such quantity studies have taught us to believe that, independent of rules of harmony, any color 'goes' or 'works' with any other color, presupposing that their quantities are appropriate."[45] I believe that's what modern painting is. So long as you only introduced diametric oppositions or gradient neighboring relations between colors, there were still laws to some extent. And Impressionism knew how to discover, to develop, to demonstrate these laws, drawing as much out of them as it could. But there was a lawless world buzzing underneath. The lawless world is when you introduce new coefficients of color, spatial energy, for example, or weighable energy. At that point, everything goes with everything if you apply the right coefficients. I really like this statement, because it's really a painter's statement: "Independent of rules of harmony, any color 'goes' or 'works' with any other color." And that's what colorism is.

There is a text by Van Gogh that I find astonishing. When Van Gogh experiments with large fields, that has a lot of practical consequences, especially compared with Cézanne: a change in the order of values. That's when Gauguin and Van Gogh—I'm not saying that they commit themselves to this—it's a turning point when they say: ultimately, the only really true thing in painting is the portrait.[46] They say: we have to go back to portraits. We have to create a modern portrait. It's an about-face in relation to Cézanne, because the Cézannian hierarchy was very clear, something he never hid and even emphasized: landscapes, still lifes, while portraits only [were at the end].[47] That makes sense given his method. No way around it. In the end, there's nothing wrong with portraits so long as you treat them like a still life or a landscape. Which is why a Cézanne portrait is so much like a still life.

But there [with Van Gogh and Gauguin], it's the other way around: a return to portraits. What does that mean? It can be totally traced back to this history of the evolution of color. Of course, there's a return to portraiture because (now I've run out of time, so that's perfect) it's no longer the diametric oppositions that count; what do you get when you've discerned the color-structure? With fields, there are bright colors [*tons*], it's still the bright regime. What are colors connected to? No longer to complementary colors, no longer to gradual neighboring transitions, but to a funny thing called broken tones [*tons rompus*]. A broken tone is two complementary colors combined; once again, you end up with grey. A broken tone is when you combine complements with one dominant over the other.[48] A broken blue is a blue/orange mixture where blue dominates. You break the tone. The same tone comes up twice: as a bright tone and as a broken tone. It's a way of overcoming both diametric oppositions and gradual neighboring transitions. That will be like the two elements of the grammar of colors: bright and broken tones, starting from Gauguin and Van Gogh.

And why does that imply or engender the return to portraiture? Not out of necessity but out of convenience: because broken tone does an excellent job of depicting flesh. Bluish hues, reddish hues, these are made with broken tones. And Van Gogh never stops repeating: the modern portrait must work through broken tones. You'll have the Gauguin formula as well as the Van Gogh formula: the great modern portrait on the field, with the field done in a bright color, while flesh and figures are rendered in broken tone.[49] At that point, whether it represents someone, whether or not it's a portrait, these are irrelevant concerns, since, in my view, there you've surpassed both the limitations of diametric oppositions and the limit of gradual neighboring transition. With the same interplay of bright tone / broken tone, and the extraordinary freedom that this produces, you've conquered a new space of color as spatializing energy and weighable energy. I'd say almost: the weight of the broken tone and the spatiality of the bright tone.

You have this formula: portrait on the field, broken tones / bright tones with, as Van Gogh says, repetition of the bright tone through the broken tone.[50] That's what is going to become the colorist formula for Van Gogh and Gauguin. And then, just leave out what you want, the figure, and so forth, but two colors will remain for which the problems are no longer decided by complementary relationships or what have you. This is also what Gauguin means when he says something directed against Cézanne: to be a colorist, yes, but an arbitrary colorist.[51] That means to have conquered the space in which the relations between colors are no longer limited by contrast or neighboring transition. The result is to create distances, infinite spaces of color.[52] So, based on this, you can leave out everything, all figuration, all motifs, whatever you like; you are left with your two elements of modern color, namely, color-structure and color-weight, or what might be called color-force.[53] Once again, if I adopt some academic terms, color-structure, which would culminate with the monochromatic field and the structure of the field-ribbon or field-section; and on the other hand, broken tone, which culminates with kinds of flesh. The interplay between color-force and color-structure is what defines this colorist space and creates a new modulation. Cézanne seemed to think that this was the direction through which modulation was eliminated. I believe we find an entirely different modulation as basis, but only as basis, defined by repeating bright color via broken tone. That's what this kind of modulation will be like. Notice in any case that there are quite a lot of these color modulations.

There you have it! Have a great rest over break!

NOTES

PREFACE

1 Gilles Deleuze, *Sur la peinture: Cours mars–juin 1981*, ed. David Lapoujade (Paris: Minuit, 2023), 7–13.

2 Gilles Deleuze, *Francis Bacon: Logique de la sensation* (Paris: Éditions de la Différence, 1981, 2 vols., out of print; Paris: Éditions du Seuil, 2002); *Francis Bacon: The Logic of Sensation*, trans. Daniel W. Smith (Minneapolis: University of Minnesota Press, 2002; London: Continuum, 2002). References to the French text are to the Seuil edition; references to the translation are abbreviated as *FBLS*, and as the text exists in two distinct editions with separate paginations, all references to *FBLS* provide both page sets, abbreviated as UM, followed by C. The masterful translator's introduction to this text by Daniel W. Smith, "Deleuze on Bacon: Three Conceptual Trajectories in *The Logic of Sensation*," vii–xxvii, serves as an extremely useful reference not only for this volume but also for the painting seminar.

3 The locations for these archives are WebDeleuze, https://www.webdeleuze.com/sommaire; the Paris-8 site, http://www2.univ-paris8.fr/deleuze/; The Deleuze Seminars, https://deleuze.cla.purdue.edu. For background on the development of these sites, see https://deleuze.cla.purdue.edu/about/ (all sites accessed 21 April 2024). References to The Deleuze Seminars sessions in the text are presented as *TDS* + abbreviated session title + session number–day/month/year (e.g., *TDS* Painting 1–310381).

4 Gilles Deleuze and Félix Guattari, *What Is Philosophy?*, trans. Hugh Tomlinson and Graham Burchell (1991; New York: Columbia University Press, 1994).

5 The translator's introduction by Daniel W. Smith is omitted from the Continuum edition.

6 For an alternate and superb reading of concepts developed in *Francis Bacon: The Logic of Sensation*, see Tom Conley, "Afterword: A Politics of Fact and Figure," in *FBLS*, 130–49 UM (omitted from the Continuum edition).

7 David Sylvester, *The Brutality of Fact: Interviews with Francis Bacon, 1962–1979*, 3rd ed. (New York: Thames and Hudson, 1987), 56, cited henceforth as *Interviews with Bacon*.

8 Deleuze, *Francis Bacon: Logique de la sensation* 93; FBLS, 82 UM. Oddly, the term is rendered with lowercase d, *diagram*, in FBLS, 100 C. Deleuze's access was to the translated text, Francis Bacon, *L'Art de l'impossible: Entretiens avec David Sylvester*, trans. Michel Leiris and Michael Peppiatt, 2 vols. (Geneva: Skira, 1976), in which the original term used in the English text, *graph*, is translated as "diagram."

9 Aloïs Riegl, *Late Roman Art Industry*, trans. Rolf Winkes, 2nd ed. (Rome: Giorgio Bretschneider Editore, 1985).

10 On the importance of this encouragement to sense philosophical concepts in the context of the temporal flow of Deleuze's seminars, see Charles J. Stivale, "Gilles Deleuze: A Man Out of Time," in *Deleuze and Time*, ed. Robert W. Luzecky and Daniel W. Smith (Edinburgh: Edinburgh University Press, 2023), 234–57.

INTRODUCTION

1 On the creation of the Experimental University Center at Vincennes, see the documentary by Virginie Linhart, *L'Université perdue* [The Lost University], Arte France, Agat Film & Co., 2016.

2 Félix Guattari, *Les Années d'hiver* (Paris: Bernard Barrault, 1986; reedited Paris: Les prairies ordinaires, 2009). [While many of these essays are available in Félix Guattari, *Chaosophy: Text and Interviews, 1972–1977*, ed. Sylvère Lotringer, trans. David L. Sweet, Jarred Becker, and Taylor Adkins (Cambridge / New York: MIT Press / Semiotext(e), 1995; revised 2009); *Soft Subversions: Texts and Interviews, 1977–1985*, ed. Sylvère Lotringer, trans. Chet Wiener and Emily Wittman (Cambridge / New York: MIT Press / Semiotext(e), 1996; revised 2009); and *The Guattari Reader*, ed. Gary Genosko, trans. Gary Genosko, Charles Dudas et al. (Cambridge and Oxford: Blackwell, 1996), the complete volume of *Les Années d'hiver* has yet to be published.—*Trans.*]

3 [IUT, Institut Universitaire de Technologie (University Institute of Technology): these institutions were created in 1966, aimed at preparing a three-year technical diploma, for immediate entry into professional programs or admission to the university.—*Trans.*]

4 On Deleuze's perception of the audience in his seminars, one can refer to *L'Abécédaire de Gilles Deleuze avec Claire Parnet* (Gilles Deleuze, From

A to Z, with Claire Parnet), dir. Pierre-André Boutang, trans. Charles J. Stivale (Cambridge / New York: MIT Press / Semiotext(e), 2012), "P as in Professor." On Deleuze's teaching at Vincennes, one can refer to chapter 19 in François Dosse, *Gilles Deleuze and Félix Guattari: Intersecting Lives,* trans. Deborah Glassman (New York: Columbia University Press, 2010).

5 The final session of Deleuze's seminars took place on Tuesday, 2 June 1987.

6 "How Philosophy Is Useful to Mathematicians or Musicians," in Gilles Deleuze, *Two Regimes of Madness: Texts and Interviews, 1975–1995,* ed. David Lapoujade, trans. Ames Hodges and Mike Taormina (Cambridge and New York: MIT Press / Semiotext(e), 2006), 166–68, first published in a collective work edited by Jacqueline Brunet, Bernard Cassin, François Châtelet, Pierre Merlin, Madeleine Rebérioux, *Vincennes ou le désir d'apprendre* (Paris: Éditions Alain Moreau, 1979), 120–21.

7 *Gilles Deleuze, From A to Z,* with Claire Parnet, "P as in Professor."

8 The aggregate of transcripts and recordings by Richard Pinhas is available on the WebDeleuze site and streaming on YouTube. [See also corrected versions of these same transcripts and links to the YouTube videos at The Deleuze Seminars (both sites accessed 21 April 2024).—*Trans.*]

9 [The recorded sessions begin, in fact, in the 1979–80 academic year, i.e., during the final year at Vincennes.— *Trans.*]

10 On the organization and content of the seminars, see Frédéric Astier, *Les Cours enregistrés de Gilles Deleuze, 1979–1987* (Mons, Belgium: Sils Maria Editions, 2006). Besides Richard Pinhas's site, the complete seminars are available on the Bibliothèque nationale de France website (https://gallica.bnf.fr/). [Accessed 28 March 2024. These recordings were faithfully made from 1979 to 1987 by a Japanese student, Hidenobu Suzuki, and the archive of the 273 cassettes and 180 separate lectures, comprising 413 hours of recordings, was donated to the BNF, which digitized them for availability through the Gallica search engine. See Preface for references to other sites where the seminar transcripts and translations are available.— *Trans.*]

SESSION 1 CATASTROPHE AND DIAGRAM

Initial translation for The Deleuze Seminars by Charles J. Stivale.

1 The first hour of the session [54:25] is devoted to questions relating to Spinoza's philosophy on which Deleuze had focused the entirety of the

seminar from 2 December 1980 to 24 March 1981. [In fact, at least one session preceded the 2 December session, on 25 November 1980, the transcript for which is furnished by Richard Pinhas at WebDeleuze with a translation originally completed by Timothy S. Murphy. See also The Deleuze Seminars for these texts.—*Trans.*]

2 [The revision in *Sur la peinture* significantly changes the sense of Deleuze's statement in the transcript, the translation of which reads as follows: "For example, we'll still have to consider eventually, on the level of materials—and here also, this might have something to do with philosophical concepts, even to things related to philosophy—[materials like] watercolor and oil, and oil and acrylics today, all that . . . well, because these are not the same things. Where is the unity of painting located? Is there a genre common to watercolor, to oil, and to acrylics today?"—*Trans.*]

3 [Deleuze refers to the final paragraph of his discussion of Spinoza in which he asserts that "the catastrophe preventing us from understanding all that [Spinoza] means is when common notions are treated like abstract things." See *TDS* Spinoza 1–310381 (time stamp: 46:00; accessed 24 April 2024)—*Trans.*]

4 On the specificity of painting compared with other arts relative to catastrophe, see *Two Regimes of Madness*: "The painter's work consists in destroying them [clichés]: the painter must go through a moment when he or she no longer sees anything thanks to a collapse of visual coordinates. That is why I say that painting includes a catastrophe, one that is the crux of painting . . . In the case of other arts, the conflict with clichés is very important but it mostly remains outside the work although it is inside the author. Except in the case of Artaud, for whom the collapse of ordinary linguistic coordinates are [*sic*] part of the work," 183–84. See also *Francis Bacon*: "Of all the arts, painting is undoubtedly the only one that necessarily, 'hysterically,' integrates its own catastrophe and consequently is constituted as a flight in advance. In the other arts, catastrophe is only associated" (*FBLS*, 84 UM; 103 C).

5 Earlier in the year, in the session on 13 January 1981 devoted to Spinoza, Deleuze already referred with great admiration to *The Eye Listens*, "an awful title, but no matter," because Claudel "suggests very curious connections between a certain kind of Spinozism and Dutch painting, notably light in Dutch painting" (*TDS* Spinoza 6–130181).

6 Paul Claudel, *The Eye Listens*, trans. Elsie Pell (Port Washington, NY: Philosophical Library, 1950): "Dutch still-life is an arrangement in

imminent danger of disintegration; it is something at the mercy of time," 48.

7 See, for example, in Claudel's *The Eye Listens*: "There is a stable, motionless background, and in the foreground all sorts of objects off balance. They look as though they were about to fall. There is a napkin or a rug on the point of unrolling, the handle of a knife ready to become detached, a little loaf of bread falling into slices as if of its own volition, an overturned cup, all sorts of vases or fruits tumbled in a heap, and overhanging plates," 47.

8 The reference is to Joris-Karl Huysmans, in *Certains* [Certain Ones] [1889]. See Joris-Karl Huysmans, *Écrits sur l'art* (Paris: Flammarion, coll. GF, 2008), 266: "childish and barbaric sketches finally, disconcerting imbalances: houses leaning on one side, like drunks; lopsided fruits in drunken pottery." [My translation from the French.—*Trans.*] It is likely that Deleuze found this reference in Henri Maldiney, *Regard Parole Espace* (Lausanne: L'Âge d'homme, 1973), 186.

9 Ten years earlier, in *Anti-Oedipus: Capitalism and Schizophrenia*, trans. Robert Hurley, Mark Seem, and Helen R. Lane (New York: Viking, 1977; Minneapolis: University of Minnesota Press, 1983), Deleuze and Guattari already referred to Turner in the same terms, but then distinguished three periods: "The paintings range over three periods. . . . The first canvases are of end-of-the-world catastrophes, avalanches, and storms. That's where Turner begins. The paintings of the second period are somewhat like the delirious reconstruction, where the delirium hides, or rather where it is on a par with a lofty technique inherited from Poussin, Lorrain, or the Dutch tradition: the world is reconstructed through archaisms having a modern function. But something incomparable happens at the level of the paintings of the third period, in the series Turner does not exhibit, but keeps secret. . . . The canvas turns in on itself, it is pierced by a hole, a lake, a flame, a tornado, an explosion. The themes of the preceding paintings are to be found again here, their meaning changed. The canvas is truly broken, sundered by what penetrates it. All that remains is a background of gold and fog, intense, intensive, traversed in depth by what has just sundered its breadth: the schiz," 132.

10 [Omitted here is the interruption by someone outside the classroom to whom Deleuze speaks briefly about a scheduling matter.—*Trans.*]

11 See Jean Selz, *Turner* (Paris: Flammarion, 1975), who relates Ruskin's statement taken from Frank Harris's *My Life and Loves*: "One day, upon

opening a carton, I found it full of drawings and paintings of the most shameful sort, depicting women's sexual organs, drawings that to me were completely inexcusable and inexplicable. I decided to find out whence came these ignominies, and discovered that every Friday my hero left his house in Chelsea and went to Wapping, where he stayed until Monday morning, living with the sailors' girls and painting them in every posture of lewdness . . . What should I do? For weeks I was tormented with doubts, trying to raise my mind to the highest moral level. Finally, like a bolt out of the blue, the idea came to me that I had been selected as the only man capable of making a major decision in the matter. I immediately burned those hundreds of lewd sketches and paintings. . . . Yes, I burned them all! Do you not think I was right? I'm proud, very proud, to have done it," 85 [Translation by Internet Archive, https://archive.org/details/bwb_KR-601-468/page/84/mode/2up, accessed 23 March 2024.—*Trans.*].

12 [Deleuze initiates this break, saying, "Fine, I am going to the secretary's office, so take a break." See TDS Painting 1-310381—*Trans.*]

13 Joachim Gasquet, *Cézanne* (1921; Paris: Encre Marine, 2002). Most of the conversations are included in *Conversations avec Cézanne,* critical edition presented by P. M. Doran (Paris: Macula, 1978), which is the edition to which Deleuze refers; *Conversations with Cézanne,* edited by Michael Doran, trans. Julie Lawrence Cochran (Berkeley: University of California Press, 2001). [Let us note that Gasquet and this text are not mentioned in FBLS.—*Trans.*]

14 This book is by Henri Maldiney, *Regard Parole Espace,* to which Deleuze refers extensively throughout the entire series of sessions devoted to painting. This is the first work published by Maldiney (1912–2013), a collection of texts published between 1945 and 1971. Longtime friends, Deleuze and Maldiney met in 1964, when Deleuze obtained a position teaching at the University of Lyon (until 1969).

15 *Conversations with Cézanne,* 124.

16 Deleuze's reading of Cézanne repeats almost integrally Maldiney's analysis in *Regard Parole Espace,* 150ff., and especially 184ff. He also cites this passage in *Francis Bacon* (FBLS, 84 and 160, note 8 UM; 102, and 185, note 8 C).

17 Deleuze specifies that he is combining two distinct texts. The two texts are located in *Conversations with Cézanne,* 114. [The Cochran translation reads "to discover the geographic strata" rather than "geological," which

corresponds to Deleuze's citation, retained here in the text. The use of *geographic* is repeated further on.—*Trans.*]

18 [The edited transcription in *Sur la peinture* omits the phrase in brackets on which Deleuze firmly insists in his statement, a phrase and sequence carefully verified; see TDS Painting 1-310381 (time stamp: 1:27:35, accessed 24 April 2024).—*Trans.*]

19 [Between the choice of "germ" or "seed" to translate *germe,* I opt for the former in consonance both with the sense of "germination" and with the choice of "germ" by Daniel W. Smith in *Francis Bacon* (FBLS, 83 UM; 102 C). However, for the expression *chaos-germe,* I opt for "germinal chaos."—*Trans.*]

20 *Conversations with Cézanne*: "And my eyes, you know, my wife tells me that they jump out of my head, they get all bloodshot," 125.

21 Letter to Émile Bernard, 23 October 1905, in *Conversations with Cézanne,* 48.

22 Sociologist and urban planner, a close friend of Félix Guattari, Anne Querrien (born in 1945) directed the magazine *Les Annales de la recherche urbaine* from 1985 to 2010. She is the author of *L'École mutuelle: Une pédagogie trop efficace* (Paris: Les Empêcheurs de penser en rond, 2005). She participates in the coordination of *Multitudes* and *Chimères,* two journals close to Deleuze and Guattari's thought. In particular, she explores the notion of schizoanalysis proposed in their joint work.

23 This allusion is to the seminar on Kant, TDS Kant 3-280378 and 4-040478, in which Deleuze developed the theory of the sublime. [Note that toward the end, Querrien's remarks are inaudible.—*Trans.*]

24 This corresponds to the mathematical sublime and the dynamic sublime, exposed respectively in § 25 and 28 of part 1, first section, book 2 of the *Critique of the Faculty of Judgment.* We can refer to TDS Kant 3-280378 and 4-040478. Deleuze often demonstrated his admiration for the *Critique of the Faculty of Judgment,* first in a 1963 article, "The Idea of Genesis in Kant's Aesthetics," in Gilles Deleuze, *Desert Islands and Other Texts, 1953–1974,* ed. David Lapoujade, trans. Michael Taormina (Cambridge, MA and New York: The MIT Press / Semiotexte(e), 2004), 56–71, in chap. 3 of *Kant's Critical Philosophy: The Doctrine of the Faculties,* trans. Hugh Tomlinson and Barbara Habberjam (Minneapolis: University of Minnesota Press, 1984), 46–67, and in an article from 1986, "On Four Poetic Formulas That Might Summarize the Kantian Philosophy," published as chap. 5 of *Essays Critical and Clinical,* trans.

Daniel W. Smith and Michael A. Greco (Minneapolis: University of Minnesota Press, 1997), 27–37.

25 *Conversations with Cézanne,* 114. Deleuze closely follows the analysis by Maldiney, who uses the same texts by Cézanne also to distinguish two main moments in the act of painting for Cézanne. See *Regard Parole Space,* 150ff. and 183ff.

26 [*Conversations with Cézanne,* 114–15.—*Trans.*]

27 See Henri Maldiney, *Regard Parole Espace,* 185ff.

28 [On this intervention, see also TDS Painting 1-310381.—*Trans.*]

29 [A brief exchange occurs here, edited in *Sur la peinture,* and on the recording, one hears Deleuze groaning as the student is contradicted by Querrien, who seems to want to initiate a debate.—*Trans.*]

30 This allusion is to the exhibit organized at the Pompidou Center, 17 December 1980–20 April 1981, with the title: *Les Réalismes: entre révolution et réaction, 1919–1939* (Realisms, between revolution and reaction, 1919–1939).

31 This is a reference to Joris-Karl Huysmans, who used these adjectives to describe Gauguin's atelier in *L'Art moderne* (1883), republished in *Écrits sur l'art*: "As for the interior of his atelier, it's in a scabby and muted color," 226. [My translation from the French.—*Trans.*]

32 Eugène Delacroix, *Journal (1822–1853)* (Paris: Plon, 1981), note from 15 September 1852, repeated on 13 January 1857: "The enemy of all painting is grey. The paint will almost always appear greyer than it is by its oblique position under the light. Banish all earthy colors." The quote was cited by Paul Signac in *D'Eugène Delacroix au néo-impressionisme* (1911; reedited Paris: Hermann, 1978), 37, a text to which Deleuze refers during the session 7 (see below, 26 May 1981). [My translation from the French.—*Trans.*]

33 *Conversations with Cézanne,* 118.

34 Wassily Kandinsky, *On the Spiritual in Art,* trans. Hilla Rebay (1911; New York: Simon Guggenheim Foundation, 1946). [While no specific reference to passive grey and active grey is available in Kandinsky's text, Deleuze seems to refer to the passage referenced in the following note in which Kandinsky speaks not only of the grey that can become "lighter, airier," but also of another kind of grey, not just "without appeal and immobile," but a grey that Kandinsky equates with the "immobility of desolation," 68–69.—*Trans.*]

35 Kandinsky, *On the Spiritual in Art,* about green-red grey: "When lightened, the colour [grey] becomes lighter, airier breathing more freely as

if in relief and with a new hidden hope. A similar grey is produced by an optical mingling of green and red which achieves a spiritual blend of passive self-satisfaction and a strong glow of activity," 69. On the grey obtained by a mixture of black and white: "A blend of these two colors, created mechanically, produces grey. Of course, a colour so created can offer no outer appeal or movement. Grey is without appeal and immobile," 68–69.

36 [Deleuze's page reference is to an edition that differs from the one cited in *Sur la peinture,* Paul Klee, *Théorie de l'art moderne,* trans. P.-H. Gonthier (Paris: Folio, 1998). Although this title appears as *On Modern Art* (New York and London: Faber and Faber, 1966), this edition only provides a translation (without translator's attribution) of the French edition's opening essay, "On Modern Art," without the "Note" in question. Hence all translations are my own. See also below, session 3, note 16.—*Trans.*]

37 The quote is located in Maldiney, *Regard Parole Espace,* 151. Maldiney borrows it from Paul Klee, *Das bildernische Denken: Schriften zur Form- und Gestaltungslehre* (Basel and Stuttgart: Spiller, Schwabe & Co. Verlag, 1964), 3; French edition: *La Pensée créatrice,* trans. S. Girard (Paris: Dessain & Tolra, 1973). One might also refer to Klee's evocation of the grey point in relation to the refrain in *A Thousand Plateaus: Capitalism and Schizophrenia,* trans. Brian Massumi (Minneapolis: University of Minnesota Press, 1987), 312.

38 We reproduce Klee's drawing in *Théorie de l'art moderne,* 73. After the brief presentation on the point in Klee, Deleuze will use this drawing in *The Fold: Leibniz and the Baroque,* trans. Tom Conley (Minneapolis: University of Minnesota Press, 1993), 15, as illustration of the concept of inflexion in Leibniz, that is, as a genetic element of the fold.

39 Through an error, Deleuze attributes to Klee this statement taken in fact from Gilbert Lascault in an article on the grey point in Klee's work: Gilbert Lascault, "Éléments d'un dossier sur le gris," *Peindre: Revue d'esthétique* 1 (1976): 212. [My translation from the French.—*Trans.*]

40 Francis Bacon, *L'Art de l'impossible: Entretiens avec David Sylvester.* [See preface, note 8.—*Trans.*]

41 This is the first occurrence of the theme of the struggle against the cliché that Deleuze initially limits to painting, as is evident from the interview granted to *Le Monde* included in *Two Regimes of Madness*: "In the case of other arts, the conflict with clichés is very important, but it mostly remains outside the work although it is inside the author," 184. The theme will later be extended to the cinematographic domain

in *Cinema 1: The Movement-Image,* trans. Hugh Tomlinson and Barbara Habberjam (Minneapolis: University of Minnesota Press, 1986), 208–15; and *Cinema 2: The Time-Image,* trans. Hugh Tomlinson and Robert Galeta (Minneapolis: University of Minnesota Press, 1989), 2–4 and 21–23; and to all the arts in Gilles Deleuze and Félix Guattari, *What Is Philosophy?,* trans. Hugh Tomlinson and Graham Burchell (New York: Columbia University Press, 1994), 203–4.

42 Francis Bacon, *L'Art de l'impossible,* 111; *Interviews with Francis Bacon,* 56. [We correct the *L'Art de l'impossible* reference from the pagination given in *Sur la peinture* (although the citation there may correspond to the combined 1995 edition); also, as mentioned in the Preface, note 8, in the original interview, the term used is *graph,* not *diagram*; the word *diagram* is substituted in brackets where *graph* appears in the interview.—*Trans.*]

43 *Interviews with Francis Bacon,* 56. We have reproduced the entire citation of which a part is missing in the session's audio recording due to a cassette change.

44 The concept of diagram appears for the first time in *A Thousand Plateaus,* 141–43, which was published a few months earlier, in October 1980. Linked to the concept of "abstract machine," it is one of the essential concepts in that work. The notion is inspired by Peirce (*A Thousand Plateaus,* 531, note 41) and by Foucault (*A Thousand Plateaus,* 530–31, note 39; 536–37, note 16).

45 Deleuze is familiar with Peirce's theory of diagrams from the collection of selected texts organized and translated by Gérard Deledalle (Charles S. Peirce, *Écrits sur le signe* [Paris: Seuil, 1978], notably, 149 and 185), and from the analysis proposed by Roman Jakobson in the article "À la recherche de l'essence du langage," trans. J. Havet, in *Problèmes du langage* (Paris: Gallimard, 1966), 22–38. Peirce's theory of signs gains decisive importance in the seminars on cinema that begin the following year, then in *Cinema 1* and *Cinema 2.*

46 See Ludwig Wittgenstein, *Tractatus logico-philosophicus* 2.0121–2.0124, trans. P. Klossowski (Paris: Gallimard, 1986), 30–31.

47 [As mentioned in the Preface, this understanding of the diagram, as containing these three aspects, corresponds to Deleuze's broad conception of the term as derived from Bacon, which Deleuze initially writes with a capital D, *Diagramme* in the French edition (93), *Diagram* in the translation (*FBLS,* 92 UM), a conception that may be juxtaposed to the

more specific conception of the diagram developed in the next session (chap. 2). Both of these conceptual uses of the diagram are evident in their succinct introduction by Deleuze in *Francis Bacon* (*FBLS*, 82–83 UM; 100–102 C).—*Trans.*]

48 [In rendering "ces idées doubles de chaos, catastrophe, germ" (in the transcript) as "these dual ideas of chaos—catastrophe and germ," the duality is understood to refer to the pair "this germinal catastrophe" ("ce chaos-catastrophe") and "this germinal chaos" ("ce chaos-germe") stated in the previous paragraph, that is, as two distinct moments now tied together "within the proposition of a notion that would be properly pictorial, specifically, a diagram."—*Trans.*]

49 [For the sake of clarity, I provide the translation of the unedited transcription at the end of this paragraph: "Van Gogh's treatment of color. And this diagram, I can date it. In what sense can I date it? Entirely like the completely different diagram that belongs to Turner. I can say, yes, this diagram of tiny commas, of tiny crosses, of tiny threes, and so on, I can show how from the start, in a rather obtuse and stubborn way, Van Gogh deliberately sought that kind of thing."—*Trans.*]

SESSION 2 PAINTING FORCES

Initial translation for The Deleuze Seminars by Alina Cherry.

1 [David Sylvester, *Interviews with Francis Bacon*, 56. As indicated in session 1, note 42, the term used by Bacon in the interview is *graph*, not *diagram*; the word *diagram* is substituted in brackets where *graph* appears in the interview.—*Trans.*]

2 See *Conversations with Cézanne*, 114.

3 In *Francis Bacon*, Deleuze refers to a text by Michel Leiris on the action of "presence" in Bacon's work, "Ce que m'ont dit les peintures de Francis Bacon" [What Bacon's paintings have told me], in *Au Verso des Images* (Paris: Fata Morgana, 1980). [*FBLS*, 155, note 10 UM; 175, note 10 C.—*Trans.*]

4 Probable allusion to the *Critique of Practical Reason*, I, i, 1, "Of the Principles of Pure Practical Reason," in which Kant distinguishes between sensible intuition as a given (*datum*) for pure speculative reason and the fact of moral law (*factum*) for pure practical reason.

5 On the distinction of the ordinary and the remarkable and on their confusion, one can refer to *Difference and Repetition*, trans. Paul Patton (New York: Columbia University Press, 1990), 47, 153–54, 189–90.

6 Deleuze has frequently used the notion of simulacrum as Klossowski conceptualized it, notably in Klossowski's research on Nietzsche (*Nietzsche and the Vicious Circle* [Paris: Mercure de France, 1969], trans. Daniel W. Smith [Chicago: University of Chicago Press, 1997]) and in his novels. Deleuze then ceased using it, as he declares in the preface-letter to Jean-Clet Martin, republished in *Two Regimes of Madness*: "It seems to me that I have totally abandoned the notion of simulacrum, which is all but worthless," 362. [As indicated in the notes for this preface-letter, it was originally published in Jean-Clet Martin, *Variations: La Philosophie de Gilles Deleuze* (Paris: Payot & Rivages, 1993). The letter is dated 13 June 1990.—*Trans.*]

7 Lucretius, *De natura rerum,* book IV. See the analysis of simulacra in Epicurus and Lucretius in *The Logic of Sense,* trans. Constantin V. Boundas, Mark Lester, and Charles J. Stivale (London: Bloomsbury, 2015), 274–87; (New York: Columbia University Press, 1990), 266–79.

8 Allusion to Oscar Wilde's essay "The Decay of Lying": "That white quivering sunlight that one sees now in France, with its strange blotches of mauve, and its restless violet shadows, is her latest fancy, and, on the whole, Nature reproduces it quite admirably. Where she used to give us Corots and Daubignys, she gives us now exquisite Monets and entrancing Pissaros [*sic*]" in *Complete Works of Oscar Wilde* (London: Forgotten Book, 2012), 986.

9 Deleuze returns to the relations between painting, photography, and cliché as seen in Bacon in *Francis Bacon* (*FBLS*, 16–18, 97–98 UM; 16–19, 119–21 C).

10 Deleuze here considers the method used by Gérard Fromanger (1939–2021) for the composition of certain of his paintings. He had given an initial description of this in 1973, in "Hot and Cool" (*Desert Islands,* 247–51), a text for the catalog of an exhibition by Gérard Fromanger titled *The Painter and the Model,* Gallery 9 in Paris. In *Francis Bacon,* Deleuze refers to a text by Michel Foucault, *La Peinture photogénique,* Gallery Jeanne Bucher, February 1975, republished in *Dits et écrits,* vol. 1 (Paris: Gallimard, 1994), 1575–83. Deleuze and Fromanger had met ten years earlier (in 1971) on the occasion of a project for an exhibit at the Gallery Karl Flinker that never occurred. Fromanger spoke of this encounter on France Culture Radio, 20 April 2002 ("Radio Free-Gilles Deleuze: Infinite Speed 1925–1995," by Jean Daive).

11 Deleuze does not return to hysteria in painting in the subsequent sessions, but this theme is the focus of chapter 7 of *Francis Bacon.* Deleuze

affirms in particular the existence of a "special relation between painting and hysteria. It is very simple. Painting directly attempts to release presences beneath representation, beyond representation. [. . .] This is not a hysteria of the painter, but a hysteria of painting. With painting, hysteria becomes art. Or rather, with the painter, hysteria becomes painting" (FBLS, 45 UM; 51–52 C).

12 D. H. Lawrence, "Introduction to These Paintings," in *Phoenix: The Posthumous Papers of D. H. Lawrence* (1936; New York: Viking Press, 1972). In fact, Deleuze had already referred to this text at the start of the seminar focused on Spinoza, *TDS* Spinoza 6-130181, to express his admiration ("[it's] the most beautiful text I've read on Cézanne") and to outline briefly the analyses to which he returns here.

13 D. H. Lawrence, in *Phoenix*: "Cézanne's early history as a painter is a history of his fight with his own cliché. [. . .] When his drawing was conventionally all right, to Cézanne himself it was mockingly all wrong. It was a cliché. So he flew at it and knocked all the shape and stuffing out of it, and when it was so mauled that it was all wrong, and he was exhausted with it, he let it go; bitterly, because it still was not what he wanted," 576. This text is cited at great length in *Francis Bacon* (FBLS, 72–73 UM; 87–89 C).

14 This refers no doubt to an exhibit at the Musée d'Art Moderne de la Ville de Paris, 26 March–26 June 1981.

15 D. H. Lawrence, in *Phoenix*: "Where Cézanne did sometimes escape the cliché altogether and really give a complete intuitive interpretation of actual objects is in some of the still-life compositions. [. . .] Here Cézanne did what he wanted to do: he made the things quite real, he didn't deliberately leave anything out, and yet he gave us a triumphant and rich intuitive vision of a few apples and kitchen pots," 580.

16 D. H. Lawrence, in *Phoenix*: "He knew, as an artist, that the only bit of a woman which nowadays escapes being ready-made and ready-known cliché is the appley part of her. [. . .] It is the appleyness of the portrait of Cézanne's wife that makes it so permanently interesting: the appleyness, which carries with it also the feeling of knowing the other side as well, the side you don't see, the hidden side of the moon," 579.

17 D. H. Lawrence, in *Phoenix*: "After a fight tooth-and-nail for forty years, he did succeed in knowing an apple, fully; and not quite as fully, a jug or two. That was all he achieved," 569.

18 D. H. Lawrence, in *Phoenix*: "Cézanne's apple is a great deal, more than Plato's Idea," 569.

19 This affirmation according to which Michelangelo is the "most capable" in art history to cause the evidence of the "pictorial fact" to be grasped is repeated at the end of chapter 17 in *Francis Bacon* (128–29 UM; 160–61 C). A bit later, in the same seminar, Deleuze corrects this affirmation and refers to Byzantium as the foundation of the pictorial fact.

20 This is an allusion to the order of the tomb of Julius II and to the project of decorating the Sistine Chapel's vault that Michelangelo judged to be too simple and for which Julius II finally authorized him to do what he wanted. See Luciano Bellosi, *Michel-Ange*, trans. H. Valot (Paris: Flammarion, 1971), 10–11. This set of comments on Michelangelo is drawn from the work cited in *Francis Bacon* (FBLS, 167, note 13 UM; 196, note 13 C).

21 Luciano Bellosi, *Michel-Ange*: "It is not, moreover, a question of indifference with regard to a religious subject but with regard to the subject in itself" (10). [My translation from the French.—*Trans.*]

22 "The Holy Family on the Tribune" (Tondo Doni) (circa 1506–8), museum of the Uffizi, Florence. Luciano Bellosi, *Michel-Ange*, 9–10.

23 This concerns a preparatory drawing (destroyed) for a fresco intended for the Palazzo Vecchio (a project ultimately abandoned) of which a copy exists by a student of Michelangelo, Aristotele da Sangallo (Holkham Hall).

24 Luciano Bellosi, *Michel-Ange*: "Indeed, when Michelangelo is made responsible for painting the Battle of Cascina on a wall of the Council Hall of Palazzo Vecchio, in 1504, he imagined something that makes one think of anything except a battle. The fresco was never executed, but the cartoon completed at the beginning of 1505 aroused such admiration that it became 'the school of the world' (Benvenuto Cellini); a crowd of young artists came running to study it such that the cartoon was reduced to pieces and crumbled in tatters [. . .]. In evidence is a group of nudes in movement at the edge of a river. If we refer to the account of the battle by the chronicler Villani, we see how the choice of representation is forced, gratuitous, and unilateral. It could be justified only by a passage from Villani recounting that, on the morning of the battle, the Florentine soldiers seeking to protect themselves from the hot weather imagined bathing in the Arno, whereupon Manno Donati demanded more decency from his troops. But there is no text on the episode mentioned by Michelangelo, namely, that the Florentine soldiery might have been surprised by the enemy while bathing. The painter therefore not

only chose a marginal fact but interpolated history to justify his exhibition of nudes, called the Battle of Cascina," 10. [My translation from the French.—*Trans.*]

25 This no doubt refers to *The Paternal Admonition* (circa 654, Rijksmuseum, Amsterdam), a painting by Gerard Ter Borch (1617–1681) that owes its title to a French etching of the seventeenth century. Art historians currently opt for a different explanation: they see in this painting instead a discussion between two lovers or between a prostitute and her customer.

26 *The Large Bathers* (*Les Baigneuses*, 1899–1906, Philadelphia Museum of Art).

27 David Sylvester, *Interviews with Francis Bacon*: "I always hope to be able to make a great number of figures without a narrative.—As Cézanne does in 'The Bathers'?—He does," 63–64.

28 This refers to Manet's *Déjeuner sur l'herbe* (1862–63, Musée d'Orsay, Paris).

29 Luciano Bellosi, *Michel-Ange*: "Like the 'Saint Anne Metterza' by Leonardo is a group of figures linked together by a play of bindings that are so developed that they form nothing more than a knot, such that the whole is transformed into a complex mechanism unfolding in a spiral, lifting upward in a twisting and 'serpentine' shape, as Michelangelo would have said. This figurative knot is much less reminiscent of painting than of sculpture produced in the 16th century," 8. [My translation from the French.—*Trans.*]

30 David Sylvester, *Interviews with Francis Bacon*: "And I've always thought about Michelangelo; he's always been deeply important in my way of thinking about form. But although I have this profound admiration for all his work, the work that I like most of all is the drawings. For me he is one of the very greatest draughtsmen, if not the greatest," 114. And see *FBLS* (128–29 UM; 160–61 C).

31 This refers to the triptych *Three Studies of the Male Back* (1970, collection Kunsthaus, Zurich).

32 Paul Klee, *Théorie de l'art moderne*: "Art does not reproduce the visible, but makes visible," 34. [The text of *On Modern Art* (1966) does not contain this quote. Rather, it is in Paul Klee, *Creative Confession and Other Writings* (London: Tate Publishing, 2013), 7.—*Trans.*]

33 Deleuze will return to Mannerism, sometimes from an aesthetic point of view, sometimes from a clinical point of view (by linking it

to schizophrenia), sometimes from a philosophical point of view (by linking it to the Stoics or to Leibniz), sometimes from a psychosocial point of view (by linking it to politeness). See, in particular, *The Fold,* 36–37, 53, 56–57. See also "Letter to Serge Daney," *Negotiations 1972–1990,* trans. Martin Joughin (New York: Columbia University Press, 1995), 75–78. Deleuze and Guattari had already referred to a Mannerism for Kafka in *Kafka: Toward a Minor Literature,* trans. Dana Polan (Minneapolis: University of Minnesota Press, 1986), 79–80 and 86–87, and returned to this notion regarding territorial distance in *A Thousand Plateaus,* 320.

34 [This reference to "paintings mentioned earlier" seems to concern the kind of painting Deleuze just mentioned, of a sleeping man painted with wonderful colors and a magnificent little bed.—*Trans.*]

35 Crucifixion is a recurring theme in Bacon. The first two date from 1933. The triptych followed in 1944, *Three Studies for Figures at the Base of a Crucifixion* (Tate Britain, London), of which Bacon will offer a second version in 1988; in 1950, *Fragment of a Crucifixion* (Stedelijk Van Abbemuseum, Eindhoven); in 1962, *Three Studies for a Crucifixion* (Solomon R. Guggenheim Museum, New York); in 1965, *Crucifixion,* triptych (Pinakothek der Moderne, Berlin).

36 This refers to *Slaughtered Ox* (1655, The Louvre, Paris).

37 Inspired by Rembrandt's *Slaughtered Ox* (1655), Soutine painted in 1925 a series of paintings on the theme of the slaughtered ox.

38 [Deleuze and Guattari refer briefly to František Kupka's works in terms of forces and sensation in *What Is Philosophy?*, 182–83.—*Trans.*]

39 The *Popes* series, largely inspired by reproductions of Velázquez's portrait of Pope Innocent X (1650, Doria-Pamphilj gallery, Rome), begins in 1946 and continues until the 1970s. [On the horror-scream distinction and the *Popes* series, see *FBLS*, chap. 6, "Painting and Sensation" (notably 33–35 UM; 37–39 C).—*Trans.*]

40 David Sylvester, *Interviews with Francis Bacon*: "You could say that a scream is a horrific image; in fact, I wanted to paint the scream more than the horror," 48.

41 In *Francis Bacon,* Deleuze deepens the links between Bacon and Beckett (*FBLS*, 36–37 UM; 40–41 C).

42 An approximate citation taken from a letter from Kafka to Max Brod, cited by Klaus Wagenbach, *Franz Kafka: Années de jeunesse (1883–1912),* trans. E. Gaspar (Paris: Mercure de France, 1967), 156: "The diabolical powers, whatever their message might be, are knocking at the door and

already rejoicing in the fact that they will arrive soon" (Smith translation, FBLS, 158, chap. 8, note 6 UM; 181, chap. 8, note 5). This sentence, quoted several times in *Kafka: Toward a Minor Literature,* returns in *Francis Bacon* concerning the scream (FBLS, 51–52 UM; 60–62 C).

43 This refers to *Figure Standing at a Washbasin* (1976, collection of the Museo de Arte Contemporáneo, Caracas).

44 [Joseph Conrad, *The Nigger of the "Narcissus,"* in *The Portable Conrad,* ed. Morton Dauwen Zabel (1897; New York: Viking Press, 1947), 354–55. On the body's escaping and also this Conrad novel and this scene, see *Francis Bacon* (FBLS, 14–16 UM and C).—*Trans.*]

45 [Deleuze is playing on the French expression *passer par un trou de souris,* which would have the English equivalent of "pass through the eye of a needle." We maintain the literal translation to follow Deleuze's effect.—*Trans.*]

46 *Painting* (1946, Museum of Modern Art, New York), reproduced in the central notebook of *Francis Bacon* (Seuil, illustration 4). [On this painting and discussion of umbrellas, see *Francis Bacon* (FBLS, 16–17 UM and C).—*Trans.*]

47 David Sylvester, *Interviews with Francis Bacon*: "I was attempting to make a bird alighting on a field. And it may have been bound up in some way with the three forms that had gone before [Bacon here refers to the 1944 *Three Studies for Figures at the Base of a Crucifixion*], but suddenly the lines that I'd drawn suggested something totally different, and out of this suggestion arose this picture. I had no intention to do this picture; I never thought of it in that way. It was like one continuous accident mounting on top of another.—Did the bird alighting suggest the umbrella or what?—It suddenly suggested an opening-up into another area of feeling altogether. And then I made these things, I gradually made them," 11.

48 The different kinds of analogy will be at the heart of sessions 4 and 5 (5 and 12 May 1981).

49 This refers to *Erased De Kooning Drawing* (1953, San Francisco Museum of Modern Art), one of the first works by Robert Rauschenberg to whom Willem De Kooning had donated a drawing, knowing that Rauschenberg was going to erase it. It was then titled and framed by Jasper Johns, friend and lover of Rauschenberg, with the following note on the back: "Do not take the drawing out of the frame. The frame is part of the drawing."

SESSION 3 CHARACTERISTICS AND DANGERS OF THE DIAGRAM

Initial translation for The Deleuze Seminars by Billy Dean Goehring.

1 See session 1, 31 March 1981.

2 Jean Grenier, "Henri Michaux: Un abîme ordonné" [Henri Michaux: An Orderly Abyss], in *Henri Michaux—Choix d'oeuvres, 1946–1966* (Paris: Le Point Cardinal, 1967).

3 [For the participants in the year's previous seminar on Spinoza, the term *puissance* will be very familiar, translated in the Spinoza sessions as "power of action" or "potential." While we retain the latter meaning, *puissance* will also be used later in the session to designate mathematical "power." On puissance as "power of action," see, among other sessions, Spinoza 3-091280.—*Trans.*]

4 See note 20 for session 1, 31 March 1981.

5 [The term "foreign" (*étrangère*) is preserved in keeping with Worringer's analysis of the Gothic line as a "northern," "barbarian," "foreign" development. Deleuze discusses this foreign will or power in *Francis Bacon* (*FBLS*, 103–15, 110–11 UM; 127, 137 C).—*Trans.*]

6 See Wilhelm Worringer, *L'Art gothique*, trans. D. Decourdemanche (1927; Paris: Gallimard, 1967); *Form Problems of the Gothic*, trans. [name not indicated] (New York: G. E. Stechert, 1920). Worringer's theme of the "Northern or Gothic line" appears for the first time in *A Thousand Plateaus*, 411 and 495–96, and then will be used in *Cinema 1* to characterize cinematographical Expressionism, 50–55.

7 [In *Francis Bacon*, Daniel W. Smith opts for "trait" or "stroke" depending on the context for the French *trait*. While there are several possible translations for *tache*—"blot" as in ink blot, or in other contexts, "stain," e.g., with reference to Morris Louis's work—we adopt "patch" or "color-patch" to follow Smith's translation in *Francis Bacon*. The discussion in the rest of the session largely corresponds to the development in chap. 12, "The Diagram."—*Trans.*]

8 [Following our translation of *tache* as "patch," this school would be "patch-ism." We retain "tachism," since this mode of painting is indeed known by this name.—*Trans.*]

9 [While we follow Daniel W. Smith in translating *agencement* as "assemblage," the reader may also understand it to mean "arrangement" or "set up."—*Trans.*]

10 In reality, this corresponds to a conversation between Paul Virilio and the editorial team at *Cahiers du cinéma* titled "Vidéo, vitesse,

technologie: La troisième fenêtre" [Video, Speed, Technology: The Third Window], *Cahiers du cinéma* 322 (April 1981): 35–40.

11 This article was then published in Henri Focillon, *Vie des formes* (Paris: PUF, 1943; reedited PUF, 2016). [*The Life of Forms in Art* (New Haven: Yale, 1942), 157–84. On this work, see *Francis Bacon* (FBLS, 124–25 UM; 154–55 C).—*Trans.*]

12 [On the easel and painting, see *Francis Bacon* (FBLS, 85–88 UM; 104–9 C).—*Trans.*]

13 Deleuze was certainly referring to the Bacon's "malerisch" period that he discusses in chap. 5 of *Francis Bacon,* a term used by Wölfflin "to designate the pictorial in opposition to the linear or, more precisely, the mass in opposition to the contour"; specifically, see FBLS (156, note 6 UM; 177–78, note 6 C). [The reference in *Francis Bacon* is to Heinrich Wölfflin, *Principles of Art History: The Problem of the Development of Style in Later Art,* trans. M. D. Hottinger (1915; New York: Dover, 1950), 3.—*Trans.*]

14 Allusion to the quarterly journal founded in 1976, which ceased publication in 1979.

15 [Deleuze clearly means the Latin word *pingere,* from which the French word is derived.—*Trans.*]

16 The quote is located in Henri Maldiney, *Regard Parole Espace,* 151. Maldiney borrows from Paul Klee, *Das bildnerische Denken. Schriften zur Form—und Gestaltungslehre.* [See session 1, note 37. Deleuze seems to be glossing several moments in Klee's *Bildnerische Denken.* To see how Klee introduces his understanding of chaos, the grey point, and the "cosmogenetic egg," see especially Paul Klee, "Towards a theory of form production," in *Paul Klee Notebooks, Volume 1: The Thinking Eye,* trans. Ralph Manheim, ed. Jürg Spiller (London: Lund Humphries, 1961), 3–4.—*Trans.*]

17 [Deleuze attributes this quote to Cézanne, but it likely comes from Van Gogh. In a letter from 1888 to his sister (Letter 626), Van Gogh writes, "And you see—this is what Impressionism has—to my mind—over the rest, it isn't banal, and *one seeks a deeper likeness than that of the photographer*" (translator's emphasis). See http://www.vangoghletters.org/vg/letters/let626/letter.html (accessed 4 April 2024).—*Trans.*]

18 On Mannerism for Deleuze, see session 2, 7 April 1981, note 33.

19 Allusion to Jean Grenier's expression to describe Henri Michaux's painting. See note 2 of this session.

20 [The instinct is correct to replace "ah, là, là" with "qu'il est raté" (this one's a failure), since Deleuze will articulate this sense shortly and again

two paragraphs later. We retain the original expression for the sake of accuracy.—*Trans.*]

21 [To provide more clarity, we have completed the text with a phrase edited in *Sur la peinture.*—*Trans.*]

22 See session 1, 31 March 1981, note 39. [The cross-referenced note indicates that Gilbert Lascault rather than Klee is the source of this statement.—*Trans.*]

23 David Sylvester, *Interviews with Francis Bacon*: "I hate that kind of sloppy sort of Central European painting. It's one of the reasons I don't really like abstract expressionism. Quite apart from its being abstract, I just don't like the sloppiness of it," 94.

24 [This textual insertion in *Sur la peinture* refers back to Cézanne's statement cited in session 1, 31 March 1981, note 21. See note 28 of this session.—*Trans.*]

25 This can be compared with *A Thousand Plateaus*: "There is no falser problem in painting than depth and, in particular, perspective. For perspective is only a historical manner of occupying diagonals or transversals, lines of flight, in other words, of reterritorializing the moving visual block. We use the word 'occupy' in the sense of 'giving an occupation to,' fixing a memory and a code, assigning a function. But the lines of flight, the transversals, are suitable for many other functions besides this molar function," 298.

26 [In this context, *plan* is translated as "plane" (following Daniel W. Smith in *Francis Bacon*) and corresponds to different kinds of "ground" in English, i.e., the background, foreground, *plan* being a pervasive term in Deleuze's career, in both solo and jointly written work.—*Trans.*]

27 See *Conversations avec Cézanne*, Cézanne's declaration in an article by Jean Royère: "At art school [*Beaux-Arts*], you learn the laws of perspective, of course, but we never saw that depth results in the crossing of vertical and horizontal surfaces, and that indeed is perspective," 188–89. [As this text is omitted from the translation, *Conversations with Cézanne*, the translation from the note in *Sur la peinture* is taken from the French edition.—*Trans.*]

28 See session 1 above, 31 March 1981, note 21, and Cézanne's aforementioned letter to Émile Bernard, 23 October 1905, in *Conversations with Cézanne*, 48.

29 [This very brief citation "un peu profond ruisseau" (shallow stream) is a reference to the last verse in a sonnet by Stéphane Mallarmé,

"Tombeau," "Un peu profond ruisseau calomnié la mort" (A shallow stream that's slandered, and named Death).—*Trans.*]

30 Henri Maldiney also refers to an "Analytique des éléments" regarding Kandinsky. See *Regard Parole Espace,* 65 and 109.

31 The portrait is reproduced on the title page of the conclusion of *A Thousand Plateaus,* 501.

32 [Whereas the different art exhibits to which Deleuze refers throughout this seminar are generally identified in *Sur la peinture,* no details on the Herbin exhibit are provided. One such exhibit was held shortly before the painting seminar, 26 February to 22 March 1981, at the Centre Culturel du Marais, not on the rue de Seine (in the 6th arrondissement), but across the river in the Marais (3rd arrondissement), on the rue des Francs-Bourgeois.—*Trans.*]

33 [The reference is to a work from 1912 published in the 1954 French translation; in *Francis Bacon: Logic of sensation,* the reference provided is *Concerning the Spiritual in Art,* trans M. T. H. Sadler (Las Vegas: IAP, 2009).—*Trans.*]

34 See Wassily Kandinsky, *Point and Line to Plane,* trans. Howard Dearstyne and Hilla Rebay (1926; New York: The Solomon Guggenheim Foundation, 1947): "The 'modern' individual seeks inner tranquility because he is deafened from outside, and believes this quiet to be found in inner silence. [. . .] But the exclusive association of the horizontal-vertical with black and white has still to take place; then everything will be immersed in inner silence, and only external noises will shake the world," 63–64. A similar citation is found in *Francis Bacon* (*FBLS,* 85 UM; 104 C).

35 We have preserved the use of the capital F for the notion of figure, a practice that Deleuze followed in *Francis Bacon,* but we have reserved it for moments when the figure seems to refer to the "temperate" (or figural) path that Deleuze addresses here.

36 Deleuze borrows the term *figural* from Jean-François Lyotard, *Discours, figure* (Paris: Klincksieck, 1971; reedited 2002). See *FBLS* (154, note 1 UM; 173, chap. 1, note 1 C).

37 [Hence the order is abstract painting, Expressionist painting, figural painting, rather than the order just stated above by Deleuze.—*Trans.*]

38 See Michael Fried, "Three American Painters: Kenneth Noland, Jules Olitski, Frank Stella (1965)," in *Art and Objecthood: Essays and Reviews* (Chicago and London: University of Chicago Press, 1998), 213–65. [This reference to Fried is presented in *Francis Bacon* (*FBLS,* 161, note 14 UM;

185–86, note 14 c). The discussion of Pollock and this section are situated in chap. 12, "The Diagram."—*Trans.*]

39 ["Shape" is often a translation for *figure,* which is particularly important in Deleuze's *Francis Bacon* (and comes up often as he discusses painting), with the French word in parentheses to avoid ambiguity. As for *contour,* we follow Daniel W. Smith in *Francis Bacon,* translating this simply with "contour."—*Trans.*]

40 See Michael Fried's descriptions in "Three American Painters": "There is no inside or outside to Pollock's line or to the space through which it moves. And this is tantamount to claiming that line, in Pollock's all-over drip paintings of 1947–50, has been freed at last from the job of describing contours and bounding shapes. It has been purged of its figurative character. Line, in these paintings, is entirely transparent both to the nonillusionistic space it inhabits but does not structure and to the pulses of something like pure, disembodied energy that seem to move without resistance through them. Pollock's line bounds and delimits nothing-except, in a sense, eyesight," 224.

41 Benoît Mandelbrot, *Les Objets fractals* (Paris: Flammarion, 1975; reedited coll. Champs, 2010), *Fractals: Form, Chance, and Dimension* (Brattleboro, VT: Echo Point Books and Media, 1977; reprint ed., 2020).

42 [In addition to Mandelbrot, the reader might recall a similar idea in Paul Klee's writings, another of Deleuze's sources. In his lecture notes, Klee describes the "linear-medial," which is "neither line nor plane, but some sort of middle thing between the two. At the beginning it is linear, the movement of a point; it ends up looking like a plane," *Paul Klee Notebooks, Volume* 1, 109.—*Trans.*]

43 We reproduce the illustration similar to the one appearing in *A Thousand Plateaus,* 487, taken from Mandelbrot's work as Deleuze and Guattari are describing fractal objects.

44 [Deleuze returns to Mandelbrot only in the final seminar, on Leibniz and the Baroque, TDS Leibniz and Baroque 2–041186 and 8–270187. —*Trans.*]

45 This is in fact what Michael Fried emphasizes in the essay that Deleuze cited previously. See "Three American Painters": "In fact until Pollock that was the most that so-called abstract painting had ever been. [...] For example, in Kandinsky's 'Painting with White Form' (1913; fig. 65), a heroic attempt has been made to allow line to work as freely as color.

But one senses throughout the canvas how the line has been abstracted from various natural objects, and to the degree that one feels this, the line either possesses a residual but irreducible quality as of contour, [. . .] or else it possesses the quality of an object in its own right [. . .] Both canvases by Kandinsky could be called nonrepresentational, but both are clearly figurative, if we compare them with Pollock's all-over paintings of 1947–50," 225.

46 This thesis already appears in *A Thousand Plateaus*, 499 and 575, note 38, in which Michael Fried is cited.

47 Deleuze here is closely following remarks in the introduction by Dora Vallier to the French edition of Wilhelm Worringer, *Abstraction et Einfühlung* [1911], trans. E. Martineau (Paris: Klincksieck, 1978), 19, note 17 (see *FBLS*, 163, chap. 14, note 9 UM; 190, note 9 C).

48 See note 6 in this session.

49 Wilhelm Worringer, *Form Problems of the Gothic*, 32–33 and 39, cited in *Francis Bacon* as *Form in Gothic* (New York: G.P. Putnam, 1927), in *FBLS* (157, note 2 UM; 179, note 2 C).

50 See Wilhelm Worringer, *Abstraction and Empathy*, trans. Michael Bullock (Chicago: Elephant Paperbacks, 1997): "The absolute artistic volition [. . .] thus did not consist . . . in the wish to copy the things of the outer world or to render their appearance. Its aim was to project the lines and forms of the organically vital, the euphony of its rhythm and its whole inward being, outward in ideal independence and perfection," 28, cited in *FBLS* (163, note 5 UM; 189–90 C). Deleuze also refers to Wilhelm Worringer, "Classical Man," *Form Problems of the Gothic*, 35–40.

51 Wilhelm Worringer, *Abstraction and Empathy*: "However, constructional relations are not illumined by a feeling for the organic, as is the process in Greek temple building, but purely mechanical relationships of forces are brought to view per se, and in addition these relationships of forces are intensified to the maximum in their tendency to movement and in their content by a power of empathy that extends to the abstract," 114. Kant is mentioned on 130. The expression ["rising to the intuition of mechanical forces"] is repeated in *What Is Philosophy?*, 181–83. [The Bullock translation of Worringer's text does not include the apparent key word here, "intuition," whereas the citation in the *What Is Philosophy?* translation, from Worringer's *Form in Gothic*, appears to contain this term (see 231, note 21).—*Trans.*]

52 See Wilhelm Worringer, *Abstraction and Empathy,* and *Form Problems of the Gothic.* [Deleuze provides partial bibliographical information in *Francis Bacon* (163, note 5 UM; 189–90, note 5 C).—*Trans.*]

53 Wilhelm Worringer, *Form Problems of the Gothic*: "Once the natural bounds of organic motion are broken through, there is no stopping; again and again the line is broken, again and again checked in the natural direction of its movement, again and again violently prevented from running out quietly, again and again diverted to new complications of expression, so that, intensified through all these restraints, it yields its utmost of expressive power, until finally, robbed of all possibilities of natural satisfaction, it comes to an end in intricate contortions, or disconsolately breaks off in vacancy, or senselessly runs back into itself," 48. Deleuze and Guattari already often use Worringer's abstract line in *A Thousand Plateaus,* 411, 415, 492–96, 498, and on the unleashed potential [*puissance*] of repetition, see 498.

54 There is actually only one painting listed under the title *Gothic* (1944, MoMA, New York), as indicated in fact by *Francis Bacon* (FBLS, 161, note 15 UM; 187, note 15 C).

55 Jean Paulhan (1884–1968) published *L'Art informel* with Gallimard in 1962. A controversy followed, in particular with François Mauriac.

56 Deleuze returns later to informal art and, in *The Fold,* he affirms, "the Baroque is informal art par excellence," 35.

57 In *Pierrot le Fou* (1964) by Jean-Luc Godard, Jean-Paul Belmondo's reading of a text by Élie Faure, taken from *L'Histoire de l'art: L'art moderne* (*History of Art,* vol. 4, *Modern Art,* trans. Walter Pach [New York: Harper & Brothers, 1921; 1924]): "Velasquez, after the age of fifty, never again painted sharply defined things, he wandered around the objects with the air and the twilight; in the shadow and transparence of the backgrounds he surprised the colored palpitations which he used as the invisible center of his silent symphony. He was no longer taking from the world anything more than the mysterious exchanges which cause forms and tones to interpenetrate one another in a secret and continuous progression, whose course is not manifested or interrupted by any clash or any shock. Space reigns. An aerial wave seems to glide over the surfaces, impregnating itself with their visible emanations in order to define and model them, and to carry away everywhere else a kind of perfume, a kind of echo of them which it disperses over all surrounding space as an imponderable dust," 124–25.

58 See *A Thousand Plateaus*: "The line is between points, in their midst, and no longer goes from one point to another. It does not outline a shape. 'He did not paint things, he painted between things,'" 298. [Deleuze and Guattari take liberties in *A Thousand Plateaus* with Faure's description (see the preceding note), and they leave the internal citation in their quote without attribution, only citing Faure in *A Thousand Plateaus* from volume 2 of *History of Art,* on Medieval Art (413). Deleuze subsequently refers to Faure regarding Velázquez with this very citation, still quite approximate, in *Francis Bacon* (*FBLS*, 85 and 161 note 11 UM; 105 and 185 note 11 C).—*Trans.*]

59 [The transcript, which we have verified as corresponding to Deleuze's recorded statements, yields two somewhat ambiguous referents: first, the pronoun *leur*, in "ça ne leur dit rien du tout" ([Abstract spiritualism] has no appeal for them at all) seems to refer to the "Informalist or Expressionist" soon to be mentioned; second, in the context of the preceding sentences, specifically the same "Informalist or Expressionist," the potentially ambiguous possessive pronoun in "sa tendance picturale" is simply rendered as "[the painter's] pictorial tendency."—*Trans.*]

60 Deleuze follows closely certain descriptions by Wilhelm Worringer, "From Animal Ornament to the Art of Holbein," *Form Problems of the Gothic,* 55ff.

61 See Wilhelm Worringer, *Form Problems of the Gothic*: "If we are filled with a strong inward excitement that we may express only on paper, the line scrawls will take an entirely different turn. The will of our wrist will not be consulted at all, but the pencil will travel wildly and impetuously over the paper, and instead of the beautiful, round, organically tempered curves, there will result a stiff, angular, repeatedly interrupted, jagged line of strongest expressive force. It is not the wrist that spontaneously creates the line; but it is our impetuous desire for expression which imperiously prescribes the wrist's movement. The impulse once given, the movement is not allowed to run its course along its natural direction, but it is again and again overwhelmed by new impulses," 49.

62 Allusion to the documentary by Hans Namuth and Peter Falkenberg, *Jackson Pollock 51* (1951).

63 Allusion to the book by Harold Rosenberg, *The Tradition of the New* (1959; New York: Da Capo Press, 1994), chap. 2, "American Action Painters." Deleuze already cited this work in *Difference and Repetition,* 91, regarding repetition and regarding the character Hamlet.

64 Deleuze was familiar with [Clement] Greenburg's texts on Pollock and on American painting through the journal *Macula* 2 (1977) that he cites in *Francis Bacon*. The journal was also accompanied by a supplement from Hans Namuth, "L'Atelier de Jackson Pollock," which includes numerous photographs of the artist at work. Let us note that *Art et culture* (1961) was translated by A. Hindry for Macula in 1988. [As indicated above in note 14, the journal *Macula* ceased publication in 1979; however, the 1988 date may be explained by the text's indication that Hindry prepared the translation at this later date "chez Macula," that is, possibly in the context of an ongoing editorial operation maintained by the original journal team.—*Trans.*]

65 Michael Fried, "Three American Painters," notably: "Pollock's field is optical because it addresses itself to eyesight alone. The materiality of his pigment is rendered sheerly visual, and the result is a new kind of space—if it still makes sense to call it space—in which conditions of seeing prevail rather than one in which objects exist, flat shapes are juxtaposed, or physical events transpire," 224–25. The term *unremitting opticality* is used by Fried to describe Barnett Newman's work, 231. In *Francis Bacon*, Deleuze emphasizes that Fried has doubts on the notion of opticality, but doubts "that he passed over far too rapidly" (*FBLS*, 161, note 14 UM; 185–86, note 14 C).

SESSION 4 DIAGRAM, CODE, ANALOGY

Initial translation for The Deleuze Seminars by Billy Dean Goehring.

1 [The translation for *tache* is a "patch" of color. See Daniel W. Smith's note in *Francis Bacon* (*FBLS*, 160 note 1 UM; 184 note 1 C). In this case, however, it is rendered as "stain" in keeping with Morris Louis's "stain painting."—*Trans.*]

2 [To distinguish between *ligne* and *trait*, the former is translated as "line," the latter as "stroke."—*Trans.*]

3 The "American critic" is Harold Rosenberg. Allusion to chap. 2 in *The Tradition of the New* titled "American Action Painters," which introduces the notion of Action Painting. See note 63 in session 3, 28 April 1981.

4 Georges Comtesse (1940–2015) assiduously attended Deleuze's courses in which he intervened frequently and sometimes at length. In 1974, he defended a doctorate of more than 1,300 pages, "The Machines of Castration: Schizophrenia and Psychoanalysis," written under Deleuze's direction.

5 [Perhaps judged as a misstatement or lacking clarity by Deleuze, these lines are edited in *Sur la peinture,* with one significant terminological reversal marked with brackets in the text. We provide the translation of the unedited text, signaling with italics the significant reversed term: "This space is classically defined as a tactile optical space. In other words, space in classical paintings is—as we'll see later, we'll come back to this point—is a tactile-optical space. Which means what? That it's a *tactile* space with tactile referents on the canvas. What are these tactile referents?" See *TDS* Painting 4-050581, time stamp: 21:34–21:55 (accessed 29 April 2024).—*Trans.*]

6 Quote from Paul Sérusier cited by Maurice Denis in an article from 1907, included in *Conversations with Cézanne,* 178.

7 See, for example, Wassily Kandinsky, *Point and Line to Plane:* "To my way of thinking, one might distinguish element from 'element': that is, the term 'element' would signify the form separated from the inner tension, and by element, the tension alive within this form. The elements are, therefore, in reality abstract, while the form is in itself 'abstract,'" 33. On tension in Kandinsky's work, see Henri Maldiney, *Regard Parole Espace,* 65 and 108.

8 These distinctions are not included, as such, in *Point and Line to Plane,* but are found in Henri Maldiney's *Regard Espace Parole,* 67.

9 Paul Sérusier. See note 6 above. [On the diagram and the code, see *Francis Bacon,* chap. 12 (*FBLS,* 85–88 UM; 104–8 C).—*Trans.*]

10 [The French transcript (with Deleuze's examples) has *vent* (wind), *dent* (tooth), *fend* (split), and *ment* (lie). To preserve Deleuze's point about phonemes, we introduce similarly spelled English words for these French words: "vent," "dent," "bent," and "meant" ("bent" substituted for the French *fend*).—*Trans.*]

11 André Martinet, *Éléments de linguistique générale* (Paris: Armand Colin, 1960). [With Guattari, Deleuze has employed the double articulation importantly in *A Thousand Plateaus,* notably in plateau 3, "10,000 B.C.: The Geology of Morals." Deleuze will later return to the double articulation in Martinet in *TDS* Cinema 4 14-50385.—*Trans.*]

12 [Deleuze is describing what is better known in English as a "binary search algorithm." The translation preserves the language of "choice" or "selection."—*Trans.*]

13 See André Leroi-Gourhan, *Gesture and Speech,* trans. Anna Bostock Berger (1964; Cambridge, MA: The MIT Press, 1993): "An anodontic

human race living in a prone position and using such forelimbs as it still possesses to push buttons is not completely inconceivable, and in certain works of science fiction we find 'Martians' or 'Venusians' who come close to this evolutive ideal," 129. [See also references in *A Thousand Plateaus,* notably 496–98 and 574, note 33.—*Trans.*]

14 Deleuze briefly considered this point earlier in the academic year in the Spinoza seminar, *TDS* Spinoza 8-270181: "Modern abstract painting wanted to establish a purely and exclusively optical world, to eliminate all of the world's tactile references" (trans. Charles J. Stivale).

15 See in André Berne-Joffroy (dir.), *Mondrian* (Paris: Réunion des musées nationaux, 1969), Georg Schmidt's observations (the reference is from FBLS, 161, note 10 UM; 185, note 10 C): "[Willem] Sandberg had a 'false Mondrian' created. The result was exceedingly instructive: he taught that, quite on the contrary, Mondrian was extremely difficult to plagiarize. Comparing the original and the imitation, one could be convinced that Mondrian's paintings are not, as one might have expected, anemic incarnations of pure cerebral invention [. . .]. However little one might understand how, in a painting by Mondrian, two black lines might cross, for example, or how multiple layers of color are arranged at right angles, we know nonetheless what eminently sensitive power, what professionalism, what writing skill characterizes Mondrian's paintings," 148.

16 Deleuze draws from excerpts of texts collected in the catalog titled *Mondrian,* published by the Réunion des musées nationaux for the exhibition at the Orangerie, 18 January–31 March 1969. This concerns the first pages from Piet Mondrian, *Réalité naturelle et réalité abstraite* [1919–20] (Paris: Editions du Centre Pompidou, 2010).

17 See Michel Butor, "Le carré et son habitant," *Répertoire III* (Paris: Minuit, 1968), 307–24. Several excerpts from Butor's texts are cited in the catalog titled *Mondrian,* published by the Réunion des musées nationaux (see note 15 above) and cited by Deleuze in *Francis Bacon* (*FBLS,* 161, note 10 UM; 185, note 10 C).

18 See Michel Butor, *Répertoire III* (311–14), which mainly concerns a Mondrian painting from 1931, a white diamond on which two black lines intersect, the vertical being wider than the horizontal (initially intended for the new city hall in Hilversum). One can refer to *A Thousand Plateaus,* which cites Butor's text, 545–46, note 89.

19 Auguste Herbin (1882–1960) conceived of his "plastic alphabet" in 1946 and exposed its principles in *L'Art non figuratif, non objectif* (Paris: Édition Lydia Conti, 1949; reedited Hermann, 2013).

20 It is probable that Deleuze meant "tendency." [However, given that this suggestion in *Sur la peinture* makes no reference to Deleuze's deliberate development of the term *tension* in the context of painting throughout this session, it is by no means "probable" that Deleuze misspoke.—*Trans.*]

21 Deleuze refers to the work by Jean-François Lyotard, *Discours, figure* (*Discourse, Figure,* trans. Antony Hudek and Mary Lydon [Minneapolis: University of Minnesota Press, 2011]), in which the distinction between the figural and the figurative appears.

22 [The shift toward the "third path" and to the analogical roughly corresponds to the shift to chap. 14, "Analogy," in *Francis Bacon.*—*Trans.*]

23 [Although in what follows, the two key Americans to whom Deleuze refers are Charles S. Peirce and Gregory Bateson, they may not represent the linguists that Deleuze has in mind in this statement. If we refer back to how Deleuze and Guattari consider linguistics in *A Thousand Plateaus,* published the previous year, two key American linguists stand forth (in opposition to each other), Noam Chomsky and William Labov (see, for example, 92–94).—*Trans.*]

24 Charles S. Peirce (1839–1914) was not English, but from the United States. Deleuze knows him essentially through the intermediary of selected texts translated by Gérard Deledalle, *Écrits sur le signe* (Paris: Seuil, 1978), the only texts available in French at that time along with *Textes anticartésiens,* trans. J. Chenu (Paris: Aubier, 1984). [The reference to Peirce as well as the entire discussion on analogy corresponds to chap. 13 of *Francis Bacon,* notably FBLS (94–97 and 162 note 5 UM; 116–20 and 188 note 5 C).—*Trans.*]

25 Deleuze hesitates regarding the word *icon* and its French gender, opting for the feminine. In linguistics and computer science, the word in principle is masculine and has no circumflex accent, but uses vary.

26 See Gregory Bateson, "Problems in Cetacean and Other Mammalian Communication," in *Steps to an Ecology of Mind* (Northvale, NJ: Jason Aronson, Inc., 1972, 1987), 369–83. [On Bateson, see *Francis Bacon* (FBLS, 162, note 7 UM; 188, note 7 C).—*Trans.*]

27 Deleuze was not aware of Bateson's death on 4 July 1980 at age seventy-six.

28 In the articles describing this theory (in 1956), it is given the name "double bind." [In the session, Deleuze calls the theory "a double dead-end" [*double impasse*].—*Trans.*] See Gregory Bateson, "Toward a Theory of Schizophrenia," in *Steps to an Ecology of Mind,* 205–32.

29 [While this is a truly minor point of transcription, the military reference here in *Sur la peinture* is transcribed as "inutilisables par les *Marines*" (useless for the *Marines*), despite Bateson's support, as was just stated, coming from the American army. Despite some laughter blocking an entirely clear transcription, we opt for *army* as a more consistent translation.—*Trans.*]

30 Deleuze and Guattari had already retraced, from a more critical perspective, Bateson's "American-style career" in *Anti-Oedipus*, 236.

31 Deleuze mistakenly said "left."

32 Gregory Bateson, *Steps to an Ecology of Mind*: "Let us call this discussion of patterns of relationship the *t* function of the message. After all, it was the cat who showed us the great importance of this function by her mewing. [. . .] The cat asks for milk by saying 'Dependency,' and I ask for your attention and perhaps respect by talking about whales," 377. [The citation from Bateson in *Sur la peinture* replaces Bateson's "*t* function" with "μ function"; whether or not this variation is from Deleuze, he loosely paraphrases Bateson in this section (cf. 370–72).—*Trans.*]

33 Gregory Bateson, *Steps to an Ecology of Mind*: "Adaptation to life in the ocean has stripped the whales of facial expression. They have no external ears to flap and few if any erectile hairs. Even the cervical vertebrae are fused into a solid block in many species, and evolution has streamlined the body, sacrificing the expressiveness of separate parts to the locomotion of the whole. Moreover, conditions of life in the sea are such that even if a dolphin had a mobile face, the details of his expression would be visible to other dolphins only at rather short range, even in the clearest waters," 376.

34 See "Postulates of Linguistics," *A Thousand Plateaus*, 75–110.

35 Anne Querrien's research relating to the construction of Gothic cathedrals is cited in *A Thousand Plateaus*, 554–55 note 26.

36 André Scobeltzine, *L'Art feudal et son enjeu social* (Paris: Gallimard, 1973).

37 [In this context, the translation follows linguistic parlance with *trait* as "feature."—*Trans.*]

38 Roman Jakobson, "Concluding Statement: Linguistic and Poetics," in *Style in Language*, ed. Thomas A. Sebeok (Cambridge: The MIT Press, 1960), 350–77.

39 Jean-Jacques Rousseau, "Essay on the Origin of Languages," in *Essay on the Origin of Languages and Writings Related to Music*, trans. John T. Scott (Hanover: University Presses of New England, 2000), 289–332.

40 Jean-Jacques Rousseau, "Essay on the Origin of Languages," chap. 4.

41 [While the translation elsewhere renders *accent* as "stress" (when Deleuze is talking about contemporary linguistics), Rousseau's translators' choices are followed here whenever possible.—*Trans.*]

42 Jean-Jacques Rousseau, "Essay on the Origin of Languages," chap. 7: "It is a mistake to believe that accent can be made up for by accent marks. Accent marks are invented only when accent is already lost. What is more, we believe that we have accents in our language, but we do not have them at all," 301–2.

43 ["On n'invente les accents que quand l'accent est déjà perdu," 378. The translation distinguishes "accents" and "accent" by referring the former to accent marks and to the latter as "intonation."—*Trans.*]

44 Jean-Jacques Rousseau, "Essay on the Origin of Languages," chaps. 8, 9, and 10.

45 Jean-Jacques Rousseau, "Essay on the Origin of Languages," chap. 10: "Mutual need united men much better than feeling would have done, society was formed only through industry, the constant danger of perishing did not allow them to limit themselves to the language of gesture, and the first word among them was not 'love me,' but 'help me,'" 316.

46 On the opposition Rameau-Rousseau, see also *The Fold,* 136 and 163, note 36.

47 Jean-Pierre Brisset, *La Grammaire logique,* followed by *La Science de Dieu,* preceded by "Sept propos sur le septième ange" by Michel Foucault (Paris: Tchou, 1970).

48 *Intervention*: There's a text by Marcel Jousse on this, *Anthropologie du geste* [Anthropology of the Gesture] where he actually traces language back to gestures, claiming that speech was created because humans were lazy and didn't want to use their whole bodies to express themselves . . .—G.D.: A text by whom?—By Marcel Jousse.—G.D.: We don't need to refer to Marcel Jousse because it's a very eighteenth-century idea. A completely standard idea, that language originated in labor and in the gestures of labor.—This text goes a little further than that, nonetheless.—G.D.: I hope so! [*Laughter.*]—Because he analyzes the function of *mimèmes,* that is, the human capacity to reproduce outward interactions.—G.D.: Fine. That might be interesting, to see if there's an analogous dimension to what he's calling interactions. But anyway, that's another topic.—There's also an analysis of language and, in particular, rhythm-melody functions.—G.D.: I'm sure there is, yes. [*Laughter.*] There's all of that!

49 The distinction between "pathic moment" and "gnostic moment" is introduced by Erwin Straus and taken up notably by Henri Maldiney

in a 1966 article, "Le dévoilement de la dimension esthétique dans la phénoménologie d'Erwin Straus" [Unveiling the Aesthetic Dimension in Erwin Straus's Phenomenology], collected in *Regard Parole Espace,* 124ff.

50 Jean-Jacques Rousseau, "Essay on the Origin of Languages," chap. 9: "Young girls came to fetch water for the household, young men came to water their herds. There, eyes accustomed to the same objects from childhood began to see sweeter ones. [. . .] There, the first festivals took place, feet leaped with joy, eager gesture no longer sufficed, the voice accompanied it with passionate accents," 314.

SESSION 5 TYPES OF ANALOGY, SIGNAL-SPACES, AND MODULATION

Initial translation for The Deleuze Seminars by Billy Dean Goehring.

1 [On the "aesthetic analogy," see *Francis Bacon* (*FBLS,* 94 UM; 115–16 C), and on molding (*FLBS,* 108–11 UM; 134–36 C).—*Trans.*]

2 On the pellicular individuation of the crystal, Deleuze refers most often to Gilbert Simondon, *L'Individuation à la lumière des notions de forme et d'information* (Grenoble: Millon, 2005), 94–95, 161, 227. [See *Individuation in Light of Notions of Form and Information,* trans. Taylor Adkins (Minneapolis: University of Minnesota Press, 2020), 89–91, 172–73, 253.—*Trans.*]

3 These critics are mainly Burckhardt, Riegl, followed by Worringer. On the crystalline laws, also called inorganic-crystalline or geometric-crystalline, we can refer to Aloïs Riegl, *Late Roman Art Industry,* trans. Rolf Winkes (Rome: Giorgio Bretschneider, 1985), 55ff.; *Grammaire historique des arts plastiques,* trans. E. Kaufholz (Paris: Klincksieck, 1978; reedited Vanves: Hazan, 2015), 63ff. [As access to the complete English translation has been difficult, citations either are drawn from the translation when a particular quote is available or are translated from Deleuze's reference to the French edition.—*Trans.*]

4 The notion of "internal mold" appears, in Buffon, in *Histoire des animaux* [1748], chap. 3. In *The Fold,* Deleuze refers to the remarks by Georges Canguilhem in *Connaissance de la vie* (Paris: Vrin, 1975), 53–54; *Knowledge of Life,* trans. Stefanos Geroulanos and Daniela Ginsburg (New York: Fordham University Press, 2008), which cites excerpts from Buffon's text [on the "inner mold"] (158, note 23). Deleuze had already mentioned Buffon in the same terms a few months earlier, during the Spinoza seminar, *TDS* Spinoza 11-170281 (time stamp: 58:00). See also *Francis Bacon* (*FBLS,* 164–65, note 20 UM; 192, note 20 C).

5 See Buffon, *Oeuvres complètes,* vol. 10, *Végétaux, Animaux,* 1 (Paris: F. D. Pillot, 1831), 287: "It can be said that this expression, inner mold, appears at first to contain two contradictory ideas, the idea that a mold can only relate to the surface, and the idea that the interior must connect here to the mass; it's as if we wanted to join together the idea of surface and the idea of mass, and one might just as well say a massive surface rather than an inner mold," 287. [My translation from the French.—*Trans.*]

6 Deleuze often resorts to Simondon's concept of modulation, each time distinguishing it from the mold. See *A Thousand Plateaus* (522, note 19, and 562, note 92); *Cinema 2* (27–28); *The Fold* (19).

7 This is a reference to the doctoral thesis of Gilbert Simondon (1924–1989). At the time of this seminar, only part of this thesis was accessible, with the title *L'Individu et sa genèse physico-biologique* (Paris: PUF, 1964). The complete version would be published in 2005 with only its initial title, *L'Individuation à la lumière des notions de forme et d'information.* As in an earlier note (note 2 of this session), our references are to the translation, *Individuation in Light of Notions of Form and Information.*

8 Gilbert Simondon, *Individuation in Light of Notions of Form and Information*: "The mold and modulator are the extreme cases, but the essential operation of form-taking is accomplished in the same way," 31. The entirety of this passage is placed under the subheading "Modeling, Molding, Modulation," 29. [While Lapoujade addresses the matter of Deleuze's citation with the preceding brief note, the matter is more nuanced: in the painting seminar, Deleuze quotes Simondon as saying they are "deux extrêmes d'une chaîne" (two ends of a chain; see time stamp: 20:38). Simondon does use this expression in *Individuation in Light of Notions of Form and Information* (while discussing means of understanding "the veritable structure of the living being" via "the basic function that depends on the first topological structure of interiority and exteriority," a function "mediated by a chain of intermediary interiorities and exteriorities. At *the two ends of the chain,* there is still the absolute interior and the absolute exterior," 252). However, the closest equivalent in the context of molding and modulating is Simondon's statement cited in *Sur la peinture* in note 11 below.—*Trans.*]

9 See note 7 above.

10 Gilbert Simondon, *Individuation in Light of Notions of Form and Information,* 30–31.

11 Gilbert Simondon, *Individuation in Light of Notions of Form and Information*: "*Molding* and *modulation* are the extreme cases of which

modeling is the intermediate case," 31. [On Deleuze's reference to Simondon, see *Francis Bacon* (FBLS, 164–65, note 20 UM; 192, note 20 C.)—*Trans.*]

12 Gregory Bateson, *Naven: A Survey of the Problems suggested by a Composite Picture of a New Guinea Tribe drawn from Three Points of View* (1936; Stanford, CA: Stanford University Press, 1965). [As for Paul Watzlawick, although he is mentioned by Comtesse, Deleuze makes no reference to him, and no details are provided in *Sur la peinture.* An Austrian-American linguist, Watzlawick started work at the Mental Research Institute in Palo Alto, CA, following on Bateson's work there, and with Donald Jackson and Janice Beaven-Bavelas, Watzlawick published *Pragmatics of Human Communication* (New York: W. W. Norton, 1967).—*Trans.*]

13 [As a gesture toward the difference between *langue* and *langage*—a difference with no comfortable English equivalent—*langue* is translated as "spoken language," with *langage* as "language."—*Trans.*]

14 [Voices are audible assuring Deleuze that Comtesse's comments support his position.—*Trans.*]

15 [In the transcription in *Sur la peinture,* the word *disjunctive* is mistakenly inserted where *conjunctive* should appear (which we have corrected), especially given the contrast that Querrien establishes here; as she continues, she deliberately insists on *disjunctive* as the second term. See TDS Painting 5-120581, time stamp: 38:26 (accessed 30 April 2024).—*Trans.*]

16 Richard Pinhas, born in 1951, musician and composer of experimental electronic music, met Deleuze at the Experimental University Center at Vincennes in 1971. While he was writing a doctoral thesis with Jean-François Lyotard, "The Relationship between Schizoanalysis and Science Fiction," he regularly attended Deleuze's seminars, as they were close friends. He is responsible for developing in 1994 the website for the recordings and transcripts of Deleuze's seminars, with Deleuze's permission, at https://www.webdeleuze.com. [In *Francis Bacon,* chap. 13 on "Analogy," Deleuze states that he borrows the analysis (FLBS, 94–95 UM; 116–17 C) "from Richard Pinhas, *Synthèse analogique, synthèse digitale* (unpublished)" (FBLS, 162 note 6 UM; 188 note 6 C), to which Daniel W. Smith adds, "A revised portion of this text has since appeared in Richard Pinhas, *Les Larmes de Nietzsche* (Paris: Flammarion, 2001)."—*Trans.*]

17 [The transcription of *Sur la peinture* indicates that Deleuze here says "rather than between 1 and 0," which we retain, but the sounds from

Deleuze do not at all correspond to these two digits (he seems to say inexplicably "3 and 0"). Hence an unclear ending persists. See TDS Painting 5-120581, time stamp: 40:23 (accessed 30 April 2024).—*Trans.*]

18 We have corrected the speaker's comments by reversing the two notions of "verb" and "substantive" in her distinctions.

19 [Given the context of this discussion, it is likely that Comtesse's disagreement is addressed to Anne Querrien and not Deleuze.—*Trans.*]

20 [For the most part, *analogique* remains as "analog." This makes sense when Deleuze is more clearly referring to technology, the difference between digital and analog synthesizers, for example. Let us note, however, that in other contexts (such as when Comtesse brings up Bateson and Watzlawick earlier), there's good reason to render *analogique* as "analogical." In fact, Watzlawick discusses the difference between so-called digital and analogical language.—*Trans.*]

21 The 1930s? The "process" in question no doubt is the development of binary code (beginning with Boolean algebra) during the 1930s for the relay and switching circuits of Claude E. Shannon (1916–2000).

22 [A note on the phrase *to plan.* A "modulation to plan" sounds too much like a "planned (future) modulation." In some contexts, *sur plan* might be translated as "to spec," as when something is manufactured according to specifications. Deleuze's wordplay is very difficult to preserve, however. *Plan*'s double meaning as "plan" or "plane" allows him to move from talking about modulating "to plan" to talking about modulating the surface ("plane") of a canvas.—*Trans.*]

23 For example, the remarks relayed by Émile Bernard: "One should never say 'model'; one should say 'modulate,'" *Conversations with Cézanne,* 39.

24 Here is the exact quotation, taken from a comment by Bonnard to Tériade, published in the journal *Verve,* founded and directed by Tériade; see *Verve,* vol. 5, nos. 17–18 (August 1947): "Avec une seule goutte d'huile Titien peignait un bras d'un bout à l'autre; Cézanne a voulu au contraire que tous ses passages soient des tons conscients" (With a single drop of oil, Titian would paint an entire arm; Cézanne, on the other hand, wanted all his painting choices to be deliberate colors) [My translation from the French.—*Trans.*]. Deleuze no doubt found the quotation in Maldiney's *Regard Parole Espace* (169, note 31): he produces its transcription error.

25 Maldiney uses precisely the same terms regarding Bonnard's comment, in *Regard Parole Espace* (169).

26 A public French network, a precursor to the Internet, created in 1978 with the purpose of transmitting data throughout the entire world, it enabled the development of telematic services. It was closed in 2012 with the end of the Minitel servers.

27 This comment probably refers to sessions devoted to the concept of "smooth space" as indicated by the rare passages in *A Thousand Plateaus* concerning Egyptian spaces and Riegl's analyses (492–95). [The "previous seminar" would in all likelihood correspond to the two years that Deleuze spent on the final plateaus of *A Thousand Plateaus,* 1978–79 and 1979–80. Since the latter seminar, the one with corresponding recordings, contains only one fleeting reference to Riegl (by a student), Deleuze no doubt introduced Riegl's works in the earlier seminar.—*Trans.*]

28 For the titles that Deleuze mentions (*Problèmes de style, Arts industriels à l'époque du Bas-Empire*), we have substituted the titles corresponding to works currently available to French readers.

29 Besides the *Late Roman Art Industry* to which Deleuze will later refer in a letter to Serge Daney, "Optimism, Pessimism and Travel," in *Negotiations* (68–79), none of Riegl's works were translated into French at that time. Since then, the works that Deleuze mentions have been translated: *Questions de style* (1893; Vanves: Hazan, 1992); *Le Portrait de groupe hollandais* (1932; Vanves: Hazan, 2008); and *L'industrie d'art roman tardive* (1901; Paris: Macula, 2014). Given Deleuze's unfamiliarity with German, it is unlikely that he had direct access to Riegl's works. To constitute his themes and analyses, Deleuze relied for the most part on Maldiney's reading in *Regard Parole Espace* (notably 194ff.) and on passages by Riegl and frequent citations from him in Worringer's *Abstraction and Empathy.* This indirect access to Riegl's works is confirmed in a comment in *A Thousand Plateaus* (492–93) and *Francis Bacon* (FBLS, 163, note 2 UM; 189, note 2 C). [In this *Francis Bacon* note, Daniel W. Smith provides this reference to Riegl's book, *Late Roman Art Industry,* trans. Rolf Winkes (2nd ed.; Rome: Giorgio Bretschneider Editore, 1985).—*Trans.*]

30 See the definitions proposed by Worringer in *Abstraction and Empathy*: "The stylistic peculiarities of past epochs are, therefore, not to be explained by lack of ability, but by a differently directed volition," 9, and "Its creators 'could' do no otherwise because they willed no otherwise," 124. [The "will at art's core" is what Riegl calls *Kunstwollen.*—*Trans.*]

31 [We restore, in brackets, the reference to Riegl that Deleuze makes, edited in *Sur la peinture.*—*Trans.*]

32 See Aloïs Riegl, *Late Roman Art Industry*: "The aim of ancient art in improving nature is still the recreation of natural objects, not in their transient natural appearance, but in their essential and final form," 238. See also Henri Maldiney, *Regard Parole Espace*: "All the stylistic laws of Egypt [. . .] converge in a single design which is also that of the rites and the sepulture: to protect the integrity and permanence of the individual—living or dead—against these forces of corruption which are space and time, milieus of universal change," 195. [My translation from the French.—*Trans.*] See Wilhelm Worringer, *Abstraction and Empathy*, 103–4. Deleuze already touched on this point at the start of the Spinoza session TDS Spinoza 6-130181.

33 Plato, *Timaeus*, 22b. This formulation about the Egyptians returns several times in Deleuze and Guattari's writing, notably *Anti-Oedipus* (222) and *A Thousand Plateaus* (450).

34 Wilhelm Worringer, *Abstraction and Empathy*: "For according to the belief of the Egyptians, the continued life of the 'Ka' was to some extent dependent upon the verisimilitude of the image," 92. On the eternity of the individual form for the Egyptians, see Henri Maldiney, *Regard Parole Espace* (194ff.).

35 Henri Maldiney, *Regard Parole Espace*: "The motif is distinguished from the background by what unites it to the background and by what constitutes it itself: contour. Whether in architecture or as ornament, in sculpture or painting, the forms of Egyptian art are always based on their limit, which is their unique foundation. This limit, while being determined, also protects," 195. [My translation from the French.—*Trans.*]

36 [For Deleuze's *corriger*—to fix, correct, adjust—the translation keeps with Jung's translation of Riegl, with "improve." See Riegl, *Historical Grammar of the Visual Arts*, ed. Benjamin Binstock, trans. Jacqueline E. Jung (New York: Zone, 2004).—*Trans.*]

37 See Aloïs Riegl, *Late Roman Art Industry*: "Man creates in art a concept of Nature, which liberates him from constant disruptions and produces an image of Nature which makes her look better than she is," 71, note 21.

38 This is the central thesis of *Late Roman Art Industry*, the only work by Riegl available in French in the period when Deleuze was working on these questions. See note 29 of this session.

39 [*Sur le plan* can also be interpreted to mean "in the plan," "according to plan." See also note 22 in this session.—*Trans.*]

40 On this point, *Francis Bacon* quotes Maldiney, *Regard Parole Espace*: "In the spatial zone of closeness, with which we are in direct contact, the

sense of sight behaves as the sense of touch, experiencing the presence of the form and the ground *at the same place*," 195. [My translation from the French.—*Trans.*]

41 Deleuze here is apparently relying on an example cited by Riegl in *Grammaire historique des arts plastiques* (130, note 24). We have revised the order of exposition in the following passage for the sake of readability (refer to the original order at TDS Painting 5-120581, time stamp: 1:40:35–1:42:40).

42 On the difference between the Egyptian fold and the Greek fold, see Aloïs Riegl, *Late Roman Art Industry* (88). Also see comments by Wilhelm Worringer, *Abstraction and Empathy*: "Thus, for example, the folds of the robes are stylized into stiffness and regularity, the fall of the drapery at the hem of the robe is transformed into a surface pattern, the same with the edge of that piece of the robe which is lifted up and anywhere else that opportunity offers, as for instance in the treatment of the hair," 92–93.

43 We have corrected Deleuze's lapse, speaking of the Greek fold.

44 ["Organic" in Jacqueline E. Jung's translation of Riegl. See Jung's preface to Riegl, *Historical Grammar of the Visual Arts*, 45.—*Trans.*]

45 Deleuze borrows the concept of "shallow depth" from the translation by Marc Chénetier in a Greenberg text, in *Macula*, no. 2 (1977): 50. The term is employed in *Francis Bacon* to qualify the junction of the planes in Bacon's work, in contrast to Cézanne's strong depth (FBLS, 163, chap. 13 note 9 UM; 188, note 9 C).

46 See FBLS: "Through the centuries, there are many things that make Bacon an Egyptian: the fields, the contour, the form and the ground as two equally close sectors lying on the same plane, the extreme proximity of the Figure (presence), the system of clarity [*netteté*]" (100 UM; 123 C).

47 [This parenthetical query is added in *Sur la peinture*, at a particular point in the recording that contains several gaps.—*Trans.*]

48 This refers to the cover of John Russell's book, *Francis Bacon* (1964; Paris: Chêne, 1979; New York: Thames and Hudson, 1993), which reproduces *Painting* (1978, private collection), reproduction taken from image 23 in the first edition of Deleuze's *Francis Bacon* (Paris: Éditions de la Différence, 1981) of which Deleuze gives a brief description (FBLS, 14 UM; 13–14 C). [The color image of *Painting* will be included as plate 4 in the Éditions du Seuil 2002 reedited volume of *Francis Bacon*.—*Trans.*]

49 Regarding the halo, Deleuze refers in *Francis Bacon* to a work by Jean Paris, *L'Espace et le regard* (Paris: Seuil, 1965), 65ff. (FBLS, 166, chap. 16, note 3 UM; 195, chap. 16, note 3 C).

50 Refer to note 45 in this session.

51 David Sylvester, *Interviews with Francis Bacon*: "DAVID SYLVESTER: Those sculptures you used to talk about wanting to do: have you more or less given up the idea now?—FRANCIS BACON: I don't think I will do them, because I think I have now found a way by which I could do the images I thought of more satisfactorily in paint than I could in sculpture. I haven't started on them yet, but through thinking about them as sculptures it suddenly came to me how I could make them in paint," 83, cited in *FBLS* (154, note 8 UM; 174–75, note 8 C). See also *Interviews with Francis Bacon,* 108ff.

52 [No passage *exactly* like this is in David Sylvester's Bacon interviews, presumably where these comments come from. The passages here are stitched together to convey the sense that Deleuze is reciting from memory, accurately, but not verbatim.—*Trans.*]

53 David Sylvester, *Interviews with Francis Bacon*: "I've thought about sculptures on a kind of armature, a very large armature made so that the sculpture could slide along it and people could even alter the position of the sculpture as they wanted" (108), cited in *FBLS* (154, note 8 UM; 174–75, note 8 C).

54 David Sylvester, *Interviews with Francis Bacon*: "It would be a kind of structured painting in which images, as it were, would arise from a river of flesh.—And what would the form be?—They would certainly be raised on structures.—Several figures?—Yes, and there would probably be a pavement raised high out of its naturalistic setting, out of which they could move as though out of pools of flesh rose the images, if possible, of specific people walking on their daily round," 83, cited in *FBLS* (154, note 8 UM; 174–75, note 8 C). [The word "figure . . . rising out of pools" is preserved in our translation, in keeping with the use Deleuze makes of the term.—*Trans.*]

55 The reference is to *Man With Dog* (1953, collection Albright-Knox Art Gallery, Buffalo). The painting is cited in chap. 1 of *Francis Bacon* (*FBLS*, 8 UM; 6 C) to distinguish three analogous sculptural elements: the armature, the pedestal, and the Figure.

56 See Aloïs Riegl, *Grammaire historique des arts plastiques,* 133ff. See also the quote from Riegl by Worringer in *Abstraction and Empath*: "It was a problem therefore 'of divesting the cubic of its agonizing quality,' of transposing the cubic into surface impressions. The pyramid stands before us as the most consistent imaginable fulfilment of this endeavor," 90–91.

57 [To make sense of the "three isosceles triangles" that Deleuze mentions, see this passage from Riegl, *Late Roman Art Industry*: "The architectural ideal of the ancient Egyptians is best expressed through the tomb-type of the pyramid. Any of the four sides permits the beholder's eye to observe an always unified plane of an isosceles triangle, the sharply rising sides of which by no means reveal the connecting space behind," 27.—*Trans.*]

58 Letter to Émile Bernard, 15 April 1904, in *Conversations with Cézanne*, 29.

59 See Henri Maldiney, *Regard Parole Espace*: "One should note that Cézanne does not name the cube. Cézannian space is not the cubic space of classical perspective," 186, note 49. [My translation from the French.—*Trans.*]

60 On the subject of Greek art according to Riegl, see Henri Maldiney, *Regard Parole Espace*: "The structure of the form is no longer governed by relations in the plane but by relations in space, by rendering visible the three dimensions. But the spatial coordinates of the individual form are those of closed cubic space," 197. [My translation from the French.—*Trans.*]

61 See Aloïs Riegl, *Grammaire historique des arts plastiques*: "There are no remains of a personal dwelling from ancient Egypt, but the scholars are undoubtedly right when they judge that the Egyptian house must not have been very different from the corncob hut of the fellah of our time: a pyramidal section, sloping walls devoid of a window," 133. [My translation from the French.—*Trans.*]

62 See the quote from Riegl in Wilhelm Worringer, *Abstraction and Empathy*: "Strangely enough, no one has so far been struck by the improbability of the process by which the first weed the artist came across was supposed suddenly to have been elevated to an artistic motif," 58–59.

63 Without direct access to *Questions de Style* by Riegl, then unpublished in French, it is likely that Deleuze was inspired by the remarks of Otto Pächt in his presentation of the only work by Riegl then available in French, *Grammaire historique des arts plastiques*, xiii–xiv.

SESSION 6 THE HAPTIC AND THE THIRD EYE

Initial translation for The Deleuze Seminars by Billy Dean Goehring.

1 Deleuze started the session with a few words of explanation concerning the two diagrams drawn on the board: "I'm in a tough spot because I'm of a mind to draw up some very basic color diagrams; actually, that preempts the subject that I'll be addressing, but I suspect that I won't have the courage to redraw them next time."

2 What we call "Goethe's triangle" does not appear in Goethe's *Treatise on Colors*. The painter Adolf Hötzel (1853–1934) first proposed the diagram in his classes, then one of his students, the German artist Carry van Biema (1881–1942), in 1930, proposed the diagram in its current form in *Farben und Formen als Lebendige Kräfte* [The Colors and Forms as Living Forces] (Munich: Eugen Diederichs, 1930).

3 Deleuze refers to J. W. von Goethe's *Theory of Colours*, trans. Sir Charles Locke Eastlake ([1810]; London: John Murray, 1840). He will present this text once again in *Cinema 1* regarding German Expressionism (49–54) and Sternberg's lyrical abstraction (93–95). He returns to the text again in the essays in *Essays Critical and Clinical*, "The Shame and the Glory: T. E. Lawrence" (115–25) and "Spinoza and the Three 'Ethics'" (138–51).

4 [In contrast to Deleuze's detailed consideration of Goethe's color theory here, he makes only passing references to Goethe in his brief presentation of color theory in *Francis Bacon* (FBLS, 106–8, 112–13, and 164 note 14 UM; 132–34, 139–40, and 191 note 14 C).—*Trans.*]

5 [The shift from "darkening of light" to "darkening of white" corresponds to the transcript.—*Trans.*]

6 [An aspect of the session that will remain unnoted for the sake of readability is Deleuze's frequent pauses as he writes on the board, embellishing the diagrams already present. His presence at the board, and thus away from the microphone, accounts for several gaps in the session.—*Trans.*]

7 [While this may well be a deliberate edit, the phrase added and placed in brackets is omitted in *Sur la peinture* yet is present in the original transcript, without which the second part of the sentence becomes unclear.—*Trans.*]

8 [Goethe's *Purpur* (which Deleuze calls here *pourpre*) predates the introduction of the word *magenta*. There's precedent for retrofitting Goethe's color wheel to include magenta instead of "pure red." For the sake of clarity, we deliberately put words in both Goethe's and Deleuze's texts by employing "magenta" or "red" for *Purpur/pourpre* and "purple" for *violet*.—*Trans.*]

9 We have omitted the passage in which Deleuze provides the diagram's numerical list of the different color triangles (time stamp: 12:25–12:45).

10 J. W. von Goethe, *Theory of Colours*: "We have remarked a constant progress or augmentation in yellow and blue, and seen what impressions were produced by the various states; hence it may naturally be inferred

that now, in the junction of the deepened extremes, a feeling of satisfaction must succeed" (§ 794, 314); and "If yellow and blue, which we consider as the most fundamental and simple colours, are united as they first appear, in the first state of their action, the colour which we call green is the result. The eye experiences a distinctly grateful impression from this colour" (§ 801–2, 316).

11 [We include Deleuze's indication about continuing to add to the drawing, omitted in *Sur la peinture*.—*Trans.*]

12 [Let us note that *primitive* is rendered as "primary" when it appears alone; here, however, "primitive" is retained because it appears alongside *primaire*, to avoid misleading the reader into thinking Deleuze has special plans for this term or is drawing a meaningful distinction between the two terms.—*Trans.*]

13 [No dotted line is found in any available sources. However, as Deleuze here develops the illustration, presumably the chromatic circle that he's drawn or is looking at has dotted lines running along the different chords (as Deleuze describes them below subsequently).—*Trans.*]

14 J. W. von Goethe, *Theory of Colours*: "Besides these pure, harmonious, self-developed combinations, which always carry the conditions of completeness with them, there are others which may be arbitrarily produced, and which may be most easily described by observing that they are to be found in the colorific circle, not by diameters, but by chords, in such a manner that an intermediate colour is passed over" (§ 816, 321).

15 [We have completed a gap, in brackets, left as inaudible in *Sur la peinture*, with text gleaned from the recording transcribed by Marc Haas, in a private communication.—*Trans.*]

16 [See J. W. von Goethe, *Theory of Colours*, § 816–17.—*Trans.*]

17 [See J. W. von Goethe, *Theory of Colours*, § 817–19.—*Trans.*]

18 Deleuze returns here to an anecdote from the art critic Théophile Silvestre related by Paul Signac in *D'Eugène Delacroix au néo-impressionnisme*: "For the application of this system, Delacroix had made a sort of cardboard dial that we could call his chronometer. At each of the steps was arranged, as around a pallet, a small pile of colors which had those immediately associated to it and those that were diametrically opposed," 58–59. [My translation from the French.—*Trans.*] Signac indeed was speaking about a chronometer and not a "chromometer" as one might expect.

19 [This brief inaudible passage consists partially of a student's questions challenging Deleuze's assertion about the reasons for Mondrian's departure from New York.—*Trans.*]

20 [In what follows, we avoid translating *ton* as "tone" given that, in most contexts in English, tone specifically refers to a shade of color. In nearly all cases, "color" or possibly "hue" is a better equivalent for Deleuze's *ton*. However, on the distinction of *tons* and *teintes*, see session 8, note 4.—*Trans.*]

21 [In *Francis Bacon*, Deleuze pays considerable attention to "colorism" and color (FBLS, 112–15 UM; 139–43 C, and also in chap. 16, "Note on Color").—*Trans.*]

22 This distinction appears in *Late Roman Art Industry*, accessible at that time only in its original version (see 196ff.). Deleuze no doubt relied on the references and comments by Maldiney on this point. See Henri Maldiney, *Regard Parole Espace*: "Colorism is opposed to chromatism, colorism endowing color with an independent value; in principle, colorism requires the non-coincidence of color and form," 190–91. [My translation from the French.—*Trans.*]

23 J. W. von Goethe, *Theory of Colours*: "They [the phenomena] show that the eye especially demands completeness, and seeks to eke out the colorific circle in itself. The purple or violet colour suggested by yellow contains red and blue; orange, which responds to blue, is composed of yellow and red; green, uniting blue and yellow, demands red; and so through all gradations of the most complicated combinations" (§ 60, 28); and "When the eye sees a colour it is immediately excited, and it is its nature, spontaneously and of necessity, at once to produce another, which with the original colour comprehends the whole chromatic scale. A single colour excites, by a specific sensation, the tendency to universality" (§ 805, 317).

24 [While this is marked as inaudible in *Sur le peinture*, we complete the gap based on the recording, time stamp: 48:12 (accessed 1 May 2024).—*Trans.*]

25 The closest citation to the paraphrase proposed by Deleuze is mentioned in Paul Signac's book (that Deleuze will use in the 26 May session) *D'Eugène Delacroix au néo-impressionisme*, in which the following statement is attributed to Delacroix: "Donnez-moi de la boue des rues et j'en ferai la chair de femme d'une teinte délicieuse" (Give me some mud

from the streets and I'll make woman's flesh of a delicious hue out of it), (86). [My translation from the French.—*Trans.*]

26 The full title is *Light and Colour (Goethe's Theory)—The Morning after the Deluge—Moses Writing the Book of Genesis* (1843, Tate Britain, London). This painting is associated with *Shade and Darkness—the Evening of the Deluge* (1843, Tate Britain, London). [See session 1 for Deleuze's earlier discussion of this Turner work.—*Trans.*]

27 [Despite the editorial decision in *Sur la peinture* to drop this exchange, Deleuze indicates clearly his interest in the student's comments, but he does not pursue them because of his own fatigue, and ultimately because Deleuze seems to realize that his response to the student's questions doesn't go very far, suggesting finally: "Oh, this is really beyond me. Put it this way, it's an exercise: how we might get nine with the chromatic circle. . . . We'll set that aside for now, but again: we're going to need it soon."—*Trans.*]

28 ["Flatness" is the most common translation for *planéité*. While "planarity" is much less common, it preserves "plan," for readers tracking plan/plane in Deleuze's works. We choose the term *flatness* here because it is Greenberg's term; see also the following note provided in *Sur la peinture*.—*Trans.*]

29 Given that Deleuze only was familiar with Greenberg then through the journal *Macula* and by Michael Fried's article, perhaps he was thinking of Fried's quote from Greenberg in the article "Three American Painters: Kenneth Noland, Jules Olitski, Frank Stella (1965)": "By now it has been established, it would seem, that the irreducible essence of pictorial art consists in but two constitutive conventions or norms: flatness and the delimitation of flatness," in *Art and Objecthood. Essays and Reviews*, 168.

30 Deleuze says "in reverse" [*à l'envers*] or backward, but the context suggests that he probably means "on" the reverse side [*sur l'envers*], as suggested by his subsequent mention of the Supports/Surfaces movement.

31 [According to *ArtForum*, "Supports/Surfaces, the radical painting movement that began in the South of France in the late-1960s, comprised a group of artists that opened works to the spaces around them by decoupling or merging painted surface and physical support." https://www.artforum.com/events/supports-surfaces-206291/ (accessed 1 May 2024).—*Trans.*]

32 [For consistency: if *planéité* is "flatness," then *planification* is "flattening" of space.—*Trans.*]

33 Paul Gauguin, *La Belle Angèle* (1889, Musée d'Orsay, Paris).

34 See note 45 in the 12 May 1981 session.

35 [Here "field" is used for *aplat* to communicate the "flat" in *à plat/aplat,* in association with *planéité* and *planification.*—*Trans.*]

36 This refers to one of the paintings in the portrait series of the postman Joseph Roulin, completed in 1889, several of which correspond to the description given by Deleuze here.

37 On the relations between painting and phenomenology, see Deleuze's comments in the 13 January 1981 session on Spinoza: "What seems quite striking to me is that Cézanne, in general, was the painter *par excellence* for phenomenologists. It's a very small aspect, too technical and without great interest, but if we understand this, perhaps we understand just a bit about Cézanne. What are the most beautiful pages written on Cézanne today? Strangely, these pages don't really appear in art criticism. There's a very good text by Merleau-Ponty. There are two or three beautiful texts by Maldiney. There are some texts by Erwin Straus. And they have in common precisely the fact of being phenomenologists. So we have here something that is linked. It's not at all surprising, since phenomenology centers itself on sensation, a phenomenology of feeling. Cézanne is no doubt the one who pushed the farthest, both in practice and theoretically, pushed farthest the relation between painting and what he himself called sensation. So, I am not surprised that philosophers like Merleau-Ponty and Maldiney had been particularly inspired or had a special relation to Cézanne" (trans. Timothy S. Murphy, Charles J. Stivale, *TDS* Spinoza 6-130181, time stamp: 14:00–15:30). See also *FBLS* (156 note 1 UM; 178 note 1 C).

38 [Deleuze cites Merleau-Ponty in *Francis Bacon* (*FBLS*, 156 note 1 UM; 178 note 1 C) from *Phenomenology of Perception* (London: Routledge & Kegan Paul, 1967), 207–42.—*Trans.*]

39 The sentence that comes closest to Deleuze's citation from memory is in J. W. von Goethe, *Theory of Colours*: "The chief art of the painter is always to imitate the actual appearance of the definite hue, doing away with the recollection of the elementary ingredients of colour. This difficulty is in no instance greater than in the imitation of the surface of the human figure. [. . .] The colour is altogether removed from the elementary state

and neutralised by organisation" (§ 877–878, 339). See also: "But we have here chiefly to speak of colour, and observe that the colour of the human skin, in all its varieties, is never an elementary colour, but presents, by means of organic concoction, a highly complicated result" (§ 670, 264–65). [In *Francis Bacon,* the discussion of Gauguin's *La Belle Angèle* and Van Gogh's postman paintings precedes consideration of flesh in different artists' work, notably Bacon (*FBLS,* 113–15 UM; 140–43 C).—*Trans.*]

40 According to Édouard Dujardin, it is Louis Anquetin (1861–1932) who creates the term *cloisonnisme* [partitionism] in 1888 in *La Revue indépendente.* Inspired by cliché images [*l'image d'Épinal*] and Japanese art, "the painter will trace the drawing by closed lines, between which he will place the varied tones whose juxtaposition must give the desired general coloring sensation, the drawing affirming the color and the color affirming the drawing. And the painter's work will be something like a painting *in compartments,* analogous to the partitioned, and its technique will consist of a sort of *partitionism*" (Édouard Dujardin, *La Revue indépendente de littérature et d'art,* 1 May 1888, 490). [My translation from the French. The French term, often preserved in English, would be "partitioning."—*Trans.*]

41 As indicated above, we have substituted the title under which Aloïs Riegl's work has been translated, *Late Roman Art Industry* [*L'Industrie d'art romaine tardive*], for the title that Deleuze gives to it, *Arts et métiers à l'époque du Bas-Empire.*

42 UER designates Unités d'Enseignement et de Recherche (Teaching and Research Units), [the equivalent of academic departments and programs.—*Trans.*].

43 This refers to a project initiated by the minister of universities, Alice Saunier-Seïté (who had the buildings of the Vincennes university campus razed at the end of August 1980, reconstituted in Saint-Denis). After having modified the composition of university councils, by granting to magisterial professors 50 percent of seats to the detriment of other categories of teachers, Saunier-Seïté sought by every means to eliminate the intervention of left-wing unions in the university bodies.

44 Let us recall that the presidential elections took place on 10 May 1981, and saw the Socialist François Mitterrand triumph over Valéry Giscard d'Estaing (resulting in particular in the repeal of the "Sauvage" law by the new minister of national education, Alain Savary, a law that had strengthened the representation of teachers at the magisterial rank at

the expense of other categories of teachers and students in university councils).

45 Deleuze is no doubt inspired by Maldiney's comment in *Regard Parole Espace*: "In the first edition of 1901, the word 'haptic' does not appear, but in a response to critics of his work (*Allgemeine Zeitung, Beilage,* nos. 92–93, Vienna, 1902), Riegl recognizes that the term 'tactile' is poorly chosen and ought to be replaced everywhere by 'haptic'" (194, note 79). [My translation from the French.—*Trans.*]

46 [On haptic and the following distinctions, see *Francis Bacon* (*FBLS*, 124–26 and 166, chap. 17 note 2 UM; 154–56 and 195, chap. 17 note 2 C). The reference is to the second edition of Riegl's 1901 *Late Roman Art History,* trans. Rolf Winkes.—*Trans.*]

47 See Henri Maldiney, *Regard Parole Espace*: "If A. Riegl was able to detect in the industrial arts of the Late Empire a radical change of the 'will of art,' it is due to having discerned beneath the apparent homogeneity of seeing two possibilities of the gaze [. . .], two types of vision articulated by two types of artistic space, which he calls optical and haptic respectively. The second term is formed from the Greek ἅπτω: to touch (for 'to take')" (194). [My translation from the French.—*Trans.*]

48 [Deleuze ends *Francis Bacon* with these words: "But the fact itself, this pictorial fact that has come from the hand, is the formation of a third eye, a haptic eye, a haptic vision of the eye, this new clarity. It is as if the duality of the tactile and the optical were surpassed visually in this haptic function born of the diagram" (*FBLS*, 129 UM; 161 C).—*Trans.*]

49 "Musicians reach orgasm through the ear, but with our insatiable eye in heat, let us taste endless pleasures," Letter to Schuffenecker, September 1980 (*FBLS*, 47 UM; 55 C). [My translation from the French. Deleuze provides no source for this quote.—*Trans.*]

50 *Conversations with Cézanne*: "And my eyes, you know, my wife tells me that they jump out of my head, they get all bloodshot," 125.

51 In the 13 March 1984 Cinema 3 session, the foreground is conceived as a means of "domesticating depth": "The Greeks of the classical age are afraid of depth. And, indeed, what will come to domesticate depth in Greek art? It is the foreground. It is the foreground which, in fact, will be the determining plane, the fundamental plane because it is the one which will determine the other planes. It is with it and in relation to it that the other planes will enter into relationships of intersection. There will be a primacy of the foreground. The figure is defined by the

foreground. It encloses the depth within its width and length. All of Greek statuary adheres to this general criterion. The most powerful instances of Greek sculpture are those which immediately appear in the foreground" (trans. Graeme Thomson and Silvia Maglioni, *TDS* Cinema 3 13–130384, time stamp: 14:00–15:00).

52 Deleuze follows closely Maldiney's analysis, in *Regard Parole Espace*, of the grave stele of Dermys and Kitylos: "Each moment is that of the appearance of a form (leg, thigh, torso, chest or neck between two braids, head) but each of these clear moments, strongly affixed in the foreground, rises from the background constituted by the hollow parts that are the spatial intervals of shadow. At the strong moments of the θέσις, represented by the luminous reliefs that surface on the same plane in the same *là*, it is necessary to add the weak moments of the ἄρσις represented by shadows," 198–99. [My translation from the French.—*Trans.*]

53 Henri Maldiney, *Regard Parole Espace*: "Despite all the talk about Greek light, the space of classical Greek art is tactile-optical space," 197; cited in *FBLS*, 102 UM; 126 C. Deleuze had already considered this point during the preceding seminar on Spinoza. See the 27 January 1981 session: "It is said that the Greeks lived in the light. That's wrong. Everything that is said about the Greeks, we can say in advance that it's false. [*Laughter.*] So they lived in the light? Not at all. The word 'eidos' is invoked for them. Everyone tells us, however, that it's a complicated word because it means at the same time 'form,' 'essence' and 'what is seen.' It is true that the Greeks invent a certain light, but I insist on this, it is not at all a pure light" (trans. Charles J. Stivale, *TDS* Spinoza 8–270181, time stamp: 1:09–1:10). In the 17 February 1981 session, Deleuze insists on the fact that rather than being Plato, it is Plotinus who reflects on pure light: "I believe that it's with Plotinus that a pure optical world begins in philosophy. Idealities will no longer be only optical, that is, they will be luminous, without any tactile reference" (trans. Timothy S. Murphy, *TDS* Spinoza 11–170281, time stamp: 1:17:00–1:17:10).

54 On this point, Deleuze follows closely the analyses by Henri Maldiney, *Regard Parole Espace* (201ff.). In the 13 March 1984 Cinema 3 session, Deleuze comments about *Regard Parole Espace*: "It is among the most beautiful things ever written on Byzantine art" (trans. Graeme Thomson and Silvia Maglioni, *TDS* Cinema 3 13–130384, time stamp: 1:53:00–1:53:10). Deleuze had already referred to Byzantine art during the previous seminar devoted to Spinoza (see *TDS* Spinoza 8–270181 and 11–170281). He will return to this distinction between Greek art and Byzantine art in the

Cinema 3 seminar (see TDS Cinema 3 12–280284 and 13–130384). [We have corrected the lapse in dates in *Sur la peinture* (to 28 February), as there was no 18 February 1984 session (a Saturday).—*Trans.*]

55 On Byzantium as the liberation of color, see Henri Maldiney, *Regard Parole Espace,* 202ff. See also Deleuze's comments at the end of the 17 February 1981 Spinoza session: "What [the Byzantines] discover is that light and color are spatializing. Thus, art must not be an art of space, it must be an art of the spatialization of space" (trans. Timothy S. Murphy, TDS Spinoza 11–170281, time stamp: 1:30:30–1:30:40). [Given that the text in *Sur la peinture* seems to rely, in part, on the transcription available at WebDeleuze, the reference to "the end of" this Spinoza session is inaccurate. This session's transcript is truncated at WebDeleuze, omitting the entire third part (26 minutes), from time stamp: 1:32:00 to 1:58:18.—*Trans.*]

56 In his analysis of Byzantine art, Maldiney mentions four colors, in *Regard Parole Espace*: "The *diatonic* scale of Byzantine colors includes four: gold, red, blue, green. They occupy the four cardinal positions of the dynamic color diagram in Goethe's theory—not his physical theory, but his phenomenological theory—which constitutes the subject of the sixth section of the *Farbenlehre* [*Theory of Colors*]" (243). [My translation from the French.—*Trans.*] See also Maldiney, 244, note 65. When he returns to the diatonic scale and Byzantine art, Deleuze will indeed mention four colors at that time (see TDS Cinema 3 12–280284).

57 Allusion to the "Quarrel of Images" (726–843), a period in the Byzantine empire during which images of Christ and the saints were destroyed and their worship was forbidden.

58 See the comments in the 17 February 1981 session on Spinoza: "Look at the mosaics [. . .], they're moved into niches; they get moved back. [. . .] And space? As is said, there is no depth in Byzantine art, but why? For a very simple reason, it's that depth is between me and the image. One of the dramas of Byzantine art is a modern drama, specifically that because of the camera—yet again, everything comes from the misdeeds of the photo—the mosaics get photographed. They are shot from only ten centimeters [four feet], and this is shameful! The photographers should be killed since, by definition, this is backwards since all of Byzantine depth is the space between the viewer and the mosaic. If you suppress this space, it's as if you were to look at a painting outside of any condition of perception. It's hideous" (trans. Timothy S. Murphy, TDS Spinoza 11–170281, time stamp: 1:16:00–1:17:10).

59 Given the examples used in what follows, the reference is to Heinrich Wölfflin, *Principles of Art History,* trans. M. D. Hottinger (1915; New York: Dover Publications, 1922). Deleuze employs this work subsequently in his research on cinema regarding depth and, in *The Fold,* regarding the Renaissance and the Baroque.

60 See Heinrich Wölfflin, *Principles of Art History.* This distinction is the central focus of chap. 1, "The Linear and the Painterly." See, for example: "The tracing out of a figure with an evenly clear line has still an element of physical grasping. The operation which the eye performs resembles the operation of the hand which feels along the body, and the modelling which repeats reality in the gradation of light also appeals to the sense of touch. A painterly representation, on the other hand, excludes this analogy. It has its roots only in the eye and appeals only to the eye," 21.

61 Aloïs Riegl, *Late Roman Art Industry*: "The connection of the individual shapes not just with the plane (which was already the aim of ancient Egyptian art) but with one another," 60.

62 The tapestry cardboard of Raphael's *The Miraculous Draft of Fishes* (1515–1516) (Victoria and Albert Museum, London) is an example analyzed by Wölfflin in *Principles of Art History,* chap. 2, 74.

63 See Heinrich Wölfflin, *Principles of Art History,* "In his treatise on painting, Leonardo repeatedly warns artists not to trace out the form with outlines," chap. 1, 41. [See *The Notebooks of Leonardo da Vinci,* ed. Jean Paul Richter, vol. 1 of 2 (New York: Dover, 2012): "The boundaries of bodies are the least of all things [. . .] Wherefore O painter! *do not surround your bodies with lines*, and above all when representing objects smaller than nature," 49, manuscript pagination, emphasis added.—*Trans.*]

64 Heinrich Wölfflin, *Principle of Art History,* for Wölfflin's comparison of Palma il Vecchio's *Adam and Eve* (circa 1520–22) to Tintoretto's *Adam and Eve* (circa 1550–53) (76ff.).

65 Deleuze is certainly thinking of the example given by Heinrich Wölfflin, *Principles of Art History,* Rubens's *Meeting of Abraham and Melchizedek* (circa 1615–18) (77–80) (of which only the engraving by Hans Witdoeck [1638] is reproduced in the first edition of Wölfflin's book to which Deleuze refers).

66 See, for example, Paul Claudel, *The Eye Listens*: "There is a stable, motionless background, and in the foreground all sorts of objects off balance. They look as though they were about to fall. There is a napkin or a rug on the point of unrolling, the handle of a knife ready to become

detached, a little loaf of bread falling into slices as if of its own volition, an overturned cup, all sorts of vases or fruits tumbled in a heap, and overhanging plates," 47. Claudel's book is already cited in the Spinoza seminar (TDS Spinoza 6-130181 and 8-270181). [Also cited in chap. 1, notes 5 and 6.—*Trans.*]

67 Paul Claudel, *The Eye Listens*: "But before a picture of Rembrandt's one never has the sensation of permanence and definiteness; it is a precarious realization, a phenomenon, a miraculous beginning again of what has already expired; the curtain, raised for an instant, is ready to fall again," 42 (cited in FBLS, 163, note 4 UM; 189, note 4 C); and "*An arrangement in imminent danger of disintegration,* it is easy to prove that that is the whole explanation of *The Night Watch,*" 48. [See also FBLS (159 chap. 10 note 5 UM; 182 note 5 C)—*Trans.*]

SESSION 7 MODULATING COLOR

Initial translation for The Deleuze Seminars by Samantha Bankston.

1 See session 6, 19 May 1981, note 53.

2 Plato, *Timaeus,* 22b. See session 5, 12 May 1981, note 33.

3 Deleuze and Guattari will develop these points in the introduction of *What Is Philosophy?,* 4–7.

4 [On Riegl, see sessions 5 and 6, 12 and 19 May 1981.—*Trans.*]

5 This expression, drawn from Heinrich Wölfflin, *Principles of Art History,* appears when the focus is on enumerating the "most general forms of presentation" (see the fifth point devoted to absolute and relative clarity) and repeatedly in chap. 5 devoted exclusively to this question, "Clearness and Unclearness," 196ff.

6 The following analyses of the funerary stele of Dermys and Kitylos (National Archaeological Museum of Athens) are again very close to those by Henri Maldiney in terms of rhythm, in *Regard Parole Espace,* 198–99.

7 An essay included in Émile Benveniste, *Problems of General Linguistics,* trans. Mary Elizabeth Meek (Miami: University of Miami Press, 1971), "The Notion of 'Rhythm' in Its Linguistic Expression," 281–88; Deleuze seems to be referring specifically to 286. The essay is also cited by Maldiney on the same question in *Regard Parole Espace,* 197–98.

8 [See session 5, especially note 4.—*Trans.*]

9 J. W. von Goethe, *Theory of Colours,* § 666, 263. [While the translation corresponds to Deleuze's rendition in French, Goethe's text is: "For, it

may be said, the nobler a creature is, the more all the mere material of which he is composed, is disguised by being wrought together; the more essentially his surface corresponds with the internal organisation, the less can it exhibit the elementary colors."—*Trans.*]

10 Deleuze will particularly cite Signac's work in which one finds a long excerpt from Delacroix's *Journal* (13 January 1857): "Banish all earthy colors [*couleurs terreuses*]," Paul Signac, *D'Eugène Delacroix au néo-impressionnisme*, 37. On the earthy, see also 38, 55, and 83. [My translation from the French.—*Trans.*]

11 An exhibition organized by the National Museum of Modern Art at the Grand Palais in Paris (22 May–24 August 1981).

12 *Les Footballeurs* [The Football Players] (Musée des Beaux-Arts, Dijon) belongs to a series of about fifteen paintings devoted to the same theme in 1952. Nicolas de Staël committed suicide three years later, in March 1955.

13 [Deleuze simply says parenthetically "je regrette presque les diapositifs" (I almost regret the slides), which could mean either regretting *having* them, or *not* having them. Since Deleuze has insisted from the start of the seminar that he would not employ reproductions, the translation reflects his intention.—*Trans.*]

14 Allusion to *La Femme étranglée* [Strangled Woman] (circa 1875–76, Musée d'Orsay, Paris).

15 Wilhelm Worringer, *Abstraction and Empathy*: "[The] psychic presupposition [of naturalism], as can be clearly understood, is the process of empathy, for which the object nearest to hand is always the cognate organic, i.e. formal processes occur within the work of art which correspond to the natural organic tendencies in man, and permit him, in aesthetic perception, to flow uninhibitedly with his inner feeling of vitality, with his inner need for activity, into the felicitous current of this formal happening," 33. One can also refer to session 3, 28 April 1981, note 50.

16 Deleuze describes Byzantine art as an optically pure art in the 27 January 1981 session on Spinoza: "Do you know who will be the first artists to have invented a purely optical space by expelling all the tactile references? [. . .] Well, it's the Byzantines; you'll have to wait for Byzantium. It's mosaic painting in particular; it's mosaic painting which gives off a pure light, but which does not emit it in some mystical way, for which all the technical processes ensure that light takes on an independence compared to form, that is, form becomes purely optical.

An optical form is a form such that, precisely, light is independent of the presupposed form; [form] is born from light. [. . .] I am not at all saying on this matter that the seventeenth century copies the Byzantines, any more than I would say that abstract painting copies the seventeenth and the Byzantines. Although between Byzantium and abstract painting today, it seems to me that there are extremely disturbing relationships. For example, in Kandinsky, it is obvious that between abstract painting and Byzantine art, there is a resumption of a kind of tradition" (trans. Charles J. Stivale, *TDS* Spinoza 8-270181, time stamp: 1:09:54–1:11:18).

17 Here, a long intervention is removed, time stamp: 1:07:10–1:11:45. [In fact, the footnote is somewhat confusing: the woman student's brief exchange with Deleuze is obviously included *before* the break; omitted from *Sur la peinture* is the intervention that she pursues *following* the break (time stamp: 1:08:35 to 1:11:50), duly indicated in brackets in the text farther on.—*Trans.*]

18 [Here, Deleuze returns from the break to discover that the student had drawn two diagrams on the board to explain her position; after she finishes speaking, Deleuze pauses while anticipating another interruption, which occurs quite promptly.—*Trans.*]

19 In *Francis Bacon,* Deleuze cites Georges Duthuit, *Le Feu des signes* (Geneva: Skira, 1962), *FBLS* (165, note 6 UM; 194, note 6 C).

20 Deleuze alludes to the 17 February 1981 session on Spinoza in which he had already briefly developed the Stoic concept of limit (see the following note). The same distinction is found in Maldiney, *Regard Parole Espace*: "Chrysippus refuses the classic definition of the Socratics for whom 'the notion is the essential and the essence of beings'; what they call the Idea only indicates the limits which a being must satisfy in order to exist, without determining more closely the nature of this being: he can be what he wants within these limits. To this type of definition, Chrysippus opposes another. The force that constitutes nature and the unity of the living 'determines the external form of being, its limits, not like a sculptor who creates a statue, but like a seed which develops its latent abilities up to a certain spatial point and only up to that point,'" 206–7. [My translation from the French.—*Trans.*]

21 See the 17 February 1981 session: "[The Stoics] are in the process of creating for themselves a totally different image of the limit. And in fact, what is their example that they opposed to Aristotle's sculptor, that is, to the exterior mold, to the optical-tactile figure? They will oppose

problems of vitality; what kinds of problems of vitality? Where does action stop? Hey, this isn't 'where does the form stop?' Answer: 'At the contour.' Form stops at contour. They are not being contradictory. But saying that holds no interest. It's of no interest because the question is not at all where a form stops, because this is already an abstract and artificial question. The true question is: Where does an action stop? And there, you aren't going to be able to designate contours. [...] What's their favorite example? It's how far does the action of a seed go? [...] I can certainly follow the seed's contour with my finger, but what will I have understood about the seed? When I then learn that a sunflower seed lost in a wall is capable of blowing out that wall, [...] something having such a small contour!" (trans. Timothy S. Murphy, *TDS* Spinoza 11-170281, time stamp: 1:00:24–1:05:52).

22 In the 17 February 1981 session on Spinoza, Deleuze briefly developed the Plotinian conception of light (see session 6, 19 May 1981, note 53). Let us note that Maldiney proposes the same references to texts by Plotinus in *Regard Parole Espace* (202–3), principally the "Treatise 29" (Fourth Ennead, book v, § 6).

23 On the analysis of two types of nudes, see Heinrich Wölfflin, *Principles of Art History,* chap. 1.

24 [We follow Daniel W. Smith in *Francis Bacon* in translating the French *trait* (feature or stroke) simply as "trait," which Deleuze distinguished from *ligne,* or line.—*Trans.*]

25 We can compare this to Heinrich Wölfflin, *Principles of Art History*: "When Dürer or Cranach places a nude as a light object on a dark ground, the elements remain radically distinct: background is background, figure is figure, and the Venus or Eve we see before us produces the effect of a white silhouette on a dark foil. Conversely, if a nude in Rembrandt stands out on a dark ground, the light of the body seems as it were to emanate from the darkness of the picture space," 20.

26 Deleuze's citation is approximative (which is also the case in *FBLS*, 165, note 4 UM; 193, note 4 C). See Vincent Van Gogh, *Van Gogh: A Self-Portrait,* ed. W. H. Auden (Greenwich, CT: New York Graphic Society, 1961): "Rembrandt works with tonal values in the same way Delacroix works with colors. Now there is a great distance between Delacroix's and Rembrandt's method and that of all the rest of religious painting," 307.

27 The quote is taken from an article by R. P. Rivière and Jacques Simon Félix Schnerb, "L'atelier de Cézanne" [Cézanne's Studio] published in

La Grande Revue (25 December 1907), included in *Conversations with Cézanne*, 87.

28 See the comment recorded by Émile Bernard: "One should never say 'model'; one should say 'modulate,'" *Conversations with Cézanne*, 39. See also the comments, *Conversations avec Cézanne*, 192–93 (and session 5, note 23).

29 See the article by Lawrence Gowing, "Cézanne: The Logic of Organized Sensation," in *Conversations with Cézanne*, 180–212. This article was reedited into a volume, first by Hachette littératures in 1992, augmented with an article "Aquarelles et dessins" [Watercolors and Drawing], then again by Macula in 2015. In the reedited texts, the title of the two paintings is no longer *Paysan assis* [Seated Peasant], but *Homme assis avec canne* [Seated Man with Cane] (circa 1900).

30 The reference is to *La Dame au livre* [Woman with Book] (circa 1900–1904, Phillips Collection, Washington, D.C.) and *La Dame en bleu* [Seated Woman in Blue] (circa 1900–1904, The Hermitage, Saint Petersburg).

31 [For these black and white reproductions, see *Conversations with Cézanne*, 191 and 200.—*Trans.*]

32 Paul Signac, *D'Eugène Delacroix au néo-impressionnisme*. [See session 1, 31 March 1981, note 32.—*Trans.*]

33 The reference is to the decoration in the Saints-Anges chapel in the Église Saint-Sulpice in Paris, composed of three paintings: the ceiling canvas, *Saint Michael Slaying the Dragon*, and two paintings opposite each other, *Heliodorus Driven from the Temple* and *Jacob Wrestling with the Angel* (1850–61). Paul Signac, *D'Eugène Delacroix au néo-impressionnisme*: "Delacroix finally reaches the crowning achievement of his work: the decoration of the chapel of the Holy Angels in Saint-Sulpice. All the progress made during forty years of effort and struggle culminate here. He has thus completely set aside dark preparations and bituminous undersides that obscure certain of his works and that now reappear, cracking and deteriorating them. For the decoration of this chapel, he painted with only the simplest and purest colors; he definitively renounces subordinating his color to chiaroscuro; light has spread everywhere," 82. [My translation from the French.—*Trans.*]

34 Paul Signac, *D'Eugène Delacroix au néo-impressionnisme*: "Because isn't the comma in Impressionist paintings the hatching of Delacroix's great decorations reduced to the proportion of small-format canvases

required by direct work out in nature?," 89 [My translation from the French.—*Trans.*]

35 Paul Signac, *D'Eugène Delacroix au néo-impressionnisme*: "But while Delacroix had a complicated palette, composed of pure colors and earthy colors, the Impressionists use a simplified palette made up of seven or eight colors, the brightest, the closest to the solar spectrum [. . .]. There is no more need for the bituminous and dark foreground that served their predecessors as a tool—even Turner—for making the backgrounds appear bright and colorful," 90–91. [My translation from the French.—*Trans.*]

36 Paul Signac, *D'Eugène Delacroix au néo-impressionnisme,* where a passage is cited from the introduction by Ernest Chesneau to *L'Oeuvre complète d'Eugène Delacroix* (Paris: Charavay, 1885), xx: Delacroix "had discovered one of the great secrets of Constable's power [. . .], that, in nature, a hue [*teinte*] which appears uniform is formed from the gathering of a grouping of various shades perceptible only to the eye that knows how to see. Delacroix felt too delighted with this lesson to ever forget it; it is from this lesson, be quite sure, that he decides on his process of modeling through crosshatchings," 68. [My translation from the French.—*Trans.*]

37 Monet's series of *Cathédrales de Rouen* is a group of thirty paintings composed between 1892 and 1894. Pissarro's series of *Boulevard Montmartre* is a group of fifteen paintings all composed in 1897.

38 The Pissarro Exhibition was at the Grand Palais, 31 January to 27 April 1981.

39 [Although Deleuze uses the term *tons,* which we translate as "tone," "tint," or "shade" elsewhere (see session 8, 2 June 1981, note 4), the translation here as "hue" accords with Deleuze's inconsistent terminology employed in the next session, that is, where he presents the same four distinctions employing *teinte* ("hue") rather than *ton* as he does here.—*Trans.*]

SESSION 8 REGIMES OF COLOR

Initial translation for The Deleuze Seminars by Billy Dean Goehring.

1 [This chalk ground is "gesso."—*Trans.*]

2 [This slaked plaster is "gesso sottile."—*Trans.*]

3 [See sessions 4 and 5, 5 and 12 May 1981, and especially session 7, 26 May 1981.—*Trans.*]

4 [Based on the four-part model Deleuze is working with, his use of *teinte* links to another of its possible translations: "hue," the "pure" color of a

pigment without any added white or black (i.e., *not* a tint or shade of the color). According to this latter usage, *teinte* is opposed to *ton* (the modification of a hue, e.g., tint or shade), despite Deleuze's own inconsistency in usage between the end of session 7 and the start of this session. As mentioned in note 39 of session 7, we opt to translate *teinte* as "hue" and *ton* as "tone," "tint," or "shade." The only exceptions are when a particular translation might mislead the reader; in such cases, the safe recourse is to use "color," when differences in value, and so on, do not figure into Deleuze's analysis.—*Trans.*]

5 See the final comments in the preceding session. [While the term *schema* is arguably less natural, it is best to avoid *diagram* due to the latter's place in Deleuze's work.—*Trans.*]

6 [This was a model specified by the Association Française de Normalisation (AFNOR)—the standards have since changed. It's been pointed out that some of these terms—*rabattu* and *lavé,* for example—do not square easily with more conventional ways of talking about color. Here the choice is for "muted" and "washed-out," respectively. See Christian Molinier, "Les adjectifs de couleur en français: Eléments pour une classification," in *Revue Romane* 36.2 (2001): 193–206, notably, 204, note 8.—*Trans.*]

7 [While it is unclear what colorimetric formula Deleuze is discussing here, i.e., what his sources are in color science, he seems to be describing a basic premise or principle of such analysis, notably that dominant and complementary wavelengths of the hues reflected by any given object share a so-called white point in common. See Janos Schanda, *Colorimetry: Understanding the CIE System* (Hoboken, NJ: John Wiley & Sons, 2007).—*Trans.*]

8 This refers to the exhibit organized by National Museum of Modern Art at the Grand Palais in Paris (22 May–24 August), mentioned in the previous session.

9 [Deleuze may have meant *gesso* in general, but he also may mean the practice of applying a second layer of slaked plaster (*gesso sottile*) atop a first layer of "rough," unslaked plaster (*gesso grosso*).—*Trans.*]

10 Xavier de Langlais, *La Technique de la peinture à l'huile* (Paris: Flammarion, 1959). Deleuze relies on the revised edition of a "study of acrylic painting" published in 1973. The work is cited as well in *What Is Philosophy?,* 232, note 31. It seems that Deleuze believes that Xavier de Langlais criticized the aesthetic evolution of painting after Van Eyck, whereas his work examined this evolution strictly from the viewpoint

of materials. Langlais simply deplores, sometimes quite virulently, the techniques used by painters to ensure the material conservation of works that he admires in fact and whose premature degradation he emphasized. Indeed, *What Is Philosophy?* cites Langlais's book from the perspective of material.

11 Xavier de Langlais, *La Technique de la peinture à l'huile,* cites in reality Maurice Busset, in *Technique moderne du tableau* (Paris: Delagrave, 1929): "This detail of execution [painting with varnish on a canvas prepared for oil], which had escaped the English portraitist Reynolds, one of the men who best studied ancient techniques, reduced to nothing the immense knowledge of this great painter. He painted with varnish on canvas, and his contemporaries were amazed at the transparency of his colors. Unfortunately, the portraits from his best period quickly faded away during the artist's lifetime. In desperation he ended up declaring philosophically: 'The best paint is the one that cracks,'" 66ff. [My translation from the French. The painter in question is Joshua Reynolds.—*Trans.*]

12 Xavier de Langlais, *La Technique de la peinture à l'huile,* states about Cézanne (whose technique Langlais links to Impressionist technique): "The large and deep cracks of his *Still Life with Soup Tureen* (breaks and crevices rather than cracks!) prove that his approach was not the right one from a technical perspective," 72ff. [My translation from the French.—*Trans.*]

13 Xavier de Langlais, *La Technique de la peinture à l'huile,* 40ff.

14 [When Deleuze says *en respectant les lignes de l'ébauche* (while following the lines of the underpainting), it is possible that he is talking about "underdrawing" rather than "underpainting." Along the same lines, "sketch" is a viable option for "ébauche." Van Eyck did use both underpaintings and underdrawings in his work. However, the translation remains "underpainting," as it is a frequent translation for *ébauche* vis-à-vis painting.—*Trans.*]

15 See chap. 5 focusing on Titian's use of oil, Xavier de Langlais, *La Technique de la peinture à l'huile,* 54ff.

16 Xavier de Langlais, *La Technique de la peinture à l'huile*: "The clear ground, no longer having any purpose, was soon replaced by brown pigment [*bistre*] preparations, more or less dark, at first with glue, then with white lead and chalk [*céruse*]. Reworking *impasto,* the 'repentance' [*repentir*] or *pentimento* became if not the rule, at least an increasingly frequent accident," 55. [My translation from the French.—*Trans.*]

17 [The typical translation for *repentir* in English is the Italian term, *pentimento.* While a translation as "to repaint" would indicate the method of working with the oils, wet-on-wet, directly on the canvas, such a translation would lose the perspective of *pentimento* as an actual technical term—for example, the "fifth leg" discussed below is a classic example of *pentimento* but is not as easily connected to "repainting."—*Trans.*]

18 Xavier de Langlais cites Giacomo Palma regarding Titian, *La Technique de la peinture à l'huile*: "And as he was discovering something that did not agree with his delicate conception, like a beneficent surgeon, he medicated the patient without sympathizing with his pain, whether it was necessary to repair an arm or to readjust some bone structures that were not properly adjusted, or even a foot that had become deformed in a bad position, and so on," 58. [My translation from the French. See, for example, the description of X-ray and microscopic evidence of just such a *pentimento* present in Rembrandt's *Portrait of Frederik Rihel on Horseback*, in David Bomford, Ashok Roy, and Axel Rüger, "Works by Rembrandt," in *Rembrandt,* ed. David Bomford, Jo Kirby, Ashok Roy, Axel Rüger, and Raymond White (London: National Gallery Company, 2006), 184ff.—*Trans.*]

19 See Françoise Bardon, *Caravage ou l'expérience de la matière* [Caravaggio or the Experience of Matter] (Paris: PUF, 1978): "The initial work consists of addressing the surface of the support. Caravaggio already knows this: for him, this surface is not negligible, nor does it serve as a mere substitute for colors, but its preparation with an umber earth base is a color with which other colors must reckon, with ocher and red placed in this black, and the act of painting located between black and shape / color," 150. [My translation from the French.—*Trans.*] See also *The Fold* (31–32) in which Deleuze reviews Caravaggio's and Tintoretto's "dark red-brown background." He draws from J. W. von Goethe, *Theory of Colour,* § 902–9.

20 See Heinrich Wölfflin, *Principles of Art History*: "Just as the drawing abandons uniform clearness, so it promotes the focusing of colour effect to make the pure colour proceed from the dullness of half or no colour," 165.

21 *Saint Matthew's Vocation* (circa 1599–1600), Saint-Louis-des-Francais Church, Rome. [See https://www.artbible.info/art/large/44.html (accessed 1 February 2025).—*Trans.*]

22 Deleuze returns to these aspects of the Baroque in *The Fold,* 31–32, linking them to Leibniz's philosophy. We have reversed the two paragraphs

that follow because Deleuze had forgotten to emphasize a point before continuing.

23 Xavier de Langlais, in *La Technique de la peinture à l'huile,* devotes chap. 4 to Rubens's technique.

24 The brief summary that Deleuze gives is located in J. W. von Goethe, *Theory of Colours,* 345–48, § 902–9.

25 J. W. von Goethe, *Theory of Colours,* 348, § 910.

26 *Suzanne au bain* (1647, Gemäldegalerie, Berlin), known also as *Susannah and the Elders.* The same example and comment are found in Heinrich Wölfflin, *Principles of Art History*: "The classic system does not know the possibility of casting an isolated red into the scene as Rembrandt does in his *Susanna* in Berlin. The complementary green is not absent, but works only softly, from the depths," 165.

27 This intervention is not included at the request of the *autrice* (woman speaker). [See also *TDS* Painting 8-020681.—*Trans.*]

28 A probable allusion to Cézanne's statement: "I wanted to make of Impressionism something solid and enduring like the art in the museums," *Conversations with Cezanne,* 122. [See also *Francis Bacon* (*FBLS,* 162, note 2 UM; 187 note 2 C).—*Trans.*].

29 This question begins chap. 7, on art, in *What Is Philosophy?*

30 This is Xavier de Langlais's conclusion regarding acrylic and vinyl paints, *La Technique de la peinture à l'huile,* 476ff.

31 This intervention is not included at the request of the *autrice* (woman speaker). [See also *TDS* Painting 8-020681.—*Trans.*]

32 [This is possibly a reference to Balzac's *Le Chef d'oeuvre inconnu* (The Unknown Masterpiece), 1831.—*Trans.*]

33 Xavier de Langlais, *La Technique de la peinture à l'huile,* 68ff, notably: "[Here's] an irritating paradox that leaves you wondering: if we had to choose among his great compositions the one which seem to us to have aged the best, we would without hesitation designate *The Death of Sardanapalus,* which was entirely restored during the master's lifetime, given how much its colors had already suffered. Repainted by a foreign hand, this canvas has no longer deteriorated," 69–70. [My translation from the French.—*Trans.*]

34 [Comtesse's words would be entirely audible were it not for ambient noise in the room, notably chairs scraping, people moving, and something crashing precisely at this particular moment.—*Trans.*]

35 [While an exact source for this Sam Francis reference on color is unclear, especially to support the claims by Comtesse, see Debra

Burchett-Lere and Aneta Zebala, *Sam Francis: The Artist's Materials* (Los Angeles: Getty Publications, 2019), 64–65.—*Trans.*]

36 See the start of session 6, 19 May 1981, when Deleuze drew Goethe's color triangle and chromatic circle on the board.

37 Deleuze says "Seurat" by mistake.

38 The reference is to Lawrence Gowing, "Cezanne: The Logic of Organized Sensation," *Conversations with Cezanne*, 180–212. [See session 7, 26 May 1981, note 29.—*Trans.*]

39 *Conversations with Cezanne*, Ambroise Vollard's account: "In my portrait, there are two little places on the hand where the canvas is unpainted. I drew this to his attention, 'If this afternoon's session at the Louvre goes well,' he answered, 'maybe tomorrow I'll find the right tone to cover these white patches. But please understand, Mr. Vollard, if I were to put just any color there at random, I would be forced to take my picture and leave,'" 10.

40 See Emile Bernard's account in *Conversations with Cezanne*: "He told me a lot of negative things about Gauguin, whose influence he viewed as disastrous. 'Gauguin loved your painting,' I told him, 'he imitated you a lot.' 'Well, yes! But he didn't understand me,' he replied furiously. 'I'll never understand his lack of modeling and modulation; it's nonsense! Gauguin wasn't a painter. All he did was make Chinese pictures,'" 63.

41 The term *virtual architecture* does not appear in Gowing's text, but in *Francis Bacon*, chap. 13, Deleuze writes (FBLS, 163, note 10 UM; 189, note 10 C): "This would be a second point common to both Bacon and abstract expressionism. But Gowing notes that, already in Cézanne, colored patches 'imply not only volumes but axes, armatures at right angles to the chromatic progressions,' an entire 'upright scaffolding' which, it is true, remains virtual (*Macula* nos. 3/4: 95)." [See Gowing, "Cezanne: The Logic of Organized Sensations,'" *Conversations with Cézanne*, 204.—*Trans.*]

42 [The translation follows the original transcript (in brackets) rather than the edited text presented in *Sur la peinture*, which folds two phrases into one, "Il n'y a plus de code de la couleur."—*Trans.*]

43 [In keeping with our previous translation choice and also with Daniel W. Smith's translation in *Francis Bacon*, *aplat* here is rendered as "field."—*Trans.*]

44 The reference is to a text published in 1816, "Sur la vue et les couleurs" [On vision and colors; *Über das Sehn und die Farben*]. One can refer to the entirety of Schopenhauer's texts collected by Maurice Élie, *Textes*

sur la vue et les couleurs (Paris: Vrin, 1986). On this specific essay from Schopenhauer's youth in relation to Deleuze's comments, see vol. 2, para. 5 (64–65) and paras. 10–11. [See also *On Vision and Colors,* trans. E. F. J. Payne, ed. David E. Cartwright (Berg; London: Bloomsbury, 1994).—*Trans.*]

45 See Josef Albers, *The Interaction of Colors* (New Haven, CT: Yale University Press, 1963; revised ed. 1971), 44.

46 Vincent Van Gogh, *Correspondance* (Paris: Gallimard-Grasset, 1960), letter to his sister, first half of June 1890: "What I'm most passionate about, much much more than all the rest in my profession—is the portrait, the modern portrait. I seek it by way of color, [and am certainly not alone in seeking it in this way]," 166, *FBLS*, note 10 UM; 194, note 10 C. [The full text cited by Deleuze is only partially cited in *Francis Bacon,* as indicated; translation also from "The Van Gogh Letters," the Van Gogh Museum, https://vangoghletters.org/vg/letters/let879/letter.html, accessed 20 April 2024.—*Trans.*]

47 [In fact, while this supplementary conclusion in brackets added in *Sur la peinture* may be accurate, Deleuze appears to suggest that Cézanne seems to reject portraits altogether: "Le portrait ne venait que tout à fait . . . hein, pour Cézanne, un portrait? Non!" (The portrait only came at . . . well, for Cézanne, a portrait? No!)—*Trans.*]

48 In *Francis Bacon,* Deleuze partially cites a letter from Van Gogh that was clearly the seminar's inspiration. See Vincent Van Gogh, *Correspondance,* vol. 2 (420), letter to Theo [letter 494, on or around 18 April 1884]: "But—if one mixes together two complementaries in unequal proportions, they only partially destroy one another, and you'll have A BROKEN TONE—which will be a variety of grey. That being so, new contrasts will emerge from the juxtaposition of two complementaries, one of which is pure and the other broken. The contest being unequal, one of these two colours triumphs, and the intensity of the dominant one doesn't prevent there being harmony between the two. Because if one now brings together similar colours in the pure state, but with differing degrees of energy, for example, dark blue and light blue, one will obtain a different effect, in which there will be a contrast by virtue of the difference in intensity, and harmony by virtue of the similarity. Lastly, if two similar colours are juxtaposed, one in the pure state, the other broken—for example, pure blue with grey blue, the result will be another sort of contrast which will be tempered by the analogy between them. One can

thus see that there exist several ways, different from each other, but equally infallible, of strengthening, supporting, attenuating or neutralizing the effect of a colour, and they involve working on what's next to it—by touching what isn't the colour itself." See *FBLS* (165, note 4 UM; 193, note 4 C). [Translation from "The Van Gogh Letters," the Van Gogh Museum, https://vangoghletters.org/vg/letters/let494/letter.html#translation (accessed 25 March 2024). However, in *Deleuze on Music, Painting, and the Arts* (New York and London: Routledge, 2003) 206 note 15, Ronald Bogue points out that, in this letter, Van Gogh includes passages (such as the one cited here) from a text by Charles Blanc, *Les artistes de mon temps* (Paris: Firmin-Didot, 1876), 65, that Deleuze inadvertently attributes to Van Gogh.—*Trans.*]

49 In *Francis Bacon,* Deleuze cites Gauguin's letter to Schuffenecker, 8 October 1888: "I have done a self-portrait for Vincent . . . The color is a color remote from nature; imagine a confused collection of pottery all twisted by the furnace! All the reds and violets streaked by flames, like a furnace burning fiercely, the seat of the painter's mental struggles" (*FBLS*, 166, note 9 UM; 194, note 9 C).

50 See Vincent Van Gogh, *Correspondance,* vol. 2 (420), [letter to Theo, letter 494, on or about 18 April 1884]: "In order to heighten and harmonize his colours, [Delacroix] uses the contrast between complementaries and agreement between analogues all together, in other words, the repetition of a vivid tone by the same broken tone" [Translation from "The Van Gogh Letters," the Van Gogh Museum, https://vangoghletters.org/vg/letters/let494/letter.html#translation (accessed 25 March 2024). Please note that this citation is found at the end of the passage that Van Gogh cites from Charles Blanc, *Les artistes de mon temps* (see note 48 in this session). As Ronald Bogue notes, given that this final sentence of the presumably cited passage is not found in Blanc's text, "it would seem that this sentence is Van Gogh's own summary comment on Blanc's passage, and that the 'he' Van Gogh is referring to is Delacroix," *Deleuze on Music, Painting, and the Arts,* 206, note 15.—*Trans.*]

51 In reality, this is a statement by Van Gogh, *Correspondance,* vol. 3 (165), letter to Theo [letter 663, 18 August 1888]: "I'll paint him, then, just as he is, as faithfully as I can—to begin with. But the painting isn't finished like that. To finish it, I'm now going to be an arbitrary colourist." [Translation from "The Van Gogh Letters," the Van Gogh Museum, https://vangoghletters.org/vg/letters/let663/letter.html (accessed 25

March 2024).—*Trans.*] Letter cited in *Francis Bacon* (FLBS, 166, note 8 UM; 194, note 8 C).

52 Vincent Van Gogh, *Correspondance,* vol. 3 (165), letter to Theo [letter 663, 18 August 1888]: "Instead of painting the dull wall of the mean room, I paint the infinite. I make a simple background of the richest, most intense blue" [Translation from "The Van Gogh Letters," the Van Gogh Museum, https://vangoghletters.org/vg/letters/let663/letter.html (accessed 4 May 2024).—*Trans.*] Letter cited in *Francis Bacon* (FLBS, 166, note 9 UM; 194, note 9 C).

53 [On these distinctions regarding color, see chap. 16, "Note on Color," in *Francis Bacon* (FBLS, notably 120–21 UM; 149–51 C).—*Trans.*]

INDEX

A UNIVOCAL BOOK

DREW BURK, CONSULTING EDITOR

Univocal Publishing was founded by Jason Wagner and Drew Burk as an independent publishing house specializing in artisanal editions and translations of texts spanning the areas of cultural theory, media archaeology, continental philosophy, aesthetics, anthropology, and more. In May 2017, Univocal ceased operations as an independent publishing house and became a series with its publishing partner, the University of Minnesota Press.

UNIVOCAL AUTHORS

Miguel Abensour
Judith Balso
Roger Bartra
Jean Baudrillard
Philippe Beck
Simon Critchley
Gilles Deleuze
Fernand Deligny
Jacques Derrida
Vinciane Despret
Georges Didi-Huberman
Manuela Draeger
Jean Epstein
Vilém Flusser
Barbara Glowczewski
Évelyne Grossman
Félix Guattari
Olivier Haralambon
David Lapoujade
François Laruelle
David Link
Sylvère Lotringer
Jean Malaurie
Michael Marder
Serge Margel
Quentin Meillassoux
Friedrich Nietzsche
Peter Pál Pelbart
Jacques Rancière
Lionel Ruffel
Felwine Sarr
Michel Serres
Gilbert Simondon
Étienne Souriau
Isabelle Stengers
Sylvain Tesson
Eugene Thacker
Antoine Volodine
Elisabeth von Samsonow
Siegfried Zielinski

GILLES DELEUZE (1925–1995) was professor of philosophy at the University of Paris, Vincennes–St. Denis. With Félix Guattari, he coauthored *Anti-Oedipus, A Thousand Plateaus,* and *Kafka: Toward a Minor Literature.* He also wrote *The Fold, Cinema 1: The Movement-Image, Cinema 2: The Time-Image, Foucault, Kant's Critical Philosophy,* and *Essays Critical and Clinical,* all published in English by the University of Minnesota Press.

DAVID LAPOUJADE is professor of philosophy at Université Paris 1-Sorbonne. He has written six books, including *Aberrant Movements: The Philosophy of Gilles Deleuze,* and he is editor of the interviews, letters, and posthumous texts by Gilles Deleuze.

CHARLES J. STIVALE is Distinguished Professor Emeritus of French at Wayne State University. He is cotranslator of Gilles Deleuze's *The Logic of Sense* and translator of subtitles for *Gilles Deleuze from A to Z,* the DVD production of *L'Abécédaire de Gilles Deleuze.* He is co-director, with Daniel W. Smith, of the Purdue University Deleuze Seminars website.